WHEN GIANTS LEARN TO DANCE

Rosabeth Moss Kanter

A TOUCHSTONE BOOK
Published by Simon & Schuster
NEW YORK LONDON TORONTO SYDNEY TOKYO SINGAPORE

Touchstone
Simon & Schuster Building
Rockefeller Center
1230 Avenue of the Americas
New York, New York 10020

10 9 8 7 6 5 4 3 2 1

10 9 8 7 6 5 4 3   (Pbk.)

Library of Congress Cataloging in Publication Data
Kanter, Rosabeth Moss.
     When giants learn to dance / Rosabeth Moss Kanter. — 1st
Touchstone ed.
        p.   cm.
     "A Touchstone book."
     1. Organizational change.   2. Organizational
effectiveness.   3. Career development.   I. Title.
HD58.8.K365   1990
658.4—dc20   90-9660
                                                            CIP

ISBN 0-671-61733-8
ISBN 0-671-69625-4 (Pbk.)

*In blessed memory of Helen Moss and
Nelson Moss, who planted the seeds
of creativity and analysis.*

*In loving appreciation of Barry Stein and
Matthew Stein, who helped me grow and
harvest them.*

*In hope and anticipation for future
generations of American leaders who
will make them bloom—and improve
upon them—everywhere.*

Gratis

Contents

Preface

*H*ow do you study the future?

One way is by listening. Amid the clatter and the noise of all the activities in today's business world, there are many notes of change. Some of the new sounds are "high notes"—innovations or strategies that generate excitement and challenge, although they may not yet be fully understood. But some of the sounds are discordant—work styles and management concepts that don't quite seem to fit, or cause disharmony. Both sounds must be listened to as keys to the future of American business.

For the past five years, in dozens and dozens of American companies, as well as some in Australia, Europe, and East Asia, I have been trying to listen. I have been trying to anticipate tomorrow's problems and tomorrow's needs in the cacophony of today by listening to people and companies exploring new frontiers—with all the hope and fear, enthusiasm and frustration, leaps forward and stumbles backward that new frontiers can entail. As greater innovation has taken place in response to the challenges of a changing economy, the notes of change I hear have grown in volume to sound more and more like a far-reaching revolution in business management. It is a revolution that I call "post-entrepreneurial," because it takes entrepreneurship a step further, applying entrepreneurial principles to the traditional corporation, creating a marriage between entrepreneurial creativity and corporate discipline, cooperation, and teamwork.

Today, the idea of at least modest change everywhere in the corporation is becoming orthodoxy. Among the most promising "themes" adopted by businesses to encourage incremental innovation are the concepts of "total quality" and "continuous improvement"— both predicated on the assumption that continual striving to reach higher and higher standards in every part of the business will provide a series of small wins that add up to superior performance. Such efforts point in the right direction—toward organizations able to learn and adapt to the demands of a rapidly changing business environment. But is "continuous improvement" enough, or are more dramatic changes in structure and systems and sensibilities required? The pressures that businesses face today suggest that more than fine-tuning is in order.

One of the major questions about the current management revolution is whether it can reach the larger, older elephantlike American corporations that so desperately need revitalization. In recent years, the creation of jobs in the United States has largely come from small organizations, and a striking proportion of technological innovation has come from start-ups, not from the corporate giants with deep pockets for research and development. Some observers argue that older, larger companies must die off, like dinosaurs, to be succeeded by a new breed better adapted to its environment, in much the same process that has characterized biological evolution. But does all change have to be via "creative destruction"? Does it come only from new entrants, or only from outside the industry? Or can even old companies mold themselves into new forms, accelerating innovation within a corporate structure?

I believe they can, if they understand the shape of things to come. That's why I decided to write a book that would use the present to explore the future.

In certain respects this book is the completion of a trilogy begun with *Men and Women of the Corporation*, published in 1977. In that book I looked inside one stagnating, bureaucratic corporation, at the factors that locked people in place and kept the business from tapping all the talent available to it. Without knowing it then, I was like a game photographer catching the last members of an endangered species. I recorded life in the big "corpocracy" at the moment before its historical dominance faded; new business models were already rising. *The Change Masters*, published in 1983, offered a comparison of the old bureaucratic change-resisters with a set of highly innovative corporations that were market leaders because they could anticipate the need for change and stimulate corporate entrepreneurs to guide it. I now see that the ideas, the changes that were just glimmers back then, are part of an ongoing rush that is truly transforming corporate life. In this book, then, I focus on a broad range of corporations—large and small, old and new—that are actively involved in this transformation. My purpose is to gain understanding and perspective on how the turbulent, fast-paced environment of global competition and constant innovation in technology and corporate structure is effecting dramatic changes in our lives across the entire business spectrum.

I began this third wave of exploration in 1983, just after the publication of *The Change Masters*, when interest in the ideas in that book opened many doors. I had the advantage of drawing on two worlds, the world of intellectual knowledge viewed from my faculty position at Yale University plus the world of down-to-earth, hard-nosed business practice viewed in the problems presented to me as a consultant and cofounder of Goodmeasure, Inc. The research was deepened and accelerated when I moved to the Harvard Business School faculty in 1986.

I chose what to study by listening to executives and other corporate members tell me what most excited them or most troubled them in the conduct of their business lives. I observed or contributed to their innovations in management, and I also investigated the disturbances or imbalances that made them seek outside help. I wanted to investigate not only *what* companies are doing to solve major business problems (the domain of strategy) but also *how* they are going about it (the domain of administrative practice, the domain of execution and implementation)—and the new dilemmas that arise as a result of new practices. By 1988, the set of studies had grown to include changing management strategies and practices in over eighty companies.

Twenty-five of the larger companies were observed closely from inside, through hands-on consulting projects (for example, working on the integration process in a merger situation) or extensive interviews and observations at repeated intervals. This group included Pacific Telesis, Digital Equipment, Apple Computer, CBS Publishing, Ford,

Navistar, Eastman Kodak, and Western and Delta Airlines; it was anchored at the small end by Teleflex (with annual sales of a few hundred million dollars) and at the large end by AT&T. In these companies, my research team studied specific management practices (such as forms of compensation or supplier relationships) as well as specific business units (such as start-up business ventures in nine big companies). Managers in another thirty companies, primarily smaller ones based in New England such as Millitech, Ocean Spray, Chemdesign, and Interleaf, were interviewed in depth for a project on innovation. Thus, I covered a broad range of industries, ages, and sizes. In some cases, the companies or the people involved requested anonymity; I report those results in only general terms, disguising identifying characteristics or using pseudonyms. But in most cases, the companies I studied reviewed and commented on my findings, allowing me to provide an insider's perspective on their changing practices.

There is ample evidence, which I cite throughout, that my findings are widely applicable and that the trends I observed are reflected in national surveys and statistical compilations. In addition to my own research, I also read literally hundreds of reports of academic research and scholarly commentary (although in this book I cite only those from which I draw specific data or ideas). There is a question, of course, of how much I can generalize across very diverse industries and company situations. As an advocate of "contingency theory"— the "it depends" view that relates management choices to the particular business environment—I worried about violating my own principles by looking for commonalities in so many different business situations. Then I realized that I was discussing broad trends and broad strategies that hold true across many industries; however, the specific ways the strategies are interpreted and used clearly depend on each company's history, environment, and current situation.

If anything, the more I learned, the more my initial generalizations were confirmed. For example, after completing the research and identifying the major new strategic premises, I was gratified to see that both IBM and Xerox are moving in many of the directions I have outlined in this book. Once such revered giants are on board, then the new practices move from the sidelines to center stage as ideals for other corporations to emulate.

But I also learned that there are no easy answers. Indeed, I conceive of the task of "managing change"—a task we perform in our personal lives as well as our business lives—as a series of perennial balancing acts. We must juggle contradictions, we must make tradeoffs between contrasting goals, and we must steer a course that does not go too far in any one direction lest events require an about-face. We are perched on a pendulum that is swinging back and forth faster and faster.

In studying and helping businesspeople with their professional balancing acts, I hope also to help America. The fate of America lies in the success of its businesses. As one of the most fundamental social institutions, business impacts on the lives of most of us. It shapes the nature of our workplaces, determines how much we get paid, and defines career routes and career possibilities that help us plan the future. Thus, changes in business practices have major social as well as economic consequences, both positive and negative. The spread of the entrepreneurial spirit, through new business start-ups and the revitalization of established corporations, affects millions of people in a positive way, providing new opportunities for them to contribute, to be rewarded for those contributions, and to increase their stock of "human capital"—the value of their skills—as a result. But the restructuring of big business in light of takeovers or attempts to get "leaner" and more agile can also reverberate in negative ways, causing career dislocation, diminished personal expectations, and disrupted family lives.

Even those who are not touched directly by corporate changes are affected indirectly. Cheering for American companies in the international marketplace is not just a matter of national pride; it is the best hope we have for ensuring that our standard of living can be maintained, let alone improved, for ourselves and our children. And the social generosity Americans are coming to expect from businesses in the wake of disenchantment with big government—from spearheading charitable fund-raising to forming partnerships with school systems to encouraging employees to volunteer for community service—rests on a foundation of healthy businesses.

I offer this book in the hope that it will help us all—chief executives responsible for the direction of business, managers who implement changes and live with their consequences, people operating in the changing workplace and planning their careers, and concerned Americans outside of the corporate world—to better ready ourselves for the future. That way we can once again be the masters, not victims, of change.

PART ONE

COMPETING IN THE CORPORATE OLYMPICS

CHAPTER 1

Small World, Big Horizons: The Challenge

"In dreams begins responsibility," observed the great Irish poet William Butler Yeats, for he understood that no lasting achievement is possible without a vision, and no dream can become real without action and responsibility.

The years ahead should be a good time for dreamers and visionaries of the business world, for the barriers to innovation, the roadblocks to inspiration and imagination, are being knocked down one by one.

For example, physical space is no longer a barrier to consummating any deal anywhere; the speed of information transmission has extended the reach of business to every corner of the globe. And smaller businesses can now do more of the things only larger ones could do in the past, due to dramatic increases in computer power at vastly lower cost and other technologies offering efficiencies on smaller scales. Furthermore, all over the world, major countries are lowering barriers to enterprise by privatizing public corporations, by encouraging entrepreneurship, by deregulating industries, by developing international standards to allow commerce to flow across borders. For individuals, too, barriers to ambition (although not always to achievement of those ambitions) are being challenged and eliminated, as women and minorities in America begin to feel that no position should be beyond their grasp. Within corporations, people can aspire to greater achievements because of a weakening of hierarchy and a broadening of participation in problem-solving and even decision-making. Business is gradually shedding the shackles of an artificial status order that told people what their place was—and to stay in it.

But tackling all these new opportunities and openings will not be easy, so the years ahead should also be a good time for disciplined, frugal pragmatists of the business world who abhor waste, can live without costly status symbols, enjoy getting projects completed, and know how to combine forces for the added boost of a joint effort. One difficulty is that the effects of other limits, natural limits, are magnified when horizons broaden. Where is the time, the capital, the energy, the skill to tackle all the new opportunities and still manage continuing commitments? And if more people, more companies, more countries can also get into the game, then resources are inherently more limited because they are spread among more players, and the industry may become crowded with too many competitors for most of them to do well.

The years ahead will be best of all, however, for those who learn to balance dreams and discipline. The future will belong to those who embrace the potential of wider opportunities but recognize the realities of more constrained resources—and find new solutions that permit doing more with less. New solutions are essential, because the business game is being played under more pressure and with a greater international scope than ever before.

THE CORPORATE OLYMPICS

The global economy in which American business now operates is like a corporate Olympics—a series of games played all over the world with international as well as domestic competitors. The Olympic contests determine not just which business team wins but which nation wins overall. The metaphor reminds us that the competition is governed by rules. Furthermore, in such combinations of games, a team's members may compete as individuals in some contests but compete as a team in others. Collaboration thus plays a role. (The analogy of a sports league has also been used by analysts to describe competition within industries—each team fighting to win each contest, but all gathering at the end of the season to establish guidelines for the league as a whole.)[1]

In the corporate Olympics, there are many different games to be entered, requiring specialized abilities and with widely varying competitive conditions. But there are common overall characteristics in those teams that can compete and win again and again—the strength, skill, and discipline of the athlete, focused on individual excellence, coupled with the ability to work well within a well-organized team.

The usefulness of these sports analogies became clear to me when I was trying to help an executive in a major communications company understand why he was getting such negative performance ratings despite his clear functional competence. "Business is like baseball," he said. "As long as I hit the ball well every time I'm at bat, I should be successful." But he missed the point. The time is long past when businesses or the people in them can succeed by just hitting the ball themselves and forgetting about the world around them. Individual excellence is not enough; responsibility for the performance of the whole team is required.

To some companies, the contest in which they are now entered seems increasingly less like baseball or other traditional games and more like the croquet game in *Alice in Wonderland*—a game that compels the player to deal with constant change. In that fictional game, nothing remains stable for very long, because everything is alive and changing around the player—an all-too-real condition for many managers. The mallet Alice uses is a flamingo, which tends to lift its head and face in another direction just as Alice tries to hit the ball. The ball, in turn, is a hedgehog, another creature with a mind of its own. Instead of lying there waiting for Alice to hit it, the hedgehog unrolls, gets up, moves to another part of the court, and sits down again. The wickets are card soldiers, ordered around by the Queen of Hearts, who changes the structure of the game seemingly at whim by barking out an order to the wickets to reposition themselves around the court.

Substitute technology for the flamingo, employees or customers for the hedgehog, and everyone from government regulators to corporate raiders for the Queen of Hearts, and the analogy fits the experience of a growing number of companies. It is getting harder and harder for executives in Alice's position to succeed by traditional corporate methods when technology, customer preferences, employee loyalties, industry regulations, and corporate ownership are constantly changing. Instead of simply keeping their own eyes on the ball, they have to watch all the changing elements of the game at once.

If the new game of business is indeed like Alice-in-Wonderland croquet, then winning it requires faster action, more creative maneuvering, more flexibility, and closer partnerships with employees and customers than was typical in the traditional corporate bureaucracy. It requires more agile, limber management that pursues opportunity without being bogged down by cumbersome structures or weighty procedures that impede action. Corporate giants, in short, must learn how to dance.

The necessities for winning the new game are pushing American corporations in ever-less-bureaucratic and ever-more-entrepreneurial directions. Across the nation, companies are attempting to unravel red tape, cut out unnecessary layers of the hierarchy, and set up new ventures in their midst that resemble small companies in order to move into new areas quickly, without having to start from scratch. They are forging closer ties with employees, suppliers, and customers, to fortify their ability to compete. They are reconsidering how they dole out rewards. And as they do all this, they are piling up the demands on their people.

The new game brings with it new challenges. The mad rush to improve performance and to pursue excellence has multiplied the number of demands on executives and managers. These demands come from every part of business and personal life, and they increasingly seem incompatible and impossible:

- Think strategically and invest in the future—but keep the numbers up today.
- Be entrepreneurial and take risks—but don't cost the business anything by failing.
- Continue to do everything you're currently doing even better—and spend more time communicating with employees, serving on teams, and launching new projects.
- Know every detail of your business—but delegate more responsibility to others.
- Become passionately dedicated to "visions" and fanatically committed to carrying them out—but be flexible, responsive, and able to change direction quickly.

- Speak up, be a leader, set the direction—but be participative, listen well, cooperate.
- Throw yourself wholeheartedly into the entrepreneurial game and the long hours it takes—and stay fit.
- Succeed, succeed, succeed—and raise terrific children.

Corporations, too, face escalating and seemingly incompatible demands:

- Get "lean and mean" through restructuring—while being a great company to work for and offering employee-centered policies, such as job security.
- Encourage creativity and innovation to take you in new directions—and "stick to your knitting."
- Communicate a sense of urgency and push for faster execution, faster results—but take more time to deliberately plan for the future.
- Decentralize to delegate profit and planning responsibilities to small, autonomous business units. But centralize to capture efficiencies and combine resources in innovative ways.

For the past half dozen years, business leaders have been saturated with tales of excellence and demonstrations of how the best companies and the best leaders do it. I have sensed growing weariness with hearing one more heroic story that simply does not match the mundane issues managers struggle with every day, the hard choices they must make. Even the best companies and the best people are dropping a few balls because they have so many in the air, and they are disillusioned with "superhero" stories—a backlash against legends of still one more Superwoman or Supermanager or Supercompany.

By now, most major companies have launched some sort of self-improvement campaign—their excellence program or their quality program or their entrepreneurship and innovation program. In a 1986 survey of nearly one hundred large corporations conducted by my research team, eighty-three companies had already devoted an average of 2.2 years to a corporate campaign of this sort. Now they are beyond the exciting (and easy) inspirational/rhetorical/philosophical stage. They are facing tough questions about whether they really mean it—such questions as Who has the power to start or block innovations? Who gets the financial returns? Some companies are stumbling over the roadblocks to perfection—the backlash, the resistance, the cynicism, and the sheer fatigue of taking on so much change. Executives are seeing the contradictions, the need to make trade-offs, the business realities. They are noticing that when everyone aspires to capital-E Excellence, it only makes the competition tougher; it does not guarantee business success.[2]

The magnitude of the problem forces more than fine-tuning, more than incremental change. It requires a serious rethinking of the way the company organizes to do business.

Wider horizons mean wanting to do more. A smaller—that is, more crowded—world means having less to do it with. Success thus requires finding new ways of managing, in our businesses and our lives, that address this central contradiction of our times. Succeeding in the corporate Olympics means operating under a new, apparently contradictory strategic imperative: to "do more with less."

THE AMERICAN CONTRADICTION: OPPORTUNITY AND CONSTRAINT

Consider the 1980s in America. The decade opened with the discovery of the entrepreneur and the promise of great wealth to be attained by the creative innovator. It opened with deregulation in key industries offering opportunities for charting a new course and reawakening the spirit of enterprise, as financial service firms, for example, pioneered new territories or "upstart" airlines offered genuine competition to the majors.

The decade threatened to close with a continuing stream of reports about layoffs, cutbacks, deficits, stock market plunges, airline safety crises, declining income, and the growth of a self-perpetuating underclass. There was low aggregate, unemployment, yes, but an enormous amount of turmoil was apparent underneath the aggregate statistics.

The decade opened with the first major public acknowledgments of the threat of foreign competition while a tax cut sent Americans on a consumption binge. It threatened to close with those same competitors owning an increasing portion of America's productive capacity, and America in debt. It opened with Ronald Reagan's proclamation that it was "morning in America" and threatened to close with former Commerce Secretary Peter Peterson's warning that it was now "the morning after." The country, Peterson said, has "let its infrastructure crumble, its foreign markets decline, its productivity dwindle, its savings evaporate, and its budget and borrowing burgeon."[3]

Throughout the recent past, there have been images of two different Americas side by side: one an entrepreneurial America creating jobs and wealth more effectively than any other nation on earth, the other a moribund and demoralized America losing manufacturing jobs, slipping in productivity growth, and decining in overall real-dollar family income. Similar contradictions are found even within the same company, the same community, the same family, and sometimes the same person, because, in fact, both the positive and the negative are happening simultaneously. Our horizons (our opportunities) have been enlarging, while our world (the resources to pursue opportunities) has been shrinking.

At the same time that the horizons of what we can aspire to—individually and in our businesses—have been expanding, the world providing us with resources to satisfy those aspirations has been getting psychologically, if not actually, smaller and more crowded. There is too much to do, and not enough time in which to do it. Too much we could be doing, and not enough resources available for tackling new things. Too many market possibilities, and too many competitors for all of them. Transportation and communication make the world smaller so "we" can sell globally—a horizon expander— but also make the world smaller so "they" can sell globally, limiting America's ability to acquire resources on its own terms.

Variations on this dilemma are common. It holds across system levels, for individuals, groups, and companies. Barriers to aspiration are falling away at the same time that difficulties in getting what is necessary to realize those aspirations are more apparent.

Increasingly, the "Having It All" generation is facing "The Limits to Growth."

A tour of the changing economic landscape makes this dilemma apparent: more opportunities along with more competition, more activities to manage, and more limited resources.

Growing Opportunities—and Competition

First, there is evidence that opportunity continues to expand—but so does the competition to exploit it. Certainly new technology opens new business opportunities, broadening the horizons of aspiration, just as it always has; many of the newest American success stories come from just those technological frontiers. At the same time, technological breakthroughs increasingly may come from anywhere in the world—as is made clear by the dominant share of U.S. patents now being issued to foreigners.

But the best indicator of expanded horizons is in markets themselves. World markets are growing, but American companies are getting a smaller share of that growth. Americans themselves are consuming more, but domestic companies are supplying less of what is consumed. For example, worldwide exports (a rough measure of the increase in international nonfinancial trade) went from about 314 billion U.S. dollars in 1970 to $1,933 billion in 1985, a better than six-fold increase. That would seem a significant opportunity, especially since overall population only went up by about 30 percent. However, for the United States taken alone, the corresponding figures are $43 billion in 1970 and $213 billion in 1985, a much smaller increase. To put this another way, the United States' share of worldwide exports went from nearly 14 percent in 1970 to just 11 percent in 1985, a significant drop in our share of that growth.[4] By 1988, the downward spiral had been stopped, but the problem was still clear.

In manufacturing, the trends are visible in statistics on the penetration ratio—the ratio of manufactured imports to total consumption in the United States. By 1987 imports had reached a record 22.7 percent of all goods consumed in the United States (excluding oil)—up from 16.0 percent as recently as 1982, an increase of more than 40 percent, and up from 6.1 percent in 1972.[5] Imports grew even faster in certain industries. From 1972 to 1984, the penetration ratio grew from 7.0 percent to 20.3 percent in apparel and fabrics; from 15.9 percent to 44.4 percent in leather goods; from 7.6 percent to 16.4 percent in electrical machinery; and from 13.3 percent to 30.5 percent in miscellaneous manufacturing (the gewgaws and gadgets that Americans dearly love).[6] Some straws in the wind point to further change. Foreign direct investment in U.S. manufacturing went from $33 billion in 1980 to $60.8 billion in 1985.[7] And it's still rising rapidly; faster, in fact, than American investment overseas. On the one hand, this foreign investment supports American industry and jobs. On the other, much of it is for foreign-owned facilities and plants, whose operating decisions and growth opportunities are shaped to external standards by those foreign owners.

In short, globalization of markets, coupled with rising standards of living around the world, means that there are wider horizons for business. But there is also more competition, and often better competition, to serve those markets.

Activity Proliferation

The second major trend involves activity proliferation—more opportunity-seekers engaged in more transactions, resulting in more work for everyone else just to keep up. For example, there are more new product ideas coming to official attention from more sources than ever before. The number of U.S. trademarks issued—a proxy for brand-new product proliferation—ran at a level of under 30,000 per year until 1980, rising rapidly through the 1980s to a level of 65,800 in 1985. Trademarks renewed—old brands and old products—stayed constant during the same period.[8] Newer products are not substituting for older ones, then; they are being added on top.

Or look at another indicator: U.S. patents issued annually. After a decade (1971–1980) at an almost constant level (roughly 109,000), the number of U.S. patent applications received annually started rising rapidly. In 1985 it reached 127,100, and the number is still rising. The number of patents issued annually, which typically lags behind applications by several years, also started to rise sharply in the 1980s, reaching 77,200 in 1985. Many of these patents were accounted for by foreign corporations and individuals. Whereas during the 1960s just under 20 percent of corporate patents issued were foreign, that figure jumped to over 50 percent in the 1970s.[9] To put it another way, *all* of the corporate patent increase in the 1970s was due to foreign corporations—a proliferation of sources of new ideas, which now come from anywhere in the world.

Transactions, too, are increasing in volume. For example, the volume of trade in the New York Stock Exchange (NYSE) went from a daily average of 11.6 million shares in 1970 to 44.9 million in 1980 and 109.2 million in 1985. The corresponding value of all shares traded for those years was $102.5 billion in 1970, $382.4 billion in 1980, and $980.8 billion in 1985.[10] Not only is volume going up, with an accompanying rise in complexity, but in some financial service industries people cannot even afford to sleep. Chicago's Board of Trade recently launched nighttime hours to accommodate Japanese interested in U.S. bond futures, so that Japanese could trade during *their* daytime hours.[11] And merger and acquisition activity continues unabated.

Consider this further indicator of activity proliferation. For all the talk of the paperless offices that would result from the spreading use of computers, the use of paper in the United States, not including packaging and newsprint, went from 11.0 million tons in 1970 to 20.2 million tons in 1985—despite the use of computers.[12]

Thus there appear to be more transactions, more paperwork, more complexity, more competition, and more balls in the air.

Resource Constraints

If there is more to do, there is also a growing sense of less to do it with. Let's look at just one realm, perhaps the most critical one—the availability of funds to pursue new opportunities around the world.

The cost of capital to American manufacturers is approximately three times the cost in Japan. And there has been a drop in private investment in the United States. Annual average investment (as a percentage of the GNP) was 34 percent less for the period 1980–1986 than it was, on average, during the three preceding decades.[13] As the Cuomo Commission on Trade and Competitiveness points out, the availability of funds for investment depends largely on national savings. Here, again, we have witnessed decline. The internal savings of businesses, which previously made possible a high degree of self-financing, have been shrinking. Indeed, private savings overall have fallen. Net private savings (as a percentage of GNP) were 25 percent less in the 1980s than in the 1970s.[14] But look at the comparison with Japan. In 1985, the net national savings rate (as a percentage of gross national product) in the United States was 3.2 percent, going only halfway to support a net national investment rate of 6.2 percent; in Japan a savings rate of 16.7 percent easily covered an investment rate of 13.0 percent—one much larger proportionally than America's.[15]

Consider two other indicators. In recent years the U.S. stock market in general, even before Black Monday, had actually performed at a very modest level. Between 1969 and 1985 it basically doubled. Compare that to Japan, where stocks have gone up sixteen-fold over the same period. Or look at deposits around the world, the fundamental source of investment capital and leveraged debt. In the world's five hundred largest banks, deposits representing U.S. interests were 33 percent of the total in 1970. In 1985, the comparable figure was 14.4 percent.

Foreign capital, particularly Japanese capital, has come to fill the gap, playing a bigger role in U.S. business financing. Eight out of ten of the world's largest banks are now Japanese, up from one of ten in 1980, when American banks dominated. Five of the top ten banks in California are now Japanese. Bank of America, once the world's most successful retail bank, was rescued from impending collapse by a Japanese consortium. Japanese banks control nearly 10 percent of the U.S. retail banking assets—up from next to nothing a decade ago. Assets of Japanese banks in the United States are so great that they now rival the combined assets of Citicorp and J.P. Morgan.[16]

In 1986, Japanese firms issued 56 percent of the letters of credit in the U.S. market, and reportedly accounted for almost 40 percent of the commercial and industrial loans outstanding at foreign banks. They financed $60 billion of new U.S. Treasury issues (about one-third of our budget deficit), and they have become major players in the municipal finance business, a market several American firms are abandoning.[17] And while American venture capitalists have pulled back from high technology, Japanese financiers have filled the vacuum. Nearly 10 percent of new funding for high-tech start-ups now comes from Japanese sources, which see involvement with these companies as a "window" on new American breakthroughs.[18]

At the same time, American companies are more loaded with debt than ever before. In the 1950s and 1960s, businesses spent about one of every seven dollars of earnings to pay interest on business debt. In the 1970s this figure rose to one dollar in every three. Since 1981, corporations have been paying more than half of their earnings to service their debts.[19]

Money and power are closely intertwined. Resources no longer abundantly available close at hand, seemingly without limit, or controlled directly by American corporations, are resources that come with more constraints. It is harder to set one's own terms, harder still to exercise control. Pacific Rim analyst Daniel Burstein argues that American business is losing power in numerous transactions because of its dependence on Japanese capital. In real estate, for example, Japanese companies dominate the financing of U.S. commerical projects over $100 million, and because of their rapid expansion in construction, they can increasingly not only buy but build without

American partners. Furthermore, Burstein holds that this trend has implications for America as a whole:

> As American debt deepens, we will continue to lose what leverage we still have in our negotiations over trade and other issues with the Japanese. It is difficult to "pressure" the people we are relying upon to finance our deficit. To put it bluntly, "You don't argue much with your banker, especially if he is also your landlord and your employer." . . .
>
> As Nobel economics Laureate Paul Samuelson suggests, the U.S., responsible for around 20 percent of the world's output today, simply cannot expect to exercise the same kind of dominant role in the world that it did after World War II when it accounted for 40 percent.[20]

A shifting balance of world financial power, coupled with highly competitive and volatile U.S. capital markets, has to come as a particularly heavy blow to some traditional, bureaucratic corporations. Top-heavy with managers, bloated with perquisites and services, and fat with assets in diverse businesses that may not fit together, they are targets for raiders and pushovers for newer, more agile competitors— whether foreign companies or domestic start-ups. Their high overhead and entitlements (such as paychecks guaranteed regardless of performance) plus the need to show large short-term profits because of capital market expectations combine to limit funds for longer-term innovations.

The Impact on People

The macroeconomic issues inevitably touch the fates and fortunes of individuals.

From the financial markets to our personal lives, uncertainty is greater, and faith in "progress" weakened. It is getting harder and harder to believe that things will always get better, that promotions will come automatically, that incomes will rise from year to year. Interest rates are volatile, stock prices swing unpredictably, companies change hands or buy and sell divisions, and personal incomes fluctuate.

It's still a world of great opportunity, and some Americans are prospering. The number of families with incomes greater than $75,000 a year (in 1984 dollars) rose by over a third from 1973 to 1984, while the number of families overall increased by less than half of that.[21] But at the same time, almost one in seven Americans was living below the poverty line in 1986. And some of the prosperity was due to a dramatic increase in the number of women in the workforce, giving families two earners—a conclusion proclaimed in the title of a Congressional study: "Working Mothers Are Preserving Family Living Standards." Between 1973 and 1983, the real income of the average thirty-year-old male fell by 23 percent, the study found; their employed wives were taking up the slack.[22]

The American standard of living has remained relatively flat on the average for the past fifteen years.[23] While some are prospering, others are going under. According to the Bureau of Labor Statistics, more than 13 million Americans lost their jobs between January 1981 and January 1986; one-third remained unemployed or left the workforce. Of those who found new jobs, almost half earned less than they had before.[24] Among the job-losers was a group that had thought they were protected from the winds of economic misfortune: highly paid corporate managers and professionals. Almost 40 percent of those the bureau classified as "displaced workers" were from the white-collar ranks: from managerial, professional, technical, sales, and administrative jobs. Between 1983 and 1987, well over 2 million people saw their jobs disappear or deteriorate due to mergers and acquisitions alone.[25] And no industry is immune. Silicon Valley in California, itself a producer of high-flying new companies and new millionaires, was supposed to be the site of America's manufacturing future. But in the mid-1980s, the semiconductor industry laid off nearly 25,000 employees after losses of $2 billion.[26]

If income has stopped automatically rising, or has risen only unevenly, then where has the money come from to pay for the increases in consumption many observers have also noted? The answer is simple: debt. The Cuomo Commission on Trade and Competitiveness referred to the United States as "a nation in hock." "If there is one word which captures the feeling of anxiety among Americans," commissioners wrote, "it is debt."[27] Total household, corporate, and consumer debt rose from $4.9 trillion in 1982 to $7.9 trillion in 1987, a 60 percent increase in five years.[28] Though the rate of debt growth is slowing, the amount of debt puts pressure on the workforce—male and female alike, with children as well as without—to keep earning just to service and pay down the debt.

Yet employment itself is no longer a certainty, no longer a

guarantee. While the United States continues to lead the world in the rate of job creation, there is also so much turnover of the population of employing organizations that careers, too, have increased in volatility. Large companies are tending to become smaller, losing rather than gaining employment; and of those smaller companies responsible for the net new jobs, many are start-ups with an uncertain future. So more Americans than ever before are employed, but that employment is less secure.

THE GREAT CORPORATE BALANCING ACT

The world is clearly more complex than ever before, and America's, and American business's, part in it is less assured. The opportunities are there, but American corporations no longer have a stranglehold on the means to exploit them—the ideas, the natural resources, the capital, or even the "home team advantage" in our own vast markets, when foreign companies build U.S. assembly plants. The opportunities and choices are great, and growing. But so is the difficulty of taking advantage of them. Being a businessperson was never particularly easy; now it's beginning to look like a feat for magicians.

Every industry is unique, of course; some are still expanding, others are being shaken down to a few dominant players, and still others are plagued by overcapacity. And there is wide variation in business strategy and product prowess among companies within an industry. Yet the imperative to do more with less is a common management theme I have heard echoed from the towers of an insurance company to the bucolic country setting of a high-tech headquarters. Budget cuts, organization-chart trimming, and programs to eliminate staff are coupled with exuberant messages about becoming more entrepreneurial and growing new businesses. Employees are not the only ones to notice the contradiction.

If we found one circumstance without the other, the management task would be relatively straightforward. Managing for resource conservation is well understood, as is entrepreneurial management in a growth environment. Even though companies have long been exhorted to try to do both—to combine cost control in the name of efficiency with investment in pursuit of innovation—for the most part, there has been a tendency to emphasize one or the other end of the spectrum. Indeed, received wisdom held that efficiency and innovation would cancel each other out. Resource-conserving management stifles innovation, the argument ran, while "undisciplined" entrepreneurial management wastes resources. But now I see businesses struggling to do both simultaneously.

This constitutes the ultimate corporate balancing act. Cut back and grow. Trim down and build. Accomplish more, and do it in new areas, with fewer resources. Can American businesses meet the challenge? Can the elephants start learning to dance? Some already have. They are the models for a new approach to managing, an approach suited to winning in the global corporate Olympics.

CHAPTER 2

Getting in Shape for the Contest: The Response

Crisscrossing America on transcontinental flights crowded with business consultants, I used to fantasize that the Westerners were carrying bundles of entrepreneurial energy to the East, and the Easterners were hauling some bureaucratic discipline to the West. At least, I hoped that transfer of models was going on, even if my geographical stereotypes were wrong. The long view across the business landscape showed that neither mode by itself would be enough to help American companies compete in the global Olympics, a competition demanding aspects of both.

The traditional large, hierarchical corporation is not innovative or responsive enough; it becomes set in its ways, riddled with pecking-order politics, and closed to new ideas or outside influences. But the pure entrepreneurial firm—the fast-growing start-up—is not the answer either; it is not always disciplined or cooperative enough to move from heady, spend-anything invention to cost-effective production, and it can become closed in its own way, too confident and too dependent on the magic of individual stars. Something new is required, something that marries the entrepreneurial spirit to discipline and teamwork, something that helps loosely managed companies get a little tighter and tightly controlled companies loosen up—a *post-entrepreneurial* response.

Take a pair of companies as diverse in industry, geography, age, and spirit as Eastman Kodak and Apple Computer—an early Industrial Age technology and one of the newest; East Coast snowbound and West Coast sunswept; mature in every sense of the word and practically newborn, growing rapidly. Yet, for all the differences between these two companies, they are converging on similar solutions to the problems of competing in the corporate Olympics. From the bureaucratic end and the entrepreneurial end of the organizational scale, they are moving toward each other as they try to build the post-entrepreneurial corporation of the 1990s—a corporation that combines the power of a giant with the agility of a dancer.

SEEING KODAK THROUGH NEW LENSES

Since its founding over one hundred years ago, the Eastman Kodak Company has been a dominant force in the photographic supplies and photo-finishing industry throughout the world. "Kodak" is one of a handful of American trade names known worldwide, adorning shop signs in dusty Third World backwaters and gracing sophisticated products sold directly to the most modern of industries everywhere.

Eastman Kodak was founded in Rochester, New York, still its headquarters city. Rochester is a capital of the snowbelt and a museum for Kodak. I first saw it, appropriately, blanketed in a foot of snow, still white because new snow falls so often in the winter. The landmarks past which we drove were monuments to the company's philanthropy and benevolence—the imposing beige brick Eastman mansion, now housing a museum of photography; the Eastman School of Music; and then Kodak Park itself, a sprawling industrial complex in the turn-of-the-century factory tradition, where lifetime employment was virtually guaranteed.

In the early 1980s, Kodak indeed seemed to have a brighter history than future. Its problems symbolized all that was then wrong with even the best of America's large corporations—it was said that mature, bureaucratic, East Coast, snowbelt corporations represented the sunset for American industry. But because of its struggle to change, Kodak now symbolizes a pathway to revitalization and restored competitiveness.

The photo giant suffered financial setbacks in the early 1980s that prompted top management to re-evaluate some of the policies and imperatives that had until then guided company action. With return on equity slipping from 20.9 percent in 1973 to 7.5 percent in 1983, Kodak's leadership recognized it had to act quickly. In many respects, the company appeared to be coming apart at the seams: Between 1983 and 1987 it dropped from fourth to seventieth place in *Fortune* magazine's annual rating of the most-admired U.S. corporations. Popular business publications between 1984 and 1987 made Kodak appear vulnerable, as if it only reacted to market events and no longer played an active role in industry:

HAS THE WORLD PASSED KODAK BY?

Once Kodak was so powerful that it controlled its markets rather than the other way around. But now the market is in control and Kodak is floundering. (*Forbes,* November 5, 1984)

KODAK SCRAMBLES TO REFOCUS

During the late seventies and early eighties, a complacent Kodak drifted while others produced the innovations it used to be known for. Sales were flat for the third year running and earnings, on a per share basis, were the worst in more than a decade. (*Fortune,* March 3, 1986)

UPHILL BATTLE—EASTMAN KODAK CO. HAS CUSTOMERS' COMPLAINTS, IT ABANDONS ITS TRADITIONS

Where Kodak once led the pack in technology, it now increasingly chases Fuji, whether in introducing faster-speed film or in marketing 35 million disposable cameras. (*Wall Street Journal,* April 2, 1987)

All through the 1970s and early 1980s, Kodak had received severe criticism for not aggressively pursuing innovation. It was losing its edge in an industry it had created and had long controlled. Kodak appeared to be falling into the trap of imitating the innovations of its competitors. Even when Kodak developed an excellent mousetrap, analysts faulted the company for being slow, as in this report from the early 1980s:

When the company finally entered the [dry copier] market with the Ektaprint in 1975, its copier was big, fast and technically superb, with copy quality better than the Xerox machines. ''It was like having the first plane you built be a four-engine jet,'' said an awed industry spokesman. But analysts estimate that Kodak could have had a highly competitive machine on the market years earlier.

When it did introduce its copier, Kodak caught Xerox at an especially vulnerable moment. . . . But instead of marketing its copier aggressively Kodak moved cautiously in expanding nationally and didn't enter the European market until late 1982. As a result, Xerox had time in which to respond, and it came out with a competitive machine in 1979. It took Kodak seven years to develop a second generation of machines. Xerox introduced better machines six months sooner.[1]

Just as Kodak ignored the photocopy machine when Xerox first pioneered dry-copying technology, the company had rebuffed Edwin Land's offer to sell Kodak the instant photography patent. When Kodak came out with its own version of instant photography almost thirty years later, the company was unable to outperform Polaroid, though some believed the Kodak product was superior, and Kodak was starting to gain on Polaroid. In fact, its product used technology similar enough in Polaroid's eyes that in 1986 Kodak lost a disputed patent infringement suit to Polaroid that could cost the company up to $800 million to resolve.

Until current leadership took action to move more quickly (witness the later successful introduction of a superior color copier), tradition-bound Kodak had displayed a lethargic attitude toward change and toward meeting competitive challenges. In the past two decades, international competitors Nikon, Canon, and Matsushita developed better, easy-to-use cameras; Fuji and Konica periodically came up with higher-quality and faster color film; and Sony and Toshiba marketed more desirable video cameras and recorders. Then, Fuji staged an upsetting coup when it beat Kodak in the bargaining process for sponsorship of the 1984 Olympics. Kodak's top leadership cadre was stunned into action upon seeing the Fuji logo emblazoned on the sides of an airship that floated above the throngs of spectators at the Los Angeles Olympics—a Japanese triumph on American territory.

By mid-1983, Kodak's leadership had recognized it had to offset stagnant revenues and sagging earnings by recapturing a solid market position in its traditional photo business as well as by making progress in new, faster-growing lines of business. Even if the company insulated itself from competitive threats and maintained its 80 percent share of the U.S. photo market, photography-related sales would grow only 5 percent a year. The June 30, 1983, appointments of Colby H. Chandler as chairman and CEO and Kay R. Whitmore as president provided a fitting beginning for a corporate turnaround.

That Chandler and Whitmore had set out to function as a team was clear to me when I first met them together in the elegant, hushed, traditionally furnished CEO suite in Rochester in December 1985. They spoke persuasively and in concert about how they were changing Kodak's business strategy and culture to bring a renewed concern for product innovation and responsiveness to market demands. They emphasized three themes. The first was restructuring through acquisitions and better integration of existing businesses and world operations to find "synergies"—interactions of businesses that would provide benefits above and beyond what the units could do separately. The second theme was external strategic alliances with venture partners and suppliers; and the third was support for employee entrepreneurship.

Kodak's new leaders acted decisively and were willing to embrace changes, no matter how painful they might be. By year's end Kodak eliminated eleven thousand jobs; by 1986, Kodak thinned top management ranks by 25 percent, and reduced the domestic workforce by 8 percent—moves that symbolized the end of Kodak's century-old reputation as a bastion of lifetime employment. Between 1983 and 1986 Kodak eliminated twenty-four thousand jobs altogether. In 1986 Kodak also shut its famed "Mother Lab" in Rochester, where 651 photo-finishers had handled problem film that photo-finishers in the field could not. Accompanying this restructuring were other efforts to reduce expenses, from not emptying wastebaskets every night to a major quality control campaign aimed at lowering manufacturing waste by more than 10 percent.

The decision to restructure the company from a highly centralized bureaucratic system—an example of what Richard Darman called a "corpocracy"—to a decentralized divisional organization brought further changes throughout the company. Kodak recognized that smaller companies were more successful at creating value and that Kodak could emulate their structure to bring that benefit to the company. Consequently, in 1984 top executives divided the company's two managing divisions into four core business groups, which consisted of a number of "entrepreneurial" lines of business. (In 1988 these became five core business groups.) With this new structure, line officers were forced to take responsibility for day-to-day decision-making, and business unit managers operated under a new charter that made them responsible for the financial performance of their divison. J. Phillip Samper, now vice-chairman, recalled the long road to internal restructuring and the culture change goals that drove it:

> Following the impact of the tremendous increase in the price of silver in the 1970s, the narrowing of technology between ourselves and our competitors, and the strong dollar treatment in the early 1980s, we did realize that a change was necessary. In fact, I was one of three who proposed the restructuring process in 1977, which was not accepted. We felt that one of the major obstacles to progress was the organization. We were a huge functional organization, with virtually no business managers.
>
> The company at that time was divided into two divisions. At the time of Colby's and Kay's appointments, I was placed in charge of the Photographic and Information Management Division, which represented roughly 80 percent of the revenues and profits of the company. After roughly one year of operation, I proposed to Colby and Kay that we work together to restructure the division. Following roughy fifteen months of conversations between first the three of us, then the top ten managers, and finally roughly 125 managers, the restructuring was announced to both employees and the public. Interestingly, no leaks occurred.
>
> The objective in all of this was to change the culture. The organization structure was an obstacle to progress. By breaking up the organization, we were able to establish a process of delegation and the building of business managers, two elements that are critical to our success.

Managers of Kodak quickly grasped the connection between organization changes and culture changes. For example, Leo J. Thomas, director of the Life Sciences Division, commented, "When our organizational structure had people reporting through their functional areas [activity specialties like finance or marketing], we needed an almost unanimous vote in order to approve anything new. It was hard to advance anything that was not a logical extrapolation of the past." Now, with fewer employees, higher quality standards, an incentive pay system, and an end to the guarantee of lifetime employment, employees throughout the organization realized that the company was changing its ways.

Kodak continued to push changes as it embarked upon a strategy of acquisitions and joint ventures that signaled that the company was moving away from its century-old tradition of relying primarily upon itself. The company sought acquisitions, used outside suppliers for services formerly performed internally, and entered joint ventures in order to fill gaps in technology. This strategy contributed to an internal culture change, and the mindset of "We can do it better inside" slowly eroded.

There were more extensive efforts at diversification. It took Kodak eleven years to make its first four acquisitions—but in 1985 alone, the company completed seven. Not all of these were praised by analysts, but they showed the company's willingness to take risks. Pursuing a strategy of investment in companies that represent a technological and strategic fit, Kodak ventured into biotechnical research and the drug business with a $45 million joint venture to develop new drugs with ICN Pharmaceuticals, Inc., in May 1986, an alliance ended in 1988, and in January 1988 Kodak made a $5.1 billion acquisition of Sterling Drug, Inc. The company entered the electronic imaging market (another form of instant photography), the potentially high-growth data storage market with the 1985 acquisition of Verbatim, Inc., and the battery business through an internal start-up company—a model for Kodak's new internal venture program—called Ultra Technologies. In 1985, Kodak also bought Eikonix, a producer of digital imaging processing equipment, and Garlic Technology, a maker of advanced digital magnetic recording heads for computer disk drives. Then Kodak invested in two high-tech start-ups that became stunning successes: Sun Microsystems, a manufacturer of advanced graphic workstations, and Interleaf, a leader in electronic publishing. In November 1986, Kodak gave a boost to its troubled photography business by buying the film processor Fox Photo for $96 million. And in March 1988, the company merged its photo-finishing operations with Fuqua Industries. The new company, Qualex, Inc., would be America's largest wholesale photo-finishing operation.

In addition to diversifying through internal ventures, acquisitions, and investments in start-ups that could be linked to Kodak's businesses, the company devoted considerable effort to lining up overseas venture partners and suppliers for goods that Kodak could not efficiently produce. The company contracted out production of 35 millimeter cameras to a Hong Kong firm and production of copiers for the medium-volume segment of the market to Canon. With this farming out of production and leveraging of marketing and distribution strengths through strategic alliances and acquisitions, Kodak developed productive partnerships with other companies.

Integration of the acquisitions and the formerly separated pieces of Kodak took place in a number of ways. One campaign encouraged "horizontal thinking"—working more effectively with peers in other functions and divisions—which helped integrate the formerly segmented organizational structure and culture. In 1986, the company created an office of the Chief Executive. Responsibility for the company was divided among a triumvirate composed of Chandler, Whitmore, and Samper, an executive who had spent most of his career in the international area, so he was "not encumbered by any of the Rochester organization," as Samper put it. Chandler was CEO and managed corporate staff organizations; Whitmore and Samper, as executive officers, split the line organizations and—literally—the globe. Whitmore took Japan, Asia, and the Middle East; Samper, Worldwide Equipment Manufacturing for Sensitized Goods and the European, Canadian, and Latin American regions. This arrangement was designed to better focus top management's attention on particular businesses—e.g., chemicals (Whitmore) and photographic products (Samper)—as well as to integrate functions and countries to aid in the search for synergies.

Another effort was to develop synergies between worldwide R&D and between global manufacturing processes. Kodak pushed to link technology strategies more directly with business marketing strategies in order to shorten time frames for the conception and commercialization of innovative products, as well as for more efficient and cost-effective technological development. Refocusing R&D helped the company get away from being overly cautious and conservative when bringing new products to market. Kodak had been criticized in the past for not paying attention to timing signals, instead adhering to goals for absolute product perfection and losing market share.

The other program aimed at enhancing synergies involved investing millions of dollars in a global manufacturing strategy that would help the company get as close as possible to theoretical limits of uniformity. The program improved the technical transfer of new formulas so that Kodak would be able to make faster market entry of new and improved products.

The top executives took as their mandate nothing short of changing

Kodak's culture. Since the internal restructuring had shortened lines of communication and made managers more accountable for their business units, more employees believed they directly affected the future of the company. The new company structure discouraged the "check with" mentality in which an individual said, "Before we take the next step on this project, let me check with someone else." Chris Tombs, U.K. manager of the company's new battery business, Ultra Technologies, has noticed the shortened chain of command within Kodak. He remarked, "These days I have nowhere to hide. There is a short decision tree. This means we can make decisions and respond to changes in the marketplace far more quickly." Chandler hoped to encourage people to think, not just work. He realized the corporation had to become more agile and responsive to market conditions and recognized that employees represented an important, undervalued resource.

Another program involved making quality an instinctive part of the company culture. In 1987, every employee was asked to make an effort to improve quality; one customer service operator vowed to answer her telephone on the first ring—last heard, she was up to thirty-seven thousand calls in a row that were picked up on the first ring. The success rate for making a perfect five-mile-long roll of photographic paper jumped from 66 percent in 1985 to 99 percent in 1987. Better-quality workmanship in production and substantial capital investment in state-of-the-art machinery account for this increase.

Kodak also altered its compensation system. Senior-level employees' automatic pay increases were reduced, and financial rewards were tied more closely to individual performance. Kodak's paternalistic, promotion-through-seniority system, which found managers almost exclusively within the company, was also revamped. Until recently, only three upper-level employees had been brought into the company—leaders for marketing communications and business research organizations and a general counselor; now, managers and consultants from outside have "infiltrated" what was once considered by the business press a "paramilitary" employment setup.

The push to delegate authority and tie pay more closely to contribution sent a clear signal throughout the organization that it was okay for the buck to stop at lower and middle managerial positions. Employees at all levels soon recognized that the company hoped to inspire an entrepreneurial spirit. That small decisions no longer percolated to the top—for example, the vice-chairman no longer took responsibility for minor entertainment expense decisions—meant that all employees had the opportunity to become more autonomous in their work roles. Chandler, Whitmore, and Samper encouraged decision-making below the top management rank as they looked to staff for new ideas and for new ways to meet production goals. For instance, within the bioproducts division, monthly pizza lunches took place during which employees and management worked out directions for future growth and improvement. "Though responsibility has been delegated," Samper said, "we all continue to drive for lower costs in the organization. We must be the lowest-cost, highest-quality organization."

The top executive team wanted to make Kodak "venture operative" and championed the establishment of a program that would help release an entrepreneurial spirit throughout the company and contribute to the development of new and improved products. In order to nurture ideas that did not fall within traditional lines of business, Kodak set aside one percent of revenues for "new ventures," which included a new venture process, acquisitions, and equity investments. The new venture organization broke new ground for Kodak as well as establishing a pioneering model other companies flocked to examine. Offices of Innovation at major Kodak facilities encourage the submission of proposals; promising ideas not falling under a mainstream business are awarded seed money to develop a business plan, which is presented to a venture board; those approved are given the capital to begin a new business, under the direction of Eastman Technologies, Inc., an "incubator" for start-ups. Fourteen new ventures have been begun this way.

The results of these changes were positive. By 1987, Kodak's return on equity had rebounded to 19 percent.

But some of the changes were revolutionary for Kodak, and therefore controversial. The controversy wasn't over style—no one could fault the company's emphasis on becoming more entrepreneurial—but over resources and rewards. I discussed this with a group of Kodak division and department heads lined up on either side of a series of long tables placed end to end in a very large headquarters conference room. Even in this rather austere, formal, and very public setting, feelings leaked out, feelings about the threat and uncertainty of this new world Kodak was entering. These managers wanted guarantees that the new ventures and strategic alliances would not dilute the talent, capital, and executive attention needed for the core businesses, the ones that represented most of Kodak. They wanted assurances that the free-wheeling entrepreneurial projects springing up in their neighborhoods would not undermine the discipline they cultivated in their organizations and the respect and status they had earned from years of slowly, dutifully, loyally climbing the corporate ladder. They wondered why proponents of marginal, offbeat ideas were getting the recognition, while they toiled anonymously in the vineyards of the cash-producing businesses. Moreover, they felt these "trivial" peripheral businesses would disappear once the gigantic film enterprise was revitalized.

Not surprisingly, Kodak's newly appointed entrepreneurs in the internal ventures had a different view. I listened to them express their enthusiasm for their businesses and their excitement about the start-up process over one of their regular dinners together, in a corner of a noisy ethnic restaurant. They applauded Kodak for the opportunity they were being given, but some wished for more—more capital, more time, more independence. They felt the urgency of the economic pressures to get Kodak into new areas, and they worried that it might already be too late, unless Kodak moved faster to unravel bureaucratic red tape and give its creative people freer rein.

I was struck by the contrast between the two groups. The same changes that traditionalists saw as "too far, too fast," were viewed as "too little, too late" by corporate radicals. What is beginning to take shape at Kodak—now visible enough to threaten some and make others impatient for more—is a new style of corporation, one whose social and economic consequences touch every person in the company.

As Kodak learns how to "do more with less" in order to compete effectively in the global corporate Olympics, the lives of Kodak's people change in significant ways. The paychecks they take home bear numbers calculated in a new way, intended to reflect not just what their job entitles them to but what their contribution is; their own efforts count for more. But as few people in a smaller Kodak attempt to take more responsibility in an environment with more complex external ties, they are inevitably working harder. A leaner organization makes more people feel stretched thin. An organization with more opportunities to contribute—and to get rewarded for it—makes more people feel like devoting more time to work, thus affecting their personal lives. But perhaps the most profound change for Kodak people is in their career expectations. Job losses have shaken the faith of managers and professionals in the security of the corporate ladder, a ladder which now has fewer rungs on it anyway. At the same time, the new venture process has opened up another, less conventional avenue for career growth—becoming a corporate entrepreneur.

While proud of the company's recent performance, top executives are quick to point out how much remains to be done. How do you teach an elephant to dance? As one observer put it, "After many smashed toes," Kodak leaders "learned the obvious: Elephants don't dance. But if you get one to walk in the right direction, he can pull a lot of weight."[2]

TRANSFORMING APPLE COMPUTER

The distance between Rochester, New York, and Cupertino, California, headquarters of Apple Computer, Inc., is measured in more than miles. It is hard to find a center to Cupertino; it seems like just one more intersection off the expressways running through Silicon Valley, identical to all the other newly constructed intersections. There is no sense of history, just endless concrete sprawl, reflecting the area's overnight growth.

Apple Computer was a revered entrepreneurial success story of the early 1980s. Created in a garage by two college dropout "kids" who were computer hobbyists, the company enjoyed unprecedented growth from its official birth in 1975 because of its pioneering ability to put personal computers in the hands of ordinary people.

In 1983, cofounder and chairman Steve Jobs lured John Sculley from PepsiCo to Apple and named him chief executive, making himself vice-president in charge of the Macintosh division (a new product line) as well as chairman. Apple's stock price rose from thirty-six dollars per share when Sculley came on board to sixty-three dollars in June 1983. The company envisioned unlimited opportunities for growth and expansion. As Sculley explained in his autobiography:

> What made it so unique was that not only were we in a relatively new, uncharted industry, but Apple was a corporation made up of a new

generation, unencumbered by the traditions of corporate America. They hadn't been schooled to understand failure, so they believed anything was possible.[3]

Terms like "vision" and "values" were common at Apple, instead of the traditional management lingo of "discipline," "accountability," "competition," and "market wants."

But even heady growth could not mask mistakes. By September 30, 1983, the end of Apple's fiscal year, net profit had fallen 80 percent in the final quarter to $5 million. By early October the stock was valued at only twenty-three dollars per share, and Sculley foresaw a future industry-wide shakeout as supply reached demand. The challenge of a changing economy necessitated a new game plan and Apple had to become more market- and consumer-oriented to be competitive.

Apple successfully launched the Macintosh in 1984, marketing it as a "tool for the mind" in a bold advertising campaign that resulted in Sculley's being named by *Advertising Age* as "Adman of the Year." But Apple faced the difficult task of entering the IBM-dominated corporate market and had little success. Compounding the company's problems were analysts' reports that claimed the seven-year-old Apple II was fast becoming obsolete. Nevertheless, the company rode on the crest of a wave of success, ignoring problems with Jobs's leadership style and failing to recognize the extent of corporate resistance to the closed architecture of the Macintosh. The Mac's design and construction did not permit modification or extension by other firms or users, in sharp contrast to the Apple II, whose open architecture had spawned both a whole industry segment and enormous user innovation.

By the end of 1984, there were many signs of trouble. Several key executives and middle managers had left the company (including cofounder Steve Wozniak) because of low morale associated with Jobs's special treatment of the Macintosh division at the expense of the revenue-generating Apple II. The Macintosh building, for example, had a grand piano in the lobby and a masseuse on call. It became increasingly apparent that the "dynamic duo" of Sculley and Jobs, as the press dubbed them, needed to discipline some of the company's "unbridled enthusiasm."

It was on a rainy Thursday in November of 1984 at Pajaro Dunes, one of Apple's favorite beach-side retreat sites near Monterey, California, that my own relationship with Apple began. My plane was late because of the weather, so one group waiting for the delayed session formed a 1960s-style "human sculpture" on the floor in the middle of the meeting room, and that reminder of California's youth culture greeted me when I arrived.

Perhaps the storm was prophetic. I had been asked to speak to a group of managers about how to handle the organizational problems of rapid growth, and my remarks elicited a great deal of revealing discussion about how Apple should handle its own future. For all the youthful exuberance of Apple people and their constant use of superlatives ("insanely great products"), it was clear there was tension at the company. Many felt it was time for Apple to move out from under the shadow of its chief founder's personality. The company's entrepreneurial style was for many people not liberating but curiously disempowering. With everyone free to suggest anything or act on anything, lines of authority were fuzzy, jobs were continually invented and reinvented, and there were few mechanisms for getting what one person wanted agreed to by anyone else—unless that one person was Steve Jobs, whose whims prevailed. Perhaps worst of all, infighting between the privileged Macintosh division and the Apple II division, the chief source of the company's sales, was draining energy from everyone.

During the first few months of 1985, I met several times with staff urgently plotting solutions to these problems (including getting Steve Jobs private MBA tutoring), and I heard the first rumblings of change at the top. On the surface, it was the same old cash-rich, free-spending Apple; our meetings, for example, were at one gorgeous California resort after another, and I was picked up at and delivered to the airport in the white stretch limos favored by Apple executives. Managers still felt Apple was totally unique—no other company could be used as precedent or model—and the party line was that the task was to preserve what was best in Apple's culture against the onslaught of creeping large-size-itis. But below the surface, Apple was a company struggling not to preserve pure entrepreneurship but to transcend it. It was a company plagued by a poorly conceived organizational structure fostering internal rivalries; a closed, arrogant stance toward the outside world, including suppliers and customers; and no clear process for developing or using new ideas.

Nineteen eighty five turned out to be a year of apocalyptic change rather than mere transition. To survive, Apple could no longer be an organization composed of visionary idealists who wanted to change the way people thought about and lived life, but rather had to consist of visionary businesspeople concerned with providing for the growth of the company. The fact was that Apple was hitting limits and constraints tempering its sense of unlimited horizons. But the company lacked strategic long-term planning. Macintosh sales plummeted, and the press hounded Apple for having no set agenda for next-generation machines. Sculley commented, "The most devastating part was that we were a new products company in a new products industry, yet we weren't pushing new products out the door."[4]

Internal conflicts increased. Strife between the Macintosh and Apple II divisions climaxed when a parts-ordering "error" in Jobs's division forced discontinuation of MacXL (the renamed Lisa), a line introduced only three months earlier. Apple suffered its first quarterly loss ($17 million) since going public in 1980. Dealers lost confidence and considered dropping the Apple line. Apple had not embraced the market realities of the industry and was not producing what consumers wanted, preferring to produce technically superior products.

In mid-1985, Apple was beginning to realize it had pursued an unrealistic strategy, assuming unlimited growth; now, more attention had to be paid to the company's bottom line: "Apple would still change the world. . . . But we had to admit the world also changed us."[5] As the personal computer industry entered a recession in 1985, gross margins shrank and inventories mounted. Management's orientation had to switch from producing machines quickly to efficient operation. But Jobs was unable to put aside his desire to push the best technology and let customers influence product design and was not good at conserving scarce resources and streamlining operations.

Sculley and Jobs were in conflict over the future direction of the company. The board expressed concern that Sculley had given Jobs too much power and had made a "monster" out of him, according to reporters:

> As a boss, Jobs was often obdurate and capricious. When Macintosh's sound quality failed to meet his standards, he threatened to remove the feature unless engineers corrected the problem over a weekend. When his group failed to make progess fast enough, he fired off irate memos and abrasively talked down middle management.[6]

The divorce of the "dynamic duo" was imminent. One Apple executive commented to me around this time, "Apple is one of the few ships that leaks at the top."

Support for drastic change came from middle management as well as the board. During 1985, Apple University, the company's training arm, held a monthly "leadership experience" at Pajaro Dunes for groups of about thirty managers. One highlight was an open dialogue with Sculley. It was clear from these dialogues that many people wanted him to exercise stronger leadership and to reshape Apple's organization. It was also clear that for all the nostalgia for the old, original Apple, many of those who enjoyed working only under start-up conditions had already left; Apple now included a majority of professionally trained people who "knew not" life in the old days.

In the middle of 1985, Sculley stripped Jobs of all operating authority, relegating him to the titular role of chairman of the company. Jobs resigned shortly after that. Despite an attempted coup against him, Sculley remained in charge and made bold moves. The boldest were laying off twelve hundred employees—one of every five people—closing plants, and writing off $43 million in losses. "The corporate dream became a living nightmare," a distraught employee told me.

The biggest sign of the departure from "Old Apple" came at Sculley's first public appearance after the management restructuring that ousted Jobs and created several middle management teams to plan a new operating style. Sculley vowed that he would try extremely hard to open up the Macintosh to third-party hardware and software companies, a first attempt at eradicating the closed and almost adversarial stance Apple had taken. This new policy still did not deviate too much from the original Apple vision; Apple would avoid moves that would enhance short-term savings (like making IBM clones or licensing technology to others) and opt instead for alternatives that would make Apple products more appealing to customers. But Apple was being repositioned as a business-focused company seeking leverage in links with other companies:

> Our perspective had been hopelessly wrong. High tech could not be designed and sold as a consumer product. . . . Consumers weren't ready to put computers in their home as easily as they installed telephones, refrigerators, televisions, and even Cuisinarts. . . . We would have to shift from being a home/education company to one that served education and business.[7]

And in another departure from California arrogance, the world was scanned for talent. Apple's country manager for France, a computer prophet in his own right, was brought to Cupertino to head product development.

The new Apple approach had three prongs, not unlike those at Kodak:

- Develop an organizational structure that would produce synergies, not conflict.
- Create more cooperative alliances with suppliers and customers.
- Find ways to maintain a flow of new ideas toward new products and new ventures.

A number of organizational changes were aimed at eliminating in-fighting and increasing synergy. In order to help the organization do more with less, a functional structure (bringing all of marketing and manufacturing back together and effectively eliminating the Mac–Apple II split) tightened management control. Plants were consolidated, and Deborah Coleman, a Stanford MBA, took the leadership in implementing a manufacturing model that lowered costs and improved reliability. Inventory was reduced drastically, even if it meant selling goods at steep discounts. Television advertising was stopped; Apple relied exclusively on a limited print campaign.

The most dramatic change was in organizational structure. In 1983, Apple had essentially been four companies under one roof (Apple I, Apple III, Lisa, and Macintosh development), with all the conflcit, waste, duplication, and in-fighting that was sure to follow when turf was staked out like that in a company whose divisions all sold similar products to essentially the same market. Instead of a team, Apple was a collection of individuals, all running their own functions. Just as the organization was rigidly segmented, all of Apple's products were segmented—incompatible with other personal computers. Later in 1983, there was an effort to take advantage of immediate internal synergies by dividing the company into only the Macintosh and Apple II divisions. However, many insiders still believed that far greater resources were devoted to the Macintosh division than was appropriate. Inequities and in-fighting resulted in a substantial exodus of managerial talent. Sculley recalled: "The tensions that developed between the two groups could have cracked steel . . . [Jobs] and his Macintosh cohorts began to openly call everyone else in the company 'bozos.' "[8]

Thus, in 1985, after Jobs left, Sculley consolidated both divisions into one and drew together an executive managerial team. As one member stated to me in typical Applelike language, "If the forces of light don't get it together like the forces of darkness have, we can kiss it goodbye." A crisis that threatened the company's survival stimulated constructive alliances and interaction, synergies that helped Apple emerge as a company that could take calculated risks and quickly adapt to new market and intraorganizational conditions. The introduction of the Apple IIgs in 1986 represented a symbolic renewed emphasis on the II product line. Internal tensions within the organization dissipated.

Apple also realized that in order to become a key player in the business market, it had to open its closed computer. One move in that direction was "AppleTalk," a network that enabled up to thirty-two users in a Macintosh group to communicate with one another; another was software that would allow the IBM PC to work with Macintoshes on a network. This was a significant enough change for Apple that it made news in the business press in 1987:

APPLE LINKS TO IBM, DEC FOR BUSINESS MARKET GLUT (*Computer World*, November 4)

IT LOOKS LIKE THE APPLE MAC HAS FINALLY RIPENED TO CORPORATE STANDARDS (*PC Week*, March 31)

APPLE STARTS SWIMMING IN BUSINESS MAINSTREAMS (*Chicago Sun Times*, March 2)

Apple also formed strategic partnerships with third-party developers, certifying many firms, which permitted the companies to call themselves Apple-certified developers and gave them discounts on Apple products. Products developed in 1988 included a hard card, which enabled a Macintosh to run IBM PC or AT programs, a hardware device that enabled the transfer of word-processing documents from an IBM PC to a Macintosh, and software that turned the Macintosh into a simulated IBM.

The third challenge for the "new" Apple was to maintain a stream of new ideas. Apple did this through an explicit process of helping new ventures to form as well as encouraging innovation in existing businesses through a greater commitment of resources to research and development.

Apple began to rely on "spinouts" to enrich the market capitalization of the parent company and keep entrepreneurs who would build new enterprises within the fold. Spinouts were different from the typical "spinoff" in that they were meant to sustain a long-term relationship with Apple; they were not unwanted assets that the parent corporation was shedding. Spinouts were intended to enlarge Apple without adding bureaucracy. Executives anticipated a future federation of companies that stemmed from the parent and explored new, related fields like systems products or markets like industrial training. Ties would be similar to ties that Apple had with third-party companies, but the companies involved would be more interdependent. As Sculley explained:

> The mothership, then, not only attempted to preserve creativity and innovation in "smaller" environments, it sought to simplify the structure and process. The fact is that new or small enterprises have been more successful at this than larger ones. We want to postpone the natural tendency for an Apple to become institutionalized. By creating the federation, it can become the mother of invention without having to give up the small company values we pride.[9]

The first spinout was Claris, which develops Apple software. Apple still owns 75 percent of the company, and Apple employees own the remainder.

To further ensure that entrepreneurial ventures could find a home at Apple, the company launched a venture capital organization in May 1986 called Apple Strategic Investment Group. It planned to invest up to $15 million in small hardware firms with emerging technologies and in software companies developing products for Apple equipment.

In 1986 and 1987, then, a major cultural change was taking place. Apple was no longer egocentric and arrogant, but was market-driven and innovative in giving customers the services and support they wanted. A more integrated structure stressing cooperation alleviated in-fighting and dissension. Having penetrated the business sector, Apple was no longer dependent on a single market. The company had a pipeline of new products into the early 1990s and recognized that customer-oriented R&D provided the foundation for success. Apple was financially stable, had hot marketing strategies, strong products, and well-established links to third-party companies whose add-on options enhanced the power and appeal of Macintosh. A "certified developer" program became the basis for a cooperative high-tech network.

As the "old Apple" was transformed into the "new Apple," a new leadership model was adopted. In Sculley's words:

> The heroic style—the lone cowboy on horseback—is not the figure we worship anymore at Apple. In the new corporation, heroes won't personify any single set of achievements. Instead, they personify the process. They might be thought of as gatekeepers, information carriers, and teams. Originally heroes at Apple were the hackers and engineers who created the products. Now, more teams are heroes.[10]

Teams rather than cowboys were clearly the heroes of a recent Apple event I participated in. It was a conference in Hawaii for the worldwide finance organization, now reporting to Debi Coleman, who had moved from manufacturing to become chief financial officer. Almost a dozen teams reported the results of several months' work assessing the challenges of the future and the kind of organization they needed to address them—a degree of integration of disparate parts of the company that bodes well for Apple's ability to work cooperatively across functions around the globe.

By 1988, Apple had proved that it can not only trim costs and improve profitability but also reposition itself and grow. After just a dozen years of existence, Apple is rapidly approaching the $4 billion mark in sales. Meanwhile, Apple managers are still working hard to integrate the entrepreneurial spirit with corporate discipline.

As a consequence, performance-conscious Apple people continue to work twelve- and fourteen-hour workdays as they take advantage of the opportunities for initiative and innovation in the more focused, more team-oriented Apple. But a new set of questions is arising in the human resources department in the wake of all these exciting work opportunities: how to promote a balanced life; how to find time for the family. There are similar questions about careers, since many people still join Apple to find an alternative to the big corporation, not to become part of one. The network of companies springing up around Apple and providing leverage for it—its spinouts, its strategic partners—is providing career options based not on climbing the corporate ladder as an employee but on growing a business or profession on one's own as a contractor or partner. The old entrepreneurial Apple is evolving into a post-entrepreneurial prototype.

THE RISE OF THE POST-ENTREPRENEURIAL MODEL

There are clear differences between Kodak and Apple, of course, even beyond the obvious differences in products and markets. They come from opposite ends of the company life cycle—mature Goliath versus young David—and opposite ends of the the country, and thus from vastly different traditions. Both faced business crises because their internal structures were no longer fit for competition in the global corporate Olympics, yet the crises themselves were totally different. Too-bureaucratic Kodak had begun to stagnate, had become burdened with a cumbersome organization that encouraged bureaucratic turf-consciousness and stifled innovation. Too-entrepreneurial Apple was mired in the problems of transition from the founder and the chaotic start-up mode, was caught in internal rivalries that wasted resources, and had not yet harnessed the achievement drives of individuals to shared purposes.

Different companies, then, at different ends of the spectrum, are meeting in the middle. As Kodak moves away from "corpocracy" and Apple away from its cowboylike start-up mode, they are converging on a new model. It is a post-entrepreneurial model that marries the best of the creative, entrepreneurial approach with the discipline, focus, and teamwork of an agile, innovative corporation.

The internal structural re-examination both Kodak and Apple carried out led naturally to reconsideration of what the company has to do by itself and what it can do through partnerships with other organizations—thus changing the employment base, simultaneously reducing fixed costs and extending the company's reach. Both struggled with their own brands of arrogance, overcoming the sense that going it alone and doing it "our way" were automatically better. More cooperation inside was matched by more cooperation outside.

Thus, as both Kodak and Apple confront the new economic realities of learning to do more with less, they have hit upon similar management strategies: restructuring to find synergies among pieces of the business, both old ones and acquired ones; opening their boundaries to form strategic alliances with suppliers, customers, and venture partners; and developing explicit programs of investment and coaching to stimulate and guide the creation of new ventures from within. These three strategies form the core of the post-entrepreneurial management revolution.

It is one thing to define these strategies, however, and another thing to make them work. Both Kodak and Apple confront new dilemmas new challenges and balancing acts, as they learn how to do more with less. And the post-entrepreneurial revolution that they are experiencing has major social and economic consequences for the American people—for the shape of the paycheck, the nature of the workplace, the connection between work life and personal life, the security of the job, and the form of a career.

I picked Eastman Kodak and Apple Computer as prototypes to introduce my themes because they represent extremes in American industry: the venerable old corporation nearly left behind by change and the young high-tech company nearly destroyed by its own success. But I could just as easily have picked another pair of seemingly dissimilar companies, Pacific Telesis in California and Digital Equipment Corporation in Massachusetts. Here, too, companies of disparate industry, age, and culture have met in the middle in the search for new organizational strategies better suited for the corporate Olympics.

PacTel was "born" on January 1, 1984, in the break-up of AT&T, when for the first time, telephone operating companies were forced to deal with the complexities of managing in a competitive environment. But of course, PacTel was really an extension of a much older company with plenty of time to get set in its ways. Divestiture from AT&T pushed Pacific Telesis into the corporate Olympics. As a result, it restructured, reduced employment, attempted to move its bureaucratic culture in more entrepreneurial directions, and formed an innovative strategic alliance with its major union. The new chairman, Sam Ginn, was the architect of a search for new ventures that took PacTel into cellular phone businesses, computer retailing, paging, publishing, and software.

If PacTel's history had been that of a protected monopoly, Digital had experienced the opposite: rapid growth as an industry innovator. But in 1984 Digital also faced major business challenges, as its position in the international marketplace slipped, and unbridled internal entrepreneurship no longer helped the company compete.

Digital brought a new focus to the business, reorganized to promote synergies between functional areas and product lines, and moved to a partnership philosophy with suppliers and customers. As Digital added a little more "bureaucratic discipline" and PacTel added a little more "entrepreneurial spirit" to their cultures, these polar opposites began to converge.

Companies like these are leading-edge examples of how a broad range of American companies are meeting the challenges of survival in today's rapidly changing business environment. Because each industry is different and each company faces unique problems, companies are moving toward the post-entrepreneurial model in different ways. But still, there is increasing agreement that the traditional corpocracy has to give way as the central image of the ideal corporation. The new management strategies are no longer radical experiments but eminently respectable business practices.

Indeed, as post-entrepreneurial responses to the demands of the corporate Olympics gain respectability, their very spread creates a need for new tools and new practices. Clearly, Americans are beyond needing still another exhortation for businesses to change. Change is already taking place, and America is already beginning to adjust. But the problem is that our action runs ahead of our understanding. Many companies, many managers, many average employees and their families are not yet prepared to cope effectively with the implications of the changes they are living through.

American business is in transition because the world economy is changing. As a result, America as a nation is changing. But what do these changes in the contemporary economy mean in practice? What are the principal ways companies implement strategies for doing more with less? What are the variations from which diverse companies in diverse industries choose as they find the form that best meets their own business situation? When are these changes handled well, and when are they mismanaged? What leadership skills and organizational structures support the new strategies? And finally, what are the economic and social dilemmas that confront all of us as businesses start to take a new shape?

We must search for the answers to these questions, not only in an attempt to comprehend the sweeping nature of the new business strategies, but also to prepare for their consequences.

PART TWO

DOING MORE WITH LESS:

Strategies for Post-Entrepreneurial Management

CHAPTER 3

Desperately Seeking Synergies: The Promise and Perils of Restructuring

Shuffling and reshuffling the organizational deck to deal a better hand for the company has always been a fact of life for American business. But today companies are changing their shape more frequently and more dramatically. In an effort to increase the value generated by their activities, they are reducing costs by becoming leaner, changing the business mix to gain greater focus, discontinuing or contracting out activities unrelated to their core competence, and more flexibly moving into and out of businesses.

By early 1988, the dollar volume of transactions involving the buying and selling of corporate assets was already twice the rate of 1987, and experts foresaw a new corporate-led, not raider-led, merger boom. Inside companies, "downsizing" (cutting employment), "de-massing" (eliminating middle management positions), and decentralizing corporate staff functions are among the tactics used by companies eager to be "seeking and destroying wealth dissipators," as a consulting firm put it.

For many companies, this involves a complex of changes rather than a single one, and restructuring is a continuing process, almost a corporate fitness regimen. An executive at a revitalized manufacturing firm summarized that company's experience this way:

> It seemed that we were changing at a pretty fast pace a few years ago, but that period pales in comparison with the present. One major effort, almost revolutionary in its proportions, is completely redesigning our compensation system to modify the relationship between fixed and variable income and giving employees a significant ownership position in the enterprise. Beginning with the merger and acquisition activity which started it all, then the name change—a significant, emotionally-charged event—through the recapitalization and now the shift to a holding company form with new leadership, we have reexamined and continue to reexamine most of the fundamental premises underlying the business.

Restructuring has an entrepreneurial thrust for companies trying to win in the global Olympics. An emphasis on innovation creates new opportunities, which in turn require a new organizational shape. The deal-making emphasis, the development of partnerships, brings with it the need for new structures to handle the new relationships. The flexibility to move into and out of ventures, reflected in part in the current wave of acquisitions, mergers, and divestitures, leads to major organizational changes. In short, while some restructuring is purely defensive—cost-cutting in response to market downturns, shedding assets in response to takeover threats—most involves not simply reducing and not simply asset-shuffling but something more: an effort to find the form that will permit doing more with less. Spending less but creating more value. Focus without fat.

The point of the current corporate shape-up boom is to achieve synergies—the value that comes when the whole adds up to more than the sum of the parts. Clearly, if the parts taken separately are worth more than the parts taken together, the raiders have a point in insisting that such companies be broken up. But synergies are notoriously difficult to achieve, even with smart acquisitions and a sound mix of activities. The track record for acquisitions is mixed; immediate financial benefits to the acquiring firm are hard to achieve.[1] And the costs of restructuring may even reduce performance.

Thus, the first challenge facing businesses as they seek the shapes and forms for value creation is retaining the value inherent in the pre-existing pieces, avoiding the perils and pitfalls that actually subtract value and make the whole worth *less* than the sum of its parts.

Whether reorganizations occur because of internal drives to increase effectiveness or because of mergers and acquisitions, whether acquisitions are in related or unrelated businesses, whether the company is adding activities or divesting them, the management task is similar: to manage the process so that value is at least retained. That provides the minimum foundation on which real synergies—value added and multiplied—can be built. Three typical examples from companies I worked with illustrate how diverse strategic intentions may result in a similar organizational task:

- As part of the effort of a major company in a mature manufacturing industry to diversify into growth sectors, a new group was formed from a potpourri of acquisitions, bought from both large companies (which themselves had acquired those pieces within the last ten years) and entrepreneurs who had built promising smaller companies. In corporate strategy jargon, many of the pieces were "cats and dogs" to their former parents, rather than "stars." The new group's executives, from the largest acquisition, faced the challenge of pulling the pieces together to meet ambitious five-year growth goals to provide a sufficient return on the purchase price. Step one was consolidation, and consolidation meant closing plants and cutting staff while investing enough in new products to be a strong presence in the marketplace.
- An aggressive consumer-oriented service business in a growing industry bought two major companies over a six-month period, almost quadrupling its size. The purchases turned out to be more costly than expected, and the acquisitions had more financial problems than were known in advance. Paying for the purchases meant integrating a number of functions to get economies of scale and letting go large numbers of managers and professionals. For the first two years, the managerial focus was almost exclusively devoted to consolidating operations, growing profits by reducing costs.
- A machinery producer facing declining markets had been through several rounds of layoffs and cutbacks, which was not enough to turn around its traditional business. Still, there was optimism because of solid performance in a second major business, and the company launched a future-oriented campaign to rally employees behind a culture of quality and innovation. Three months later, the company announced the sale of its core business to a competitor in order to

concentrate on the other business. An eighteen-month transition began
that would result in a newly named company with half the revenues
and less than half as many employees, because most of the corporate
staffs would now be unnecesssary. After so many promises of "no
more layoffs," how could the company get through still one more
bloodletting while strengthening the remaining business?

Each of these restructurings was plausible from a strategic
standpoint—more value could be created through the reconfigured
organizations. The first made business sense because the company had
to diversify to survive, acquisition was the quickest route into a
desirable new industry, and the combination of smaller companies
could gain strength in unity. The second made business sense because
of the great growth potential in the industry and the excellent fit
between the companies. The third made business sense because the
divested core business would be better off as part of a larger merged
entity, and the remaining company would be leaner and more focused.

But strategic rationality was not the issue for the people who had to
work with the new pieces or for the people displaced by the changes.
For them, the first task was simply to retain the value that already
existed in the organization, as the foundation for creation of new value
in the future.

In situations like these, top management typically *overestimates* the
degree of cooperation it will get and *underestimates* the integration
costs. Two executives said about the restructuring process in an
instruments company:

> It was a friendly acquisition. At least, I thought it was. I found out later
> we didn't have as many friends as we thought we did. [CEO]

> We underestimated the problems of bringing the businesses together in
> one major market, of a successful introduction of [the other company's]
> products in our market, and of getting each company's sales force to sell
> the other's products. [group vice-president]

Middle managers, for their part, said that lack of commitment was the
problem:

> We've been bought and sold and consolidated before. People don't
> believe anything issued that says "management." We all come from

companies that made a commitment for the future. [division general manager]

Why should anyone care if this becomes a great company? [president of acquired subsidiary]

What are the rewards, the incentives for doing this? There's no training and development, no career promises. Taking a risk, making a suggestion, starting a new project—that could be a career-limiting move. [division controller]

I come from an organization that said, "We're committed to you," while unbeknownst to me, they were putting us up for sale. Now here we are. [division vice-president]

Should we write the list of our locations in pencil? [division manager]

Numerous studies have shown that acquisitions do not generally improve the financial performance of acquiring firms in the short run. One study, covering 103 active acquirers from 1965 to 1979, showed that, on the average, the firms deteriorated in competitive position within their industries, and the extent of deterioration was associated with the number of acquisitions (but not with the degree to which acquisitions were related to the core business).[2] Explanations for the failures of synergy include: resistance by managers of acquired businesses to the consolidation of activities; reduced motivation after the acquisition; expenditure of energy on acquisitions leading to neglect of the pre-existing businesses; and too much acquisition activity overloading the management systems. In short, the way the acquisitions process is implemented makes a difference.

Robert Tomasko makes a similar point with respect to downsizing—that attention to the *process* of change is critical to retaining instead of losing value: "The slash-and-burn approach to streamlining may produce significant overhead reductions in the near term. And a combination of fear and adrenaline might even keep the survivors on a common course for a while." But Tomasko argues that *sustainable* downsizing that will result in a well-functioning organization is a different matter, requiring more leadership attention than a one-time cost-saving through layoffs.[3]

Among the many by-products of significant organizational restructuring are *discontinuity, disorder,* and *distraction.* There are gaps between what was once appropriate and what will now be appropriate—until the next change. There is uncertainty about what should be done and the standards to apply. And restructuring produces distractions in the organization; it diverts people's attention from the critical focus. At the same time, leaders may be less available to counter these three dangerous *D*'s. Managers have important immediate tasks to perform and decisions to make. They are called away for meetings, they are engaged in secret deliberations. They are so swamped by urgent *content* priorities (decisions about what to do) that they simply do not have time or attention for *process* matters (observation of how things are going).

If mismanaged, restructuring can all too easily make people feel helpless, anxious, startled, embarrassed, dumb, overworked, cynical, hostile, or hurt. Restructuring thus produces a window of vulnerability, a time when exposure to disease is increased at precisely the same time as the corporate body is temporarily weakened. This threatens not only current productivity, but also the foundation for the future, the organization's credibility, culminating in a *crisis of commitment and a need for people to reaffirm their membership.* Every time the basis of the relationship of employee and company changes, a recommitment is necessary. It is especially ironic that more commitment is needed at the very time when the basis for commitment itself is temporarily weakened.

THREATS TO CURRENT PRODUCTIVITY

Restructurings can provide a long catalogue of threats to value retention.

The costs of confusion. People can't find things, they don't know their own telephone extensions, and the letterhead hasn't arrived.

Misinformation. Communication is haphazard. Some managers do a better job than others of keeping their people informed. Rumors are created and take on a life of their own, especially when it is not clear who has the "right" information. Some of the rumors are potentially destructive.

Emotional leakage. Managers are so focused on the tasks to be done and decisions to be made that they neglect or ignore the emotional reactions engendered by the change. But the reactions leak out anyway, sometimes in unusual behavior.

Loss of energy. Any change consumes emotional energy—especially if the restructuring is perceived negatively. People become preoccupied with the current situation. They feel guilt about the people who are losing something. The mood becomes somber, morale sinks, and it is hard to maintain the usual pace of work. For example:

> It's very hard to work when you have no idea what will happen next. "Final" changes are replaced by new ones every other week. So even when you're told you survived a "final" round of cuts, you know you can still get another turn next month. No one can really know what's coming down at his level until they settle who's where on the top floors. Right now it's so chaotic you can be demoted if you stay on, but also called disloyal if you go for the exit package. Most of the people leaving looked relaxed, like now they can stop worrying about what's happening here. The ones who can't get out or want to stay anyway are the most nervous and upset.[4]

Interviews Paul Hirsch conducted indicate that feelings of anxiety, uncertainty—even being terrified—persist three years after restructuring, even for a group with high productivity not directly affected by downsizing. Sometimes the effects are bizarre. Some people come to work in an almost catatonic state, starting no new programs; others who have been let go continue to come in to the office.

Loss of key resources. Some companies handle consolidations in bureaucratic rather than human ways, by establishing uniform policies administered uniformly, to be "fair" to everyone and to avoid difficult or time-consuming decisions. But across-the-board cuts mean that inevitably some very good people are lost who could serve the company in other roles.

Also, attention to the immediate and acute, to the cutting and reshaping and moving, leads to a rush to take care of the people being displaced and neglect of the people being *kept,* the people on whom the future depends. Even the most people-conscious organizations often focus on their cutting decisions and on services such as outplacement for those let go, and not on the positive decision about whom to keep. Under those circumstances, some people whom the organization would have liked to keep will decide to leave.

Breakdown of initiative. Because of the uncertainty and the clear message that top management is redefining its mandates through restructuring, people below become passive and wait to be told what to do. Initiative and spirit are lost. Production of ideas declines, because people say, "Why bother? It's out of our hands. Everything might change again."

Weakened faith in leaders' ability to deliver, and the need for scapegoats. Management can lose credibility because of the shock of a restructuring crisis or the apparent "lurches" in the business strategy. These may represent shortfalls of leadership. The ghosts of false reassurances can come back to haunt leaders. Implicit problems made now seem to be broken.

During restructuring, it is difficult enough to retain the value that exists, let alone rally people behind the quest for improvements in performance. The further removed people are from the leadership ranks, the greater their cynicism. "Management is more gullible than the troops," one manager who had been through several acquisitions told me. "Managers will line up behind any banner."

Rents in the Social Fabric: Power Differences Made Visible

All the anxieties and uncertainties of the transition process can pale in comparison with another, more permanent by-product of restructuring: awareness of the realities of limits to individual power. Restructuring threatens to disempower large numbers of people, illuminating and enhancing the power of "commanders" and making other people feel more dependent and less valued in the process.

Some restructurings divide people into conquerors and vanquished. When one group clearly "takes over" another group in a merger or internal restructuring, the conqueror inevitably parades its power in front of the others: "After all, wasn't our ability to buy you a sign of our superiority?" Imagine hearing an executive tell managers from an acquired company that "You are frogs we will teach to be princes." Or imagine watching the acquiring company dismantle the other company's boardroom, taking the best furniture and silver to outfit its own headquarters.[5] Both of these real examples may be extreme, but the same feeling of being "colonized" like a defeated country exists in many groups that are merged with a more dominant entity. Sometimes the "colony" has expertise that the "conqueror" should use, but the power dynamics preclude this. As analysts put it, "The parents' desire to help the new subsidiary and their confidence about their own capabilities often lead to a misappalication of management systems which reduces the chances for the acquisition's ultimate success as a subunit of the parent firm."[6]

The acquisition of different parts of the Ziff-Davis publishing organization by both CBS and Rupert Murdoch provides an interesting contrast with respect to this issue. As *Forbes* magazine argued, "Rupert Murdoch did a better job with the Ziff-Davis publications that he bought than CBS did, because he runs such a lean operation that couldn't impose a bureaucracy on top of another, 'proving smart enough not to tamper with the hands-off management style their editors and publishers had grown used to.' . . . At CBS, by contrast, executives attempted to superimpose a corpocracy culture."[7]

Arrogance and organizational chauvinism on the "conqueror's" part lead to defensiveness and concern on the other side. People sense a loss of power to determine their own fate. When Chevron took over Gulf Oil, Gulf people found Chevron leaner, more centrally run, and more clannish, leading to widespread fears that they would lose autonomy and find Chevron blocking promotions for Gulf people.[8] At the same time, managers in the conquering unit express impatience that they cannot go even further in using their power. In a consumer products company which I advised after it acquired a group of small-volume products, a manager told me that her company was going *too far* in trying to empower the group they bought. "Looking for ways for them [the acquired company] to be of help to our organization isn't a good use of time." Worried that so many small products would diffuse management attention, she concluded: "We bent over backwards to make them feel welcome. We should have just said this is the way it is . . . I'm sick of apologizing for our differences. I've heard a lot of bitching about our rules. Well, I think we've been too nice."

"This is the way it is." Restructuring makes clear the realities of power. This is particularly difficult for pure entrepreneurial companies. Many young organizations are designed to be empowering—to provide the information, resources, and support for people to speak up and to initiate action, with a minimum of distinctions between categories of people. Of course, every time someone innovates, someone else is made the responder, but on everyday matters, there's a rough reciprocity. Still, despite this participative atmosphere, power

differences exist. When all is said and done, some of the most important life-shaping and work-shaping decisions are made by just a handful of people. Everyone else is on the receiving end.

In traditional corporations, this is well understood. But in younger, smaller companies, even ones with a strong leader, there is a tacit agreement to pretend that the differences between people have nothing to do with power—to pretend, for example, that the leader's strength derives from superior qualifications, not from power over the fates of people. Power is easier to forget, for the day-to-day absence of constraints masks the ultimate realities of power. The mandate to take responsibility, the pretense of equality because of the absence of visible status markers, and the frequency of open and honest dialogues across levels make it easy for some people to ignore power differences.

But then major change makes the realization hit. Those in control of restructuring decisions have much more power than others, even managers with a geat deal of local autonomy. A man whose company was undergoing drastic restructuring told me, "Despite my modest ownership share and strategic centrality and voice in decisions, I can still be faced with a shift in direction not of my own making. I can still be reviewed out of my special project budget."

At one computer company, layoffs—the first the company had faced—killed forever the fantasies some people held about the company. The period of innocence was over—and none too soon, other people thought. The layoffs came unexpectedly, followed by a boardroom coup and a reorganization. There was a brief moment of wondering whom the board would back when the CEO wanted to fire a key executive with strong personal backing on the board, but soon the answer was clear. It was now the CEO's company. The reorganization confirmed it. This new reality, with power out in the open, was hard to swallow for some of the managers I spoke to. Even though the other executive had been, in their view, more domineering and whimsical than the CEO, and the CEO was a better listener, the myths of life "before" had made these managers feel they could do anything, take the company anywhere.

Restructuring, in short, increases the likelihood of unilateral managerial action, which is exercised on everything all at once and further disempowers the rest of the people. Of course, because of all the distruptions, it is more important at times of restructuring than during normal times to make clear that someone is in charge. But some managers interpret this need as the need to take drastic steps and make dramatic decisions quickly. They feel that there is no time to explore options or consider ideas from the troops. So people are reminded of their marginal status; signals tell them their positions are vulnerable. Perhaps the press gets announcements and briefings regularly and items run in the media before employees hear about them. Middle managers look dumb and uninformed. Employees feel left out. No one looks or feels good. For example, morale plummeted during one General Foods cutback because insiders heard about the changes from outsiders (consultants or stockbrokers)—sometimes incorrectly.[9] In situations like this, values regarding participation, involvement, or concern for people seem to fly out the window as luxuries of good times. Inevitably, cynicism about the ''culture'' grows along with distrust of leaders.

Thus, overzealous or misdirected attempts to ''solve'' restructuring problems can easily exacerbate them, turning relatively minor irritations into genuine and enduring crises for the organization—the struggle to retain value turning into actual loss, into value subtracted.

VALUE SUBTRACTED: THE DANGERS OF THE ''MEAN'' WITH THE ''LEAN''

Turning ''lean and mean'' is one way American managers have expressed restructuring goals of cutting out the fat and getting in competitive shape by finding the proper mix of businesses. The rhyme is cute, but the sentiment it expresses can be pernicious. The first requirement in finding synergies is to remove the barriers to successful restructuring, and hostile internal competition is foremost among them.

I saw this issue nearly destroy a company when I observed the misfortunes of a high-flying financial services firm I'll call ''Fastbuck.'' The company had enjoyed rapid growth and seemed positioned well to take advantage of deregulation. Then trouble struck when a new business was acquired. At least in retrospect the acquisition was the problem; at the time many observers said that the strategy was a smart one, a perfect fit, a great way to get synergies. The new business was to be a form of balance and a hedge against downturns in the core business, as well as a source of new service packages that would boost both businesses.

The difficulty was not in the strategy but in its execution. The two businesses were almost immediately set up to compete for resources and the attention of the CEO, and the two business heads were told to fight for the big prize—the CEO's job. One business would be swallowing the other when it became clear where the fortunes of the company lay.

The CEO, known around Fastbuck as a "gunslinger" type who liked "shooting from the hip," thought this made the most business sense. He wanted to push both groups to do their utmost, and he knew no other way. So each business had a totally separate organization, and nothing was done to create ties between the people in each. It was thought to be healthier to allow each to push its point of view and argue for its own needs, even in the same market. There was no shared past to provide a basis for relationships anyway. The new business brought newcomers with it—a staff with little knowledge or experience of the original business. Moreover, the key executives of the new business were attracted by subtle promises that they were the future of Fastbuck and that soon they would be running the whole thing. Naturally enough, they made their understanding clear to anyone who would listen. Their behavior was arrogant, and their attitude toward their peers in the original business was patronizing.

The organizational competition was matched by the strong rivalry between the heads of the two businesses, whom I'll call Fred and George. In fact, the old business/new business competition was often personalized as a battle between Fred and George. At management events, everyone watched to see how the CEO treated each, who got more time and attention, whose hand showed most strongly in the agenda, whose interests were best served by policy announcements.

The CEO was clearly attracted by the glamour of new business, a higher-risk gamble that appealed to his sense of daring. Besides, he could take the old business for granted; its revenues were assured and predictable. Furthermore, he still felt he had to court the new executives in order to keep them, as he could not count on their loyalty as he could count on that of Fred and Fred's people, most of whom had grown up with the company. Consequently, when people read the cues, they thought all signs pointed to George and his business as the clear winner.

Fred, too, read the signs (he thought), so he stopped arguing for the needs of his business. He became passive and took it as inevitable that he would soon be reporting to George anyway, because the CEO, from whom he was accustomed to taking direction, had said nothing to the contrary. Fred started avoiding his boss, confining contact to the minimum necessary.

George, in contrast, became even more feisty, outspoken, and aggressive. Promoting the virtues of coming from outside, he called himself the voice of the future, the iconoclast who had to overcome the limitations of tradition—and thus did not need to know much about the original business. He lobbied everywhere for his conviction that the new business was clearly the only bet for Fastbuck's future—so much so that the original business should be gradually dismantled or turned into a mere service center for the new one. He took every opportunity to push himself or his people. He approached the CEO often with suggestions and recommendations. Soon he appeared to have the ear, and the total confidence, of the CEO and the board.

There was just one niggling fly in the ointment. Who was winning the internal competition had little to do with who was better positioned to help the company win in the global marketplace. Fred's business, the traditional business, was still responsible for 90 percent of the company's revenues and all of its profits, and it was expanding to more overseas locations. The original business was the cash generator and the new one was the cash consumer, since it was still in a start-up mode with heavy investment requirements. So the idea of the new business as company savior and company future was still pie-in-the-sky, an unproven proposition. If George's business "won," what would happen to the company's only reliable source of revenue?

That was the real problem. The original business was in danger of collapsing as a result of the internal competition. Fred's unit was starved for capital. Because Fred did not fight back in public or combat George's aggressiveness with countermoves (Fred claims he was too busy running his business), his managers assumed that their business was indeed being phased out. Faced with a perception of themselves as the losers, they too dropped out. They stopped planning for the future and became passive in their own operations, taking care of immediate issues as a holding action but not taking the steps to ensure that the original business would continue to flourish. Feeling demoralized, as losers generally do, they retreated into a hostile defensiveness, blaming every glitch in business results on someone else. Many key managers began dusting off their résumés to look for other jobs, working only halfheartedly. And, what was even worse from a performance standpoint, they assumed that they would soon be reporting to George, so they let him and his lieutenants begin to dictate terms. They gave in (albeit reluctantly and resentfully) when their peers in the new business made demands on their own resources, which only weakened the core business further.

Soon revenues in the original business were declining, and earnings were on the wrong side of flat. This was a troubled company, financially as well as organizationally.

A self-reinforcing cycle was in motion. The original business was being pummeled and bled by the new business warriors. But as things got worse for the old business, George used this as still more ammunition for his argument that he (and his business) should take over the whole thing.

George was sure he was winning, but that's not how things turned out. Within six months of the time that subtle competition turned into open warfare, Fastbuck hit a major financial crisis. Because both revenues and profits were down, the stock price plummeted, and 20 percent of the employees were laid off. The CEO had to do something dramatic to rescue the company, and it was clear that the present organization was a source of problems, not solutions. So both George and Fred were fired, and the company was reorganized to integrate the two lines of business into a single market-facing entity. An executive was brought home from an overseas assignment to head the newly combined entity, because he was seen as above the fray, untainted by the competition. Another half year after that, pieces of the new business were sold as the CEO decided to concentrate on the original business. But now Fastbuck was weaker and created less value than it had before.

It was a clear case of the limits of a style of management favored by "gunslingers"—"management in the OK Corral."

The Problems of Cowboys as Managers

In the stampede to restructure, to become "lean and mean," is American business in danger of uncritically embracing "cowboy management"? Some companies believe in that romanticized picture of the virtues of rugged individualism and unbridled competition. The cowboy is viewed as the ultimate entrepreneur and the frontier metaphor is invoked frequently at those companies. Consider these comments to an interviewer by a veteran of a service-based company:

> It's like an old Western movie where the [field manager] is the sheep herder and the [headquarters] guys are the cattle ranchers. Everything

was sort of peaceful until [headquarters] wanted some fences put up for the cows while [the field manager] wanted the whole prairie for his sheep to graze. Someone had to move or there was going to be a shoot-out.[10]

Cowboy management makes heroes out of hipshooters who fire before aiming. In the every-man-for-himself world of cowboy management (the male designation applies), rules are there to be broken by daring frontierspeople who do not hesitate to bootleg funds if they feel they know better than the sissy city folks at headquarters. What a cowboy manager likes best is being alone out there in the wilderness with a few trusty pals, no constraints (like government regulations, family obligations, or corporate reporting), and a few foreign savages to fight.

Of course, it is dangerous out there. Masked raiders are ready to commit hostile takeovers against the unwary, and great natural disasters like restructurings threaten to eliminate jobs. So law and order is maintained in the tough, survival-of-the-fittest style of the frontier: through performance shootouts at high noon, in which the best gunslinger emerges victorious. Cowboy managers seem to like the sight of blood, so they deliberately set up groups inside their companies to slug it out in structured competitions. Or they pit new hires against each other in life-or-death struggles—like the head of an electronics firm who told his lastest batch of recruits, "Only half of you will be here in two years."

Cowboy mythology holds that corporate citizens are supposed to enjoy combat, and they are supposed to be tough enough to take it. It glorifies the rough-and-tumble fight-it-out style. Cooperation, in turn, is seen as "soft," as something for "sissies," or as something imposed by "citified" bureaucrats. "Tough" management styles are regularly glamorized in the press, as in *Fortune* magazine's listing of the "ten toughest bosses in America."

Such ideas lurked behind the new business/old business competition in the case of Fastbuck, the financial services firm. The "gunslinger" chief executive thought that anything else was a sign of weakness. He thought that being impulsive—shooting from the hip—was a sign of how smart he was, and he expected similar behavior from his managers. He had made it to the top by besting external competitors, and he felt that everyone thrived on competition—even when people were supposedly on the same team.

A more Machiavellian purpose also drives in-house competition:

using competition to gain short-term political advantages. Such advantages accrue especially to the overseer of the battles. For the boss who defines the competition and chooses the winners, power is temporarily enhanced. He can use the competition to keep people off balance, to keep them scrambling to curry favor with him, to watch them expend energy weakening each other while he remains fresh.

Finally, in-house competition can be the unintended result of other management practices. The new chief operating officer in a Midwestern manufacturing firm was minted in one of those companies known for its reigns of terror, managed by large doses of public humiliation. When the operating results of each of his divisions were discussed in executive committee meetings, he badgered and needled those with poor results until they felt thoroughly embarrassed in front of their peers and unable to defend themselves adequately even when there were good business reasons for the numbers. At first this behavior created a kind of perverse peer solidarity among the division heads. I passed by a set of them one day as they were waiting to go into the boss's office for individual reviews of their strategic plans. They were comparing notes about who "got it" last time, how the first person's review had gone, and what they might do to avoid getting hit. But still, it was possible to detect a secret joy for some of them in seeing the punishment heaped on someone else. Soon the desire to deflect punishment led to whisper campaigns by the more ambitious against their peers, leaking tidbits about the performance of other divisions to the boss.

From Shootouts to Rodeos: Varieties of Cowboy Competition
Cowboy competition can come in many guises. For a number of different reasons, often tied to restructuring, groups are put into direct competition, their fate determined by how well they do relative to an internal rival. For example:

The parallel start-up. In this situation the company already has a successful line of business in a particular market, but it adds a competing product line in-house to make sure the market is adequately covered. In one such case, the chief executive of a multidivisional consumer products firm was dissatisfied with the performance of a major division. So he authorized the ambitious general manager of another division to develop a competing line of products. One way it could gain market share was by reducing the share of the existing business.

The "replacement" business. In one example, a high-tech company had grown rapidly on the strength of one major product line, and its founder-chairman was eager to see a new family of products developed that would be an even more spectacular success. A division was set up to develop, manufacture, and market the new line, with his personal blessing and clear personal interest. The new division quickly saw its mission as replacing the old product—even though they would occupy very different market niches, and the company would have need for both. There was a similar situation in an energy firm that acquired a new business to cover downturns in the market for its core business. Because of the way the acquisition was introduced and managed, its leaders (inaccurately) saw themselves and their business substituting for the traditional business, with the old one to be reshaped into a service center for the new one.

Creeping market boundaries. A classic example of this was found in General Motors before its 1983 reorganization. The five car divisions were originally oriented toward different price segments of the market, but over time the offerings of each gradually expanded to overlap with those of the other divisions until the range was virtually indistinguishable and the market image of each blurred. In another case, in a publishing company a reorganization to integrate some acquisitions left a major area of market overlap among three divisions that otherwise needed to have separate identities and product lines. All three were prepared to go after that market segment.

Even when lines of business are nominally distinct, some companies encourage cowboy management by regularly holding rodeos—public testing of the strength of groups of managers under difficult conditions. These might be called by names like "operations review," but participants know they are involved in a rodeo. They will be judged on how well they handle the difficult trials set in front of them—defending numbers, making strategic leaps forward, answering unexpected questions, grappling with fellow contestants—and their performance in the arena will be compared with that of their peers. Managers subjected to rodeos guess that their fate is determined as much by their public performance as by the overall results they produce.

Sometimes the rodeos are held on paper, like the ones that organizations stage when they compare businesses or facilities or people. Many companies regularly rank-order their manufacturing facilities on productivity and quality, or their sales offices on volume, or their service departments on calls successfully completed—with the corporate equivalent of blue ribbons going to the winners. A few prominent companies include individuals in these contests, engaging in a practice known as "stacked ranking." Every single person in a particular category is numbered in order of excellence, from number one on up. High-level groups may spend days developing the list and arguing over the relative position of people on it. Though generally people are not supposed to know their numbers, the word gets out. And what was originated as a way to be "fair" to people, by making salary and promotion decisions on an objective basis, instead treats everyone as though they were directly competing—the impact of being ranked rather than assigned to broad categories. So they do indeed start to compete.

The sheer amount of change with which companies are dealing today makes in-house competition more likely to arise. The sources range from corporate restructuring to personal ambition:

- Acquisitions that put former external competitors under the same roof.
- Pressure for performance, because of intensified external competition, that leads to the comparisons of internal units as a supposed basis for motivation.
- Slower growth in some sectors, and outright decline in others, reducing available internal resources and causing areas to fight over them.
- Removal of hierarchical layers, which reduces the number of opportunities for promotion.
- Decentralization and greater divisional autonomy, which creates strong local pride and identity—and identification of other divisions as rivals.

Add to these the "natural" competition that occurs when any collection of people defined as a group compares itself to other groups, and we can see that rampant competition could easily dominate an organization.

Why In-House Competition Is a Value Subtracter

There is a two-fold rationale for competition, a rationale embedded in American mythology as well as in management philosophies. Competition is supposedly a spur to performance, and it theoretically stimulates the development of alternatives. But more often, in-house competition has the opposite effects: depressing performance and decreasing alternatives.

For several decades social psychologists have been studying the effects of competition on performance and productivity. A few conclusions are unequivocal. Excellence and victory are conceptually distinct, as Alfie Kohn put it.[11] Competitive situations—in which several people or groups are seeking the same end, but not all of them can achieve it—tend to be less efficient and result in poorer-quality products. This is especially true where tasks are interdependent and tends to be less true when performance is totally independent. When interdependence is low, so that people require little or nothing from one another, competition has a very slight advantage because of the motivational push from the knowledge of relative gain. This is probably why sales contests work so well. In the simplest situation, sales representatives have independent territories, and how much one sells has nothing at all to do with what another might sell. Overlaps are few, so that one's sales do not deplete another's, and there are possibilities for synergy through joint action. This simple situation aside, the minute people need anything at all from the efforts of others, or share a future fate, cooperation has all the advantages.

This finding has been known since Peter Blau's studies in the 1950s. In a comparison of two groups of interviewers in an employment agency, one highly competitive, the other cooperative, people in the first group hoarded job notifications because they were so personally ambitious and concerned about productivity. This then became a self-perpetuating defensive strategy as others did it. Performance was lower in the competitive groups. Other researchers have also found a negative correlation between individual competition and achievement by executives and managers.[12]

But while cooperation *inside* the group of organization results in higher performance, competition *outside* can add an important stimulus. After reviewing 122 studies, University of Minnesota researchers concluded that cooperation within, coupled with competition without, was the ideal combination for maximum productivity.[13] This is why major American companies that were fat and lazy for decades have been galvanized into action by the effects of foreign competition. An external challenge can certainly push up standards. Problems arise, however, when the "external" competition is seen as the other divisions, or the next department, or the other members of the planning committee—or as "everyone else but me."

What's wrong with in-house competition is the way it undermines goal achievement, sometimes in blatantly obvious ways.

One of the more hair-raising examples of the destructiveness of infighting occurred a few years ago at the U.S. Centers for Disease Control's Atlanta AIDS laboratory. Highly placed professionals were accused of tampering with their internal ''competitors' '' experiments, slowing publication of key results, and throwing away rivals' research materials. As a result, turnover reached almost 80 percent among senior scientists in the lab's first three years, and many junior positions remained unfilled. Connecticut Senator Lowell Weicker triggered a National Academy of Science investigation, and the *Wall Street Journal* issued a lengthy report.

When flasks with delicate virus cultures were rearranged and contaminated by human spit, and when other material for experiments wound up in the garbage, in-house competition had moved far beyond the point where it could be considered a spur to performance. Instead, jealousy and rivalries colored decision-making on nearly every issue. One of the major splits was between researchers (''real scientists'') and administrators (''just physicians''). Researchers showed contempt for the scientific knowledge of administrators, resisting their authority even though the administrators were nominally in charge. In retaliation, administrators ordered certain lines of research started and forbade others.

As in many such tales, there was no real winner. Eventually everyone involved in overt sabotage was called to account for it, and those victimized by it left. But sadly, there was a clear loser—the American public. Not only were large sums of federal money wasted, but knowledge of a possible AIDS prevention step was withheld from publication an unnecessary six months—a period during which thousands of people were newly infected with the disease.[14]

As this example illustrates, when internal competition gets out of hand, we can forget about performance excellence and innovation. There are five reasons why competition can depress performance, five signals of destructive rather than constructive competition.

The first sign that competition has become destructive is that *the players pay more attention to beating their rivals than to performing the task well*.

Social psychologists have demonstrated that competition decreases ''intrinsic motivation''—that is, interest in the task itself and concern with meeting one's own standards. When people are encouraged to compete at an activity, they begin to see that activity as an instrument for winning. And winning—or avoiding losing—becomes more important than doing the job well.

It is common to assume that competition is a performance stimulant, inducing people to do their best, but recent evidence disputes this. When Allan Cohen and David Bradford asked several thousand managers about circumstances in which they did their best, competition was rarely mentioned. Instead, they talked about goals that were exciting and challenging, some autonomy and ownership, high visibility or accountability, and an exciting task.[15] In short, the thrill of danger or excitement helped provoke "intrinsic motivation," but competition was irrelevant.

When winning becomes an end in itself, absolute or ideal performance standards lose meaning. It is hard to encourage people to do better, to meet a higher standard, as long as they know they are ahead of their rivals. Why bother to reduce the failure rate from three per hundred, if the nearest rivals' failure rate is four per hundred? Doing the least to stay ahead becomes the goal, not doing the most to meet the highest standard. No wonder competition-focused U.S. companies—whose quality standards were pegged relatively to doing better than others, rather than absolutely to an idea of perfection—were surprised by the sudden onslaught (and victory) of Japanese companies with much better performance records—because those Japanese companies sought perfection.

If winning is the goal, those determined to win develop a preference for incompetent rivals—even if they want the pretense of "tough" competition to make their victory seem valuable. In competitive situations, people tend to like being surrounded by others who are less competent, because it enhances their own chances to win. Highly competitive managers may then be tempted to advance the careers of weaker rather than stronger people, to give subtle boosts to the less talented in rival areas—to the detriment of overall company performance. Similarly, dominant companies in an industry may find ways to encourage weaker competitors that they know they can outperform while still maintaining the illusion of a competitive market, while hoping to drive stronger competitors out of business. This strategy might make it possible to win, but the high performance standards that competition is supposed to produce disappear in the process.

Eliminate strong players, encourage weak players, and forget about performance excellence—what a prescription for corporate disaster when the competition is taking place among members of the same large team.

A second sign that competition has gotten out of hand is that *"friendly competition" among people who respect one another is replaced by mistrust, suspicion, and scorn.*

What may begin as a limited competition—two divisions introducing different products that serve the same customer need, for example—can get out of bounds, spilling over to infect every other relationship between those divisions. One division goes from being a fellow player in a game both enjoy to being an enemy whose existence is responsible for anything that might go wrong. As the rivalry intensifies, negative characteristics of the other division are exaggerated until they begin to deserve the enmity. This makes it possible for the first group to justify its desire to eliminate the other group—not in the selfish terms of its own need to win but in "altruistic" terms of doing a favor for the whole corporation by removing a negative factor.

Psychoanalyst Erik Erikson gave this process a name—"pseudospeciation." A group driven to dominate treats its rival as though it were a different species, less than human, therefore not deserving normal human consideration. While this seems a strong statement to make about everyday business competition, I hear echoes of Erikson's idea in the scorn heaped upon counterparts in the traditional division of one company by those who thought they were the "new breed" replacement business. Even their use of the term "new breed" signified the strong distinction they were making between the two groups. Once rival groups see themselves as different breeds, they can suspend those courtesies that would be extended to a member of one's own breed: "Why bother to explain? Those bean-counters in accounting would never understand anyway." And they can easily feel the need to erect barriers against social intermingling, not to mention taboos against "intermarriage."

One major danger of rivalries that get out of hand in such situations is that the competition spills over into the marketplace in destructive ways. In one information services company, a second division was authorized by the boss to develop an offering close to that already on the market from its flagship division. One of the ways the second division, a highly aggressive group, decided to prove its mettle quickly was to go after some of the same talented (and critical) software designers used by the first division. As the "new breed," representatives of the second division conveyed their utter disdain for the "dinosaurs" in the original division. But to the designers, this was all one company. The in-house hostilities made them question whether they wanted to work for either group. When the internal battle is for external customers, the financial consequences of infighting-that-goes-public can be disastrous.

The NIH (not-invented-here) syndrome, which causes groups to resist importing ideas from outside their borders, is worsened when competition turns destructive. Even if the reason for establishing the competition was to generate many new ideas and then select the best for all groups to use, the purpose is defeated when anything "tainted" with the hue of the "others" is automatically rejected.

Despite the tendency for hostile competitors to reject anything originating on the other side, still, a third consequence of destructive competition is that *imitation may drive out innovation.*

Here's another irony of in-house competition. Though designed to provide variety, to stimulate differentiated alternatives, it often does just the opposite. For fear of missing out on something good that rivals do, and concerned about leaving out a tactic the rivals use to make their case, each party starts looking over its shoulder at what the other is doing. Spying and copying begin to replace the search for creative new options.

Creativity appears to require a measure of security, not the constant insecurity brought about by competitive dynamics. Risk-taking can be too dangerous when rivals are prowling the bushes waiting to pounce, so it is easier to choose a safer course. Indeed, social psychologist Theresa Amabile found, in a series of controlled experiments, that when an externally induced need to compete for scarce resources is replaced by income security, creative performance is enhanced; but in conditions of insecurity, creative performance declines.[16]

When each party is tempted to settle for only minor variants of the other's ideas, alternatives are, in fact, limited rather than increased. Imitation is a likely response to competition under conditions of great uncertainty about criteria for judging performance—so it feels safer to stay closer to convention. I watched two product development teams in one company turn their quest for a new food-processing technology into a game of copycat. Neither was sure what would please the higher-ups or work in the marketplace, and their faith in their own technical competence was shaken by the knowledge that another group, nearby in the same large facility, was working on the same thing. As soon a word got out about what the other group was doing, the first would decide to mount a project in that direction, too, so that the rivals would not get too far ahead. But, of course, the rivals were doing the same thing. What began as the pursuit of two different techniques soon converged on a single process—but for political, not substantive, reasons.

Competition can also depress performance and limit options for a fourth reason. *The weaker party may give up rather than continue to fight.*

In destructive competition, the performance of weaker competitors is likely to be depressed rather than stimulated. For one thing, laboratory studies show high levels of anxiety in people who compete, which in turn is correlated with inferior performance.[17] Furthermore, if elimination of the rival becomes the goal, and the competition is seen as a fight to the death, those least able to destroy their rivals may simply surrender. They lack any incentive to keep trying. Continuing to fight depletes what small reserves they have left. And why bother to meet performance standards if the game is already lost?

Weaker competitors have many ways of giving up. Individuals simply leave. Groups begin to act as if they have already been conquered, allowing their triumphant rivals to dominate decisions, dictate terms, have first call on resources. They withdraw by retreating to the minimum performance level necessary simply to survive, and they back away from planning their future, instead carrying out only the things put in front of them today.

Unfortunately, in destructive competition cooperative moves look weak to parties bent on total victory. Competition drives out cooperation, as many experiments using game theory show. It is dangerous to be playing a cooperative game if one's opponent is playing a competitive game. Thus, weaker competitors cannot easily join forces with stronger ones (a cooperative strategy) if the game is structured as a destructive competition.[18]

When weaker competitors start dropping out, the fifth issue in destructive competition comes into play. *The stronger party begins to feel dangerously invincible.*

There's a fine line between the strength that comes from pride in demonstrated achievements and the arrogance that comes from vanquishing obvious opponents. If stronger parties feel that they can rest easy, that they no longer need to perform according to standards as long as they are clearly winning the battle, then their performance may also deteriorate. There is a suggestive analogy in a study of influence tactics in intimate relationships. Skewed power distribution, especially with respect to control over resources, leads to bullying by the stronger party and manipulation by the weaker.[19] This is why many American companies that dominated their markets before the game became truly global grew lazy and complacent—and missed seeing that new foreign competition was chipping away at their share.

Those who manage by competition hope that it will spur performance and generate alternatives. Yet, as we have seen, the impact of in-house competition that crosses the line into combat is just the opposite. Performance standards often decline, attention is distracted, weaker parties allow their performance to deteriorate, and options are narrowed rather than increased.

Furthermore, the obvious risk of playing each game as a hostile competition is that there is some still-larger game waiting to be played in a still-larger arena, in which today's rivals will find themselves on the same side. Today's competing parties may be jointly vulnerable to an as-yet-unrevealed competitor who can easily overtake both of them, because both are battle-weary or have focused too much attention on exploiting each other's weaknesses instead of learning to play the game better. The weaker party who has become passive is no help, and the stronger who felt falsely invincible has created no defenses against a new threat and does not know how to take advantage of anyone else's good ideas. The legacy of bitterness from hostile rivalries adds a barrier to cooperation. And if the stronger parties have succeeded in eliminating their weaker rivals, then there's nobody left to mobilize for the bigger game.

Some analysts would say that this scenario is an accurate description of what has happened to many U.S. companies in recent years. Excessive infighting within corporations and rivalry with competitors close to home has weakened everyone for the larger game with international competitors, has made it more difficult to marshal the necessary cooperation, has reduced innovation, and has maintained lower performance standards. It remains as a further danger for those companies drawn to the cowboy management style with its heavy reliance on in-house competition.

The issue, then, is to become lean without becoming mean, to reshape the organization for the global corporate Olympics without destroying the morale and the contributions of the separate parties composing the organization. This is preeminently a matter of developing and increasing commitment to the whole organization.

THE COMMITMENT CHALLENGE

The potential loss of commitment in restructuring, whether from cowboy competition or from poor management of transitions and their aftermaths, is a serious threat to any company. The post-entrepreneurial corporation is taking new shape in order to pursue growth opportunities while cutting the costs of its continuing operations—to do more with less. But it cannot achieve that goal unless it is able to maintain the commitment-during-change that allows synergies the opportunity to develop.

Commitment-building management practices involve the active recognition that the way the transition phase of restructuring is handled makes a major difference in whether the new structure produces the desired results. The creation of Unisys out of Burroughs and Sperry is an often-cited case of maintaining continuity, avoiding "we-they" cowboy dynamics, and creating a new, shared identity quickly. When Southwest Bancshares in Houston merged with Mercantile Texas Corporation in Dallas to form MCorp (which became the eighteenth-largest banking organization in the United States), twenty-one different restructuring task forces were formed a few months after the announcement but well before the merger, each with three to four subtask forces. Participants attributed the absence of conflict and the retention of customers to the cooperation engendered by this activity. One explained, "The officers saw their bosses cooperating with the counterpart at the other bank to come up with a recommendation for a policy. A certain spirit developed that had the effect of alleviating the personnel issues."[20]

Excellent management also helped Delta Airlines' 1987 acquisition of Western Airlines become an industry model. I met Western's then-Chairman Gerald Grinstein in December 1986, on the day the merger was approved. Soon after, Cynthia Ingols and Paul Myers, two members of my reserach team, went to Los Angeles, Salt Lake City, and San Francisco—major Western locations of the company—to observe firsthand how Delta and Western managed during the period from announcement in December 1986 to full integration on April 1, 1987.[21]

Three years before the merger, few observers would have believed that Western could long survive, let alone succeed, in the increasingly competitive, deregulated airline industry. Western had been losing $100 million a year since 1981 and was near bankruptcy in the late summer of 1985. Gerry Grinstein called those times "the dark days of 1984."

And they were certainly bleak moments. Everyone, including pilots, flight attendants, customer service representatives, and ramp workers, sacrificed to save the company. A "Competitive Action Plan" was introduced, in which all employees, union and management alike, took wage cuts of 20 to 50 percent, adapted work rule changes, and eliminated positions. The concessions were part of a quid pro quo worked out between Western and its unions. Each of four unions was given a seat on the company board of directors, and all workers became eligible for new profit-sharing and stock ownership programs.

The financial concessions of Western employees allowed its management team to restructure the debt. In addition, fortuitous events in the business environment, like the strike at United Airlines and the reduction in the price of oil, helped to boost Western's load capacity and to reduce further its operating expenses. The cumulative effect of this series of events was record profits of Western in 1985, leading to the distribution of profit-sharing benefits to all employees in February 1986.

Western had now become a prime target for takeover by other carriers, and the company's top executives began to meet privately with a small number of suitors. In a whirlwind round of secret meetings held over Labor Day weekend in 1986, Western Chairman Grinstein struck a deal with Delta Chairman David Garrett. Within days, the respective boards of directors met and approved the merger, and on September 19, Delta announced that it would purchase Western for $860 million, making Delta the fourth-largest carrier in the industry.

Then the tough job of transition management began. Both Delta and Western did their part to create cooperators rather than cowboys by managing feelings about the past, the future, and the present that would build commitment.

Managing the Past: Mourning the Losses

Issue number one in managing a difficult transition smoothly is to allow employees to mourn the past, to grieve over their losses. After all, employees make major emotional investments in their companies and in their jobs.

In 1986, when Western celebrated its sixtieth birthday as a company, many employees celebrated their own long-term employment with the firm. One pilot who had flown with Western for twenty-two years could call seven thousand of Western's ten thousand employees by name. Another employee, who started out by cleaning planes for the firm twenty-three years ago and by 1986 assisted in managing one of the bases, said that "it's a business that gets in your blood." In an industry colored with romance, Western employees regarded their firm with great affection. Several remarked that the reality of the merger had not fully set in until they watched the company logo being removed from the airplanes. And one special employee group was affected in a particularly jarring way: Western retirees were issued new Delta retiree travel passes—they became retirees of Delta, on paper at least, although they had never worked one day for that company.

The sense of personal loss was accentuated by the state of upheaval experienced by approximately two thousand Western employees—those who had been employed at the company headquarters in Los Angeles but now had to transfer to Atlanta. Many of Western's middle managers had been demoted as a result of Delta's efforts to integrate the new workforce without creating redundant positions. Leaving behind families, friends, and memories and pulling up deep roots are traumatic in any case; when one loses a job, a lifestyle, and one's company as well, the sadness is amplified.

Western executives not only allowed but encouraged a period of mourning, to help people bury the past. For example, Tom Greene, a vice-president–general counsel and an eighteen-year Western employee, eulogized the firm in a testimonial distributed to all employees: "A final wish for the lives of us who mourn is to go on with joyful memories."

Managing the Future: Positive Visions

The second key to commitment building during the restructuring process is getting the survivors excited about the future—offering a positive vision to compensate for the loss. For example, Mitchell Marks, a consultant to Western during the merger process, brought to the merger an awareness of the power of formal ceremonies to bridge the gap between loss and vision, based on an event he had designed for another company:

> Each of the eighty attending managers was asked to write down the three worst things that could happen to them personally as a result of the merger. Then the managers were given sheets of their former letterhead and business cards. The group was led outside and assembled around a wooden casket. A band was playing a funeral march. One by one, the managers were asked to crumple up their statements, cards, and letterheads and toss them in the coffin. Suddenly, a hundred-ton paver emerged from around the corner. As it approached the coffin, the band broke into a rendition of "On Wisconsin," and the group cheered wildly as the paver flattened the coffin and its contents. Next, the group was whisked back inside where they were given academic caps and gowns to put on. They marched into an auditorium. There the boss gave a graduation speech, resembling any college ceremony: "You are the architects of our future; our destiny lies in your generation's hands!" After the speech, the name of each manager was called. They walked across the stage, shaking hands with the regional manager and receiving a "Doctorate in Merger Management" and a share of company stock as a graduation gift.

Delta stressed its version of a great future immediately by creating a slogan for the merger that made Western people feel valued: "The Best Get Better."

Despite the seemingly tragic changes that faced Western employees, the transition time preceding the merger was kept upbeat and optimistic. The merger brought stability to a workforce that had made enormous sacrifices to help Western avert bankruptcy and become more competitive in the deregulated airline environment. Grinstein commented that Western was bought by the "Rolls-Royce" of the industry, and that the financial community regarded Delta as a sound, strong, well-managed airline. In the words of one union leader, "Western's employees deserve this merger with as fine a company as Delta. They'd gotten the s—— kicked out of them since 1981. That period was hell on them. There was no stability." Western employees recognized that although they had worked hard to turn their company around, long-term viability as a midsized independent carrier did not seem likely for Western, given industry conditions.

When the merger was announced Delta took an additional step to reassure Western's workforce, to reinforce their expectations of stability. Delta promised to honor industry-recognized "labor protective provisions," which included a pledge to offer every full-time Western employee a job at Delta at a rate of pay not less than what they were currently receiving from Western. This pledge eliminated the anxiety surrounding the question, "Am I going to get an offer?" Instead, all Western workers knew there were jobs for them at Delta if they wanted them. (The company voluntarily chose to follow the protective provisions, rather than being required to do so by law or labor contract.) By its actions, Delta also strongly indicated that it planned to treat its "adopted siblings" the same as it treated the other members of the Delta family.

Managing the Present: Reducing Uncertainty

Issue number three involves the transition period itself. Transitions engender uncertainty not only with regard to employees' careers and daily work but also in terms of bills, mortgages, families, and lifestyles. Delta reduced uncertainty by its methodical, forthcoming, and, with few exceptions, concise style in communicating about the merger process. At the same time Western executives minimized discontinuity and disorder by stressing "business as usual," making sure they came into the office for regular workdays to create a reassuring presence. Delta's style was first shown in a memo sent by Telex to each Western work location and shortly after to each employee's home just after the merger was approved. That letter, in early January 1987, outlined Delta's plans for managing the details of integrating the two companies and their respective employee groups. For example, "During the week of February 16, 1987, a bulletin will be distributed containing the following information . . . ." As announced, on February 13 a thirty-page bulletin was issued that included details about when job offers would be made, how traveling and moving expenses would be reimbursed, and general information about the transition from Western's benefit programs to Delta's.

Keeping a promise is key to keeping commitment. Throughout the months that followed, Delta did what it had said it would when it said it would. One employee commented that "Delta hasn't once had to back up and say 'Hey, that's wrong. We did it wrong.' They're methodical—not fast. But when they give us information it's good, solid.'' The well-planned and carefully executed merger process alleviated employee stress and uncertainty. Even when workers did not have the facts and the details at a certain time, they knew when the information would be forthcoming and that it would be reliable and certain.

During the transition period, Western continued its established pattern of openness and communication. The airline's regular newsletter, called "Update," was renamed "The Best Get Better"—Delta's slogan for the merger—two weeks after the first merger announcement in September. Regular features included articles describing Delta's plans for the merger process and comments by Delta and Western officials.

Employees received news from other formal sources, too, rather than from rumors. A toll-free phone line, started in 1984 to give updates on the Competitive Action Plan, switched messages shortly after the merger announcement. Western employees could then receive weekly recordings about the merger and leave their questions. In turn, those questions often became the subject of subsequent updates.

Finally, Western used the structure and services of its Health Services Program (HSP) to deal with employee stress and anxiety caused by the merger. The HSP had been established in 1984 through joint union-management efforts to deal with employee problems with substance abuse and wage concession–related stress. The program used counselors, rap sessions, pamphlets, and other educational aids to help employees work out their emotional difficulties. After the merger announcement, HSP personnel began to develop programs, including seminars and videotapes, to address employee anxieties about the merger.

Overall, the success of the merger process at building commitment was a result of Delta's policy and style of implementation on the one hand, and Western's proactive communication and counseling on the other.

Even so, after the transition period, there was still a great deal of integration to manage. The culture at Western was "Californian," informal, intimate, and participative, while Delta was perceived by some Westerners as "Southern conservative" and "paternalistic."

Some Western people felt "conquered" and disempowered by Delta, subject to its rules and dress codes. Largely nonunionized Delta faced a labor challenge even before the merger was complete, from a union representing Western employees that sought recognition by Delta.

But the merger got off the ground quickly and effectively because of good management, and value was retained. Now the promise of synergy could become a reality.

RESTRUCTURING AS A BALANCING ACT

If the purpose of a corporation is to create value for its stakeholders—certainly its stockholders, but also its employees, customers, creditors, and others with a legitimate stake in the future of the enterprise—the first step in creating that value is to avoid dissipating the company's resources. Restructuring—the reshaping of a business through mergers, acquisitions, divestitures, and internal reorganizations—is often done in the pursuit of new sources of value, but if managed poorly, restructuring threatens a loss of value.

To achieve the synergies that the post-entrepreneurial corporation desperately seeks, post-entrepreneurial managers need to be sensitive to the process by which changes are introduced, and especially sensitive to the needs and concerns of people, in order to ensure involvement and cooperation. Instead of creating cowboy competition, winners and losers, conquerors and colonized, or rivals for the same tidbits of power, post-entrepreneurial corporations will raise performance standards by building commitment to shared goals and enhancing the ability to work together. If the post-entrepreneurial corporation is indeed to be a flexible instrument that can quickly reshape itself when the terms of global competition change, then the people who run it must learn how to carry out enormous change while retaining productivity and cooperation.

Only time can tell what the long-term impact of the current restructuring of American industry will be. It will be positive for business if it results in a clearer focus, a better fit between parts, and the flexibility to keep innovating. In the short run, however, managers face a number of dilemmas. They must confront and remove the subtraction of value that cowboy management brings, at the same time that restructuring itself threatens to set up internal competition and create winners and losers. They must be aware of the effect that the reshaping of American companies has on the workforce; rearranging jobs and moving players around inevitably means letting some of them go, while confronting the survivors with discontinuity and distractions.

From a human standpoint, not all restructuring results in loss, of course. The survivors of staff cutbacks often find themselves with enlarged responsibilities and opportunities. The employees of business units that become independent companies feel even better. One's fate in a restructuring obviously determines one's reactions to it. Lucky Stores, for example, accelerated a restructuring in order to fend off a takeover threat from corporate raider Asher Edelman; it sold one division to a large corporation that intended to dismantle it and spun off another as an independent business. The employees of the first division had baseball caps printed with a picture of a screw, followed by the name Edelman; but the second division now hangs a picture of Edelman next to that of its founders.

Although post-entrepreneurial organizations need the flexibility to make such structural changes, they also need the commitment of their people—the full engagement of their capabilities—if they are to retain the value that existed before the changes. But while commitment comes from certainty and security, restructuring causes uncertainty and insecurity. This realization entails a major corporate balancing act: managing the inevitable organizational changes of the post-entrepreneurial era in ways that build, rather than jeopardize, the bond between people and organizations. Such bonds, in turn, are a key asset in helping companies find the synergies they so desperately seek.

CHAPTER 4

Achieving Synergies: Value Added, Value Multiplied

*B*uild a better mousetrap, the old saying goes, and the world will beat a path to your door. Build a better mousetrap in the traditional corporate bureaucracy, however, and the story might unfold a little differently. Here's how I imagine it:

> You're very excited about your mousetrap and eager to get it to consumers. But first, the Mousetrap Department manager, her boss, and her boss's boss insist upon thorough reviews, each one asking for some changes before taking it to the others, and then the whole thing goes to the vice-president of the Mouse, Mole, and Skunk Traps Division (MMSTD). The price is marked up way over costs to cover the charge for the company volleyball court, executive dining rooms, middle manager training in how to conduct downward and upward reviews, newpaper subscriptions and lounge chairs for the internal press clipping group, and other overhead charges.
>
> At last, the Better Mousetrap brand is ready to go to market, so an elaborate research project is begun in three rodent-rich cities in three

different countries. Unbeknownst to you, the Chemicals and Pesticide Division (CPD) has already collected extensive market data for the launching of its new Mouse Repellent, which is being sold through exactly the same channels. (You learn this from reading the accident report filed by one of your MMSTD truck drivers who almost ran over one of CPD's truck drivers.) And Animal Services, the company's innovative new lease-a-pet acquisition, has completed a psychological profile of the mouse-averse for its Kittycat product line, which points out the desirable features for mousetraps, a profile they are careful not to show you.

Meanwhile, costs have mounted, there has been no way to build on what the other divisions have already done, and the Better Mousetrap gets to market later and at a higher price than the offering of a spiffy new mousetrap specialty start-up. Wall Street, which had once praised your parent corporation, Unrelated Holdings, Inc., for its smart move toward synergy by acquiring three companies with a common interest in rodent control, reacts unfavorably to the news. The stock drops precipitously. Raiders see that the break-up value of UHI is higher than its current stock price; after all, the three mouse-oriented divisions are gaining nothing by being together anyway, and "corporate" requirements are a drag on their performance.

Then your boss calls you in for a heart-to-heart. "Sad news, Better Mousetrap Builder," she says. "The company has to cut its losses to avoid a takeover, and since your product isn't doing too well, we're letting you go."

Post-entrepreneurial corporations, in contrast, make the search for synergies a central part of their strategies. Slowly but surely, they are learning how to accomplish more (exploiting new opportunities quickly) while using less (keeping expenses down). They clear the "clutter" out of the way, such as unnecessary oversight loops that delay action. They get rid of extraneous activities. They make sure each area contributes something to the others. The leaner, more focused, more cooperative and integrated organizations that result help each unit add value to the others. The "whole" contributes something above and beyond the value of the parts.

This sounds straightforward, yet the implications of taking these steps are revolutionizing corporate structure.

VALUE ADDED: RETHINKING "ADMINISTRATION" AND "CORPORATE SERVICES"

At the same time that post-entrepreneurial companies are restructuring their lines of business in the search for focused combinations that build synergies, they are also re-examining their internal structure to make sure that all activities, all departments, "add value." For example:

- Interested in cutting costs as well as improving delegation downward, a telephone company—once among the most intricately graded of organizations—has almost eliminated an entire managerial level (promotions now jump people from level three to level five just below the officer ranks) and has doubled supervisory spans of control in its largest unit, which covers 75 percent of all employees.
- An auto giant took its first step toward streamlining by banning all one-to-one reporting relationships (a boss responsible for only one subordinate).
- A widely respected household products manufacturer has gradually thinned its line management ranks by creating "high-commitment work systems" in which employee teams take full responsibility for production, without requiring managers.
- A pharmaceutical company is "delayering," as they put it, to reduce unnecessary levels that were indeed "delayers" of decisions and actions; it has distributed to all departments a kit of instructions for rearranging the organization chart to work without at least two levels of management.
- An oil company, calling itself an "elephant learning to dance," is trying to become more agile by collapsing several levels of the management hierarchy.

The principal targets of this kind of reorganization are corporate staffs and middle managers. But restructuring to ensure that every management layer and every corporate service adds value to the organization also raises profound questions about what it means to be a corporation. How much management from the top is really needed? What activities should be under the company's hierarchical umbrella, as opposed to being purchased on the market?

There are two kinds of roles included in the "corporate" category: supporters and interveners. The questions about supporters are the more easily resolved. Some supporters, whether financial planners or management trainers, are indeed facilitators and integrators who add value by improving the way business units operate or transferring knowledge and expertise among them. Supporters also include the vast armies of clerks and quasiprofessionals whose role is to handle the paperwork and the documentation involved in business transactions. But the ranks of supporters are being thinned anyway by two intertwined forces: information technology and the growth of specialist firms taking over corporate support functions. A leading electronics company, for example, anticipates that computer networks will reduce a purchasing staff of three thousand, doing largely routine work, to a mere hundred professionals negotiating contracts and establishing systems. "Eighty percent of our transactions could be ordered directly through the requisition system on terminals, and bank-to-bank funds transfer could support them," a purchasing executive reported. For other companies, the road to smaller internal staffs is to turn routine transaction processing over to specialist firms that do nothing but handle the payroll or manage accounts receivable or keep the records.

Interveners are a different matter; their role and contributions are more controversial. To some companies, they are the necessary links in a chain of control. To others, they are the principal source of "fat" to be reduced to get in shape for the corporate Olympics. Over the years, corporate bureaucracies have come to include large numbers of people whose primary task is to check up on others, to ensure that "standards" are being met. These range from middle managers that oversee other managers who direct the work, to staffs that establish procedures and then monitor how well other managers carry them out. As the same purchasing executive put it, "Controlling the number of purchase orders, checking up on how many parts were ordered, and nitpicking over which day we want it to come in ends up being intervention rather than value added." In short, interveners serve to slow the work process by adding loops in the decision-making chain or hurdles to cross. The rationale for interveners is that they improve results. Some do. But the growing conviction is that most of them add costs without adding clear perceived value.

"Value-added analysis" is now used in many companies to determine if each step in a work process or decision sequence augments the preceding steps. If it does not, perhaps it should be eliminated. It is this kind of reasoning that cuts out middle-management positions—of the traditional kind. If we look at the traditional managerial responsibility, it is clear why the position cannot always withstand this kind of scrutiny. The traditional manager was a link in a reporting chain—a gatekeeper to ensure that things stayed within bounds, an interpreter to the troops below of the sentiments of those above, and a message-carrier to high levels. Did middle managers add value? In too many cases, as administrators they subtracted value rather than adding it, by taking extra time, by telling eager subordinates that the upper echelons would never approve their proposals, by dampening enthusiasm and preventing direct access.

There are delicious ironies in the term "overhead" for administration and other corporate services. The original meaning of the word clearly involved the physical surroundings in which work took place—the roof over workers' heads. As corporations grew fat and complex, however, "overhead" began to signify something else to employees: "the people who can go over my head to second-guess my decisions." And looming first and foremost among those second-guessers, in the eyes of many producers, are corporate staffs. In most companies, "I'm from corporate and I'm here to help you" is considered as fraudulent a statement as "I'm from the IRS and I'm here to help you." In both cases, they feel they'll be taxed.

In fact, in many companies I deal with, those running business units wonder whether they would do better if they were independent—and in some cases, the evidence supports them (for example, leveraged buyouts by managers of their own units that produce dramatic increases in performance). In the traditional corporation, a business unit would often have to justify itself to the parent corporation, to explain why the corporation would want to keep owning it. Now, in an interesting reversal, the onus is often on the corporate entity itself—the entity that exists above and beyond the business unit—to, in effect, justify itself to the business unit, to explain why the business should bother to belong to it.

In theory, there should be benefits to business units from their corporate affiliation; post-entrepreneurial corporations can find these sources of added "corporate" value:

- Scale economies from sharing certain functions or facilities.
- Management competence, including a larger talent pool for business units to draw on and sources of expertise to help the unit make better decisions.

- Broader career opportunities, to help attract and retain the best people.
- Staff services dedicated to the specific needs of the corporation's business units.
- Information exchange about technology or markets, broadening the intelligence base available to each business.
- The capacity to look ahead and consider the future across an array of businesses, while business units are immersed in daily operating pressures.
- Common values and standards that raise performance.

Johnson & Johnson, for example, is widely praised for its form of corporate organization. Well over one hundred decentralized companies pursue specific product-market charters as part of the corporate family; new companies are spun off from old ones when separable products reach critical mass; and each has an internal board of directors. Value-added by the corporate level comes not only from the cultivation of a managerial talent pool and career opportunities across companies but also from the J & J credo, a statement of values that builds a common cultural focus on serving customers.

While post-entrepreneurial corporations seek ways to add value to their business units, many traditional corpocracies wind up taking more from the business units than they give to them. If they are to compete in the global Olympics, companies can no longer afford to support anything that does not add value to their central business focus. Corporate services must be either restructured to add value or eliminated. Companies have a choice of methods:

Decentralizing and redeploying. Putting more responsibility in the hands of business unit managers and reducing the need for approvals or checkpoints make it possible to operate without so many layers of hierarchy, and by extension, with fewer people. Andrew Grove of Intel, for example, wants his company to be an "agile giant"—big enough to win global wars of products, technology, and trade while moving like a small company. To achieve this, he has decentralized approval and eliminated middle-management layers. Other companies have cut the number of corporate service personnel while increasing the effectiveness of their activities by breaking up large central departments, relying instead on business unit staffs to do the work. This eliminates redundancies and tends to replace a watchdog orientation with a service orientation; instead of "controlling" from the top, these staffs are now linked closely to the needs of particular businesses. What remains at the corporate level are minimal staffs carrying out future-oriented tasks such as environmental scanning, professional development, and facilitation of cross-business-unit information exchange.

An alternative to cutting staff, then, is to redeploy them. Offering new jobs in a more vital sector (along with attractive early retirement options) can, of course, encourage people to leave voluntarily to ply their trades elsewhere. But it also puts those who remain to better use, making them a source of added value. IBM, for example, embarked on an enormous retraining effort after a 1985 business downturn, enabling a whopping twenty thousand or so employees to change jobs—engineers moving into sales, plant workers into systems engineering and, as in other companies rethinking staff, corporate services providers into the field.[1]

Contracting out. Of course, companies can decide not to manage certain activities themselves at all, and many are doing so in the name of "focus." For a widget company to be running a cafeteria and a print shop and a law firm, the reasoning goes, is not the best use of widget managers' time. It increases staff, which adds complexity and hierarchy, and anyway, there are specialist firms out there concentrating on running superior cafeterias and print shops and law firms. The company should use their services and concentrate on widgets. The strategy here is to divest all but the solid core. Cut staff to the bone, do without some amenities altogether (who needs to manage a fleet of jet planes?), and contract out for everything else.

The extreme of the contracting-out strategy is represented by companies that are essentially marketing and financial shells working through vast networks of suppliers and dealers. Examples are found in publishing, apparel, and other fashion businesses that have long needed the flexibility to make changes quickly, effected by lean core organizations using external specialist organizations for particular tasks. For example, Benetton, an Italian apparel producer, owns outright very few of the assets involved in bringing Benetton clothes to consumers; manufacturing is contracted out to numerous small factories, and retail outlets are licensees. Indeed, Benetton is part of a surge of entrepreneurship in Northern Italy based on networks of small firms allying with one another. In 1982 Benetton contracted out work to 220 production units, which employed ten thousand people; many were partially owned by Benetton managers as individuals, but

Benetton itself owned only nine facilities as a company.[2] In another sector, Lewis Galoob Toys, maker of "micromachines," board games, and Star Trek toys, contracts out almost everything, including accounts receivable, running a thirty-one-year-old company with almost $70 million in sales with only about one hundred employees.

Berkeley Business School Dean Raymond Miles calls this managerial style the "corporation as switchboard," the company acting as central information center and command point for a network of other organizations.[3] This is clearly one strategy small companies can use to grow "big" in market scope and power very quickly. But it is also on the increase for much larger companies, as post-entrepreneurial strategies take hold. It is not a long leap for companies that consider their manufacturing and sales functions to be "staffs" for business units that are essentially marketing arms to begin to think about whether they should continue to own so many plants and employ so many salespeople when working through contractors would give them more flexibility.

To put it another way, the *corporation-as-department-store*, a gigantic entity with every conceivable aspect of the production chain and every service it uses under its own roof, is being replaced by the *corporation-as-boutique. Focus* is the key word.

Turning services into businesses. In some cases, rather than divesting themselves of staff services, companies are converting them into profit centers, which sell their services on the outside as well as the inside. This is the ultimate post-entrepreneurial, market-oriented response. Let those staff bureaucrats be entrepreneurs, and let the market decide if they add value or not. Among the companies thus deriving revenues from their own corporate services are Control Data, selling personnel services; Xerox, logistics and distribution services to customers; General Motors, employee-training programs; and Security Pacific Bank, data-processing and information systems.

Even when corporate staffs are not set loose in the outside market, companies are still starting to treat them as internal vendors who must compete with outside vendors to get their services purchased. General Foods recently put on a pay-as-you-use basis the "overhead" charges for corporate staff services, which were formerly assigned uniformly to users and nonusers. Of course, under the old system use was mandatory; for example, product managers in the past had to go through up to eight layers of management, including corporate staff, to get business plans approved.[4] But now, those same staffs must prove to their internal customer's satisfaction that they add value. There are sometimes thorny questions of managing internal transfer payments and whether to set rates at market levels, but the principle is clear: Staffs are no longer considered "overhead" but potential sources of value; they are not watchdogs and interveners but suppliers serving customers.

In short, to use the language of prominent economist Oliver Williamson,[5] companies are dismantling the very management layers and service staffs that helped create the corporate hierarchy in the first place and gradually replacing some of them with marketlike relationships. Many employees are either being replaced with "outside" contractors or becoming contractors themselves.

Thoughtful Restructuring Versus Mindless Downsizing
There are two principal mistakes some companies make in staff restructuring.

First, they exhibit strategic blindness, turning the quest to ensure value added into mindless downsizing and delayering, on the assumption that leanness automatically equals effectiveness. They focus only on the "less" of the "doing more with less" imperative, as if the only good staff were a small staff. They fail to differentiate departments and business units in terms of their future contributions and resource needs; while some can be reduced or stabilized, others might profitably grow. Or their goals are cost-driven instead of effectiveness-driven— get the expenses down instead of the performance up. Or they view employees primarily as costs rather than valuing them as assets, and they fail to see the value (in skills or experience) that walks out the door with terminated staff. At a machine tool company that has become the subject of a popular Harvard Business School case, a new president from outside was so incensed by high wages in Cleveland that he downsized there and moved the bulk of production to a new plant in the South, only to find productivity lowered because of inexperienced employees. Manufacturing costs were ultimately higher in the South than in the "high-wage plant" where employee experience raised productivity.[6]

Second, some companies assume that if a little cutting is a good thing, a lot must be even better. They starve themselves into a state of organizational anorexia, the disease that occurs when companies become too thin. Cutting people to cut costs, if poorly managed, can actually increase some costs, such as the hidden costs of overload—tasks haven't disappeared, just the people to do them. It would have been better to review the tasks to see what unnecessary or outmoded work could be eliminated—as Exxon U.S.A. did when it conducted its "hog law" review (a Texas expression for rules and procedures) to see what red tape could be cut forever.

Furthermore, an organization that is too thin risks numerous implementation failures and dropped balls because of lack of follow-up and follow-through—from the inability to return phone calls to customers to making plans without communicating them to all the departments that will have to change something as a result. In general, when anorexic companies starve themselves, they also starve innovation. The pressure of activities the company is already committed to drives out the ability to think about preparing for the future; there is insufficient preparation for tomorrow. If an organization gets too thin, it tends to lack depth in people for backup if a crisis hits, or for development and succession. One company boasted of the money saved by eliminating all but the most experienced middle managers; seasoned people, they reasoned, would save training costs and be able to manage larger groups. But then some of the experienced managers left for better opportunities (after all, they were the most marketable), and the company found itself with no internal succesors. Recruitment and training costs shot up. The "leanness" strategy backfired.

Finally, companies that are lean because they substitute outside contracting for internal employment find themselves engaged in another set of difficult management tasks: They must work with other organizations to make sure the work is done to their specifications on their schedule, and they are vulnerable to the whims of other companies on which they rely—along with other dilemmas I take up in the next chapter.

Even managers who push downsizing and delayering as the best assurance of value added are aware that they are walking a tightrope. In a publishing company that had, in an executive's view, "built up fat during the good years," over a thousand people who "added no discernible value" were cut during a time of profit pressures. Now, he said:

> There is no money for good people who are being asked to do more with less. We need to keep this core. After two years of cutting, we could either boom or fall flat. A move of our headquarters will be the last

straw. We are running the risk of hitting the bone. First one layoff, then another, then shrinkage, then relocations. All of this equals risk to the division.

To counter the risk, he must increase the effort to create teamwork among the remaining staff—teamwork that will help each contribute to the work of the others.

The challenge, then, is not simply to get lean for the sake of doing so, but to build the kind of cooperation that helps the more-focused corporation get maximum value from all of its remaining resources.

VALUE MULTIPLIED: THE PAYOFF FROM SYNERGIES

The structure that is "right" in theory, the "right" combination of parts, is still not enough to produce synergy. A business mix that is good from a strategic analysis standpoint brings benefits in practice only if the relationships and processes are established to ensure cooperation and communication—with managers of every area committed to contributing value to one another.

The only real justification for a multibusiness corporation, in my view, is the achievement of synergy—that magical mix of business activities that are stronger and more profitable together than they would be separately. The "portfolio" or "holding company" approach—in which each part stands alone and needs to be different in order to compensate for the weakness of other parts—has been increasingly discredited. For example, strategy expert Michael Porter's longitudinal data on a set of Fortune 500 companies showed that most could not digest acquisitions unrelated to their core business; over 70 percent of the firms divested such unrelated units after about five years.[7]

Sometimes companies have moved away from a portfolio strategy for defensive reasons: the costs of administering diversity or the vulnerability to takeovers engendered by the ease with which the pieces could be unbundled and sold at a premium. But more often, the quest for value multipliers comes from growth goals. There is a growing conviction that doing-more-with-less is possible when the right combination of parts, working together in the right way, can actively contribute to one another's success.

Nowhere do synergies seem more important than in global technology companies, which face brutal, fast-paced competition. PPG Industries, for example, knew this when it launched a Biomedical Products Division out of diverse worldwide acquisitions. Edward Voboril, the group executive, put "teamwork" number one on his priority list, and he convened the first management conference of the group to build the foundation for it.

From the noncommittal expressions on the faces of the audience as he opened the conference, I could see that he had a hard sell ahead of him. On paper, the fit between the parts was excellent. But he had to cajole suspicious managers from different nations and different businesses out of their territoriality. "The eggs have gotten scrambled, and we can't unscramble them," he said, to remind listeners that they had better accept the situation. "But now we've got the raw materials to succeed on a bigger scale than any of us have seen," he continued, to appeal to their ambition. And then the real pitch; "We must turn our attention to the goals we have in common. We can pool our strengths instead of dissipating them." He had a few carrots to offer them: higher R&D funding than any of the businesses separately had ever known, a worldwide marketing and sales organization to expand the sales of what had been geographically localized products. But still, the formal programs and structures would not be enough unless heads of different business units from different parts of the world agreed to cooperate.

In the global Olympics, this is indeed what differentiates winners from losers. As international management researchers Christopher Bartlett and Sumantra Ghoshal show, the best competitors in world markets know how to build cooperation at the business unit level.[8] Instead of either dictating everything from headquarters (the "centralized" strategy) or allowing every country and every business to go its own way (the ultimate "decentralized" strategy), multiproduct transnational companies like Procter and Gamble, Philips, NEC, and, increasingly, Colgate have created a balanced organizational strategy. Such a balanced approach helps the separate parts see shared goals, develop common values and standards, communicate among themselves (Colgate uses, among other things, a creative video magazine), pool resources for some activities, create joint ventures and projects, build career paths flowing across their borders, and divide responsibility for innovation.

PPG Biomedical Division's goal was to be among those world-class companies. For the next three days, the assembled managers talked about their businesses, identified areas of overlap with potential for cooperation, found solutions in another corner of the world to the problems plaguing them at home, and built the foundation for continuing communication. By the end of the conference, some teams had formed to explore matters of mutual interest, and there was an agreement to divide the innovation labors—for example, one country taking the lead in development technology that many countries and many divisions could use. "The work has just begun," Voboril commented afterward. "My job will be to keep pushing those synergies, to help each division take advantage of the knowledge and the marketing inroads that their peers develop. We'll keep sliding back, and I'll keep pushing."

Cross-selling, product links, combining expertise, improved market intelligence, and leaps in efficiency are some of the outcomes of synergy. For example:

• *Cross-selling.* By 1986 Prudential expected over $30 million in commissions from sales shared by stockbrokers and insurance agents, up from $4 million two years earlier.[9]

• *Product links.* General Foods, after restructuring to decentralize, wanted to keep the benefits of a whole company identity. Chairman Philip Smith set up a task force of marketing executives to work on integrative programs aimed at retailers that would get more shelf space for all products. This led to a program, Team Up for Kids, tying in a number of products.[10]

• *Combining expertise.* Pillsbury applied the expertise of its packaged food researchers to help revitalize its Godfather's Pizza chain, developing new food products for sale in the restaurants. (Individually packaged slices of pizza was the first such product.) Similarly, Pillsbury used the expertise and resources of the restaurant group in finding sources of, storing, and distributing fresh vegetables to open the possibility of a Green Giant line of branded fresh vegetables for supermarket sales. Similarly, coordinating research and development on a worldwide basis allowed Procter and Gamble to take advantage of the varieties of expertise found in different countries to speed new product development.

• *Market intelligence.* A technology company got its multinational product divisions to alert one another to market signals, a practice that helped make product launchings in new countries more effective than ever in the company's history. Each product division served a different array of countries. Combining experience and data through communication across divisions, the company saw immediate payoffs in world market share growth.

• *Leaps in efficiency*. Combining operations of several divisions allowed Shenandoah Life Insurance to increase productivity and quality dramatically. Before: One form was routed to thirty-two people, across nine sections and three departments, taking twenty-seven days. After: The job was done by one self-managing clerical team of six people handling 13 percent more work faster, with fewer errors and 80 percent less supervision.[11]

Such benefits have led companies with a cowboylike tradition to develop new structures aimed at achieving synergies. For example, Procter and Gamble's traditional emphasis on internal competition grew out of a respected organizational innovation by Neil McElroy, later chairman, over fifty years ago: the assignment of a single marketing manager, a "brand manager," to each product. The rationale back then was that each product should receive distinctive treatment, treatment more likely to produce creative ideas, and that the company would grow faster by competing intensely against itself. In the early 1980s, in light of a changing marketplace and a proliferation of categories and brands, Procter and Gamble moved away from this cowboylike stance to a greater reliance on business teams. Now, as an observer put it, Procter and Gamble's brand managers "no longer operate like mini-czars but are assigned to teams with manufacturing, sales, and research managers, people they once outranked." CEO John Smale explained the business team to the *Harvard Business Review* as "a concept that says, 'When you're going to address a problem, get the people who have something to contribute in the way of creativity if not direct responsibility. Get them together.' " Teams are credited with turning around the sales of a losing product (Pringles potato chips), with packaging inventions, and with speeding the process of getting a new product to market.[12] A network of "organizational effectiveness consultants" trained in skills for facilitating team formation supports the search for synergies.

One especially comprehensive and successful case of a concerted effort to build value multipliers is American Express. In 1986, roughly 10 percent of American Express's net income came from cross-selling and other synergies. The one *big* success was selling life insurance, but there were also many "singles and doubles instead of home runs," as CEO James Robinson put it. Robinson made achieving synergies a priority in 1982, emphasizing that American Express was "one enterprise" united by common overall goals and asking senior executives to identify two or three promising "One Enterprise" synergy projects in their annual plans. A manager of corporate strategy watched over this, issuing a One Enterprise report among one hundred top executives, giving visibility to those engaged in collaboration. Evaluations and incentives were tied to this program: The Chairman of American Express Bank received one of two 1985 bonuses for efforts such as selling travelers checks for the card division and introducing brokerage services to its overseas clients. And by 1987 the company had sifted through about 260 ideas for collaboration between businesses, about 70 percent of which have worked. Among these ideas were sharing of office space, data processing capabilities, and marketing expertise among departments and also cross-marketing of products.[13]

American Express's search for synergies rests on an entrepreneurial foundation—a set of rather autonomous and focused business units concentrating on their own businesses, with a corporate staff of about eight hundred auditors, lawyers, and public relations experts. The One Enterprise program is an attempt to convey that American Express is "one big family" of entrepreneurial companies. Each unit or division is trying to maximize its profit, and if its leaders see that help from someone else in another unit is going to aid them, they will seek it out and try to convince the others that it is in their best interest also. This approach is based on decentralization with voluntary cooperation, not centralization with top-down commands. The synergies the company finds tend to be ways of augmenting what one unit wants to do rather than forcing all units to rely on a single method or a single corporate function. American Express never thought that one sales force could cross-sell life insurance, annuities, stocks and bonds, and credit cards, but the One Enterprise approach means that each company can find occasional marketing leads for the others.

There are nice cash bonuses and recognition for the people who work on One Enterprise projects—something they often have to do after hours and in their spare time. These were among the winning One Enterprise projects for 1987:

- A ten-person team representing all four major business units (Travel Related Services, IDS, Shearson Lehman Hutton, the American Express Bank) and a data processing unit (First Data Resources) negotiated a deal with AT&T for major price reductions. The team discussed the telecommunication needs of their respective companies, pulled the information into a coherent plan, and then worked with AT&T, saving tens of millions of dollars.
- Jim and Malcolm of TRS expanded business opportunities for the whole company by introducing other units to key TRS contacts—for example, a large airline that might be able to use SLH financing for the purchase of new planes.
- Katie, Pete, and Julie of IDS developed a new investment service for Trade Development Bank customers in Luxembourg.
- Gustavo of TRS supported SLH in developing a Financial Management Account product for Latin America, after SLH requested the help of TRS people who were familiar with the cultural differences and business expectations of the area.
- Craig and Ramesh of TRS and Jack of IDS assisted in the development of an Investment Management Account for American Express credit card holders, using IDS expertise to find ways to sell mutual funds to TRS customers.

Two forms of synergy seem most common at American Express, one externally oriented (marketing leads) and one internally oriented (efficiencies from using another company's "back-office" information-processing capacity). For example, the TRS marketing organization that places traveler's checks with banks and other institutions to sell them helps IDS market financial planning on a mass basis through those banks. Similarly, TRS or Shearson professionals who have relationships with the chief financial officer or controller of companies planning large restructurings can pave the way for IDS to offer financial counseling to employees deciding whether to take early-retirement options. "When they help IDS, they sort of expect that the favor will be returned," Harry Freeman, executive vice president, observed. "This starts a cycle of internal synergies that build on each other and create a companywide spirit of cooperation."

Back-office collaborations might take the following form: IDS may want to create a new mutual fund which will require an information processing capacity; by going to Shearson to see about using its Boston Safe subsidiary, a very efficient back office for mutual funds, IDS can save a substantial amount in setup expenses while compensating Shearson for use of the system; Shearson gets a source of additional return on its investment.

But even when synergy is a stated goal, there are many roadblocks. In other financial services companies, for example, synergies such as cross-marketing and the development of financial supermarkets seem limited by territoriality—the unwillingness of salesmen representing different products to work together. When Prudential first experimented with joint sales programs involving insurance agents and stockbrokers, the efforts were "crashing failures," according to George Ball, head of the brokerage unit. Or the attempt to achieve synergy is hurt by the unwillingness of executives to share customer lists, as with American Express's charge card people's initial reluctance to share their lists with the brokerage. Or internal cooperation and cross-marketing can threaten external relationships. Sears wondered whether to give its merchandise group access to the Discover credit card customer list because other merchants who have accepted the card could be upset.[14] All of these roadblocks were internal, having nothing to do with any unwillingness of customers to change their habits.

Similar problems are by-products of the very decentralization that also gives some companies their entrepreneurial strength. But without the ability to cooperate across areas, the units might as well be split up into independent businesses. This was the dilemma faced by the $200 million technology development company I will call "Firestar." In 1986, a new president put the issue of internal competition high on his list of things to change:

> There are natural competitive forces in a technology business. With the breadth of technology we have, it is easy to look at one area, e.g., electronics, and say that that group might do work in electronic materials, while the materials group might feel like that business is part of its scope and mission in life. Another example is the Computer Integrated Manufacturing Systems (CIMS) market. Our manufacturing technology *and* information systems groups have the technical knowledge to compete against each other for business in that market—or they could work jointly.

In his view, each of the six sectors of Firestar saw itself in competition with the others. Compensation to senior managers had been based on the performance of their sectors vis-à-vis the others. There was no incentive to cooperate internally, and as a result, the business sectors didn't "see the whole company" when making decisions. The groups acted independently rather than with a shared interest in the division. The president remarked that "I didn't see everyone's oar in the water at the same time." Some cooperation did exist from time to time, but it was not encouraged enough; if it happened, it happened by chance more than by design. "We don't have a bunch of Machiavellian types running around screwing their buddies," he said, "but we also are not getting enough synergies."

"Turf battles" had clearly arisen between business sectors in this company. For example, two groups separately approached the same customer, without a coordinated effort—"The left hand didn't know what the right was doing." As the president put it:

> Group A had studied the problem, decided it wasn't a good opportunity for us, and did not bid on the contract. Group A was the main line technology group for the type of problem involved here, the next best suited to evaluate the project. Unbeknownst to Group A, though, Group B looked at the same project and made a bid. The bid is still pending, but it probably won't be accepted. When Group A found out what Group B had done, they were livid, outraged. You may ask, "How could a group feel a charter to make a bid like that?" Well, Group B could see it as part of its mission.

Another example was even more vivid:

> Last year we established a new Aerospace office to be closer to an air force base, one of our biggest customers. This new office appeared to me to be in direct competition with several business sectors here at headquarters. In fact, they could have been in competition with all of the other divisions, that is how broad their mission statement was. This has set up a "we/they" mentality. As it was, we had three other groups in competition for aerospace business: the materials and electronic groups and the business development staff. This had to be changed. The new office staff are supposed to be our point people on the scene, not to compete with us but rather to use all the company resources to solve the customers' problems.

Then there were the minor instances of rivalry—minor, but no less irritating and costly, such as two different groups investing in the same piece of equipment, each purchasing one when instead they could have shared one.

Seeing these barriers to synergy, the president made the search for value multipliers in Firestar his major priority, shaping his approach to every aspect of the business, from strategic planning to compensation.

Successful efforts to increase synergy generally have three components: a focus from the top and the development of methods and managers to find value multipliers; shifts in incentives and rewards; and a culture of communication and cooperation resting on a foundation of personal relationships.

Providing Leadership and Vehicles to Identify Opportunities

The first ingredient in the search for synergies is a familiar one: leadership from the top. American Express's Jim Robinson made identification of synergies a priority in 1982, when he asked senior executives to define two or three One Enterprise projects in their annual plans. Executives are quick to point out that One Enterprise is not *forced* on anyone; projects must be in the best interests of the business unit. But Robinson's leadership is also clear. Consider Harry Freeman's view:

> Over the years we have managed to achieve a lot of useful synergies. Useful synergy does not come from directives from the top. It really comes when somebody in one of the business units thinks he can do a hell of a lot better, or make more money, or introduce a much better product, and really needs somebody or sees that some unit in another business unit can be really helpful. He then tries to convince the other guy that it is in his or her interest. What you try to do is create an environment of entrepreneurship about the whole place. One Enterprise was never meant to be the total program. The main driver of synergy does not come from directives. It comes from shared self-interest.
>
> Jim Robinson is a great One Enterprise guy. If you go outside the company and were using someone else's system, you'd better have a very good answer ready for him. Now if your answer is good, he'll say, "Terrific," or he may call up those other guys and say, "Hey, why don't you get more reasonable?" There is a certain amount of executive pressure to cooperate. But if you do go outside and find it cheaper for the same quality, Jim Robinson is going to say, "Go outside. We are in business for the profit of the shareholders."

Once top management identifies synergy goals, a "synergy czar" may then swing into action, serving as chief cheerleader and recorder of the efforts to find value multipliers. Sometimes the corporate strategy office plays this role, nudging cross-area projects into strategic plans, suggesting areas of overlap offering joint possibilities, convening task forces and councils to hammer out ways to maximize the payoffs from joint resource use, and encouraging collaborative efforts. This alone represents a striking shift of mind-set for many strategic planners, who are more accustomed to identifying the value of assets before an acquisition or divestiture than to finding ways to gain the benefits of internal collaboration.

At Pillsbury, the appointment of a synergy czar was a valiant attempt to shore up some ailing businesses by bringing the resources of various units together to create value multiplier effects. Then-CEO John Stafford realized that segmentation of the food industry required giving each division great autonomy; at the same time, someone was needed at the top to pull things together in order to capitalize on new opportunities that might cut across division lines. In March 1986, Stafford assigned James Behnke to the new position of senior vice-president for Growth and Technology—or, as Behnke put it on business cards he had printed, "Senior Vice-President, Blurring."

Behnke's business development group worked with the divisions to marshal all of Pillsbury's resources, which in practice meant getting restaurant divisions to help food divisions, and vice versa. As a result of Behnke's efforts, new business opportunities opened up. For example, when Green Giant (specialists in canned vegetables) decided to develop branded fresh vegetables, they lacked three critical resources, which Burger King helped provide: year-round supply, a distribution system, and food service customers. Behnke extracted three lessons from Pillsbury's experience:

First, it must be a win/win situation. If company A wins 10 points, and company B loses 5 points, Pillsbury gains 5 points, but it will never work. Both companies A and B must gain points, even if it is only 2.5 points each.

Second, if you go too low down an organization, then it gets tougher and tougher to cross disciplines. At the lower levels, people are more provincial, more guarded, more defensive. If the effort is important enough—you should tackle only the big projects—then the negotiations need to go on between the top levels of the organization. More senior people must be involved.

What makes it work is the chemistry of the people. There can be no systems, no rules, no manuals—people hate that stuff. There can be no pressure, only suction.

Unfortunately for Pillsbury and Stafford, the search for multipliers came too late to dilute the effects of other business problems. Mounting losses led to the return of the former chairman, Stafford's resignation in 1988, and frequent mention of Pillsbury as a takeover target. The search for value multipliers is a long process that cannot guarantee the quick rescue of failing businesses.

Realizing the importance of a concerted long-term effort to build synergy, the president of Firestar, the technology development company, built a number of planning and action vehicles. First, he and his senior managers shifted their strategic planning exercise from a near-term outlook (which leads to pressures to "beat your buddy in competition") to more long-term goals. They reviewed the standard business plan questions—Where are you now? Where do you want to be? How are you going to get there? But they added a twist of their own, approaching planning on two levels. Each sector came up with its own business plan; then, working together, the groups wrote strategic plans for different market areas, such as the industrial market and the defense business.

The president also created an investment council, comprising Firestar's senior business sector leaders and the business development staff. The council was guided by the strategic direction of each sector and of Firestar as a whole. It evaluated investments in R&D, capital equipment, and human resources (hiring needs). The goal was to change the past practice of tactical investing to a more strategic, holistic approach; for example, instead of having the manufacturing sector tactically purchase a piece of equipment, that purchase would now be considered a more general investment, an item with potential utility for other sectors as well.

Both components of the strategic planning were part of an effort to struggle against the forces that make a diverse technological company's sectors compete single technology with single technology. Instead, Firestar wanted to become a more fully integrated company, gaining power from a multidisciplinary approach. The company's strength was always its broad technological offerings; to capitalize on this required cross-business-unit cooperation. As the president put it,

"A good materials company is limited to only materials. We can do materials, but also do process design, environmental impact—we can provide our customers with many ancillary support services. We take a systems approach to the problem." His goal was to "foster a culture in which everyone gravitates toward working together to create synergy."

Incentives and Rewards

The approaches necessary to build synergy could not be more different from the shootouts of cowboy management. Destructive competition is set up so that the losers lose as much as the winners gain. There's a single prize, which the winner takes; but in addition to missing the prize, the losers also incur costs. What drives the competition in a negative direction, then, is largely fear of losing. The destructive side of the battle stems as much from avoiding punishment as from seeking rewards. Cooperation is likely, however, when there are incentives for performing well, regardless of who comes in first. If one of the goals of competition is to develop options, then it is important to reward the generating of alternatives, not just getting the right answer. Some rewards come from playing the game well, even if the ultimate prize goes to someone else. Joint incentives, which give everyone something if anyone reaches high levels of performance, make cooperation even more likely.

The creation of an inter-business-sector development fund was one of Firestar's new president's first moves. He held a reserve of funds for use in projects that spanned the boundaries of two or more sectors. Previously, if a sector was going to work with another sector, it had to invest by itself—only one sector put up the money, though the other would also get some benefits. This situation did not encourage cooperation; why help support a competitor? The president found these new funds to be an immediate incentive for joint projects. The atmosphere at the company soon began to reflect this emphasis. As he said:

> In an environment where team play gets rewarded, we now openly discuss the pros and cons of major bidding decisions. The decision making is more holistic. If two separate groups think they should both bid on a contract, they'll put together a joint proposal. The problems in the past have arisen when one group thinks bidding is a good idea and

another does not. Then I bring the two groups together for a meeting to discuss both sides of the decision. When sectors can't agree, I help them resolve the problems by making the ultimate decision.

Although some of this crossing of lines did happen before, there was no necessity or drive to do so. Now there was *incentive,* as opposed to just a hope that cooperation would happen.

A second approach is to add team incentives to senior managers' evaluation and compensation. American Express has a variety of ways to reward achievement of synergy goals, starting with special awards, bonuses, and publicity for specific One Enterprise projects, available to contributors at any organizational level. Synergy goals are also built into top management incentives. Incentive compensation awards (called portfolio awards) for senior managers in one of the businesses are determined primarily by the performance of their business unit, but a significant chunk of each award is determined by the performance of all the business units. For senior corporate managers, the portfolio award is divided into quarters, and 25 percent is determined by the performance of each of the major business units. Furthermore, a large number of employees own shares in the company, and a large number of officers have stock options. This package of incentives and rewards directs people's attention to the performance of the whole company, not just the performance of their own business.

Firestar's new president had to revise both incentive and evaluation systems. He began to ask the question, "How much business did you develop for the rest of the company, not just for yourself?" Sector leaders were asked to develop inter-sector markets and programs. In the past, managers hadn't been evaluated on the combined results of two or three sectors together. Now that was part of the evaluation. This provided an incentive for sector leaders to work together and avoid one-to-one competition; they could be rewarded for working together and across sectors. Managers were now encouraged to bring back leads for others, to market for the entire division. "Instead of dangling the carrot in front of each sector manager, I've put the carrot between organizations," the president said.

Similarly, at Bankers Trust, the heads of corporate banking and corporate finance review the proposed bonuses for each other's officers and can influence the amount if an officer has been uncooperative. If trends toward synergy incentives and rewards continue, there is also a need for new measurement systems that can permit attribution of the benefits from collaboration.[15]

Communication, Relationships, and the Foundation for Cooperation

Communications is the third key to achieving synergies. Many opportunities for synergy come in the form of information sharing; thus, the channels need to be established to enable managers and professionals from different business units and different parts of the world to communicate. Post-entrepreneurial companies tend to be characterized by more frequent events that draw people together across areas—executive conferences, meetings of professionals assigned to different businesses, boards and councils that oversee efforts in diverse places and transmit learning from them. Training centers and educational events are a potent means for increasing communication. General Electric's facility in Crotonville, New York, is much more than a corporate college; it is in effect a synergy center than helps people identify shared interests across businesses and tackle common problems together.

Computer networks and other information systems can enhance the communication that knits a company together in pursuit of synergies. But systems—no matter how easy to use—do not necessarily guarantee cooperative communication without the knowledge of one another than people develop through face-to-face relationships. For this reason, Digital Equipment Corporation runs a helicopter service to and from major New England facilities to permit people to get together to transmit information and pursue joint projects. People develop relationships with one another this way faster than they do through electronic mail, as important as systems like that are for making communication easy and instantaneous; and those relationships make cooperation possible.

It is harder to get the benefits of cooperation and easier for rivalry to get out of hand when there is no history of past relationships to draw on to give the rivals understanding of one another, when there are no shared experiences to prevent mistrust and hostility—or worse, when past experiences have been negative. Cooperation flourishes on a foundation of shared experience. Even in encounters involving strangers, relationships make a difference. For example, players in laboratory games like "prisoners' dilemma" do better when given the chance to talk with one another beforehand.[16] Friendships help. After first encountering resistance to joint sales programs involving stock-brokers and insurance agents, Prudential made the programs work by encouraging joint efforts where there seemed to be natural affinities on the basis of friendship.[17]

Synergy is also difficult to achieve when there is a clear and apparently unbridgeable structural separation between areas. Their activities are not intertwined, they seem to need nothing from one another, and their apparent independence is reinforced by separate career paths or communication patterns or reporting relationships. Cooperation, in contrast, is engendered by structural links that make the parties interdependent. Awareness of mutual need reduces rivalries to a friendlier level. So do integrating mechanisms that remind the parties of joint interests—for example, liaisons between groups or people with a foot in each camp.

Expectations also help. The anticipation of a shared future dampens the killer instinct. Even in competition, there will be more cooperative relationships among rivals when the competition is viewed as tempo-rary, when the composition of the opposing team is known to change regularly, when today's losers can join winners in another effort toward another goal. Robert Axelrod's computer simulations of prisoners' dilemma games found the most successful strategy to be TIT for TAT, a strategy that began by cooperating and then simply reciprocated the opponent's last move. He argued that cooperating was most likely when people or groups knew they would have to deal with one another again in the future.[18]

In short, cooperation is encouraged when people perceive a shared fate. They see that they and other rivals have a joint stake in a larger outcome—advancing their joint enterprise as a whole. This idea was behind James Robinson's One Enterprise program at American Express. Another CEO stressed "dual citizenship" to all his manag-ers, making them members, simultaneously, of both their business unit and a corporate project team, with "citizenship responsibilities, rights, and rewards" stemming from each.

We have come full circle in the search for synergies. To get value multiplied requires removing the sources of value subtracted. Tilting the balance toward cooperation offers the possibility of tackling new business opportunities as well as eliminating the costs of in-fighting. Encouraging cooperation even among nominal rivals helps organizations gain the synergies that come with the transfer of good ideas from one unit to another. It makes it easier to focus on standards for quality performance and to concentrate organizational energy where it should be concentrated, on achieving the goal, not on eliminating rivals. And it offers flexibility; today's friends can more easily be tomorrow's collaborators.

There is so much competition already inherent in most organizations—from the "pyramid squeeze" that means that not all of the talented people can rise to top positions, to the natural pride that one department takes in doing better than another—that the task of managers is often not to fuel the fires but to dampen them.

The real danger of performance shootouts is that someone you need may die of the wounds.

THE CORPORATION'S NEW SHAPE

Striving for synergies is essential to managing the do-more-with-less imperative of the corporate Olympics. Fewer resources, intelligently combined, can work together to bring greater payoffs and to pursue new opportunities with greater speed. A stress on synergies can help companies save on fixed costs and tackle new opportunities at the same time.

Getting there, however, requires the corporation to take on a new shape. The company that achieves synergies looks and operates very differently from the swollen, lethargic "corpocracy" that many large American businesses allowed themselves to become. No longer does the typical corporate organization chart resemble the Eiffel Tower—a broad pyramid of productive activities on the bottom and a tall, narrow hierarchy of many levels of managers piled upon managers, stretching all the way to the top. The model for the post-entrepreneurial corporation is a leaner organization, one that has fewer "extraneous" staff and is thus more focused on doing only those things in which it has competence. In the post-entrepreneurial company, there are fewer and fewer people or departments that are purely "corporate" in nature; more responsibilities are delegated to the business units, and more services are provided by outside suppliers. And fewer layers of management mean that the hierarchy itself is flatter. Thus, the "vertical" dimension of the corporation is much less important. At the same time, the ''horizontal'' dimension—the process by which all the divisions and departments and business units communicate and cooperate—is the key to getting the benefits of collaboration.

The post-entrepreneurial corporation represents a triumph of process over structure. That is, relationships and communication and the flexibility to temporarily combine resources are more important than the ''formal'' channels and reporting relationships represented on an organizational chart. *In Olympic contests requiring speed and dexterity, what is important is not how responsibilities are divided but how people can pull together to pursue new opportunities.*

Management sage Peter Drucker recently used the image of a symphony orchestra to describe the new model of the leaner, flatter corporation.[19] In the orchestra, performers with different skills concentrate on perfecting their professional competence, while a single conductor coordinates the overall performance; performers with similar specialties form self-managed work teams, operating without a bureaucratic hierarchy above them. The image is useful and evocative as far as it goes. But for corporate players to make beautiful music together they must achieve a balance between concentrating on their own areas of skill and responsibility and working together with others. They need to do their own jobs well while keeping one eye on what might be useful for someone else. They need to understand enough about the company's other areas to identify possibilities for joint action and mutual enhancement. They need to simultaneously focus and collaborate. They must function in many roles: as soloist, ensemble players, and members of the orchestra.

CHAPTER 5

Becoming PALs: Pooling, Allying and Linking Across Companies

One of the lessons America's mythologized cowboys supposedly learned in the rough-and-tumble days of the American frontier was that paranoia was smart psychology. You couldn't trust anybody. They were all out to get you, and they would steal from you as soon as your back was turned. Staking out an ownership claim to a territory or to a herd was necessary (though not sufficient) to guarantee that you would get your piece of the action. Indeed, one did not even have to travel very far west to find other cultural support for the paranoid world view. "Self-reliance" was the best-known phrase associated with the influential New Englander of the nineteenth century, Ralph Waldo Emerson. "Good fences make good neighbors," New Englanders thought, as poet Robert Frost quoted to his readers a century later.

Good fences make good corporations, the translation to traditional management assumptions could read. If you don't own it, if it hasn't been branded with your mark, you don't control it, and it might hurt you. What you own is "inside" the fence; everything else is "outside," to be treated as a potential enemy or adversary unless brought under your domination.

How times have changed. Today the strategic challenge of doing more with less leads corporations to look outward as well as inward for solutions to the competitiveness dilemma, improving their ability to compete without adding internal capacity. Lean, agile, post-entrepreneurial companies can stretch in three ways. They can *pool* resources with others, *ally* to exploit an opportunity, or *link* systems in a partnership. In short, they can become better "PALs" with other organizations—from venture collaborators to suppliers, service contractors, customers, and even unions.

This friendly approach contrasts sharply with the adversarial system ingrained in American business management. The adversarial mode for dealing with "outsiders" has had a long time to take root. Like the "paranoid style of American politics" labeled by Richard Hofsteder, the "paranoid style of traditional American management" evolved as a major means of survival in the fiercely competitive atmosphere of the late nineteenth century and reflected corporate conditions then, not now. It has pervaded relationships with organized labor. It has been immortalized in folk wisdom like "caveat emptor"—let the buyer beware. The paranoid world view has even dominated textbook discussions of organization theory and behavior, in which organizations are seen as being resentful of "resource dependencies" that force them into relationships with other organizations and seeking any way they can to increase their own advantage in the relationship.

The adversarial mode with its paranoid world view centers on images of domination and fear of being dominated. It stands in stark contrast to the cooperative mode better suited to the challenges of the global Olympics, a mode that seeks opportunities for growth by allying with other organizations. For post-entrepreneurial strategists, distinctions like inside versus outside or us versus them have less meaning when teaming up might produce benefits for each group.

For example, the adversarial model long dominated purchasing in American corporations. The goal was to minimize price by maintaining a large vendor base, frequently shifting the mix of purchases from each vendor, and operating through short-term formal contracts with frequent rebidding.[1] As recently as 1984, an American textbook on procurement defended such arm's-length arrangements:

Generally, caution must be exercised when purchases by any one customer exceed 10% or so of a supplier's sales. If purchases appreciably exceed this amount, the purchaser begins to assume a moral responsibility for the economic well-being of the supplier. The purchasing firm loses needed flexibility in such a situation.[2]

Avoiding such "moral responsibility" for the well-being of another company and getting the lowest price was the purpose of the adversarial model. While price was, in fact, generally minimized, so were incentives for supplier innovation or quality, beyond agreed specifications. But over the last decade, the inadequacies of this model have become much clearer to American companies. For one thing, by 1980, throughout all U.S. manufacturing, purchased materials and services accounted for 60 percent of the total cost of operations (indicating major strategic leverage to be found). Furthermore, the role of supplier relations in the superior quality of Japanese products had been noted. The Japanese model involves the supplier as "coproducer," fewer suppliers per customer and customers per supplier, long-term relationships, close interaction among all functions, physical proximity, and blanket contracts.[3]

The choice companies were once thought to have in dealing with any "external" entity was either to fight with it and keep it outside, or swallow it up to bring it inside—protecting boundaries through adversarial relationships or through acquisition. Today there is increasing interest in an intermediate arrangement involving coalitions, one that keeps more options open—cooperation through alliances and partnerships.

FROM ADVERSARY TO ALLY

In the face of heightened competitive pressures and the worldwide scope of both technology and markets, many U.S. firms have established new cooperative agreements with other organizations at home and abroad that involve unprecedented (for them) levels of sharing and commitment. While American firms, particularly small ones, have always allied with other firms for specific purposes, the extent as well as the diversity of such activity has grown in recent years, moving from the periphery to take a central place in some companies' strategies. Indeed, international alliances and partnerships are associated with competitive strength: entered into by larger firms, by those more experienced internationally, and in strategically important industries by those with strong domestic positions.[4]

In 1987, more than forty coalitions between Ford Motor Company and outside commercial entities were identified by Harvard professor Malcolm Salter. There were more than eight thousand person-visits by U.S.-based Ford employees to Japan—and so much traffic between Detroit and Tokyo in general that many U.S.–Tokyo flights now originate in Detroit rather than Chicago. Indeed, by 1986 General Electric had more than a hundred cooperative ventures with other firms, and even IBM, long known as one of the "great independents," had established formal partnerships with a number of other organizations, including Merrill Lynch and Aetna Life and Casualty. IBM was also trying to ally with potential competitors through agreements making them "value-added resellers"; McDonnell Douglas Automation, for example, would sell IBM products to their customers, adding their own to the package. In some sectors, there were more joint domestic ventures announced in a single year in the 1980s than in the previous fifteen to twenty years combined.[5]

These relationships with "blurred boundaries," to use Joseph Badaracco's term,[6] overlay or even replace market relationships with organizational ones, often creating close, even intimate connections between separate organizations. Firms do not lose their legal identity; they retain their own culture and management structure, and they can pursue their own strategies. But they reduce their autonomy by strengthening their ties with other organizations, thus sharing authority over certain decisions. And sometimes the interpenetration makes it hard to distinguish employees of one organization from employees of the other. At Eastman Kodak, one of its suppliers staffs and runs a Kodak office supply room.

When an alliance has existed for a long time, the bonds between representatives of the two cooperating organizations can sometimes be even closer than those within their own organizations. The advanced development division of a major defense contractor I worked with has had a long-term partnership with the Department of Defense that has resulted in a joint entity that functions like a single operating unit with both corporate and government employees. In terms of any measure except formal employer, the contractor and customer form an organization with stronger internal ties than those either group has to its own official "owner." Some of the DOD program managers have been in that role more than twenty years, guiding the corporate team in decision-making. Both sets of people participate fully in regular review meetings, turning them into working sessions exemplifying their joint commitment to the products. They attend each other's recreational and educational events; indeed, at a recent divisional management development retreat, it was impossible to distinguish the customers from the hosts.

The initial bonds in this particular relationship grew out of a legal requirement for secrecy, which immediately set both contractor and customer apart from their parent organizations and gave them a shared mission. But over time, a set of working relationships evolved that gradually institutionalized the alliance. Formally, the relationship is governed by a series of contracts, entitling the customer to shop elsewhere if not satisfied. Informally, however, a web of overlapping projects, joint planning, career incentives, and social relationships bind the parties more thoroughly.

Yet, despite examples like these, the fragility of some kinds of partnerships is as striking as their growing frequency and extent. Independent studies by McKinsey & Company and Coopers & Lybrand show that perhaps 70 percent of joint ventures or formal "strategic alliances" are disbanded or fall short of expectations. Of course, dissolution of a partnership is not de facto evidence of failure; it may mean that the alliance *achieved* its purpose.[7] But even for those that work, the management complexities are enormous. So why would companies elect to enter into partnerships or alliances rather than choose the simpler options of building their own internal capacity or merging with another organization?

The "do-it-yourself" option has limitations in a fast-paced, highly competitive environment. It is costly in terms of both resources and time, even assuming that the organization has the capacity to handle the new task successfully. Acquisitions are similarly costly; and they entail an obligation to manage all that comes with the package. Furthermore, it is harder to move in and out of full-fledged ownership positions than more limited arrangements that offer more flexibility. Acquisition in the form of vertical integration may create organizational rigidities that prevent innovation (for example, former external vendors with so much security they lose the motivation to innovate) or make it difficult to keep up if industry technology changes dramatically. For example, auto-makers who were vertically integrated with carburetor manufacturers were slower to change when electronic fuel injectors began to substitute for mechanical carburetors.[8] While the power to set terms and conditions may come with ownership or domination, this strategy can also limit the flexibility required for innovation and fast technological progress.

Besides avoiding the risks and costs of acquisitions, partnerships that allow organizations to retain nominal independence also provide the motivational benefits of "ownership" of each one's piece of the territory—something particularly important to smaller and more entrepreneurial companies—instead of the loss of identity that a full merger implies. And then, of course, in some spheres, for some kinds of alliances, building your own substitute or taking over the other organization is not even an option. A company cannot "take over" an existing union; it is legally safeguarded. And antitrust rules still prevent some mergers while permitting alliances among those same organizations for more limited purposes.

Analog Devices, for example, has two reasons for preferring partnerships and joint ventures over outright acquisition of small companies with the new technology Analog needs. Acquisitions would require changes in Analog's organizational structure every time a company was bought, changes that would have to be undone if an acquisition turns sour; and acquisitions would soon amount to an increasing portion of the company.

Another justification for partnerships is their dynamism. Some partnerships that begin as an alternative route to gaining a capacity or a resource may end with at least one organization better able to provide that resource for itself, so that it no longer requires the partner. Dependency is decreased over time, and the partnership dissolves. But other partnerships have the opposite dynamic. What begins as a limited alliance may move toward greater degrees of interdependence, and end with the organizations merging. Some analysts have compared "strategic alliances" to marriages, but they are really more similar to living together.

There is something entrepreneurially appealing about cooperative arrangements among firms. These relationships can help little firms compete with big firms. They offer flexibility and speed of access to new capacity. Getting the benefits of what another organization offers without the risks and responsibilities of ''owning'' it is the ultimate form of leverage.

Of course, the benefits and issues that partnerships create depend on the purpose of the alliance. I have distinguished three categories of such partnerships: multiorganization service alliances, opportunistic alliances, and stakeholder alliances. The first type involves the least overlap and smallest sphere of cooperation between the partner organizations; the latter involves the most. Yet it is the third kind of partnership that seems to have the greatest potential for enduring benefits to the allies.

Service Alliances: The Cross-Company Corsortium

In service alliances, a group of organizations with a similar need, often in the same industry, band together to create a new entity to fill that need for all of them—an industry research consortium, for example. The service is one that is too expensive or difficult for a single organization to provide for itself, and it cannot be purchased on the open market. So several organizations ally to establish a new organization, which they jointly control, to meet the need.

The resulting consortium requires the fewest changes in each partner of the three types discussed here, because interdependence among partner organizations is low; at the same time, the difficulty of getting the diverse partners to agree on the service that suits all of them can make these entities very hard to manage and loss of interest or commitment a common problem. The limited purpose of the consortium makes it possible for even nominal competitors to ally (both legally and strategically) in ensuring that a service is available across the board to all members for the purpose of lifting the performance level of the whole group. By definition, a consortium is a group formed to undertake an enterprise beyond the resources of any of its members that will provide benefits to all of them.

Consortia thus try to offer the benefits of larger scale through resource pooling. Each member gains some of the benefits of larger scale while still retaining its independence with respect to every other activity. For this reason, consortia are especially attractive in areas in which the development of new technology is particularly important and particularly costly.

The National Cooperative Research Act of 1984 loosened antitrust restrictions to allow joint development through the prototype stage. By

1985, at least forty R&D consortia were being organized nationwide, taking a number of forms. Pradco, organized by Borg-Warner, Dresser Industries, Ingersoll-Rand, and TransAmerica to design new boiler pumps for power plants, spreads research tasks among its own members. The thirty-three members of the Semiconductor Research Corporation, including AT&T, GM, IBM, and DuPont, sponsor research at a number of universities, as do the seven members of the International Partners in Glass Research. The Center for Advanced Television Studies, formed by ABC, CBS, NBC, PBS, RCA, and five other companies to improve the quality of television transmission, spends its $1 million yearly research budget through MIT; and the Guided Wave Optoelectronics Manufacturing Technology Development Program, organized by six companies, conducts its research on fiber optics at the Battelle Memorial Institute in Columbus, Ohio.

Still other consortia have created new, stand-alone organizations. Two of the better-publicized examples are Bellcore and MCC. In 1984, the regional telephone companies spun off from AT&T formed Bellcore, a research center with a $900 million budget established to carry out research and development benefiting all seven companies. In 1983, twenty-one computer companies formed the Microelectronics and Computer Corporation in Texas, an industrywide research center with a budget of up to $700 million over ten years and a staff of four hundred drawn in part from member companies.

Research consortia predate the current high-tech competitiveness frenzy, although the pressure for rapid technology development still appears as a driving force. The Electric Power Research Institute, a nonprofit, semipublic organization managing research and development for the entire industry, was established in 1973. Since its founding, its engineers have turned out more than 430 products: hardware, software, manuals and guides, electrical devices, and entire electric-generation systems. About four dollars in quantifiable benefits have been generated for each dollar invested.

While R&D consortia are by far the most identifiable, they are not the only examples of this form of organizational cooperation. In 1986, thirty-four companies, including IBM, General Electric, and Chase Manhattan, anted up $10 million each to form American Casualty Excess Insurance Company, a company that would provide them with insurance they could not otherwise obtain. Even more significant are consortia designed to allow smaller companies to gain joint purchasing or market clout—such as the Independent Grocers of America.

Consortia are stronger versions of the weaker alliances (such as trade associations) that companies in the same industry form to conduct research or take action at the industry level. Membership is generally more restricted, membership costs are higher, and the corsortium itself has more strategic significance; it is expected to produce specific benefits for specific companies, rather than generalized or abstract benefits. The stake in consortia is much higher than the stake in trade associations, and participation in governance is thus a more significant issue. But still, compared to the next two types of alliances, consortia maintain the lowest degree of joint commitment. This low commitment level is often pointed out by skeptics, who claim that companies withhold their best people and best ideas.

Opportunistic Alliances: The Joint Venture
A second cluster of partnerships is best labeled "opportunistic," with all the positive and negative connotations of that term. Organizations see an opportunity to gain an immediate, though perhaps temporary, competitive advantage through an alliance that gets them into a new business or extends an old business. The goal is venture development. The alliance opens up possibilities that would not have existed for either of the partners acting alone. Once that opportunity is exploited, it is not always clear whether there is any basis for the relationship to continue. It is this kind of alliance that the McKinsey and Coopers and Lybrand studies saw dissolving frequently.

Joint business ventures are the generic example of the opportunistic alliance. The partners get from each other a competence that will allow them to move more quickly toward their own business goals. For example, CBS formed a number of joint ventures in the 1980s— with IBM and Sears to develop and market Videotex, an electronic information service; with Twentieth Century Fox to develop video-tapes; and with Columbia Pictures (Coca-Cola) and Home Box Office (Time Inc.) to develop motion pictures. Digital Equipment Corporation strengthened its hold on the manufacturing automation market by developing an alliance with Allen-Bradley, an industrial controls company.

The addition of the partners' competence is the answer to the question of why organizations would want to pursue a business opportunity with full-fledged partners, instead of more passive lenders or investors. The ability to attain larger scale is one motivating factor, though a weak one, tending to be confined to mass production industries with lower rates of technological innovation.[9] Instead, the two principal driving forces behind this kind of alliance are competence-enhancing ones: technology transfer or market access or both—especially where technology and markets are rapidly changing. And that is often the trade: one partner contributes the technology in return for the other partner's access to particular markets. But then, once one of the partners has gained experience with the competence of the other, the alliance is vulnerable to dissolution—the opportunity can now be pursued without the partner.

Many joint ventures form because one partner is eager to learn something from the other—get a piece of technology, learn how to manage a process, gain technological expertise. This is one way to prepare quickly for new global contests. Indeed, international joint ventures for R&D purposes were the fastest-growing subcategory of cooperative arrangements by U.S. firms in the 1980s, replacing wholly owned subsidiaries. But how much "jointness" is involved in many of these alliances is an open question, and one that makes direct comparison of costs and benefits difficult. In two advanced-technology companies where my research team gathered data, creating a partnership with a newer, smaller company was a primary way that each got access to new technology. But the twenty-four alliances we found all involved different degrees of investment and proportional ownership.

A second opportunistic use of joint ventures is to gain fast access to new markets. A number of studies have pinpointed the considerable odds against success, at least in the short term, when companies try to enter product markets in which they have not previously competed. Experience with similar products is not sufficient to compensate for lack of customer base or market experience.[10] Finding a local partner to provide access to a foreign market is particularly appealing to U.S. companies. After deregulation, for example, AT&T allied with Philips and Olivetti to gain access to the European market.[11]

Joint ventures are not always start-from-scratch efforts to pursue new opportunities. Sometimes a joint venture is designed as the solution to a business problem involving prior commitments by the partners. This was the case in an international technology venture I worked with that I will give the pseudonym of "Grotech." Grotech's partners represented several companies from several countries with different levels of investment and different interests in the venture's success. Grotech had been a poorly performing subsidiary owned outright by one of the partners, linked to the other partners by licensing and marketing agreements going back over a decade. When its parent announced that it was seeking a buyer for Grotech, the Country X partner knew that (a) it needed Grotech for access to some technology and markets, and could not let it fall into competitors' hands but (b) the Countries Y and Z partners would not allow X to buy Grotech outright for the same reason, and (c) Country X could not afford the purchase anyway. The outcome of a series of frustrating negotiations was the launching of Grotech as a venture jointly owned by all the companies, including the original parent. But relationships among the partners were strained, because of personal antagonisms, historical rivalries, and a suspicion that everyone was in it to protect past investments, not to promote Grotech's success.

Grotech is the ultimate opportunistic alliance, since none of the partners had much interest in the others, and they were keeping their share of the venture to ward off competition as well as to build a growth company. Yet I have found that even start-up joint ventures often involve tangled histories of prior dealings between the partners. The new alliance is simply a new form of an old relationship.

Other joint ventures can be even more complex. Alcan, the Canadian multinational giant, has a series of relationships with a Delaware start-up company developing advanced ceramics, a technology of interest to Alcan. Alcan owns 20 percent of the Delaware corporation itself and 40 percent of a limited partnership holding the start-up's patents, and it jointly runs a third company, which commercializes products using the start-up's technology and Alcan's materials. Meanwhile, the start-up has similarly complex relationships with a large chemical company. The opportunities that joint ventures represent can make many companies want to have their fingers in the pie.

Stakeholder Alliances: Suppliers, Customers, Employees

Stakeholder alliances are defined by pre-existing interdependence. They are ''complementary'' coalitions between a number of stakeholders in a business process who are involved in different stages of the value-creation chain. Stakeholders are those groups on which an organization depends—the people who can help it achieve its goals or can stop it dead in its tracks. They include suppliers, customers, and employees.

Such complementary alliances tend to be both quality-driven and innovation-driven. Quality for one company's products is often a matter of actions taken by another organization that supplies parts or labor; gaining more control over quality may mean influencing those other organizations. Furthermore, major innovations in technology or organizational systems require longer-term investments. When they also require similar investments from stakeholders, to ensure compatibility of systems, for example, then the basis for an alliance emerges. These stakeholder alliances resemble other forms of long-term relationships between companies with separate ownership: franchiser-franchisee relationships, for example, or the "quasifirms" of building contractors and their subcontractors in the construction industry.[12]

Suppliers. Facing imperatives to cut costs and improve quality, leading American companies are creating closer relationships with their suppliers. "Outsourcing" is one way American high-tech firms are addressing productivity issues—buying more instead of making it in-house; 41 percent of the firms in a 1988 American Electronics Association survey planned to increase the value of the product outsourced, while only 18 percent intended to decrease it. But those same firms saw *quality* as their number one competitive factor.[13] To ensure quality while buying from outside firms calls for a redefinition of the vendor relationship. Arm's-length relationships do not produce the motivation for suppliers to invest in technology to improve quality or manage the complexities of just-in-time inventory.

Thus, leading companies are starting to treat suppliers as their "partners." John Marshall, vice-president of TRW Safety Systems Division, told George Lodge about this change at TRW's automotive divisions:

> In the past we sought bids from a number of suppliers, and price was the principal issue. Now we want flexible relationships with a few suppliers, and we want our suppliers to help us in a variety of ways. We want better quality. We want them to help us reduce our inventories. We want their help and ideas about how we can improve the final products. It is not unusual these days for two or three engineers from our suppliers to be working in our plants for a while. We network through computers. I might call one of our suppliers and urge them—if not help them—to locate a plant near us.[14]

In addition to making possible joint investments in technology and compatible systems that improve quality and reduce waste, supplier input into product design can generate innovation by taking advantage of the suppliers' expertise in the potential of their technologies. At the same time, helping suppliers manage better also has payoffs. Polaroid saved $27 million over two years by helping vendors to improve their cost structure. To do this required knowing the suppliers' businesses well and showing them ways to operate more efficiently.

NCR has a particularly well-developed set of alliances with its key vendors, designed to ensure that the partnership works to their mutual benefit. To maintain its computer products based on the Intel 80000 family of integrated circuits and microprocessors, NCR established an internal role called the "Intel advocate," which has been so effective that Intel has assigned its own in-house advocate to manage its relationship with NCR. The NCR "supplier advocate" program involves the ten suppliers with the most important strategic implications for the company. NCR works closely with those organizations to make sure not only that the relationship is sustained, but that they each benefit from the other's particular strength and expertise. NCR also has a series of technological agreements with suppliers for developing and sharing knowledge on a worldwide basis. Executives say that they see such agreements as part of a broad commitment to supplier and customer education, which improves the transaction of the moment while laying a foundation for enhanced relationships in the future.

Customers. Partnerships with customers are just the flip side of supplier partnerships, of course. There have always been strategic advantages to staying close to customers. Good customer relationships reverberate not only in current sales but also in future effectiveness and growth. Satisfied customers are the single best source of new business. Timely knowledge of changing customer requirements makes it possible to guide production more efficiently, reducing waste, inventory costs, and returns. And experience shows that customers are also one of the major founts of ideas for innovation. In some industries, as much as 80 percent of all important industrial innovations have originated with users.[15] These are among the reasons that innovation-conscious high-technology companies go beyond emphasizing customer service to create more formal ties: user councils, inviting customers to consult on R&D projects, joint promotions, and the ultimate partnership step, joint development projects.

Harvard marketing professor Benson Shapiro has been following the evolution of the sales functions in manufacturing companies from single transaction–oriented sales, to systems selling, to account management, to what he calls "strategic partnering"—the "close encounter of a fourth kind." He comments:

> Even account management with all of its opportunities and rewards, as well as significant investments and costs, cannot satisfy the evolving need for closer, more permanent vendor/customer relationships. Joint products, service, and infrastructure development have led to an even more intimate buyer-seller relationship.[16]

One example Shapiro cites is the alliance between Electronic Data Systems (EDS, acquired by General Motors in 1984) and AT&T Information Systems (ATTIS). EDS has substantial skills in integrating computers, telecommunications gear, and software into customer systems. ATTIS sells telecommunications gear, computers, and related equipment. It does not, however, have sufficient systems integration skills to satisfy all of its customers. EDS and ATTIS therefore signed an agreement under which EDS will be considerably more than a routine supplier to AT&T; it will also play an important role as a systems integrator for other AT&T customers.

At Ford's initiative, IBM has also departed from its past modus operandi with customers in winning a $200 million contract for office systems at Ford Motor Company. Ford had "asked to start with a blank piece of paper and redefine how the relationship between the two companies should work. So we did," reported an IBM executive. Under the new relationship, a team of fifty Ford and IBM employees is designing the system to fit Ford's needs and is jointly overseeing installation.[17]

Technology is not the only basis for customer alliances. I helped a consumer products company experiment with another form of customer partnership with large retail chains. It is making part of its sales force available to store managers to provide a number of in-store shelving services.

Employee organizations. A third form of complementary partnership is that between labor organizations and management to set policies jointly or administer an area of company operations. The planning for General Motors' Saturn subsidiary, for example, has been conducted jointly with the United Auto Workers. The plans include a network of management-union committees running the plant; representatives of the UAW sit on all planning and operating committees, including the strategic advisory committee formed by Saturn's president and staff.

In addition to those in the auto industry, several well-publicized but unstable labor-management alliances have occurred in air transportation. Eastern Airlines made a deal with its unions in 1984 to exchange employee stock ownership, union seats on the board of directors, and a workplace participation program for wage concessions. The alliance fell apart in bitterness when Eastern asked for further wage concessions and was ultimately taken over by Texas Air. Western Airlines developed a less-publicized but dramatically more successful partnership with its unions to cut costs; this alliance helped Western recover and then find an acquirer in Delta.

Union-management alliances are occurring in industries undergoing rapid change, as a means to permit innovation—to collaborate in changing work rules or job conditions to improve competitiveness. Thus, it is no surprise that telecommunications is joining autos, steel, and air transportation in seeking new relationships between labor and management organizations.

Of all the changes that occurred in telecommunications organizations since the breakup of AT&T on January 1, 1984, and the formation of seven new regional telephone operating companies, perhaps no change is more remarkable than the speedy and effective change in which Pacific Bell, the largest part of the newly formed Pacific Telesis Group, and Nevada Bell, its tiny sister to the east, established a new "business partnership" with their major union, the Communications Workers of America. This business partnership—Pacific's term—was considered vital to realizing its strategic goals of superior financial performance in a competitive environment. The economics of the business meant that PacTel needed to introduce labor-saving technology and new operating methods in order to be effective in the growing sector of the market, the business customer, and in order to keep costs down for price-sensitive services now that they were no longer a protected monopoly. But the business changes the company foresaw implied changes in employment levels and workforce skills as well. Thus, the cooperation of the union would make a difference in whether or not the company could act on its strategy.

While the idea of a dramatically different relationship with the union was seeded in the first year after divestiture, partnership activities got under way in the spring of 1985. Between May 1985 and September 1986, the following was accomplished:

• A Memorandum on Employment Security was developed by Pacific Bell officers and CWA local presidents and ratified by the CWA membership in August 1985. The company agreed to undertake a variety of actions to save jobs and avert layoffs in exchange for greater flexibility in deploying people. A layoff of more than one thousand people was averted immediately.

• "Local common interest forums" (LCIFs) were established to continue to discuss employment security issues—which were now broadened to include company discipline policies, introduction of technology, contract labor, and new venture development. These forums consisted of every company officer and the union local presidents representing the employees in their organizations. Meeting monthly since the fall of 1985, they began gradually to include the next echelons in their activities, and by the fall of 1986 were beginning to act as policy boards or steering committees guiding a number of task forces working on specific organizational changes.

• Pacific Telesis conducted its first independent (postdivestiture) bargaining with its unions in the summer of 1986. Though AT&T and other regional telephone companies had strikes, Pacific and the CWA signed their contract a week before the contract deadline, and it was later ratified overwhelmingly by the CWA membership. The local common interest forums contributed ideas to the bargaining team, a pioneering concept in negotiations of a union and management. The contract itself set forth the principles for deepening the business partnership. The company gained several ways to cut costs through flexibility in labor deployment and the exchange of a portion of fixed compensation for pay and benefits that would partially float with company performance.

The Pacific Bell–Communications Workers of America partnership is an example of management-driven labor relations[18]—labor relations to realize management's strategic agenda, with union involvement as an aid to management's operational decisions at the worksite level. This does not mean that the union is getting hurt; indeed, the union may gain in power. But the origin of the PB–CWA partnership lay in business necessity, and the new role evolving for the CWA in California and Nevada was to serve their membership through helping management design programs and shape policies—and protect their members' interests in the process.

The decision to seek a new relationship with the CWA was a strategic business decision championed by Lee Cox, executive vice-president for Operations. It was not done to "improve labor relations" in the narrow sense, and was not union-driven, and it was not even staff-driven by the labor relations and human resources function, though Ben Dial, executive vice-president of Human Resources, played a major role. It was not a matter of mounting an "employee involvement program," but rather of creating a partnership with another organization—the union—through its official leadership. Such union-management partnerships are another form of alliance across organizational lines.

Overall, stakeholder alliances represent the closest tie between companies of all of the three forms of partnership. The relationships establish the largest sphere of jointness—the greatest area of overlap between the activities of the partners.

PARTNERSHIPS IN ACTION: THE SUPPLIER-CUSTOMER CASE

The intertwining of the partners' organizations is well illustrated by the supplier partnerships at Digital Equipment Corporation. The move to establish supplier partnerships at Digital has brought the company clear benefits, at the same time that it increased the areas of overlap between Digital and its partners. Digital managers describe the differences between their former arm's-length relationships and the new partnerships in these terms:

Manager A: There is a much clearer understanding of the need to build better relationships with suppliers. In the past, suppliers were people who filled orders. Today, we see them more as partners in contributing to the success of the company. We are tending to focus much more on the relationship between us and our supplier and what would be mutually beneficial than simply order-filling. I think that is a significant difference.

Manager B: Our goal is being the customer of choice, which means identifying the suppliers we want to do business with, talking with them, finding out what their needs and wants are, and sharing what our needs and wants are. By the way, I do mean suppliers; we used to call them vendors but we really want a differentiation as we try to put them on a level with us instead of one down. Our behavior has changed as we ask them what they need to be successful and don't just give them an order and say have it filled by next week.

Manager C: In the strategic alliances we are forming with suppliers, we have promised not to treat them as subordinates. We work with them—not against them.

Of course, as a savvy Digital observer pointed out, the new alliances still reflect a goal rather than universal everyday practice:

> The relationship is a growing two-way street whereas it used to be "We are the customer up here and you are the vendor down there. We have power and you do not." There isn't an equalization of power, but there is a beginning trend toward partnership. To some degree, these are dreams, they are visions. Not everything is in place and we are screwed up on systems, but there are clearly stated objectives of improvement and we are clearly working hard at them and making inroads in many areas.

Digital began to focus on partnership philosophies in 1984, after a very bad quarter in which the stock price also fell dramatically. Costs were too high, and there was a pervasive sense of missing opportunities to benefit from the technology developments of its suppliers. Digital had four to five suppliers for nearly everything, inventory was three to four times too high, and administrative spending (from office supplies to travel) nearly equaled manufacturing inventory spending.

There were several ways Purchasing vice-president Ron Payne saw in which partnerships with suppliers would help Digital regain its edge and do more with less. As in many companies seeking flexibility, speed of action, and a lean, cost-controlled organization, Digital managers recognized the need to treat suppliers as an extension of the company. "In the future," one manager said, "we are not going to be able to build everything that we will be selling. We just don't have the resources to do that. We had better rely on other than Digital employees to help us deliver goods and services ourselves."

This reliance on other organizations, which shifted certain fixed costs outside of Digital, also meant that purchased goods and services were a significant and growing part of Digital's budget—in the 30 percent to 35 percent range in 1987. So supplier relationships also offered leverage for cost reduction. "Digital recently focused more attention on the money that went out of the company, and this put purchasing in the limelight," another manager commented. "Purchasing could take more dynamic initiative in terms of cost savings to the company's bottom line. To do that, we realized we couldn't have thousands of suppliers, where we'd get the same part from so many places we wouldn't even get volume discounts. Our competitive edge has to come from new supplier relationships which make suppliers feel like a credible extension of Digital."

Furthermore, supplier partnerships could support product innovation and process improvement—the *more* side of doing more with less—by providing ideas and information at the design stage. Long-term Digital professionals see many examples of these innovation advantages:

> We realize we can't work independently and expect to thrive. An example involves a buy-make decision for a printed wire board. We wanted to develop a smaller, faster, and better functioning product. We recognized that although demand for the product was low at the time of development, it was a key technology. Therefore, we decided to buy the technology. Five years ago, decisions were made more by the seat of the pants—they were certainly short-term and based on the present supply-demand relationship. Since we decided to buy a technology that was so sophisticated and state-of-the-art, we also needed a better, different relationship with our suppliers.

Sometimes the innovation advantage came about at the supplier's, not Digital's, initiative:

> We dealt with a supplier recently who showed us how to cut costs. It was a fan assembly and we had designed an item for them to produce. They told us it could be manufactured for substantially less and deliver exactly the same requirement had we included them in the design process. They showed us another one, sitting right beside it, that they were given by another company. The other company had said, "Great, we need this amount of air flow, we need it to fill this amount of space, this is the power requirement, and we don't want it to make more than this amount of noise." And then the supplier went off and designed it. it met their process and they could therefore run it down an existing line and use

parts they already used in their business—not specials. It did exactly the same thing and was considerably cheaper. The supplier recognized they had more to offer us and came to Digital and said, "Hey, we can do this for you. Include us in the process next time." Now we do.

Five years ago, had the company come to us with a similar proposal, they would not have gotten in the front door unless we were specifically looking for it—which again, we probably wouldn't have been. It is now okay to come to Digital and say, "You are wasting money and this is why you are wasting money: You design it for us and it doesn't meet our processes and needs. We will continue supplying it to you, if that is what you want." Then, we get to make the decision. The decision these days is usually, "No, I don't want to do it that way anymore." Before it would have been, "You don't understand what meets our needs. Keep doing it the way it has been."

In some cases, Digital's partnership with suppliers is formalized; in others, it shows up as a philosophy guiding behavior. For example, Digital's cooperative marketing program with its software suppliers is formal, involving joint selling and joint appearances at trade shows, which has led suppliers to "feel much more an adjunct to Digital than a distant supplier to us," a manager observed. In other cases, what he called a "shortened arm's-length relationship" to suppliers has evolved over time without formal agreements. But the cooperative attitudes are similar.

To reap the benefits of partnership ties to gain competitive advantages, Digital has to engage in joint planning with suppliers, sharing an unprecedented amount of information about its business in order to encourage suppliers to move in directions compatible with Digital's future needs. Suppliers, for their part, hope Digital will help them forecast new technologies and stay on the cutting edge. An experienced manager with a corporation-wide perspective notes that,

We are telling stuff today which I'm sure if the old purchasing manager of two years ago knew we were doing, he would roll over in the grave. He'd think we were giving all the information away and weren't being competitive. The game is changing; you no longer play the card game with a very tight fist of cards, never letting a number down until you know what the other person has got.

The information flow is supplemented by technical assistance to suppliers and, in return, Digital is given the opportunity to get a thorough look at the supplier's business. As one purchasing executive said:

> We are trying to have longer-term contracts and in order to do that we are trying to give suppliers information about our future business so that they can be more prepared for their lead times. We are also giving suppliers help on their own manufacturing process. We want to understand their business as well as they do.

Another manager put it this way:

> We are starting to talk about the technologies the suppliers are planning on using in their products and processes so that we can better understand how we can take advantage of what they have. We want to share with them; if we find out we are not in line with where they are going, we explore the issue and see if one of us is going in the wrong direction or if we're just simply growing in different directions. This working relationship helps avoid bitter feelings if and when we stop using a particular supplier because he knows why we are no longer "partners."

While acknowledging the benefits of information sharing, Digital managers still understand that there are lines not to cross. Sometimes the company is reluctant to reveal data because it is state-of-the-art, not yet even envisioned elsewhere. But even so, the new spirit of partnership pervades those instances in which the company has to withhold information. Those involved with suppliers are expected to explain the reasons for setting limits and to be willing to modify those limits after discussions with suppliers. Overall, Digital managers feel they are more open than most companies.

Joint planning at the *strategic* level and technical data exchange at the *professional* level are augmented by direct data links at the *production* level. Digital and its suppliers thus have integrated information systems that permitted them to operate as one continuous entity rather than as a set of separate organizations. Such systems cut down on paperwork and create much faster response time, but they also reinforce the longer-term nature of the joint commitment. As one observer framed it:

> You can bet your life that if Company *X* has an electronic connection to Digital and they know they are going to get all the business from Digital

on the terminal, they're going to be committed to providing us the best service they can. That is what being the customer of choice for them can do for us. In doing so, they become a supplier of choice.

Other programmatic aspects of Digital's partnership with suppliers involve activities virtually indistinguishable from how a corporation might treat one of its own divisions. Digital holds regular forums with key suppliers to review business plans, technology changes, and results. An internal Digital team is organizing a training program for suppliers. But perhaps most symbolic of the new relationship is a performance-appraisal process for suppliers akin to the process for employees. This "Vendor Performance Management System" measures suppliers on quality, delivery, price, and flexibility across the whole company. A manager explained:

> We have suppliers who deal with fifty different sites. In the past, Phoenix would call and say, "Hey, we want to give you more business—thank you," and then the Boston plant would call and say, "The quality of this last shipment stunk, get your acts straight." Now we meet quarterly with our major suppliers and say, "Here's what the report card says and this is how you have done for Digital. Let's talk about why you haven't done well in these areas." In many respects, it is a two-way street now. We may say, "The quality on 50 percent of your lots is 80 percent and we want 100 percent. What is going on?" Well, they may say, "Wait a minute, Digital, how you spec the piece parts is not clear. We interpret that 20 percent as per your spec." We are both working together toward an ultimate goal of saving money.

Such management system links across companies allow customers to be more demanding of suppliers, raising performance standards in a way that would be impossible without the spirit of partnership. At Digital:

> We started a program a couple of years ago in which we wanted delivery performance from our suppliers to be plus or minus one day. Suppliers didn't like that, already aware that they had trouble getting within a monthly window. We told them the monthly window meant we had to order five or six weeks in advance and carry five or six weeks' worth of inventory. Some of them came back and said they'd like to try plus or minus one day and some came back and said plus or minus five

days—they went all over the map. What we were really after was a goal that we could measure them to—consistency and predictability. Talking to suppliers after the fact, we found out they didn't want to get into the agreement and thought it was one-sided. They eventually admitted, "What the arrangement meant for us, however, is that we have much better control of scheduling our product, getting it off the dock on time, and can predict our payments more accurately. We are also now able to offer that to our customers. Some don't know what to do with it; some think it is great." Many suppliers have come back to us and said, "Hey, thanks for doing that to us."

In short, Digital can let suppliers know its goals and work with them so they can meet those goals. The power of customers to set standards is a two-way street, however. Partnerships rest on reciprocity. Digital's managers are therefore aware that gaining the commitment of "suppliers of choice" means striving to be "customers of choice" by such behavior as paying the suppliers' bills on time.

Reciprocity is a particularly salient issue at Digital because, as with many big companies, some of its key suppliers are also key customers. (Reciprocity is also a legal issue, with laws governing the extent of such dealings.) As customers, they want from Digital what Digital demands of them as suppliers. "Some of our suppliers who have met our plus-or-minus-one-day delivery agreement are also our customers," a manager explained. "They are saying, 'Okay, I did it; when are you going to do it?' " Without reciprocity, these companies would lose motivation as *both* customer and supplier. On the other hand, generous dealings with suppliers could convert them into customers as well. An active participant in many of these relationships reported that:

> There is much more synergy, interaction, and sharing with our suppliers. They really do look to Digital and say, "Digital, how are you doing it? We would like to learn from you." Every day we get those questions. In Purchasing, we have been out to talk to DuPont and Kodak and Batelle Labs about what we are doing with our Purchasing systems and what we plan to do in the future. So, they are customers in addition to being suppliers. In some cases, they have stopped what they were doing and waited for us to develop our stuff.

Once Digital managers began to realize that customers are key suppliers of important information—regardless of whether they also supply specific goods and services—they "worked on getting an information flow that showed us positive and negative aspects of our supplier relationships," a senior executive said. His example (disguised for obvious reasons):

> ABC is a major hotel chain where most Digital employees stay. However, XYZ was a key Digital customer and we learned our ABC hotel policy was having a major impact on our relationship with XYZ. XYZ wanted Digital people to use their hotel and wanted to know why not. The only reason we were aware of was that some executive years past had chosen ABC. Purchasing recommended that Digital let field people pick the hotel that they wanted. We gave both companies lists of all employees eligible for a Digital discount and each advertised and tried to recruit "customers." This new policy helped us leverage our sales relationship with XYZ.

The growing partnership orientation is also, then, heightening the interdependence between the purchasing and sales functions even short of such fully joint activities as cooperative marketing with software suppliers.

Digital has gained a variety of advantages from becoming PALs with its suppliers: cost savings, quality improvements, early access to new technology, the capacity to develop new components without having to make everything in-house, and marketing payoffs. Yet, even for a model company like Digital known to be on the forefront of change, the new alliances represent a change of corporate philosophy and a territory for competitiveness improvement only barely explored—a frontier in the post-entrepreneurial management revolution.

CHAPTER 6

Putting Power into Partnerships

What does it mean to be PALs?

The strategy involves more than a mere handshake. The development of formal alliances with ''external'' parties also changes internal roles, relationships, and power dynamics for the organizations entering into them. The greater the sphere of cooperation between organizations, the greater the magnitude of the changes within each one, and the greater the disruption to the traditional hierarchy. The degree of change is likely to be minimal, of course, when the alliance is an actual, stand-alone organization (such as Bellcore or Grotech) that can operate somewhat independently from the partners' ''home'' organizations, but important and significant when the partnership's activities overlap with other ''home'' organizational activities, as in the Digital overlap with suppliers. In general, service alliances such as research consortia would have the least internal impact, while stakeholder alliances would have the most. Roy Shapiro's comments about supplier-customer partnerships make this clear:

> Consider a company that enters a long-term cooperative relationship with a supplier. The company purchasing department no longer performs the

essentially clerical task of renegotiating short-term price-based contracts based on precise specifications. Instead, purchasing becomes a focal point for efforts to learn about the supplier's capabilities, aid in improving them, coordinate contacts between design personnel in the purchaser's firm and the counterparts at the supplier, and perhaps even finance equipment and inventory at the supplier. The purchasing department will grow in size and surely grow in expertise and responsibility, and important decisions may well be shared with the suppliers.[1]

The most important degree of change is in *power*. The redefinition of power begins with a rethinking of the company's role vis-à-vis its stakeholders, a re-examination implied by the very notion of "strategic partnership." "Partners" are welcome allies, not manipulated adversaries. An enhanced role for allies can be accomplished only via a sincere company acknowledgment that such influence is warranted. This requires a new attitude among those who might feel that kind gestures toward stakeholders are a management "gift," not a partnership, in which they temporarily agree to "give" the stakeholder some of the company's rightful power, to bequeath something voluntarily in order to win cooperation, something that can be withdrawn at will. Such a paternalistic attitude can undermine the core of the partnership effort and its future potential.

Even in alliances with different origins and goals, the impact on a partner's home organization is profound. This was illustrated in three partnerships I observed closely. They can be arrayed along a continuum of prepartnership status, from the most to the least adversarial. The first, the Pacific Bell–Communication Workers of America union-management "business partnership," was initially a highly adversarial relationship and thus faced the greatest amount of internal change as the parties moved significantly closer. Furthermore, the sphere of cooperation was great. The Digital supplier partnerships involved previously arm's-length but not severely adversarial relationships now moving closer; there was an intermediate amount of change and an intermediate degree of overlap. In the third case, the "Grotech" joint venture, the partnership grew out of a pre-existing but limited alliance for particular products. There was, therefore, the least internal change when the joint venture was established, and the least overlap, since the joint venture was a complete business separate in large part from that of the parent companies. But even so, there were concerns that a closer partnership would involve some of the same consolidation and cutbacks as a full merger.

As a general rule I found that the greater the change in external relationship, the greater the shift in internal power resulting from the partnership:

• *The labor-management partnership* shifted the action away from events favoring professionals in the union and toward the events favoring local presidents; away from processes favoring the national union and toward processes favoring local decision-making; away from treatment of workers on a mass basis and toward differentiated treatment of individuals and local worksites. And the local common interest forums added new arenas for defining union strategy, arenas in which local presidents represented the union.

• *The supplier-customer partnership* shifted the attention of staffs from routine administration of strategic considerations, empowered the purchasing department, and necessitated a more collaborative web of interfunctional relationships across departments inside the company.

• *The joint venture* shifted the locus of power from the traditional management hierarchy to those who could effectively influence the partners and represent the home organization's strategic agenda.

THE SHIFT IN POWER

The power that devolves on partnership managers is seen most directly in those cases where pre-existing arm's-length relationships are converted into partnerships. For many of the managers and professionals involved in partnership dealings, the empowerment is clear and direct. They have increased access to top management, whereas previously they were not included in strategic deliberations. They are given information and data allowing them to better understand what drives business decisions, and they can get questions answered with a single phone call to a previously inaccessible executive. They are consulted on matters of business significance to the company, before decisions are made. They are handed an opportunity to educate management about the pressures on allies—suppliers, venture partners, or customers. And they increasingly know things before the rest of the company management does, even becoming a source of information and influence for others in middle management.

The empowerment of Digital's purchasing department is a clear outgrowth of the shift to a partnership orientation. At the senior levels of management, there is definitely a higher expectation of the role Purchasing can play in the financial and customer performance of the company. Purchasing "controls" billions of dollars of company money; there is a responsibility to see that the corporation leverages that. Senior-level people are heard to say, "We can't spend as much money doing things inside; we have to do more with the supply base. Let's talk about how Purchasing can help us do that." That is a new discussion for Digital. Furthermore, plant managers are involved in supplier review, which had previously been relegated to the lower-level buyer. As plant and senior management begin to participate in such activities, a reciprocal shift is starting to happen in the partner companies.

The strategic role for Purchasing grew in senior executive councils because of the importance of supplier partnerships, as these comments show:

> Management at Digital now looks at Purchasing and asks us, "Which companies will we be working with in the future?" (They want to know from both technical and cost points of view.) They wonder, "Does management need to give more time to championing relationships with these companies?" What often happens is a top manager will say, "I will give Purchasing thirty hours of my time this year which you can use to schedule meetings with top-level people from supplier companies." If he feels Purchasing has used his time wisely, next year he may give us fifty hours. Each year, people at higher and higher levels of sponsorship are getting involved in building these new strategic relationships.

In one case, a purchasing manager accompanied a senior executive and some professionals on a tour of more than fifty suppliers around the world, meeting with their senior management. They explained the new strategy, including Digital's desire for "an equal relationship where we tell each other what we are doing right and what we are doing wrong."

For their part, the CWA union local presidents in the Pacific Bell partnership contrast their greater access to senior management with how it used to be: "We've only gotten together for once-a-year meetings over the last four to five years, which was usually a report from the company. We were always met negatively, as potential grievances. We lacked the ability to present the union's concerns. We weren't as aware of business issues." Certainly, access other than the most strictly formal and official was missing. "I've never had access above the department head through the grievance procedure," a CWA local president recalled, "and I'd never met a company vice-president before. They were untouchable; they wouldn't know what's going on here with employees; they're driven by revenues . . . that's what we thought." Said another:

> There are still some side deals, but now managers are coming to the union presidents to "flex" the contract. I have lots of phone calls coming in from third-level managers just before an LCIF [Local Common Interest Forum] meeting, to get *my* help to influence the management team on their behalf! . . . This is a return to the kind of subtle influence old unions had, prior to the advent of hard union times. We are now back to the union presidents having some control.

This new access to company officials gives union local presidents more power in the union hierarchy above them. They are more central in the communications flow because of their direct links to company officers, and they often have information earlier and more completely than district-level or national union officials. They are also more broadly connected with company management than many PacBell middle managers were, because the structure of local common interest forums means that local presidents sit on more than one company officer's forum.

But cooperative relationships impose their burdens, too. With the power comes responsibility. Adversarial relationships make it easy for people to complain, to throw stones, to withdraw, without having to play any role in improving the situation. If prepartnership Digital didn't like what a particular supplier did, the company could complain vociferously or simply shift its business elsewhere. Now, with partnership philosophies prevailing, Digital works with the supplier to solve the problem. All partners must be part of the solution. One insightful union president involved in the Pacific Bell partnership framed the matter well:

This is a much more difficult way to deal with each other. [Before] if we didn't like the decisions, we just complained. It was very easy, very comfortable, anyone could do it. Now, we must make advance decisions, exercise judgment and live with it, which is much harder and places much more responsibility on us. . . . It's all new territory.

Questions about the meaning of the power bestowed on those directly involved in the partnership dealings also arise at the levels below. Partnerships often mean a reduction in power for those not involved. Stronger links tying organizations together in a cooperative fashion pose dilemmas for the remaining hierarchies inside each partner's home base organization. A variety of political problems develop. First, in the cases I observed, partner representatives agreed that it could be difficult or dangerous to report much to others of partnership deliberations. They could report *outcomes* to their "home team," but not the *process* by which the decision was made. Sometimes the issue is pure process: why so much time was involved, and why consideration of various issues took so long, as well as concerns that attempts to share this information could create more confusion or misunderstanding. In other instances, representatives needed to maintain the partner's confidences or show solidarity, especially at times of delicate negotiations, therefore requiring the representatives to mask the actual process. This is as true in a joint venture as it is in a labor-management partnership. But the impact is the same: to make those left out of the partnership sphere, with middle managers foremost among them, feel isolated and disempowered.

For example, the opportunity for direct contact between union presidents and company officers that is provided by the Pacific Bell local common interest forums effectively eliminates a whole slice of the middle management chain of communication. In certain respects, the LCIF is a vehicle to circumvent or end-run the standard management chain of command. In some instances, vice-presidents say *they* are getting problems brought to them that middle managers used to tackle. And at times, Pacific Bell middle managers find themselves in the position of learning more about emerging company issues from union representatives than from their own superiors. One officer sees the LCIF process as producing a "squeeze" at the middle and bottom levels that requires a redefinition of the appropriate first-level management role. "Middle managers see this as a joke," a union president asserted, claiming that communication with them was the key to success. The presidents recognized the impact of the LCIF on the management hierarchy. "Pre-LCIF, local presidents didn't meet with PacBell vice-presidents, except very rarely," a CWA-er reported. "Now our meetings make the district managers nervous, but they are all very authority conscious, so they don't complain."

Company officers are aware of the need to be sensitive to middle managers' needs and feelings, and to not undercut them, but they are not sure how to go about this. Newer roles do not so much have to be learned as to be defined in the first place. This creates a dilemma. To accomplish this also requires opening up the LCIF process to wider involvement, something that itself had to be approached cautiously, given the initial agreement to keep LCIFs small and to retain information within the LCIFs in order to build a foundation of trust. One LCIF set up a task force to look at how to communicate to those outside the LCIF, "in contrast to the previous sensitivity regarding circulation of LCIF minutes," commented an officer. "LCIF members didn't want them published to anyone but us. Now we realize we can't stay an island."

The importance of middle manager involvement in all kinds of partnerships stems not just from the potential for hurt feelings, but also from the material harm these managers can inflict on the process if new roles are not invented for them. Said a manager in the Grotech joint venture, "The next level people make it difficult if they're not on board. Our venture partner's president and I wrote letters to customers saying we had no anticipated shipment problems when a plant manager was planning a slowdown for equipment changeover, making us look foolish."

The people involved in a partnership, then, face the problem of selling those around them and below them on partnership decisions— decisions that by definition can involve some deviation from the pure pursuit of the home company's short-term interest. There are intensely political considerations in the minds of all the partnership players as they try to convince members of their own organization that they are not "selling out" when their decisions appear to offer benefits to the partner, and at the same time convince the partner that they are not "caving in" to parochial organizational interests when they argue their own company's case. It is a balancing act. The Grotech joint venture head deliberately fought hard on symbolic issues of importance to the people below him, even though the fight put the partnership at risk, because he felt that his troops needed to see him win a few victories in order to support his leadership.

The union presidents in the PacBell-CWA partnership had a particularly delicate balancing act. While LCIF participation brings local presidents greater influence with Pacific Bell, it also makes presidents vulnerable to charges of neglect from their membership or to isolation resulting from disagreement with their peers. In response to the new challenges presented to union presidents by the LCIFs and to avoid attacks by their constituents, they developed new ways of selling the concept and new techniques to involve their rank-and-file membership in the process. The need for active selling is clear, given the shift in traditional roles that the LCIF represents—and the vulnerability of presidents who need to be re-elected. As one president put it, "Compared to the traditional [union] role, some members' secondary leadership may see the cooperative effort as selling out." So he redoubled his efforts to be sensitive to the dynamics within his local, and he has intensified internal communication efforts:

> There are feelings of powerlessness that influence the LCIF process, so I route the associated paperwork through the secondary leadership. However, our rules to limit the circulation of minutes until they were approved also caused problems. We are winning the battle in proving that we're not selling out or sleeping with the company. Through internal communication we are seeing results.

A number of presidents attempt to address these issues by further empowering those around them to act on their behalf. They delegate more, have secondary leadership represent them on LCIFs, and hold "shadow" LCIF meetings in the union.

Involving other organizational players is important in order to sell them on partnership strategies. But it is also important to delegate downward for another reason. Partnerships between companies add to the time demands on key players. The collaborative nature of the relationship—from joint planning to exchange of technical data to the need for awareness of the latest developments in both the home and the partner business—requires more meetings and more travel than arm's-length relationships. Participants are thus outside their regular bailiwicks more of the time, spending time on the partners' premises.

This occurs in all the partnership types, including the union-management partnership. Senior executives at Pacific Bell, for example, attend meetings at union halls and become conversant with the ins and outs of the CWA contract. They learn about career issues and work conditions for the unionized workforce, and the "teaching" often comes directly from union presidents. In short, partnerships bring their representatives onto one another's territory both literally and figuratively.

THE CHANGING NATURE OF STAFF ROLES

More line manager and senior manager involvement in partnerships does not necessarily mean a *diminished* role for staffs, but it does mean a *different* role—and often one with fewer people.

The traditional mode was characterized by a single point of contact between one organization and its "external" constituencies: the purchasing department to manage procurement, the sales department to deal with customers, the labor relations department to handle the union. That manager or department served as "gatekeeper," patrolling the boundaries and including, if not determining, what could come "in" and what would be sent "out." All information flowed through that gate, and the gatekeepers monopolized the management of the relationship.

Partnerships, in contrast, simultaneously make the activities involved in "external" relationships more important and reduce the former gatekeeper's monopoly over them. They can increase the number of functions and the number of people involved with those "external" relationships. For example, where strong customer alliances prevail, both product designers and production workers get directly involved with customers. In a union-management partnership, line managers relate directly to union officials, without any labor relations staff involvement. The former "boundary managers" can gain importance from the strategic significance given to their area, but they lose monopoly power and must change how they operate. If they do not, they risk being bypassed.

The change in traditional staff roles is apparent in Digital's purchasing department. Jobs are being upgraded, as routine administration and an emphasis on meeting specifications are replaced by a need for more experienced people who can be involved in every aspect of a business process and handle complex negotiations. Instead of rewarding staff for never running out of parts, the department now emphasizes meeting broader time-to-market and profitability goals. Instead of using the purchasing staff as an opportunity to promote less-sophisticated clerical personnel, the department seeks people who can effectively take more complete business responsibility for their decisions, represent the company in strategy discussions with partners, and even carry out such specialized professional tasks as writing contracts without using lawyers. While these are more *significant* tasks, they can also be done by *fewer* people, especially as advanced technology replaces purely routine paperwork. As one manager put it:

> Think for a moment of what it is like to live if you have a thousand Purchasing people and half of them are just sitting at a desk expediting orders, making calls, and writing up pieces of paper. If you can get rid of that functionally and do EDI [Electronic Data Interchange] where when a requisitioner wants a hundred pens, he presses a button, and it goes right to the vendor and the vendor ships it in, nobody has to expedite and write purchase orders. What, in effect, we are trying to do is eliminate the more mundane and routine jobs and create a stronger base of business partnering and vendor relationship building.
>
> It is sort of like making cream. Jobs are separating. The less important stuff is going to the bottom and the significant stuff, the cream, is rising to the top. If I had my wish, five to ten years from now, you would have the same amount of senior people in Purchasing and less junior people because those tasks will have gone away. So where is the fun? The fun is in working relationships and working as a business partner who contributes to the success of the business—rather than how many P.O.'s you process today.

Similarly, the role of the Labor Relations staff at Pacific Bell has undergone two subtle shifts that cumulatively result in a significant role redefinition. In the past, LR provided counsel and support to managers in contract interpretation and, when grievances arose, stepped in at the later stages of the grievance resolution and arbitration procedure. With the advent of a business partnership with CWA, however, two things changed. First, the LCIFs would have a hand in addressing the conditions that might previously have led to grievances. Second, the LCIF presidents, that is, the company VPs and the CWA local presidents, would now be intimately involved in the development of contract proposals and language. No longer are Labor Relations personnel the principal company actors involved in the two primary processes of formal union interest. Yet, rather than seeing a complementary decline in the volume of its work as the number of formal grievances declines, the Labor Relations department finds itself increasingly called upon by managers for counseling, advice, and support in the handling of interactions with the union and unionized personnel.

Clearly, the task of staff departments in a partnership is to integrate and coordinate rather than dominate. Indeed, partnerships generally tend to increase the requirements for intraorganizational integration. With multiple ties connecting partners, communication can be unmanageable or inefficient unless each partner is itself well-integrated. The intertwining of partnership interests with many aspects of the business also creates a need for early consultation across functions and closer working relationships. For departments to work in isolation could mean negative reverberations of their actions for the partnership. Furthermore, decisions may require the intelligence or expertise brought by those in touch with the partners.

This showed up strongly at Digital. The shift to supplier partnerships meant that the purchasing department was getting more involved in discussions and collaborations with other functions. For example:

- *Engineering*: The business we are in is much more competitive and as a result, Engineering and Purchasing cannot afford to be independent of each other. The best way of producing new products is not to have only the engineer who is developing the item design it and search for suppliers, but Purchasing should get involved and examine other existing technologies and suppliers. Now Engineering is realizing Purchasing is significant leverage if managed properly and allowed to do the job that it is here to do. For the most part, when the engineers want to know what is out there in the supply base, they will call us and we will outline some of the options. We play conduit for communication between our engineers and suppliers as we outline what houses are out there that can do what they want to do or some of the houses that maybe are on a different platform but want to get on the Digital platform.
- *Manufacturing*: Manufacturing looks to us to give them the guidance on the options that they have so that they can make the right decision.

They make the decisions but it is our job to bring all the information to the table that they need to evaluate which package is best and what direction they should go for the next generation. We are now involved in looking at the next generation of a system that Manufacturing wants to consider three years from now, i.e., do we develop it ourselves, do we have a third party do it, is Company X the one that we want to ask to do it? We are right in the thick of it.

• *Marketing*: In the areas where we are doing a lot of work in building relationships with third-party suppliers, various marketing groups use our folks to help them select the supplier, to decide how good their product is, and to see how it should be positioned. Through our marketing organization, we are also looking at increasing the number of cooperative relationships we have with software suppliers. We want them to do more on the Digital platform so we communicate better with our customers.

THE CHANGING NATURE OF JOB SKILLS

Overall, the development of strategic alliances is one more force toward politicizing the role of managers, making it essential for them to be able to *juggle constituencies rather than control subordinates*. The great management theorist Chester Barnard recognized long ago that the task of leaders was to develop a network of cooperative relationships among all those people, groups, and organizations with something to contribute to an economic activity.[2] Alliances and partnerships multiply the complexity of this task. For example, after leading Teknowledge, Inc., producer of expert systems software, in development alliances with six major corporations, including General Motors, Procter and Gamble, and FMC, President Lee Hecht told a *Business Week* reporter that he feels "like the mayor of a small city. I have a constituency that won't quit. It takes a hell of a lot of balancing."[3]

That balancing act was not required in the traditional corporation. Whatever its shortcomings in practice, the traditional adversarial style had one advantage for control-conscious managers: It preserved the illusion of decision-making autonomy for the corporation as a whole. Executives could move quickly, could make unilateral decisions without needing to consult any of the other organizations that would be affected by the decisions. There might be negative consequences later—for example, a labor union calling a strike after an unpalatable management announcement, or customers switching to another manufacturer after a price rise—but at least there were few apparent constraints on action. It might be smarter management to consult with stakeholders and take their interests into account in making decisions, but it was not required.

Partnerships, in contrast, require this kind of consultation as a matter of routine. The illusion of autonomy is lost. Unilateral action decreases. The number of forums for cooperative decision-making increases. The shift from arm's-length relationships to more intimate partnerships thus requires a different set of skills, especially for those working closely with a component of the partnership.

This became clear to me as I watched and listened, and as I saw who failed in partnership roles. In the PacBell-CWA case, the LCIF structure placed union presidents (who represented all the employees in a geographical area) on forums with nearly every company officer (responsible for functions); union presidents were able to compare the officers and their LCIFs. The lowest marks were given to a PacBell executive with a very curt, no-nonsense style, who had risen from a marginal role in the company and thus seemed always trying to prove that his current job was deserved. This led to a very authoritarian, "know-it-all" attitude. As a result, this officer's forum was the only one bogged down in contentiousness. The officer's major use of the LCIF was to ramrod through an agreement to push employees to sell services even more aggressively. Within less than a year, however, the sales push was a failure and a public humiliation for the company, an event they vowed not to repeat.

Unlike relationships in a hierarchy, relationships in a partnership are ostensibly more egalitarian. Representatives of one organization cannot "order" the other to do anything, the way they could issue orders or directives to subordinate divisions or employees. One Digital manager uses the image of boss-subordinate relationships to describe how partnership behavior is different:

> There is a big difference from a boss-subordinate relationship where the boss tells the subordinate here is the task at hand and please complete it, and one where the boss says, "We have got to win and here is what winning is as we see it. Is this how you see it?" In this new relationship we say let's talk about the work that has got to get done and let's divide

up the tasks in a fashion that makes sense. There is a very different way that you are going to be motivated and approach your work with that second scenario. I think the suppliers that I have visited feel that difference of inclusion, of desire to partner to get stuff done, of the desire to help each other out and be sensitive to each other's needs. I think with 60 to 70 percent of our vendors, there would be a vast improvement in what they think of us now as compared to five years ago.

Discussion of goals and a search for consensus, then, become more important than who has the upper hand. Indeed, even when one partner company has the power to make its will prevail, it is considered very dangerous and damaging to the relationship to try. The formation of a partnership almost by definition calls for partici- pative skills—gathering information, resisting preconceived ideas, listening to others, testing assumptions, seeking consensus. Tradi- tional managers sometimes find it hard to adjust when their companies build strategic alliances.

Managers who are accustomed to acting decisively and presenting full-blown plans (in part to look good to *their* underlings) need to learn the patience that consensus building requires, and they need to learn to present half-formed ideas for discussion *before* making decisions. "Coming in with prepared documents" and "not fully consulting and collaborating" were two reasons why union presidents came to resent and distrust one company officer in the PacBell-CWA partnership. Because the process was far less amenable to packaging or control by any one player, managers accustomed to always having their home- work done and their case flawlessly persuasive found that such behavior could be seen as manipulative, disingenuous, and counter- productive. Instead, the LCIF process rewarded managers who were prepared, yes, but more important, flexible, informed, forthcoming, and candid.

One of the sources of tension in the Grotech joint venture grew out of the inability of one partner to recognize the importance of a collaborative process. The joint venture agreement gave that partner an increasing ownership share over time, and that partner's representa- tive, who also chaired the venture's board, interpreted this to mean that he could set the meeting agenda single-handedly and confine discussions to what was on that agenda. Furthermore, he disparaged all attempts of the more freewheeling representatives to bring up new items, follow unanticipated issues, and write new ideas on flip charts as they arose. Antagonized by this form of leadership, the other partners started holding side meetings and challenging the chair on his favorite issues. The resulting squabbling deflected attention from important strategic questions facing the joint venture—questions that should have been discussed in open-ended, less structured sessions.

The participatory standard can easily make an executive who likes to look as though everything is fully under control feel vulnerable and exposed. And it creates dilemmas even for those who handle it well, because sometimes junior partners carry old expectations that senior partners *always* know what they want. For example, the manager of the Grotech joint venture attributed hidden agendas to the majority shareholder's CEO, who was genuinely opening up an issue for discussion—in part out of disbelief that this executive would *not* have a preset agenda.

Because of the premium placed on group leadership skills, those managers who had more experience with participative leadership or had received formal training in it and who felt more secure about their position in the company were better able to handle the PacBell-CWA LCIF role from the beginning. For them, the new roles came more naturally, and they were better able to share power with the union presidents in their LCIF. Thus, in some LCIFs the company officer did not set the meeting agenda, as happened more typically in others. Instead it was jointly determined. Furthermore, in the "high-participation" LCIFs, the chair rotated between the company officer and each of the union presidents. In addition to participative skills, of course, this process required more participative attitudes, a gut feeling of basic equality. As one of the high-participation officers said, "We're all just a bunch of people trying to do our best."

Clearly, respect in a partnership does not come automatically with rank. The same close working relationship that builds trust also gives each partner firsthand knowledge of the actual competence of the other's representatives. Participation demystifies potential authority figures by showing them as real people. Awe is replaced by data.

One union president made this clear in praising Pacific Telesis Chairman Don Guinn and Pacific Bell President Ted Saenger as people who did not need the traditional trappings of authority to win respect. He used descriptions such as "not rigid, wears light-colored suits, more liberal, freer with people," and then went on to compliment them for their "job knowledge, they could walk you through the technologies, tell you how they work and why."

Thus authority gives way to influence, and command to negotiation. Success at resolving issues within a partnership and at leading discussion toward the outcome a representative seeks is dependent on both his relationships within the alliance and his personal communication skills, as well as on his understanding of how best to manage group decision-making. One experienced joint venture participant recognized this important new dynamic: "In voting by consensus, it's not whether you agree, it's what you can live with. This is not so good when strong feelings exist, or are not expressed, that push people to act independently in their own area rather than carry out a common solution they didn't feel good about—instead, you need to take the issue apart in small groups." This dynamic also places a premium on face-to-face contact rather than communication by faceless voices on the telephone—increasing the necessity to spend time with the partners.

In negotiations signals and symbols are very important, and partnership representatives benefit from the ability to read them—and use them. The experienced people in the partnerships I observed are very adept at "reading" signals that indicated whether partner representatives can be trusted. This was true not only of the union "politicians" who rose to their positions through elections in the PacBell-CWA joint venture, but also in the Grotech joint venture, in which many managers had also clearly learned to tune in to people of different nationalities. In the Pacific Bell-CWA LCIFs the union representatives distinguished "vice-presidents who are serious" from others "who were just reading the script." They looked not for rhetoric but for concrete evidence of management's sincerity, such as one officer who kept people in their jobs despite negative financial implications that could lower his incentive pay. While commenting favorably on such gestures, the union representatives also pointed out contradictions and inconsistencies—for example, when management asked them to help sell a new program in terms whose credibility was undercut by another management action elsewhere. In Grotech, managers of one shareholder company questioned the sincerity of managers of the other when the second company's officers were sent minutes from a major joint meeting to review, with the first company getting a later, "revised" version. In another case, managers interpreted the placement of two of the venture partner's managers in key positions in their company as sending "hostages and spies."

Nearly every managerial action in a partnership seems to carry the additional weight of being scanned for "messages" about "real" motives, attitudes toward the partner, and sincerity. Thus managers in partnerships need to pay attention to a new range of details, signals, and danger zones, as well as develop a greater self-awareness about the impact of their behavior. The Grotech joint venture, because its partners and operations span the globe, frequently encounters problems because of managers' reading their own cultural messages into gestures intended quite differently. Although relationships between the venture's own management, derived largely from its former parent's ranks, and the majority partner company from Country X were strained from the beginning, it has been getting worse. Unthinking behavior of the venture management is misread as insult by the Country X team—for example, leaving a meeting in the middle to return urgent phone calls. The Company X people think this means that Grotech managers who came from Company Y are ignoring what they have to say. At the same time, Country X representatives set meeting agendas in advance without informing Grotech management (a gesture Grotech takes as confirming Country X's intention to buy out Grotech and replace them all). Perhaps these interpretations of the cues are not altogether false, either. But still, the venture is close to falling apart in conflict and antagonism because neither side chooses to exhibit sensitivity to cultural signals.

Sensitivity is most important when the partner organizations are very different in culture and style. For example, the Pacific Bell officers involved in the company-union partnership are learning to perceive the nuances of union members' reactions to things company people would take for granted or regard as trivial. The managers are becoming aware of a range of details that do not "normally" or "traditionally" concern an officer—from making sure to hold meetings in unionized hotels, to being aware of protocol in terms of who gets meeting agendas first, to anticipating the reactions of union members when they see photos of their leaders smiling alongside managers. In relationships that move from hierarchical or adversarial to egalitarian, partners look for the symbols of equality, and one important one is each honoring the other's values.

Self-awareness is important in partnerships for other reasons, too. Personal styles play a greater role than in arm's-length transactions. "Personalities" become more important when closer working groups are established and people debate issues face to face. And it is more likely that personal compatibility will make a difference in how well (and in which direction) issues are resolved. The success or failure of Grotech as a joint venture, for example, was assumed by participants from the beginning to turn on personalities. The venture's general manager and the venture board chair were so different that nearly every action was misinterpreted, and the misinterpretation provoked retaliation. The more the two got to know each other, the worse this became. Similarly, the LCIF process, a union leader observed, "makes things that were not important before important now—for example, whether I like a vice-president or not. Before I could judge them on actions alone." While the autonomy and empowerment of the LCIF made certain external influences (like the hierarchy above) *less* important, the intimacy created made interpersonal attraction *more* important.

This dynamic also necessitates role redefinitions for managers who are accustomed to brisk, no-nonsense, no-time-wasted, task-oriented styles. If the effectiveness of a partnership must rest on a strong foundation of trust, this means that people must come to know one another beyond their "official" presence and image. The time spent chatting over coffee and doughnuts in a union hall before a Pacific Bell LCIF meeting is thus not just "filler" until the meeting begins, but a helpful adjunct to the process, a signal that people are willing to make gestures toward one another as people. One company officer recognized this need when pointing out the benefits to the LCIF of "pure exposure to each other—uncovering motivations and building trust." It is one way of "making sure we have the same goal"—a union president's phrase for an ingredient in making the LCIF work. In contrast, in the Grotech joint venture the middle levels of the partners and the venture staff got together occasionally for golf outings and conferences at resorts where there was informal social time, but the board—the source of the antagonism and squabbles—held business-only meetings followed by a stiff and formal dinner. The attempts of one partner representative to organize social gatherings were rebuffed. Was it surprising, then, that the Grotech business was suffering from lack of clear direction?

THE CHALLENGE TO MANAGEMENT

Strategic partnerships form because they bring value to the organizations entering into them. But their existence also changes how the individual organizations operate and how their managers manage. Unless partnership activities can be segregated from other organizational activities (as in the formation of a stand-alone, arm's-length unit that is the only sphere of cooperation), the need to relate to partners in ways that reap the benefits of partnership inevitably changes how each partner operates.

Thus, in profound ways, the new alliances may change how American business operates. I have seen evidence of a number of changes inside partners' home organizations: in the roles of top management and the behavior required to succeed; in communication and decision-making channels; and in the influence and role of staff functions. Furthermore, the goals and strategies of each organization now embrace the goals and strategies of the partner. Alliances with high degrees of interpenetration—in which each partner becomes involved in processes formerly "internal" to the other—change the nature of the management task.

Perhaps one of the major reasons that the number of interorganizational partnerships is still relatively small is the management difficulties they entail. For each partnership, there are three areas of management challenge: managing the inherently fragile relationship between partners and managing the changes in each of the partners' own organizations. Until these new management challenges are mastered, corporations will not be able to take advantage of the benefits of strategic partnerships.

The kinds of partnerships I have outlined still represent only a small proportion of all American corporate activity, by any measure. In 1985, cooperative research represented only $1.6 billion of the over $50 billion corporations spent on R&D, including the $1.4 billion spent by research organizations serving noncompetitive electric, gas, and telephone utility companies, according to Professor Herbert Fusfield, director of New York University's Center for Science and Technology Policy.[4] Investment in joint ventures is a drop in the bucket compared to the multiple billions spent on mergers and acquisitions. Union-management partnerships are identifiable in a few large companies, but are still relatively rare. It is impossible to count those supplier-customer alliances that do not take the form of an identifiable joint venture, since they represent a more cooperative extension of an existing relationship. They are probably the most common and the most stable alliances—but they are unlikely to be announced in press releases that allow researchers to count them.[5]

Yet a great deal of important strategic improvement in competitiveness may be taking place in coalitions—rather than "inside" the "boundaries" of one organization. This makes it especially important to understand what it takes to manage organizational partnerships—why so many, begun with high hopes, fail to produce what they promised.

DIFFICULTIES BETWEEN PALS: VULNERABILITIES OF PARTNERSHIPS

The fragility of interorganizational alliances stems from a set of common "dealbusters"—vulnerabilities that threaten the relationship. Partnerships are dynamic entities, even more so than single corporations, because of the complexity of the interests forming them. A partnership evolves; its parameters are never completely clear at first, nor do partners want to commit fully until trust has been established. And trust takes time to develop. It is only as events unfold that partners become aware of all of the ramifications and implications of their involvement. For one thing, the very success of a partnership in transferring knowledge may threaten the relationship by making the partner less essential over time.

All relationships have vulnerabilities. But for strategic alliances, the issues arise more often, and their impact is more severe.

Strategic Shifts
An alliance is formed to suit one strategic purpose; but what then happens to it when business conditions change? Any significant shift in the strategy of the organizations forming an alliance is a potential threat to the relationship.

In the simplest case, one partner simply exits the business that provided the rationale for the alliance. Not surprisingly, the partnership of the German company Siemens with RCA ended when RCA got out of the computer business. A former Siemens vice-president recalled that RCA informed Siemens that it was no longer in the computer business in a surprise phone call: "Okay, we were just in a board meeting and we decided to get out of computers."[6] In other cases, the interests of partners begin to diverge as their businesses move in different directions; the relative importance of the partnership and the goals for it may change. Bellcore, for example, the R&D consortium for the former AT&T regional telephone companies, was in operation only two years when it received pressure to shift from a generalized research agenda supposedly serving all seven companies to proprietary research for one at a time. No sooner were the seven companies divested from AT&T than their interests began to diverge, and divergence tears the fabric of partnership.

Uneven Levels of Commitment

The vulnerability of alliances to strategic shifts simply points to another source of fragility: differences in the commitment of the partners to their joint activity. For one partner, the alliance may be central to its business, but for the other, it may simply be a peripheral activity. This asymmetry is particularly apparent in alliances between larger organizations and smaller ones, for whom the partnership matters more when it represents a larger relative proportion of their business. The success of a union-management partnership is also more important to the labor leaders than to the managers involved, for the union's only *raison d'être* involves its relationship to the company as employer, but managers have many other business areas in which they can demonstrate their prowess. Furthermore, union leaders face periodic elections.

If one partner incurs greater risks in establishing a partnership, that partner becomes more dependent. The least-committed gains a weapon for exercising power over the more-committed: the threat of withdrawal. To solve this problem and ensure mutual commitment, some joint ventures involve what *Business Week* called the "corporate equivalent of hostages"—contracts forcing companies to buy from each other.[7]

Unevenness of commitment stems from basic differences between organizations entering into partnerships, and these differences can cause other inequalities of power.

Power Imbalances 1: Resources

When richer organizations ally with poorer organizations, the richer ones often end up subsidizing the poorer ones in conducting the activities that will allow them to hold up their end of the partnership. For example, Mazda has more than a hundred engineers whose full-time job is to work inside suppliers' organizations, educating the suppliers' staff, making sure their procedures match Mazda's, and instituting such programs as statistical process control. In union-management partnerships, resource imbalances frequently mean that the company pays for support services such as education and training or staffs of facilitators to help implement joint decision-making. This leads to such anomalies as General Motors undertaking to provide company-paid training to United Auto Workers members in labor history and the union ethos, along with problem-solving and business decision-making, as part of getting ready to work in the new Saturn facility. When management pays for courses in union matters, is union independence eroded? (But perhaps partnerships transform the very meaning of "independence.")

This additional cost incurred by richer organizations can also get them additional control. Because they are providing resources on their own terms, they may be able to ensure that they are used in ways that make the poorer organizations conform to their standards. In exchange for strengthening the poorer organization, the richer one may be intervening in its decisions.

Over time, it is likely that the structures and practices of the organizations entering into partnerships with this kind of resource imbalance will develop similar structures and practices to facilitate coordination. The smaller or resource-poorer partner may begin to be organized more like the larger or resource-richer partner, and to internalize more of the richer party's business philosophy and operating practices. Some of this was visible even in the first year of the Pacific Bell–Communications Workers of America business partnership. Pacific Bell offered training to CWA leadership, in order to close the knowledge and skill gap around partnership decision-making. Local union presidents were aware of their resource disadvantages, particularly their lack of the large staffs that prepared many of the company officers on issues. One local president was looking forward to the time when he would have a similar staff—funded by Pacific Bell.

The company, in turn, was beginning to show signs of interest in the selection of the CWA officials who worked with them. Because of the greater importance of the local presidents, now that they would be involved in partnership activities, management was gaining a different stake in union elections. In interviews, some savvy Pacific Bell managers regretted they could not aid strong candidates, because this was not an appropriate role for the company. But, as union leaders played a role in organizational decisions, the company was concerned about their expertise and business skill, not simply their political ability to get elected.

"Qualifications" are important in a "business partner" in a way they are not in an adversary; the stronger organization wants more competent people on the other side of the table—and also the "gratitude" and cooperation of those people, since they gain strength from the first partner's resources. The stronger management is also more concerned with the continuity and stability of the partner's organization, since turnover can mean additional investments in training to bring newcomers up to speed and can also make it more difficult to work on issues requiring longer-term effort.

The creation of a strategic alliance does not equalize power, then. Resource dependencies may instead increase as the richer side contributes to the poorer side. The "stronger" party has a stake in strengthening the "weaker" party so that the latter can do the work the partnership needs (like Polaroid deploying consultants to suppliers); but this resource infusion may bring with it more control by the richer organization.

Power Imbalances 2: Information
Two kinds of information are required for effective partnership participation; technical knowledge that permits contributions to decision-making, and "relationship" knowledge—understanding of the partner, knowledge of partnership activities, political intelligence—that provides the background for successful negotiations. A comon problem in union-management alliances, for example, is union leaders' lack of information about matters on which they will be deciding. As one union official put it, "Stocks, bonds, notes, debentures—that's the language of corporate types, not the working person. In that territory, they have the advantage."

One of the many reasons given for the lopsided benefits Japanese firms derive from their joint ventures with American companies— assimilating their U.S. partner's skill, then squeezing him out—is a key information gap. Japanese managers tend to learn English, while very few American managers speak Japanese. Furthermore, some joint ventures have no American managers at all![8] To address this difficulty, Celanese Corporation trained two employees in Japanese and assigned them to Celanese's joint venture with Daicel Chemical to observe and learn.

A balance of power certainly helps sustain a partnership, and at least one company has taken the next step, attributing economic benefits to the avoidance of power imbalances. Corning Glass is known as a particularly successful practitioner of strategic alliances, and Corning executives seem particularly concerned with equalizing power with their venture partners rather than monopolizing it. "Mutuality" is the operative word. Declared former Vice-Chairman Thomas MacAvoy, "If I tried to gain the upper hand in a joint venture, my boss would reprimand me."

Imbalances of Benefits

Even if allies begin on an equal footing, with all parties close together in resources and information, the structure of the deal may still favor some over others. *The New York Times* branded U.S.-foreign alliances the "high tech giveaway," claiming that they have resulted in a "largely one-way flow of technology and other critical skills from the U.S. to foreign nations, especially Japan."[9]

In joint ventures benefits may diverge because of differences in how each partner derives revenue. In 1982 CBS, Time Inc., and Columbia Pictures (later acquired by Coca-Cola) formed Tri-Star Pictures, a movie production studio; each partner put in a total of $100 million in equal shares to get a steady flow of movies for Time's HBO (a cable station), CBS's broadcasting, and Columbia's theater distribution. But in less than three years, Columbia was able to take cash out of the deal (revenues of $26 million over six quarters) while CBS, and Time to a lesser extent, had to keep putting more in; Tri-Star as an entity was only beginning to move from significant losses to very modest gains. This happened because Columbia already had a large international distribution system and simply locked in a fee structure for distributing Tri-Star's movies through it, while the deal obligated CBS to keep buying $60 million worth of movies—whether it needed them or not.[10]

Premature Trust: Absence of Institutional Safeguards

"Even paranoids have real enemies." Sometimes parties to an alliance are naive in trusting their partners too soon, before a solid basis for trust is established, and without any legal or contractual safeguards. They give away too much too early. For example, Acme-Cleveland Corporation licensed Mitsubishi Heavy Industries to manufacture and sell one of its machine tools, only to watch Misubishi become its rival in the U.S. market. Somehow Acme-Cleveland had "understood" that Mitsubishi was going to confine its efforts to Asia. Having learned its lesson, A-C is now writing market restrictions into its licensing agreements.[11]

Union leaders are particularly vehement in warning against premature trust. Robert Lemire, shop steward for Eastern Airlines employees belonging to the International Association of Machinists and Aerospace Workers, testified before the Massachusetts Governor's Commission on Employee Involvement in 1987 about events at Eastern before it was bought by Texas Air Corporation. Eastern had launched a well-publicized "employee partnership" in 1984, which traded employee stock ownership and representation on the board of directors for wage concessions. After widespread praise, this partnership fell apart in a blaze of conflict, paving the way for the Texas Air takeover. Lemire offered his conclusions in the form of a parable:

> Whenever I contemplate this subject, I am put in mind of the story of the kind elderly woman who on her daily stroll one winter day came across a snake frozen in the snow. She picked up the snake and brought it back to her modest cottage where she made a place near the fire and nursed the serpent back to health. One day soon after the snake had recovered, the elderly woman brought it some food. As she reached down, the snake struck, delivering a lethal dose of venom. As the woman slipped into a coma preceding death, she said to the snake, "How could you do that? If it were not for me you would have perished." The reptile looked up at her and said, "You knew I was a *snake* when you picked me up." If I were to replace the elderly woman with the faithful employees of Eastern Airlines and the snake with the Eastern Airlines Board of Directors, you would have an extremely accurate account of our experience.

Lemire felt that the company managed to progressively water down contract agreements by invoking the "spirit of cooperation," and then when economic circumstances became hostile, management could turn its back on the partnership agreement.

Conflicting Loyalties

The flexibility inherent in allying with other organizations rather than merging with them is sometimes accompanied by a singular drawback.

Unless the agreement specifies an exclusive relationship, with all the additional costs that entails, each party to the partnership may still maintain relationships outside the alliance, including relationships with competitors. These other ties pose conflicts of time and attention and raise questions of how proprietary or potentially harmful informtion is to be handled.

In the simplest case, ties outside the alliance may divert the attention of partners from providing each other with the services that form the basis for the alliance. For example, Hewlett-Packard bought 11 percent of Cericor Inc. for joint development purposes, to move more quickly into engineering-design software. But Cericor had a similar relationship with Data General. H-P soon found that its 11 percent ownership bought it only 11 percent of Cericor's attention. (H-P eventually bought the whole company.) Cericor itself was sought out by Computervision in an alliance that competed with Computervision's joint venture with Metheus.[12]

Because each partner organization maintains other ties, it may shift allegiances if disappointed with the alliance or if promised a better deal elsewhere. According to reports, Olivetti was apparently disappointed in its partner AT&T's ability to sell the Olivetti PC6300, which may account for Olivetti's making a separate distribution agreement with Xerox.[13]

Then there's the question of "insider" information. To make a partnership work, a great deal of information has to flow to and from the partners, some of it proprietary business information or information that could give competitors an advantage if it leaked out, such as the sales forecast information Ford shares with suppliers to help them plan their own production. Pacific Bell officers, for example, are well aware that their "business partner," the CWA, also represents employees at competing organizations such as AT&T and Northern Telecom, and the local union presidents who participate in Pacific Bell decision forums are also working on behalf of people employed elsewhere. One goal of establishing the partnership is to prepare effectively for technological changes; but technological information is just what the company wants to keep proprietary. In the first year of the partnership, there were no leaks of confidential information, but at least one officer wondered out loud when the problem would start to arise. "At the very least," he mused, "someone will try to use what they learned from us as a bargaining chip with our competitors."

One high-tech company faced this situation in reverse—liability problems when its people appropriated confidential partnership information. As a company manager put it:

> In the past, engineers would have called the suppliers and asked, "Can you do this?" There were issues of liability and of confidentiality. We have had some engineers that got into some problems. There weren't any nondisclosures in place and six months after contact took place between one of our engineers and a software supplier, we came out with a new product that looks similar to what that supplier offered. They say, "Wait a minute, I talked to that engineer and then you all came out with that software package. You took my idea." Then we are in court and we don't want that. We are not out to steal people's ideas. Since we now manage this relationship, we avoid potential problems. Engineers are not sensitized to some of the emerging legal issues around intellectual property. Ideas are owned by people who develop them. It is not uncommon to have things look similar when people never talked, but if people did talk, there is always the question. We have to manage that process a lot better.

A solution to this problem, of course, is for the organization with multiple ties to segregate those working with the partnership from all other personnel, to create an island of concentrated attention and information security. But this may destroy the very reason for partnership—more integration between the allies. And this does not prevent the parent organization from acting in another relationship in ways that are contrary to a partner's desire.

Undermanagement

Some partnerships founder because of difficulties of implementation and execution. They are not organized or managed well. According to a study by accounting firm Coopers & Lybrand, nearly half the time top management spends on the average joint venture goes into creating it. Another 23 percent goes into developing the plan, and only 8 percent into setting up management systems. When former Transportation Secretary Drew Lewis was brought in by American Express to head Warner Amex Cable Communications in 1983, he found "a company out of control. You had two companies with diverse views on almost everything that came up, and we had people all over us from both companies trying to call every shot."[14]

One typical management difficulty is the absence of "tiebreakers." Companies that would balk at the mere suggestion of "democracy" inside their own ranks establish alliances with equal representation from each partner and a requirement for consensus.

Hedging on Resource Allocations

Related to undermanagement is starvation of the partnership by not feeding it with sufficient resources—from inadequate levels of funding to mediocre staff to insufficient rewards for the people from each company who have to make it work. This is one way companies show their ambivalence toward a strategic alliance. Since alliances often start out of ambivalence anyway—"We're not sure we want to do it ourselves"; "Can we find someone else to share the risk?"—this is hardly surprising. Fed less than it needs, the relationship gradually atrophies because it cannot do all the things it was formed to accomplish.

One form of starvation is the failure to provide internal incentives for cooperation with partnership activities. Instead, even those people directly participating may pay more attention to other activities. A former Siemens vice-president felt that an alliance between Siemens and Texas Instruments foundered because TI's decentralized structure made line managers whose activities affected the partnership's success "only interested in quarterly profits and quarterly shipments. They're not going to spend time or resources on something that won't improve the balance sheet tomorrow."[15]

The reluctance of member companies to commit much to the alliance is a particular issue for research consortia. Observers have noted that cooperative research ventures by nominal competitors are stimulated primarily by threat (MCC, the computer research consortium, by concerns about the Japanese and IBM; the glass bottle makers' alliance by concerns about plastic bottles). Rather than seeking positive goals, these partnerships seem to be seeking to avoid negative consequences. Partners express their ambivalence by various forms of hedging—for example, MCC members reportedly were unwilling to provide their best researchers to the venture.

Conflicts Over Scope

Another matter for conflict involves the scope of the alliance—what is included under its purview, and what is not. Partners may reserve for themselves the right to act unilaterally in certain areas, or they may define the domain of the partnership in ways that exclude certain key items. Sometimes this reflects hedging—skepticism or lack of commitment—and sometimes merely differences in partners' needs and goals.

Decisions about what is covered by the alliance can be cause for conflict because they shift the advantage toward or away from one or another of the partners. For months after CBS and Twentieth Century Fox announced their intention to form a joint venture to produce videotapes, discussions centered on whether the venture would be confined to home videos or whether cable would also be included. The decision to exclude cable was widely seen as a setback for CBS, for whom it would have been an opportunity to revive its money-losing cable operations. CBS clearly assumed that cable was squarely in the middle of the domain of a video partnership. Said one former CBS executive, "To go ahead with the venture without CBS Cable is like buying Ford but leaving out the automobile plant."[16]

Decisions about what to include in or exclude from the partnership are clearly part of striking the initial bargain, but they are also a continuing concern. Like all dynamic social arrangements, strategic alliances evolve, and as they evolve, they stumble into territories that one ally may not wish disturbed, or they bump up against limits that bother other members. Partnerships are vulnerable when one party wants to hedge more than the other about shifting the agenda to encompass new issues. The partnership domain was a sore point for the Grotech joint venture, for example. The Country *X* partner wanted the Country *Y* partner to reduce the license fee Grotech paid for *Y*'s technology. But this was one of a number of matters that *Y* refused to discuss.

Union leaders in the Pacific Bell–Communications Workers of America partnership were also concerned about this issue of hedging. After the intense activity of the partnership's first year—a successful agreement on employee security and a popular contract helped by union-management committees and ratified overwhelmingly by members—attention focused on the agenda for the union-management "business partnership." Could the partnership move from protecting employment security and company flexibility through creative use of the current system to more proactive action in finding new sources of business and, hence, creating new jobs?

The creation of new jobs was a topic much on the minds of leaders involved in the partnership. The union local presidents were especially eager to move into their new, more statespersonlike roles as business partners by influencing company strategy with respect to the introduction of new technology, the evaluation of jobs, and the creation of new ventures. But more than one president worried that the company did not want the partnership to get involved in this vital area, despite its importance to union members. Suspicion that company officers did not really want any of this on the partnership agenda was confirmed by one officer who was adamant that the partnership should stay out of company strategy, from financial matters to technology choices to marketing tactics. But once having established a partnership process and asked union leaders to be involved, how could management draw the line at an issue of vital concern to the union? Issue hedging threatened to undermine the credibility of the partnership itself.

The IBM-Ford supplier-customer partnership for office systems provides an example of how a lack of hedging produced more business for the supplier. IBM is even including proprietary product information in partnership discussions:

> To discourage Ford from shopping around, IBM is lifting its usual shroud of secrecy about future products. "Now we don't have to second-guess them by reading trade magazines and listening to the oracles who watch IBM," says Ford's director of information systems. In some cases, he adds, the confidential information has encouraged Ford to wait for an IBM product instead of buying from a competitor. Ford's reactions to IBM's plans also are helping the computer company refine product ideas.[17]

Insufficient Integration and the Absence of a Common Framework

Benson Shapiro argues that strategic partnerships between suppliers and customers to develop new products require five types of integration: strategic, technical, organizational, personal, and financial.[18] Without mechanisms that allow the partners to work together, it is difficult for alliance to live up to its promise.

In addition to the potential differences in strategies, commitment, and power that I have already described, partner organizations also differ initially in organizational structures, processes, procedures, and style. Some of this difference stems from differences in generic type: big firm–small firm differences, union-management differences, or national differences in law, traditions, and language. Some stem from common cultural differences between organizations even of the same basic type.

The partners can, in fact, remain so different that common procedures are never adopted. They can fail to develop a legitimate process for joint decision-making, so that every decision is slowed by misunderstanding and conflicts. Partnerships can fall apart because systems fail to match, because people fail to agree, or because no institutional supports are built around the partnership to shore it up during difficult times.

Insufficient integration has both a short-term and a longer-term cost. In the short run, it means that the infrastructure is not in place for the partnership to carry out its activities efficiently and effectively. In the long run, it means that the partners have not developed a sufficient stake in each other—the kind of stake built up by years of tailoring systems to fit those of the ally—to reinforce mutual commitment. Insufficient integration can also make it easier for one partner to capture more of the benefits from the relationship.

Internal Corporate Politics

If all the other vulnerabilities of partnerships are not enough, they also fall prey to the enemy of all innovation—the politics within each of their member organizations. The issue can range from someone feeling that the partnership threatens his or her territory, to the partnership's chief sponsors losing power.

A joint venture between Syntex and Genetic Systems to market Genetic's monoclonal antibodies expertise reportedly foundered in part because Syntex researchers, who prided themselves on their own expertise, felt bypassed.[19] Similarly, in a moderate-sized advanced technology firm I observed, the company's joint venture agreements are under constant attack by corporate researchers who feel that the resources being poured into the venture partners for risky new product development should instead go to them to build extensions of existing products that are the bedrock of the company's profitability.

An alliance's sponsors can leave, fall out of favor, or turn out to have had little power in the first place. James Towne, president for the first six months of a joint venture between Metheus, a tiny producer of computer-aided engineering systems, and Computervision, gigantic in comparison, attributed problems of the partnership to internal conflicts between senior people at Computervision. "It ended up that our champions were unpopular. I was being walked all over as people were racing to hit somebody else," Towne recalled. (Slightly over a year later, Computervision swallowed Metheus completely, folding it into its operations.)[20]

THE "SIX *I*'S" OF SUCCESSFUL PARTNERSHIPS

Managing the fragile relationships in partnerships and strategic alliances is indeed a delicate balancing act. Corning Glass Works is one of the few companies that has mastered the art. In 1987, about 50 percent of Corning's $207.5 million in net income came from more than twenty partnerships, most with fifty-fifty ownership. Furthermore, that year sales for such equity companies increased 16 percent while core company sales declined. Corning has had successful partnerships for more than five decades, including the venerable Owens-Corning Fiberglas Group owned with Owens-Illinois. Its largest current partnership is Dow Corning, with Dow Chemical, but other partnerships include Nutrisearch, with Kroger and Eastman Kodak; Ciba Corning Diagnostics, with Ciba-Geigy; Pless-Cor Optronics, with Plessy of Great Britain; and equity venture companies in France, Australia, West Germany, and China, among others. Even its joint ventures have joint ventures: Siecor, the company formed by Corning and Siemens, has just formed an alliance with Kaiser Aluminum.

The flexibility with which Corning approaches its partnerships— letting the form be determined by the goals, and letting the ventures evolve in form over time—is one factor in its success. But even more important is the time and effort by Corning executives to create the conditions for long-lasting, mutually beneficial relationship. According to retired Vice-Chairman MacAvoy:

> We spend a lot of time building trust and a personal relationship with the chief officer of the partner. Commitment at the top is more important to us than formal legal documents. The choice of partner is extremely

important. We look for those firms with complementary cultures—we'll get along better when they're like us. . . . We would have problems, for example, with a company that is much smaller than we are (they may feel defensive or even offensive) or with a company that is much larger (they might get condescending). The partner must bring something to the party. And not just money; we can get that anywhere. I mean technology or knowledge that fits with our needs.

We look for fifty-fifty ventures. We won't argue about specific percentages, about whose patents are worth more than the others'. We think of the venture as a marriage; we're both in it for the long haul. We believe in sharing rather than control. There seems to be a whole mentality among many business leaders that they don't want to give up control. Partnerships can't survive when one partner is always using its power against the other. Don't get me wrong—we're not idiots. We argue with our partner if we think we're getting screwed.

From cases like Corning, we can see what it takes to make alliances work over the long term. Successful partnerships tend to have "six *I*'s" in place.

• The relationship is *Important,* and therefore it gets adequate resources, management attention, and sponsorship; there is no point in going to the trouble of a partnership unless it has strategic significance.[21]
• There is an agreement for longer-term *Investment,* which tends to help equalize benefits over time.
• The partners are *Interdependent,* which helps keep power balanced.
• The organizations are *Integrated* so that the appropriate points of contact and communication are managed.
• Each is *Informed* about the plans and directions of the other.
• Finally, the partnership is *Institutionalized*—bolstered by a framework of supporting mechanisms, from legal requirements to social ties to shared values, all of which in fact make trust possible.

These *I*-factors reflect a different way of thinking about the management and organizational tasks of a modern corporation. For companies to gain the benefits of allying with other organizations— from the power of combination to flexibility and innovation—these must serve as the basis for a new, more cooperative philosophy for American enterprise.

"The rewards of these things must be incredible to justify all the extra short-term costs that go along with them," one of my Harvard Business School colleagues commented at a seminar discussing organizational cooperation. Yet for the organizations forming strategic alliances, whatever the costs, the rewards are longer-term but still tangible. Partnerships represent one of the ultimate post-entrepreneurial balancing acts—a way for one partner to leverage its own resources by joining forces with others, a way of encouraging others to invest in developing the things that will bring future benefits to the first organization. In the future, if an increasing amount of economic activity continues to occur across, rather than within, the boundaries defined by the formal ownership of one firm, managers will have to understand how to work with partners rather than subordinates. And that alone promises a revolutionary change in the way America does business.

CHAPTER 7

Cutting Channels: The Push for New Business Streams

One of the best fitness exercises for companies trying to win the global Olympics is stretching in new directions.

But pressures to innovate confront businesses as well as people with another demanding balancing act: keeping up with the activities we are already committed to, to reap the benefits of our investment in them, while at the same time starting new activities that will be of benefit in the future. While caught up in the mainstream, we must also generate "newstreams."

Mainstreams have momentum. Their path is established, the business flow already developed. They have the prestige and legitimacy of the already-established and already-understood. A variety of commitments have been made to keep the mainstream flowing, and these commitments—from budgets to schedules to job definitions to expectations—push along the people swimming in the mainstream.

The same momentum that gives mainstreams their power also makes it hard for them to change. Yet, as the stream image tells us, the flow is not guaranteed even with the power of establishments.

Particularly today, mainstream businesses can easily dry up, stagnate. Thus, companies must seek new sources of revenues, find ways to change course. They must explore opportunities to pioneer in new directions, seek innovations that will improve or even transform the mainstream. And in order to do this, they need to tap newstreams.

The newstream issue used to be relatively straightforward—it was the province of departments whose job was either to invent (research and development) or find acquisitions (strategic planning or "business development" staffs). In the traditional company, segregated staffs specialized in finding or developing new ideas at the behest and under the direction of mainstream business imperatives. The model was a highly functional and linear one—specialists carrying out one step in a process. Leaders of the mainstream business controlled these staffs, and when the staffs were finished, the results—a new product or a new acquisition—were handed over to the mainstream, although occasionally they found something big enough to warrant building a new division around it.

The people involved—the R&D scientists or the start-up managers or specialists—were not considered heroes. Often, quite the opposite. They were hidden and isolated, perhaps so their experimentation would not contaminate the mainstream. I remember the distaste with which some executives talked about "entrepreneurs" ten years ago, as though it was a dirty word; "creativity" had much the same flavor. At a meeting at IBM in 1981, in what now seems like the distant past in light of subsequent changes at IBM, I asked for feedback on research I was conducting on innovation; I was told not to use the word "entrepreneurial." "To us," one manager said, reflecting the bias of the time, "that means people who have beards, hang out in basements, and are undisciplined."

Several things have happened during the global Olympic contests of the 1980s to challenge this traditional view. Dissatisfaction with the old ways has grown, while tantalizing examples of new ways are praised on the business advice circuits.

First, the dissatisfaction. Volatile markets with more competitors and more rapid product obsolescence underline the weaknesses of the traditional bureaucratic model. It is too slow, and mainstream direction too conservative, to allow companies using it to compete successfully. Growth-oriented companies began to turn to internal ventures as well as acquisitions to open new markets.[1] One industrial products company with a dominant market share began to slip because its

engineering department consistently failed to meet product development deadlines by a large margin. The solution was to turn each major
product development project into an autonomous business unit, called
a "Tiger Team," with its own home in a separate building and a full
complement of manufacturing, marketing, and sales people. IBM did
something similar to develop its personal computer quickly. It set up
an independent cross-functional team on its own turf in Florida, far
away from headquarters and far away from the R&D department, with
a mandate to do whatever was needed to create the product and
establish the new business.

When IBM does something countercultural, it makes news. In this
case, IBM's Boca Raton venture simply added to the news already
being broadcast. By 1983, the entrepreneur was the new culture hero.
And among the hero stories told and retold in the popular press were
stories that created some defensiveness in established companies—
stories of lost opportunities, of enterprising employees with good
ideas who had been turned down by their companies and left to start
their own. Steve Jobs and Steve Wozniak, founders of Apple
Computer after Hewlett-Packard said no to their idea, were the
best-publicized as well as the most dramatic successes. But every
company has its stories, and those stories help justify later investments
in newstreams. At Raytheon, where a New Products Center was
eventually founded to push newstreams, the story is told of a salesman
in a California company that Raytheon bought in the 1960s, who had
an idea for a product that is commonplace today but was laughed at
then. "He had this crazy idea," an executive recalled. "Maybe we
could connect cash registers to a computer to do the inventories and
all. That salesman ended up getting fired, and then later this huge
business developed out of that idea."

Sometimes it is hard to pin down the lost opportunities, but the
feeling of something being missed nags at executive minds, especially
when start-up businesses with innovative ideas outpace the growth of
larger "establishment" corporations. In a typical meeting at one such
large corporation, the mixture of defensiveness and interest I saw was
particularly vivid. The youthful vice-president of strategic planning
was explaining to me why he might put "developing new ideas" on
the agenda for the annual division general manager's planning
conference. His electronics company was successful, he said, though
not growing as fast as it used to—but still successful, he kept
repeating. With growth, however, some of the old entrepreneurial

spirit that had created a steady stream of new products and opened new markets seemed to be lost—not entirely lost, he hastened to correct any mistaken impression, just less common. The division presidents play it safe, and a recent study uncovered a widespread feeling that mistakes were punished. Not that the company was having problems, he reiterated, but the executive committee wondered whether it was missing something. Was the competition going to leap ahead? But all that was background to his real concern, reluctantly but finally expressed. The company had recently sold several weaker businesses to its managers in leveraged buyouts. The LBO's had transformed lackadaisical managers into go-getters. They were experimenting with new markets, speeding up the rate of new product entries, and they had already moved the ventures in innovative new directions. "Why couldn't *we* have done that?" the strategic planner lamented. "Where were the new ideas when *we* ran those businesses?"

The continuing publicity about the benefits of new ideas programs and the already-existing models has helped start a minirevolution in America's business management, one aimed at speed and agility in Olympic competition. Established corporations want to move faster. They want to improve mainstream business performance, certainly; but they also want to plunge into newstreams quickly, seizing rather than losing new opportunities.

Join dissatisfaction with a new model, and the seeds for change are sown. Many companies are extending opportunities for invention well beyond the R&D department, and opportunities for new venture development well beyond the acquisition specialists. Newstreams are beginning to flow beside mainstreams. More companies are joining those already seeking ways to cut even-deeper channels for new ideas to flow.

This is far from the norm, of course. Entrepreneurial rhetoric is always more common than action. In 1984, a survey of 198 representative U.S. companies asked whether their innovation mode was tied to their existing business or oriented to the creation of new ones; two-thirds of the companies said they did neither, though 60 of the companies had 77 official innovation programs.[2]

The absence of formal newstream programs does not necessarily represent resistance to new ideas, however, as my interviews showed. Some business executives like to think they don't have to do anything special. They think they already encourage risk-taking and entrepreneurship. They think innovation will arise spontaneously if they hire the right people—and they read the press clippings about determined corporate entrepreneurs bootlegging funds, inventing on their own time, refusing to take no for an answer, and developing a lucrative new product. They see the lack of experimentation in their companies, ipso facto, as a sign they have the wrong people. They think if they exhort their managers enough about the need for new ventures, that will do the trick. Anything more formal, in their minds, would just "add bureaucracy."

That reasoning is still voiced in executive suite discussions about building new lines of business from within, more actively pursuing outside technology partners, or more aggessively seeking employee ideas. But by now, it is voiced less frequently and with less conviction by the leaders I see. Leaders are beginning to understand that one process cannot easily push both mainstream and newstreams simultaneously.

In a case that is typical of this evolution in thinking, the new president of a restructured company in a rapidly changing industry was himself an aggressive pursuer of new opportunities, and he wanted the division managers reporting to him to behave the same way. He told them that repeatedly—generally at the end of monthly operations review meetings in which deviations from budget and failure to meet shipping deadlines and other operational details were attacked rather venomously by the financial officers. Then he complained that his managers never took risks, never brought him new ideas, and ignored the need to invest in new ventures. It was only when he finally saw the connection between the demands of the operations reviews and the failure to develop new projects that he acted. He changed the focus of the monthly management meetings to marketplace changes and future opportunities, and he created set-aside investment funds to be used to pursue newstream opportunities outside of mainstream budgets.

Without special support, new ideas can easily get lost in the momentum of the mainstream, in the sheer surge foward of an already-established business flow. Swept along in the demands of the mainstream business, people may lack the time, energy, or enthusiasm to think about—let alone start—something new.

Through the last few decades, newstreams have ebbed and flowed in terms of official corporate attention. One formal approach to newstreams, the "new venture development department," has come and gone recurrently. Norman Fast estimated that between 1965 and 1975, almost one-fourth of the Fortune 500 companies had such a department.[3] His case studies of the evolution of a few of them showed that they rarely remained a viable channel for new ideas. Their fate was to disappear altogether, after a disappointing performance (Zenas Block's studies showed a corporate venture failure rate of 80–90 percent);[4] to fade into the strategic planning department, becoming analysts rather than activists on behalf of newstreams; or, if they did produce one viable business, to become a mainstream division running that business, stopping all other newstream efforts. A single big idea can consume all the resources, set expectations too high, or make it easy for the company to feel finished with new ventures for a while.

More often, though, it is neither success nor failure that causes newstreams to wane but simple neglect. Ambivalence about publicizing the opportunities, wariness in committing resources, and fuzziness about the proposal-to-decision-to-authorization process send signals to people in the company that newstream activity is not really where the action is. Still other companies are wary about turning their newstream experiments into a "permanent program." "We want to self-destruct in a few years," said the management sponsor of one employee ventures program. "We want to become a way of life, the way everyone handles their everyday job." But where will the funds come from, if they are not set aside? Where will the support be, if there are no official sponsors and allies? Where will the time come from, if the effort is not officially recognized outside of department priorities? What will be the incentives, if there are no special rewards?

An official emphasis makes a difference. Channels for newstreams are all too easily closed or silted over by the force of mainstream currents, by what the mainstream throws off. The channels need to be dug again and again, the commitment renewed explicitly.

We can look to the seacoast to demonstrate the universality of this need to bolster newstreams. Along the Atlantic coast, economically valuable shellfish grow in tidal ponds; in many places, the powerful ocean moves sand to build up beaches that close off the ponds' pathway for the vital nutrients the ocean brings. I have watched this struggle of nature year after year on Martha's Vineyard. Every few months, a work crew arrives with jeeps and bulldozers to make a deep cut through the beach from the pond to the ocean, to allow the water to flow and the pond to remain a nurturing environment for new life. Within as little as a week, the ocean—nature's "establishment"—moves enough sand over the cut that it disappears, leaving the pond again closed off and on its own. One hot July a few days after a cut was made, I found a shellfisherman digging into the channel with a hand shovel, trying single-handedly to stop the cut from closing, to keep the ocean's resources flowing into the pond.

Individual corporate entrepreneurs, who are expected to keep newstreams alive by dint of their own efforts with no formal company support, are like that lone shellfisherman—trying futilely to do with a shovel what can only be done by a large crew with bulldozers at regular intervals. Formal programs are the corporate equivalent of the channel-diggers with heavy equipment. Sheer determination to get out there regularly to keep the newstream channels open is the best way to counter the force of the mainstream.

Mainstream momentum was exactly the problem Lennox Black saw at Teleflex, a Pennsylvania-based manufacturer. It was the problem that led him to conceive of Teleflex's New Venture Fund even before he became chief executive. Black describes himself as "an operations guy," aware of the pressures of keeping the established business going. "In good times," he said, "you're concerned with getting the product out the door, and in bad times, you're trying frantically to get things moving again. So how could we develop a constant pool of resources, in good and bad times, to encourage experimentation?" In the late 1960s, Black asked the then-CEO for extra funds for a project to invest in new ideas in Black's area, the instrumentation business. Both the project and the business grew. When Black became CEO in 1972, he decided that such a fund was important everywhere. By 1988, the fund had gone through a few changes but was still producing results, getting credit for helping shape about 80 percent of the current Teleflex product portfolio.

Programs like Teleflex's New Venture Fund are the vehicles that cut the channels through which newstreams flow. As post-entrepreneurial challenges move innovation from the periphery to center stage, the number and kind of such programs proliferate. While it is hard to get data on trends, the impression of many observers is that more companies are deliberately forming units to nurture new-streams, these units are playing a larger role in corporate strategy, newstream projects are more often competing directly with the mainstream for attention and loyalty, and more people at more levels have the opportunity to become involved in newstream creativity.

Newstreams grow out of the combination of invention and investment—new ideas and the resources to develop them. Newstream programs bring together inventors and developers with investors and sponsors. Some focus more on the invention side, stimulating the ideas themselves, while others focus more on the investment side, distributing the resources among projects. Programs also differ in the extent to which newstream projects are physically and organizationally separated from the mainstream. Sometimes there are separate "incubators" for new businesses, "skunkworks" for maverick inventors, or "reservations" for creative people. But sometimes newstream projects are carried out without leaving the mainstream home base. By examining all of these types, we can discern the requirements for success.

While a formal emphasis is necessary to get newstreams flowing—from official encouragement, to funds and rewards, to leaders championing projects and freeing people's time to do them—there are also dangers in excessive and narrow formality. A "program" can constitute still one more rigid set of procedures, or set of inappropriate hurdles, or package of constraints that take away the spontaneity and creativity that are the essence of newstreams.

After observing the failure of many companies to organize effectively for newstreams because of just this ridigity, Timothy Tuff, President of Alcan's U.S. unit responsible for new business development, decided that he should use every single vehicle that could be conceived of to encourage and nurture new ideas. He moved from Cleveland (U.S. headquarters for this Montreal-based company) to Cambridge, Massachusetts, to signify a new direction and to be close to sources of new technology. Corporate staffs for the mainstream businesses report to Tuff, but his primary team consists of business development managers whose job is to champion new ideas and find their appropriate home, depending on the project itself. Alcan newstreams can live close to or far away from the mainstream—an advantage of Tuff's access to both. They can involve acquisitions, financial investments in external start-up businesses, joint ventures and alliances with other companies, internal ventures to open new lines of business, or innovation projects within the mainstream businesses themselves. The new ideas themselves are more important to Alcan than the method for getting them; all sources can be tapped.

Newstream programs arise from a mixture of motives, evolve from various roots, and serve a variety of strategic purposes. They are generally "overdetermined," to use the psychiatric phrase, in the sense that there is rarely a single clear purpose or a single measure of success. I can distinguish two types in the abstract: programs designed to grow revenues through separate lines of business, and programs oriented to bring innovation to the mainstream. But in practice, the picture is more complex. Some programs are designed to capture people as much as ideas—to provide a home for entrepreneurs who might otherwise leave, to serve as a training ground for people who can take entrepreneurial skills back to the mainstream, or to serve as model and inspiration for mainstream managers. And many have more than one goal, making evaluation as difficult for the people managing them as for those of us from outside.

The origins of newstream programs are just as varied. Some evolve from classic R&D units, like Raytheon's New Products Center, where an inventor's desire to contribute directly to building new business played a role. Some evolve out of mechanisms for employee voice, like Ohio Bell's Enter-Prize Program, which traces its ancestry to a suggestion plan and before that a complaint process. And a third group evolves out of acquisition-oriented strategic planning offices, like the enterprises division of "Barton Machines" (my pseudonym for a company preferring anonymity). Each illustrates a different way that a newstream channel gets cut.

A HOME FOR CREATIVITY

In the mid-1960s, George Freedman, a materials engineer with Raytheon, and a group of his colleagues were moved by two unrelated series of events to pressure the company to allow them to form a separate new products group. The first of these was their growing discomfort at working on defense contracts at the height of the Vietnam War. But the more fundamental impetus for the formation of the New Products Center was an aptitude for and love of creating new product ideas shared by all of these engineers. Their frustration arose from the fact that too often they were reduced to "bootlegging"— working on projects on the sly, using funds appropriated from other, officially sanctioned projects. George Freedman noted that because the money was so scarce and piecemeal, "bootleg projects are the world's most beautifully managed projects."

It took three years for Freedman and his colleagues to get approval for the New Products Center because it was such an innovative concept for its era. Four factors facilitated the ultimate decision by Raytheon to support it in 1969:

- Over several years, Freedman had become friendly with people throughout Raytheon who had problems in the materials area. He soon had a portfolio of ideas and problems that could begin to justify the support of an innovation unit by Raytheon.
- The microwave oven, which was introduced in 1967, was a huge success that proved the value of innovation and creativity. Such a visible success made Freedman's search for a corporate "champion" much simpler.
- Freedman found a champion in the person of a former MIT classmate who had risen to one of Raytheon's twenty-five vice-presidencies, a man described as a frustrated inventor.
- Freedman threatened to leave Raytheon.

Yet even these conditions were not sufficient to bring about the creation of the NPC. Feeling that he had reached an impasse, Freedman contacted a friend in the public relations department, showed him a couple of products that had been successfully developed, and suggested that perhaps this would make an interesting news story. His colleague agreed, and the news broke in the newspaper that the NPC had been established when, in fact, it had not yet been approved. The materials group got a lot of attention and immediately began to receive calls. Even if Raytheon had wanted to stop it, the newstream center was in motion. When the story appeared on television, Raytheon's stock rose four points! "My boss couldn't stem the tide so he decided to ride it out," said Freedman. "He conceded, 'You've got your New Products Center.' "

Freedman and his colleagues had to do something in a hurry, so they rented two trailers, which the NPC would continue to occupy for a number of years. There was no real plan, but since the company expected the NPC to be self-supporting, Freedman's portfolio of ideas soon came into play. For the first seven years, the NPC led a hand-to-mouth existence characterized by the provision of engineering support, which would occasionally lead to the development of new products.

Staffing the NPC at the outset did not prove to be difficult: Freedman had instinctively hired people like himself, so he already had five or six people in place when the NPC was created. Subsequently, staffing consisted of "picking up some orphans"; finding the "parent" of ideas that had been shelved for one reason or another.

Raytheon's demand that the NPC be self-supporting was complicated by the unwillingness of managers to risk their budgets on an untested group of entrepreneurs. Engineers prefer to solve their own problems, so their acceptance of the NPC's services was additionally hindered by a resistance to anything NIH: "not invented here." Until Raytheon's top management was persuaded to furnish the NPC with its own budget, Freedman found himself looking for creative sources of funds to support the NPC, such as grants from trade associations.

The NPC currently operates as a discretionary expense center on a yearly budget of about $3 million. The NPC services primarily Raytheon's major appliance business segment (Amana, Caloric, and Speed Queen), accounting for about one-sixth of Raytheon's $7 billion of annual revenues. The NPC has moved from trailers to aging office space in a rundown industrial park to, in 1987, a new facility, the first time a building had been specifically designed to house it. It also clearly has a life beyond Freedman; in 1988 he retired, handing the leadership to another "father of invention," Robert Bowen. But Freedman left an impressive set of results on a small base: dozens of new products responsible for $100 million in incremental sales and a flourishing Industrial Microwave business started by NPC staff.

TURNING EMPLOYEE VOICE INTO EMPLOYEE INNOVATION

Ohio Bell's Enter-Prize program grew out of a new corporate philosophy that followed the breakup of AT&T, when telephone companies faced competition for the first time. President Ed Bell wanted every employee to feel a sense of ownership and responsibility for the success of the business. He believed that Ohio Bell provided better technical service than competitors; but its customers could easily switch to the competition if they had a conversation with a "rude, impolite, or unhelpful" Ohio Bell employee.

To encourage employee identification, Ohio Bell began a major participative management and quality of work life program, seeded by their AT&T parent in 1982–83. A Suggestion Plan was an outgrowth of these programs—an attempt to solicit employee ideas. At the time, most of the suggestions made were minor and job-oriented. But after divestiture from AT&T, Ohio Bell found itself—along with its sister companies—playing a new game with new rules. While Ohio Bell had been 2 percent of AT&T, it was now 20 percent of the new Ameritech. To be truly valuable, an employee suggestion plan had to have significant impact on the company's bottom line. Ohio Bell needed to generate new revenue, find new lines of business, and seek more effective, less costly ways of doing business. In July 1985, Jim McGowen, a vice-president, determined that the Suggestion Plan initiated in 1981 was not sufficient to generate the kind of innovation the company needed, and that Ohio Bell needed a new program to go beyond the simple small-scale Suggestion Plan. He looked to Henry Fletcher, originator of the Suggestion Plan, and one of Fletcher's staff members, Christine Miller, to design such a program.

Fletcher is credited with coming up with "Enter-Prize," the catchy name of the program, and he sees himself as the chief architect of its formal guidelines. McGowen had given him an assignment, but no parameters. "I knew that the game was wide open," Fletcher said. "There wasn't a set of procedures for me to follow. We hadn't done anything like this before. I told myself, 'The sky's the limit—let's see what I can create.' "

Shortly after the Enter-Prize program had been conceived, word about an employee project currently in development reached its staff. Paul Karas, an electrical engineer on the support services staff, was trying to improve the electronic network of the Ohio State Lottery system (the State of Ohio is Ohio Bell's biggest customer, next to AT&T). Miller remembered, "We were chasing Paul during the early days of the program. As we were trying to develop a process, he was in the middle of developing his ideas. So we built our process around his efforts. We were constantly modifying the process; even now, as we encounter different kinds of ideas and projects, we are still modifying the procedure." She felt that part of the success of Ohio Bell's innovation program came from being designed around a live project. In its first eighteen months, Enter-Prize sponsored seventeen projects, one that was already a major new revenue generator and others that had already brought several million dollars to the bottom line with minimal use of company funds.

Ohio Bell now advertises the Enter-Prize program through company newsletters, posters, and pamphlets. But each of the first seventeen projects emerged by a different route. Some people resurrected "suggestion winners" from the old Suggestion Plan (for example, how to recycle surplus material). Others had already developed an invention, had it working, and then were asked to join Enter-Prize (for example, a new piece of test equipment). McGowen likes the variety, proclaiming, "Formalization is equal to failure. We're trying to avoid the red tape; it's a danger we are trying to guard against."

FROM ACQUISITION TO VENTURE CAPITAL AND PARTNERSHIP

Nurturing ideas from within—whether from a group of creativity specialists or from employees at large—is one form of newstream channel. Almost diametrically opposed is another approach, one that relies on external sources of new ideas, seeking to acquire positions in other people's start-ups and form alliances to exploit other people's technology. In this case, the corporation comes to resemble a venture capitalist, investing in new business rather than creating it. Here the financial stakes are higher than in the New Products Center or the Enter-Prize Program, but so are the risks; and disappointment is more common.

"Barton Machines Enterprises" (BME), for example, a division of "Barton Machines, Inc.," both pseudonyms for a company in my study, manages a portfolio of eleven investments in support of Barton's corporate diversification strategy. BME's stake in the companies that make up the portfolio varies from 10 percent to 70 percent, but there is a common thread that binds these investments: BME's mission of exploring and gaining access to new technologies so that they may be incorporated into Barton's strategies for growth.

BME has a history of technology transfer and growth through investments in and acquisitions of companies developing technologies critical to BME's success. In 1969, for example, it became clear that

Barton's future success would be predicated on an entry into the semiconductor and integrated circuit area. Barton provided start-up capital to entrepreneurs looking to form an integrated circuit company. In return for the financial support, Barton retained an acquisition option, which was later exercised; this start-up is now generating $250 million annual revenues as a core business. Soon after this initial investment, Barton identified a related opportunity; a similar path was pursued and the seed money has turned into a $100 million core business.

During the 1970s, investments of this nature continued. Barton began to acquire a reputation as a company willing to invest in partnerships with smaller high-tech firms. It started to receive unsolicited requests for funding from small companies. At this point a debate emerged over the most appropriate way to take advantage of the opportunity for growth. Barton's president was uncomfortable with outright acquisition of the companies, preferring partnerships, for all the reasons I outlined earlier. Barton did not have the resources to single-handedly develop the technology necessary for the company to maintain its growth throughout the 1970s and 1980s; partnerships would help Barton extend its reach without the costs and risks of acquisitions.

The solution to the dilemma came from a large Southern manufacturer. Barton's initial contact with the manufacturer had come in 1977, when it provided Barton with funds for investment. Then in 1980, looking for a safe investment with a "guaranteed" 15 percent return, the manufacturer agreed to fund the formation of Barton Machine Enterprises. Under a five-year agreement beginning in 1980, the investor annually provided BME with up to $10 million in investment funds. BME invested these funds in emerging high-technology growth companies whose technologies and products complement Barton's long-term interests. In return for each advance of funds to BME, the manufacturer received Barton preferred stock, which it could later convert to common stock.

When BME was launched at the end of 1980, the company as a whole was in the latter portion of a second five-year plan. As a result, for the first year or so of BME's existence, its leader was "flying by the seat of his pants." It was only after the five-year plan for the period 1982–87 was complete that BME had a clear strategic direction.

When the agreement with the manufacturer expired in 1985, it was not renewed. During this period, the investor had undergone two changes in management, and the company's new director of corporate development felt that the investment in BME was inappropriate, because unlike Barton, the manufacturer got no technical leverage, and the investments were too small to bring significant payoffs to such a large company. But BME survived, and the diversification strategy that it now serves is designed to expand Barton's distinctive competencies into technologies that will reinforce and develop Barton's position in its industry, so Barton itself supplies the funding.

The mission of BME is to invest in young high-technology companies with high growth potential that can eventually expand Barton's technological base. Using the expertise of Barton's corporate marketing staff, BME studies submarkets of the high-technology industry, learning about their structures, product opportunities, and market segmentation. From this analysis comes an identification of "emerging companies who appear to have a distinctive competitive edge," as BME proclaimed in its 1983 progress report. BME's head describes the process of negotiation with potential portfolio firms:

> We have no preconceived notion as we approach the business. We sit down and try to understand the ambitions and motivations of the entrepreneurs. The dialogue can sometimes go on for six months, during which we try to work out a way we can make an arrangement that moves us to our strategic objective and meshes with their goals. There have been cases in which we have been unable after months and months of discussion to come to an arrangement.

Once the decision has been made to invest in the candidate company, an agreement is drawn up that provides BME with monthly profit-and-loss statements and balance sheets, supplemented quarterly with reports containing greater detail. BME places a director on the company's board, and retains absolute "visitation rights": the company is at all times accessible to BME scrutiny. The BME executive is quick to point out, however, that:

> We have nothing to do with the day-to-day decision-making or the creation of the culture within the companies. We don't try to manage the company or try to get in the way of the entrepreneur. We do take pains to establish formal and informal channels of feedback [for example,

regular board meetings, and occasional phone conversations for which a Barton representative "comes up with a reason to call]". Whether this works is a function of the openness and integrity of the CEO of the company.

The flow of information critical to the monitoring of the companies' progress is completed by twice-quarterly meetings between BME's controller and the portfolio companies' VPs of Finance. According to the head of BME, "Surprises are brought to my attention more quickly than the news would break on the outside."

BME's head claims that "it is too soon to make a judgment of the ultimate impact" of BME; another Barton manager once remarked that "portfolio performance has ranged from horseshit to mediocre"— but followed up by agreeing that it is too early to evaluate the success or failure of BME. "When the BME history is written," the venture unit's executive said, "I have a hunch that what will prove workable are those deals in which we invested in companies whose technologies can be exploited by our core component business. The technology transfer options, joint R&D rights, and marketing rights are where we should get leverage. On the other hand, we'll probably conclude that investments to put Barton into divergent businesses just don't work."

So far, the financial payoffs have not come. By 1987, Barton had invested $40 million in companies now valued at $29 million, and had taken $7 million in write-offs. Barton's chief financial officer confesses that "from a financial viewpoint BME has been very painful and will continue to be for some time. BME represents, at best, 10 percent of nonproductive assets for the near term, so if you are interested in return on equity, it has been a tough time." He is careful to point out, however, that the real benefits to Barton are not primarily profit-oriented; in fact, he says, "If all we ever do is make money on this by buying low and selling high in liquidating the portfolio, then the program has been a failure." The true objective, in his eyes, "has been to build Barton's knowledge base through technology transfers:

There are two aspects to technology transfer. First, we have the right to design products on their processes. We've introduced at least one new product to run on one of the portfolio company's processes.

In the longer term, actually practicing their technology, you have to get beyond a point indicated by a "make or buy analysis."

In time . . . the benefits of the diversification of the product line will lead to sale growth and ultimately to profits.

Barton's newstream strategy of external investments, financially driven, has been a source of controversy within the company (the reason I have given this otherwise excellent company a pseudonym). Many managers feel that if the only payoff is in learning technology, Barton is getting an awfully expensive education.

Barton is not alone in questioning the wisdom of a purely investment-oriented newstream strategy.[5] Post-entrepreneurial corporations will not succeed by being arm's-length venture capitalists but by knowing how to contribute more than cash to the development of new ideas.

TURNING A TRICKLE INTO A FLOOD: ENCOURAGING MANY NEWSTREAMS

The decision to invest in newstreams is the first step. The second step is to ensure that there will be many ideas flowing.[6] Companies do this in three principal ways: by *scouting* (seeking ideas that already exist), *coaching* (encouraging people with embryonic ideas to develop them); and *inspiring by example* (offering visible role models).

Scouting

The scouting model is simple: a few people to scan the internal and external environment for promising ideas who can then give them the funding to move forward.

Gus Tschanz, vice-president of Engineering for Teleflex, talked about Teleflex's New Venture Fund (NVF) while he walked through a training center designed to nurture newborn businesses. Sport-shirt informal, Tschanz began the tour at his modest corner office, an office with a drafting table out among the other engineers in a partitioned cubicle. His project records were equally informal. One list of forty-six projects funded from 1979 to 1983 was handwritten in pencil on an accountant's ledger sheet. After the project name were listings for dollars allocated, dollars spent, dollars remaining in the account, and the outcome. Many were labeled "failures," with notations such as "too expensive," "product in inventory but no sales," or "couldn't be manufactured." But there were a critical few that read "in production." "At that time," Tschanz recalled, "we were funding 80 percent of the proposals we got, and maybe 20 percent of those could be termed successes. But we're not looking for the sure winner; those the divisions should be funding. I want to encourage more off-the-wall proposals, much more risky ideas"—with, he hopes, high reward potential. "We try almost to build up a cult around the fund," commented Lennox Black, Teleflex's CEO and NVF's founder. "We talk in terms of 'attack' and 'defend' units. The fund is an 'attack' unit."

Teleflex employs more than thirty-five hundred people worldwide, in forty facilities. Its Technical Products group makes custom components and coatings for aerospace, defense, and medical industries. The Commercial Products group services the automotive, pleasure, marine, outdoor power equipment, and fluid transfer markets with less complex, high-volume products. Black, CEO since 1971, is an energetic man in his mid-fifties, clearly a hero to many of his employees.

Money for the NVF is automatically taken from the sales of all the divisions—one-half of one percent. Black considers that a "smart move." In 1986, with net sales of $218,146,900, the fund contained $1,300,000. Black says that the NVF is one "vehicle for top management to force a company to grow." The monies create "subtle pressure on line people to reinvest for the future." The reward or incentive system at Teleflex, as at most other companies, in Black's view, is "both bottom line and short term." The NVF is one way that Black encourages the others on his management team "to spin plates."

The NVF is intended to allow any person within Teleflex who has a new idea to pursue that idea by obtaining funding outside normal budgetary channels. Until 1987, the fund was administered from the corporate level. Anyone in the company could apply for funding to the committee that reviewed funding requests. Membership in the committee rotates among senior managers; in 1986 the committee was composed of the chairman, the CEO, the vice-president of Marketing and the vice-president for Engineering. Requests for funding, which ranged from one thousand dollars to two hundred thousand dollars, were made by writing a one- to two-page memorandum to one of the committee members. Often the idea was discussed with a committee member in the hallway before being put out in memo form. The memos sometimes had supporting materials attached to them, but almost invariably the attachments were such things as advertisements for competitors' products or a simple drawing. There were never long, detailed financial justifications for the funding requests. The analysis was of the "back of the envelope" variety, just the way most start-up firms operate.

Black and the other top executives wanted the application for NVF to be quite informal. Once someone had an idea, they should chew it over with their fellow workers, boss, and Black, although Tschanz, the chief engineer and roving gadfly, also would meet with people over lunch. Black believes that "most people have crude ideas—not very sophisticated." He wants a process that encourages them to bring forth these "crude ideas." It also fits with his style of spinning plates. "Here's four thousand bucks, see what you learn, and call us in June." For a lot of people this process "separates the wheat from the chaff." "Formality is death," he says.

Recently, Black decided that the distribution of NVF monies should match more closely the decentralized structure of the organization. So he gave the presidents of the various divisions sums of NVF funds for which they are responsible. For example, Dave Boyer, president of the Commercial Segment, was allocated two hundred thousand dollars for 1987, which was invested in six projects. The net result of the new policy is to give the presidents of the divisions the responsibility for distributing a set percentage of NVF. Another portion, referred to around Teleflex as "Bim's Mad Money," is still reserved for corporate investments in new opportunities.

The first of two primary uses for the NVF is product development. For example, a team from the SemeTech division wanted to see if they could apply the SemeTel coating to sheets of steel (up to seven feet wide and continuously rolling) that could then be cut to use for consumer products like washing machines. There were four specifications that the engineers needed to meet for the process to be "successful," but they could only achieve three. But the engineers all said that "we learned a lot about coatings in the process of experimentation," and this learning resulted in a new line of successful coatings.

The second major use of the NVF has been market research. One important success is a system for the U.S. Navy known as the RMVA, an opportunity that would have never come to fruition without NVF scouts' rescuing it from oblivion. In the 1970s two Teleflex engineers were in the bowels of a U.S. Navy ship and saw parts of a valve system lying on the floor, broken and rusted. Since Teleflex knew how to coat metals and design cable and control systems, the engineers thought that they could build cable/valve systems for the Navy and create a new market niche for Teleflex. One subsequently left the company. In 1979 Black contacted the ex-Teleflex engineer and urged him to return, but did not assign him to the RMVA. From 1979 to 1982, the project moved from division to division; the returned engineer continued to be involved on the periphery. By 1983 it was apparent that the RMVA project was on everyone's back burner. Scouts for the NVF saw the RMVA as a major new business opportunity that was getting lost in mainstream business priorities. The technology was there; the next step was to learn the market and shape the product to fit market needs. NVF funded it, putting the returned engineer in charge and moving it out from under a mainstream division. The project's success has opened the military market to Teleflex.

Smaller amounts of money (five to ten thousand dollars) have been used for myriad other projects. The president of one division, for example, is encouraging his director of communications to apply for new venture funds. During the past year, part of the responsibilities of the communications director has been to promote communications among employees at nine different plants spread across the United States and the United Kingdom. With home video machines, employees in plants in the United Kingdom talked with employees in the U.S. plants and vice versa. Now the goal is to develop a more sophisticated video system to use for customer services. NVF dollars permitted the hiring of summer interns in communication from a local college to produce a professional video.

People applying for new venture funding are not competing for scarce resources within their own divisions or departments. Because each business unit contributes the same percentage of its sales to the fund, competition to "recoup" some of that money is encouraged. Managers of each business unit therefore have an incentive to support and encourage their people to develop the kind of innovative new ideas that might receive approval for new venture funding. While the project is still under development, funding comes from the corporate level so it is not an expense to the individual business unit. And if the project fails, because it is a corporate expense it has no adverse effect on an individual manager's bottom line. Indeed, "failure" also has little impact on a person's career. Black reported, "After one recent failure, the key person was promoted. After it was clear it wasn't going to fly, a report was made on what we learned from the experience—so it's valuable even in failure."

The stress of the New Venture Fund is on the word "new." One thing Teleflex does not want to encourage is people seeking some of this "free money" to do what they should be doing anyway as a normal part of their operations. Therefore, funding will not be given for product proposals that would be natural evolutions or extensions of existing product lines. Likewise, the fund will not pay for new equipment to improve current manufacturing processes, although occasionally funding might be approved for equipment to test new products or processes. The test is that if it is something an operational group should be doing as part of its continuing efforts, then it is not eligible for new venture funding.

Communication about the New Venture Fund is just as informal as the application process and, as a consequence, it may be underpublicized and underused. Black reported that monies are more frequently "left over, rather than overspent." The president of one division had yet to allocate his 1987 funds by April. And a division chief engineer often labeled "a genius" was upset that so little was known about the fund below the top two or three layers of the organization. The lack of communication is deliberate. One division president feels that if more people know about the fund, more people will apply, and as a result he will have the problem of turning some people down. "And then I must deal with the bad feelings that causes," he said.

Scouting, in short, is a conservative approach to getting newstreams flowing. Scouts seek ideas that are already developed enough to be attractive candidates for further development, but they do not attempt to broaden the base of new idea proposers.

Coaching

A more active step in getting the ideas to flow is a coaching process to encourage those with embryonic ideas to come forward and to guide them in appropriate directions. Sometimes this takes the form of a training program, such as Lutheran Hospital's "ICE" (for Ideas

Create Excellence) program, given throughout the thirty-four-facility chain to show people how to develop new business ideas and take them forward. Sometimes coaching is a matter not of training but of outreach.

Members of Ohio Bell's Enter-Prize staff serve as coaches, helping develop and refine an idea, find subject matter experts to assess and improve it, and devise the appropriate "sales pitch" for those managers who will have to sponsor the idea, including the employee's own supervisor. The staff coaches applicants on presenting their ideas to senior management and then continues to stay in touch after approval, helping make connections to other consultants with technical expertise. The legal staff is also available to advise employees. This is particularly important in cases in which the business idea requires an outside vendor or involves new technology that the company will license to outside manufacturers. (Several Enter-Prize ideas have resulted in Ohio Bell's licensing products and technologies to companies as important as Hughes Aircraft.)

Coaching at Eastman Kodak is even more elaborate. Kodak's New Opportunity Development process is a carefully constructed and extensive process to identify, develop, and obtain sponsorship for new ideas. There are three tiers in the process, corresponding to the evolution of an embryonic idea into a full-fledged business: (1) individual initiative; (2) seed financing for ideas that warrant further development; and (3) development of the business as a separate subsidiary. The structure is overseen by a Venture Board, a senior management group whose mission is to foster innovation and entrepreneurship. Reporting to the Venture Board is the New Opportunity Development Staff, an organization of about fifty people that serves to guide innovative efforts and to enhance the likelihood of success. Robert Rosenfeld and Robert Tuite, known as "the Bobs," created much of the process.

Coaching takes place via the first tier, a network of twenty Offices of Innovation throughout the corporation. Any employee with an idea can approach an innovation office and receive support, guidance, and access to a network of internal consultants who can advise whether the idea has merit and how to proceed. At this stage, the idea originator is assumed simply to be seeking advice and is kept anonymous if desired. But he or she is also expected to be the champion who will push the idea forward.

For ideas that survive this individual initiative stage, the coaches help find sponsorship within the existing organizations in the company. If an already existing Kodak business won't or can't provide funding, the originator is steered to the New Opportunity Development office. There a staff of six reviews proposals, with the ability to provide the most promising projects with up to twenty-five thousand dollars in initial seed money. Before a full business plan is written, the idea is run by appropriate line organizations one more time in an attempt to get sponsorship within existing organizations. Then, it goes on to the Venture Board with a staged financing plan. If approved, the project gets stage-one financing and a home in Eastman Technologies, the company's incubatorlike venture subsidiary.

Kodak is a gigantic company, and by overall Kodak standards, the amount of money involved in the new opportunity process is small; the process represents less than one percent of total corporate investment. But for a fledgling venture, the funding can be substantial: from a few hundred thousand dollars to over $10 million. Even more important is the stimulation provided by the active coaching. Innovations are solicited, and ideas are steered in an effective direction. The presence of the offices of innovation and their facilitators has led to a steady rise in the number of ideas submitted, from 40 in 1979 to 960 in 1986.

Some Kodak venture developers have needed only minimal coaching; they were already working on a new business idea, and the New Opportunity Development program gave them just the boost they needed to turn concept into reality. Elena Prokupets is a typical example, if anything about Elena can be considered "typical." A Russian engineer who emigrated to the United States with her husband, Ruvin, and their three-year-old son in 1978, Elena was a fount of high-tech ideas. She worked out one of them in her spare time with Ruvin, a Kodak engineer, and Ted Perkins, a colleague at a small company where Elena was employed. It was a unique concept: storing high-quality photographs on a computer screen, a process that would be useful for security systems, among other applications.

For two years, the Prokupetses and Perkins planned the project—on weekends and almost every single weekday evening late into the night. The venture capitalist they approached wanted too much ownership and too much control. So when the Kodak program was started, the team went right to Kodak and were coached on how to take the next step. Their proposal, submitted in April 1985, was approved by October, and their new company, Edicon, was born with Elena as president because, as Ruvin said, "she is the best person for the job." In December 1985, Edicon moved into a building and hired two people. The product was developed quickly—faster than the business plan, Elena recalled—and about a year after start-up, there was a product on the market. By June of 1988, Elena was projecting $10 million a year in revenues. Customers included the Los Angeles Police Department, NASA, Merrill Lynch, Boeing, and government users in Israel, Belgium, France, and Dubai.

Inspiring by Example

The third way companies encourage newstreams is through publicity—putting forward examples of employee heroes and how they did it. Written publicity is one method, like Lutheran Hospital's catalogue of innovations or Banc One's book of quality improvement projects. But even more effective is offering opportunities for active contact with innovators. For Ohio Bell, it was important to spread the word to literally thousands of people.

From the fall of 1985 to the spring of 1987, innovative employee ideas had contributed several million dollars to Ohio Bell's net earnings under the Enter-Prize program, and the company was eager to show this off. So in late April 1987, Ohio Bell staged Innovation Fairs in office buildings in Columbus and Cleveland to display seventeen prize-winning ideas to the rest of their employees. Just as in any well-executed trade show there were thirty-inch television screens, computer terminals galore, crisply executed graphics displays, gold-cloth-covered display tables, neatly arranged booths, and lots of people milling around to talk with exhibitors.

Unlike similar fairs at other companies, Ohio Bell's was open to all employees. Its purpose was to "make innovation contagious," to get fourteen thousand employees excited about their potential to do what the first batch of Enter-Prizers did.

Thousands of Ohio Bell people, at all levels, wandered through the fair to view the eight ideas already brought to successful completion and the nine others underway. They saw how Paul Karas's invention helped the Ohio Lottery to operate more efficiently by enabling workers to identify and turn off faulty lottery ticket machines in a matter of minutes. They talked to Roger Hixon and Tom Penty, who saved Ohio Bell over a million dollars by consolidating a basic software tool with a network already up and running that had extra capacity. They heard about Walt Bailey's and George Badziong's company within a company—the venture that commercialized a software package (familiarly known as "MacFig") to generate engineering documents much more quickly than they could be done manually—that worked with an outside vendor to sell it on the open market. They saw John Aulicino waving a piece of cable like a magician with a magic wand to show how his Glocator—an infrared laser light—can find breaks in telephone lines.

Carol Twigger, an assistant manager of installation and maintenance support, stood next to her manager while a small crowd gathered in front of her booth to offer congratulations and satisfy their curiosity about what she did. Over and over in the course of the day, without getting tired of repeating herself, she explained the details of her mechanized installation productivity measurement system and how she developed it. She had been working on the system for two years, at home in her spare time, before she heard about Enter-Prize, and even then, she wasn't sure her project was suitable for it, until her boss encouraged her to apply. She received twenty thousand dollars in funding, which helped her bring the system on-line, and a flow of supportive phone calls from the Enter-Prize staff. So far the company has saved two hundred thousand dollars from her idea. "I'm really impressed," she said. "I didn't realize how much interest there is from other employees. I can't believe all this is happening to me."

The exhibitors clearly loved the attention, loved explaining what they designed—a reward almost as good as having been chosen in the first place, and in some cases nearly as meaningful as the percentage of the net proceeds they were to receive. Al Wallenhorst, designer of an elegant system to rehabilitate old equipment, was proud that after his forty years of service he would be leaving a tangible legacy. The winners' bosses chimed in, proud of their connection to the stars of the day. From press interviews to showing off their accomplishments, the fair clearly made heroes out of employees with initiative.

The fair-goers liked it, too. It was fun, it was a change of pace, and it dramatically symbolized the push to move beyond bureaucracy. "Under the old suggestion system," a twenty-one-year veteran from the cable tracking department recalled, "I won fifty dollars for a plan to improve fire drills. The new program is better. In the past, someone would come up with an idea, and management would capitalize on it. Now it's your baby."

THE SIGNIFICANCE OF CUTTING NEWSTREAMS

Carving out channels for new ideas to flow and to develop into new business streams has significance beyond the number and magnitude of the projects that emerge. Companies support newstreams for a variety of officially stated reasons, ranging from the purely economic (hoping that investments in new ventures will bring financial returns, regardless of any other payoffs) to the purely cultural (seeking to set norms about the search for innovation in every aspect of the business by visibly funding and rewarding a few model projects). In the middle are a mixture of other official goals: getting a window on technology, developing managerial skill at innovation. Ironically, the projects that begin small and with "cultural" goals often generate greater proportional financial returns than those with "economic" goals.

Regardless of the stated goals, however, the very existence of newstreams sends a signal about the search for new ideas—from any source—to help the company compete in the corporate Olympics. The opening of newstreams cements the marriage of entrepreneurial principles and corporate structures that results in the post-entrepreneurial corporation. While focused and disciplined in its pursuit of mainstream business success, the post-entrepreneurial corporation is also flexible enough to have new ideas ready and organized enough to get new ideas moving *fast*.

CHAPTER 8

Swimming in Newstreams: Mastering Innovation Dilemmas

*O*nce promising ideas have been scouted or solicited from inside or outside the company, and people have been encouraged to step forward, lured by the opportunity to grow their ideas, the new development stream is ready to flow.

At Eastman Kodak, for example, the heads of the ventures that have made it through the new opportunity screening process move into the company's incubator, the renovated red-brick warehouse with the label Eastman Technologies, Inc.—a new environment with new space to make their own. At Ohio Bell, the favored Enter-Prize winners generally stay at their posts in their home departments, although their official assignment now involves leading their project to fruition. But even when the physical setting does not change, the experiential setting changes dramatically. The innovator is now swimming up a newstream.

And here the tensions begin. Newstreams have needs and requirements different from those of mainstreams. The operating logic of a newstream often conflicts with that of the mainstream. Mainstreams and newstreams differ in performance criteria, predictability, and the need to shed the burden of the past.

Mainstream activities, first of all, are commonly evaluated by whether they are profitable, offering a return on past investment. It is appropriate to seek efficiencies to lower costs to in turn increase profitability. But newstreams may require a great deal of investment without a clear prospect of immediate return. Rather than seeking efficiencies, they may seek market position almost regardless of costs—to get the new flow established.

Second, mainstream activities benefit from having a history, an experience base. This provides data for predictions about the future which, in turn, allow some degree of planning, scheduling, and most important, smoothing—the spreading out of highs and lows over the calendar. Newstreams, however, have no such base. Their rhythm is not clear. Newstream events may be totally out of synch with the mainstream calendar.

Third, mainstreams carry in their wake a hefty accumulation from the past. This accumulation might include sunk costs (investments already made that have to be held to derive the expected return); commitments (labor contracts, promotion promises); or expectations and traditions. Newstreams, however, are starting fresh. The mainstream's accumulation is a burden to the newstream, a burden that may unduly encumber an infant venture. The newstream may not need costly corporate services designed for the mainstream. The newstream may prefer to run lean, investing in its project goals, rather than paying for corporate overhead.

Overall, effective management depends on knowing which stream you're swimming in. What it takes to develop and launch the new is very different from what is acceptable and appropriate for managing the already-established. The two streams have two different logics.

Creative projects, regardless of type, share a set of characteristics, and these characteristics shape the newstream workplace. Among the experiences common to writers, artists, task force leaders, development engineers, and new business creators are:

- The need to move quickly when opportunity or inspiration strikes.
- Missed deadlines and encounters with the unexpected.
- The constant need to justify the project, especially as new options come up that sound even better.

- Extreme emotional swings: numerous frustrations and moments of despair coupled with clear highs.
- If it is a joint effort, the difficulty of keeping up with what everyone else on the project is doing and thinking.
- An all-encompassing and absorbing project world, which makes it easy to get disconnected from the surrounding world.

It is the nature of newstreams to be uncertain, bumpy, boat-rocking, controversial, knowledge-intense, and independent—seeking their own course. These characteristics make them vulnerable to unique dangers. And in addition to the problems all start-ups share, newstream activities face additional vulnerabilities when they are carried out in the midst of a powerful mainstream.

For George Freedman's new product developers at Raytheon, for Carol Twigger at Ohio Bell, for Elena and Ruvin Prokupets at Kodak, and for other managers of newstream projects next to mainstream businesses, the managerial agenda for newstreams is formed by three compelling characteristics: high uncertainty, high intensity, and high autonomy.

HIGH UNCERTAINTY

Newstreams are, by definition, uncharted waters, and the course through them is bumpy rather than smooth.

When anyone creates something new, results are always a little uncertain—what resources will be consumed, when they will be needed, exactly what will come out, when the project will be finished, and how it will be received. And the newer it is, the more likely that there will be little or no precedent, little or no experience base to use to make forecasts. Timetables may prove unrealistic. Anticipated costs may be overrun. For example, in two pharmaceutical companies the ratio of actual to expected cost of new products was 1.78:1 in one and 2.11:1 in the other; the ratio of actual to expected time was 1.61:1 and 2.96:1, respectively.[1]

Furthermore, the final form of the "product" may look different from what was originally envisioned. To add to the uncertainties, the creation process is nonobservable; it is carried on inside people's heads. And unlike established activities in which a reservoir of experience makes it possible to "do it right the first time," innovation makes progress by "mistakes": false starts, dead ends, blind alleys, and failed experiments that build their own reservoir.

A newstream project at GTE, which ultimately generated a $70-million-a-year revenue flow for the company, was almost terminated because of the uncertainty factor. The project was developing and marketing an electronic mailbox system. The idea came from a corporate entrepreneur who, with support from the company's new ideas program, put a project team to work in an old warehouse in Dallas under a plan and schedule endorsed by mainstream executives. But the project soon fell way behind. Like many innovations, the product employed technology so unknown in the marketplace that prospective customers were not receptive to it, and several rounds of replanning were necessary to get the right product configuration. Even assumptions about the scope of the test market had to be changed in the light of experience. What the team had originally imagined as a local test had to be rethought across the time zones—thus necessitating a national test. This change in tactics paid off. Although only six of the new TeleMessenger units were sold after a local mailing of sixty thousand letters, two hundred were sold at one crack to a multinational company immediately after the test went national.[2] Still, it was a fight to get mainstream approval for the extra time, the extra cost, and the deviation from plan to turn this into a success.

GTE's TeleMessenger ultimately became profitable (and part of the mainstream) faster than many "big ideas" for new ventures. While "small," less complex ideas can often bring short-term returns, as Ohio Bell's Enter-Prize projects have, history tells us that bigger corporate ventures may take from seven to twelve years to become profitable.[3] Thus, newstreams have to be managed with a degree of faith that the uncharted waters indeed lead to a desirable destination. They require balancing patience and speed—the ability to persist and also to move quickly when the right path does present itself.

Innovations often engender secondary innovations—a number of other changes made in order to support the central change.[4] As necessary, new arrangements might be introduced in conjunction with the core tasks. Methods and structure might be reviewed, and when it seems that a project is bogging down because everything possible has been done and no more results are on the horizon, a change of structure or approach, or a subsidiary project to remove roadblocks, can result in a redoubling of effort and a renewed attack on the problem.

This conclusion is confirmed by a study of innovation in Japanese and European as well as American firms. Multiple approaches, flexibility, and speed are required for innovation because of the advance of new ideas through random and often highly intuitive insights and because of the discovery of unanticipated problems.[5] Project teams need to work unencumbered by formal plans, committees, board approval, and other "bureaucratic delays" that might act as constraints against the change of direction.

The newstream situation thus requires:

- Committed visionary leadership willing to initiate and sustain effort on the basis of faith in the idea.
- The existence of "patient money"—capital that does not have to show a short-term return.
- A great deal of planning flexibility, to adjust the original concept to the emerging realities.

But these requirements can run counter to typical mainstream practice in established corporations that are organized to seek certainty for mainstream maintenance rather than support uncertainty. For example:

- Detailed analysis in advance of resource commitments. In one company, the list of analyses to be done itself runs ten pages.
- Fairly rapid returns on investment or a very high probable revenue base from the activity. Several prominent packaged goods companies, for example, declare themselves uninterested in products with a revenue potential of under $100 million a year.
- Short time horizons. There is a common "mismatch" between the newstream time frame—a longer time from conception to profitability—and the time horizons of managers who have to prove themselves in the short term.
- High-level sign-off on a plan, and agreement to a series of procedures or steps, with the expectation that they will be followed without deviation. "Adherence to plan" is a common measure of managerial performance in established corporations.

Newstream need and mainstream management are thus in conflict.

HIGH INTENSITY

Newstream projects rush forward, absorbing mental and emotional energy as they go. They breed intensity in a number of ways.

First, the development process is knowledge-intensive. Creation not only relies on the application of existing knowledge via human intelligence, but also generates new knowledge at a rapid rate. New experiences accumulate; the learning curve is steep. There is a lag between the awareness of this knowledge in the minds of the creators and its application to the task. The creators' knowledge is not always codified—put into a form in which it can be transferred to others. Sometimes it is not even codifiable because it is elusive; it is a matter of "feel" based on the experience that is piling up. And whenever a group work together on a development task, their ability to share this rapidly accumulating knowledge makes a difference in how effectively they can work toward the common goal. One of the requirements for teamwork to develop the new is what James Brian Quinn called "interactive learning."[6]

All of these characteristics make newstream work intense and absorbing. People become absorbed in creative activities more easily than in routine ones. The rhythm of a newstream workplace involves, literally, "going with the flow"—continuing to work as long as the creative juices are flowing, unwilling to stop for fear of losing the almost-formed concept. Curiosity is also aroused by exploring uncharted waters; people get absorbed in seeking what's around still one more bend. When the newstream pursuit is a team effort, the inherent attraction of the work is multiplied by the need and the desire to learn what others are learning.

The concentrated bursts of high energy expended in newstream projects result in a work rhythm hard to fit into the mainstream pattern of predictable days of standard duration with occasional "overtime." "Overtime" has no psychological meaning in a creative effort, since stop-time derives from the task itself, not from an artificial construct like the end of the official workday.

Newstream work rhythms are more likely to show periods of high intensity and long hours followed by lulls. The swings are greater, the peaks higher, and the valleys lower than in the mainstream. At one budding newstream business, the contrast with the mainstream is clear. As one participant said, "For the main company, the seven-hour workday is the norm. It is *not* the norm here. From day one we've put in eight or eight-and-a-half hours or more. People don't have the approach of seven-and-a-half hours and then go home. We don't follow that rule. But other policies are also generous. We haven't run into people-abusing policies. The sick time and vacation time have worked," he concluded, "to compensate for the periods with long workdays." Another manager in another company's newstream program was proud that his venture unit was free from "Corporate Goof-off-itis," an imaginary disease of the headquarters staff, characterized by an 8:15 to 4:45 mentality (and with a 9:30 to 10:00 coffee break and work ceasing at 3:45 on golf days). The long hours at such venture units reflect the intensity of the work. In contrast to the mainstream, "We have a much more highly motivated group here; the levels of excitement, enthusiasm, and motivation are high," one newstream human resource director reported. At Raytheon's New Product Center a team member confided, "Sometimes I have to laugh. I get paid for this. I enjoy it so much . . . It's having all the fun with relatively little effort."

The commitment and drive of innovators can be so great that they have to be almost literally torn away from the work. Bob Bowen, George Freedman's successor at Raytheon's NPC, spoke of having to "shoot the engineer and pry his fingers off a project." An Ohio Bell Enter-Prize winner estimated that she had probably been working more than sixty hours a week for two years developing her idea (doing her forty-hour-a-week job *plus* working out her idea after hours and on weekends) before even bringing it to Enter-Prize.

The intensity of the newstream work style derives not just from individual absorption but also from the need for communication. The "teamwork" requirement for newstreams transcends what is normally meant by that term. Not only do people have to collaborate, they have to be able almost to get into one another's heads. The great minds necessary for newstreams do literally have to run in the same direction. In a sense, the whole team has to become conscious of what each member knows. The science fiction writer Arthur Clarke described the next stage of human evolution as involving "mind-sharing," perhaps a farfetched idea. And yet, the group working together on the act of creation does learn more mundane and practical forms of mind-sharing. In the building of System 75 at AT&T, a state-of-the-art telecommunications system, venture mastermind Alec Feiner built a remarkable number of communication links among the hundred project engineers, using computerized project notebooks for real-time data-sharing in imaginative ways, as well as selecting people whose shared values and willingness to interact would help them understand one another quickly.

Besides selecting for compatibility and encouraging communication, newstream managers may foster knowledge-sharing by organizing to create overlap between what people do. NEES Energy has a lean and flat organization with one job description for everyone, much staff latitude, and a preference for overlap, "to get everybody to work together as a team." Everyone wears several hats and works at about five subprojects at once. Similarly, at Raytheon's New Product Center there are more work stations than engineers because most participants juggle four or five projects at a time. In addition to the ease with which people can share their insights in the loose, informal atmosphere of the NPC, formal weekly brainstorming sessions ensure that everyone is in touch with others' latest thoughts.

For all these reasons, newstream projects are particularly vulnerable to turnover. There are sometimes good reasons, from a project's standpoint, for people to leave: inadequate performance, interpersonal tensions, the wrong skills, stale ideas from having been part of it too long. (Ralph Katz holds that two to five years is the ideal length of service for members of R&D teams.)[7] But every loss and replacement can jeopardize the success of creations.

Each person *leaving* removes knowledge from the pool, knowledge that has not yet been routinized, systematized, or codified, inspiring the fear that he is taking "secrets" with him—private knowledge that has not yet been transferred or built into the product. Each person *entering* deflects the energies and attention of the others from knowledge development to education—transferring the experience base of current staff to avoid reinventing the wheel. Sometimes this is helpful; it causes participants to pull together what they have learned, making it tangible and transferrable in the process. But telling about it is time-consuming, and it is no substitute for having been there. Inevitably, there is another small-scale start-up.

Turnover in power positions can be especially disrupting. Each new boss is a new beginning. Key managers entering in midstream are likely to change course in order to establish their own power, put their own stamp on the project. Or because new management does not understand the enterprise, they make changes that cause interruptions.

A senior executive of a major instruments manufacturing company recalled one of the company's venture failures—a new product start-up in one of the divisions. He had been the venture manager for the first six months. "I think about this often," he said, "because if

I had stayed I think I could have made it work.'' Six months into the project, he was offered a promotion up several levels—from managing fifteen people in the start-up to managing six thousand people in an established division. The career implications were clear: Take it now or lose his place in line. The rewards were also clear: ''The corporation rewarded the person running a stable $200 million business more than someone growing a business from zero to $20 million, which is much, much harder.'' Even so, he remembered, ''I wanted a week to think about it. I felt torn.'' Eventually he took the promotion. Members of the start-up team understood the corporate career message, but they still felt abandoned. The new manager sent in to replace him simply did not have the ''feel'' for what it would take to get his business going. Even more than loss of leadership, it was loss of experience that hurt this project.

Loss of key team members is not the only loss that hurts newstreams. One manager pointed to the importance of continuity in the mainstream's representative to the newstream:

> A lot [of success] has to do with the relationship and the interface between the manager of the line and the manager of the new business. It's like an umbilical cord. You can kill a new business by changing the people it is interfacing with in the [mainstream] organization. If you have just one sponsor for the new business and that sponsor leaves or changes jobs, the new business dies.

This newstream situation thus requires:

- Concentration and focus during the development stage, to capture elusive knowledge fragments.
- Close, team-oriented working relationships with high mutual respect and commitment to joint goals, to encourage rapid and effective exchange of knowledge.
- Stability among the participants in collective creation.

It's a paradox: Creating change requires stability. But established corporations often exacerbate the vulnerabilities of their infant enterprises by the instability, the constant motion, they encourage in and around them. For example:

- Reporting requirements that disrupt project activities and distract participants by asking them to prepare special analyses for upper management or to take on tasks and attend meetings unrelated to advancing the work of creation.

- Assignment of people to groups without regard to their degree of belief in the effort or their compatibility.
- Regular turnover of managers because of a lock-step career system that ties rewards to promotions and thus requires job changes in order to "advance."

HIGH AUTONOMY

Newstreams seek to go their own way. Even when they emerge from mainstream sources and will eventually rejoin the mainstream, newstreams push for their own paths and need the autonomy to do so. Because of the uncertainty factor, newstream projects want independent control over their resources, to move quickly or change course easily when necessary. Because of the intensity factor, newstreams want to develop their own rituals and identity, to build the high levels of commitment and communication they need. Of course, because the newstream rhythm is so different from that of the mainstream, many mainstream practices do not fit newstream needs anyway. Furthermore, part of the point of generating a newstream is to provide the opportunity for a fresh perspective or a fresh start. So newstream project leaders often want to go outside the company to find ideas, staff, and services.

The first sign of autonomy, for newstream participants, is a separate place dedicated to nothing but newstream experimentation. Managers at one new venture unit insist that the only way they had any chance to develop their countercyclical business was to have their own building and create a new culture from scratch. Certainly their building could not be more distinctive. Their offices are more cluttered and less opulent than corporate headquarters. The restroom is used for storage, as is the conference room; boxes are piled high. One senses the atmosphere is characterized by urgency and a sense of mission, compared to the trappings of specific position within the hierarchy seen in other officers' spaces. Similarly, Elena Prokupets of Kodak's Edicon believes in the importance of her venture's having its own building. From the beginning, Edicon was in its own place, in the downtown area of Rochester separated from both mainstream Kodak and the other newstream ventures. There were a snack bar and a shower on the premises; employees didn't have to leave even to eat or wash up—a virtue in light of newstream intensity and team communication. "That gave us a sense of standing on our own," Elena recalled. When Edicon grew and she moved its operations to a modern glass building (of the type common in high-tech areas like Silicon Valley but unusual for Rochester), she had to convince Kodak management that the morale benefits balanced the expense.

The term "skunkworks" has been popularized to refer to the places where newstreams begin. The word comes from a Li'l Abner cartoon, was adopted by Lockheed, and was spread by *In Search of Excellence*.[8] Ken Stahl at Xerox grabbed the imagery, developing an array of hats, signs, and puns from the notion of skunks to promote his new idea unit. In more reserved language, others have provided similar analogies. Jay Galbraith used the term "reservations"— havens for "safe learning" managed by a full-time sponsor. Reservations can be internal or external, permanent or temporary. Galbraith found that some innovations were perfected at a remote site before being discovered by management; thus "the odds [for innovation] are better if early efforts to perfect and test new 'crazy' ideas are differentiated—that is, separated—from the . . . operating organization."[9]

Overall, high-innovation companies in the United States, Europe, and Japan tend to be characterized by flatter organizations, smaller operating divisions, and smaller projects. Typically, small teams of engineers, technicians, designers, and model makers are placed together in units dedicated to the new venture with no intervening organizational or physical barriers to developing the idea to the prototype stage.[10] Even in Japanese organizations widely (and often incorrectly) supposed to have elaborate (and slow) consensus-building processes, innovation projects are given autonomy; top managers—for example, for many years the founder of Honda—often work directly on projects with young engineers. This approach eliminates bureaucracy, allows fast and unfettered communication, enables rapid turnaround time for experiments, and instills a high level of group loyalty and identity by maximizing communication and commitment among team members.

Even more important than separation of place is separation of style and procedures. "We ignore all the rules," one newstream manager said. "We're allowed to get away with a lot. We hardly ever write memos here. Procedures still get in the way of the mission of the venture." Said another:

I don't get a whole lot of direct feedback [from corporate]. There is very little or no involvement. I consider us to be an outside organization. We don't have as much synergy as we could have. Most of the people we hire come from outside the organization. Unfortunately we don't have the same corporate structure. There are rules and procedures we don't know about and unfortunately it causes problems. It sometimes means that we can't take advantage of certain aspects of the system because we don't know about them.

Newstream style is reflected well in Raytheon's New Product Center. The staff at the center is described by others at the corporation as often nonconformist; people who don't like to work normal hours or necessarily follow procedures; difficult to manage for the above reasons; generalists, and extremely versatile. "They're a freewheeling group, they are not constrained," says John Baronofsky, director of Raytheon Laser Products. Another manager commented:

Now you have to understand that for a company like Raytheon to have an NPC, given the style and operation of the company, is an interesting concept. It's not like R&D. I worked in R&D for four years. It's independent, but R&D is done on a very structured P&L [basis]. It's break-even, with the funding from the government and the corporation. But the research is defined things to work on—that's the normal nature of the Raytheon beast. The NPC is allowed to freelance. That's not normal . . . The NPC has more freedom than other departments/ divisions, and will work on off-the-wall things, for fun. They develop a lot of ideas, and have access to expertise. . . . [The relationships between NPC and appliance divisions] are informal; they have to be. If they were structured, like R&D, they would become constrained. You don't have the free thinking [in R&D]. The NPC is unstructured compared to the rest of Raytheon—they have looser goals.

The push for newstream autonomy shows up most sharply in the desire of venture participants to ignore or avoid the use of corporate procedures and services. For example:

There is some conflict with the purchasing department. They always did the negotiations before, but they are not geared up for what we need. They can't negotiate the way we need to. They always rely on the name, the ability to draw bids. So, we're infringing on their territory, and there is always some conflict. But for us to be profitable, we must have control over purchasing equipment, determining which contractor to use. We have to have tight control. That is still an unresolved issue, one we have to work out in the system of checks and balances, the process of evolution. They have gotten more used to us, and we have gotten used to them, but sometimes things drag the mud up again. . . . We can get better prices because we can pay faster [than corporate].

At another company, a newstream engineer explained his negativity toward corporate services by an example of the slow-moving personnel department and corporation-wide policies. He described a venture ''star'' who wanted to take a graduate course that met during working hours. Corporate policy states that missing work for a course is prohibited. The manager hesitated to give his blessing for fear that ''we would step on toes.'' While he looked for a solution, the ''star'' received a job offer from a competitor, with the chance to take the course. ''Two days later we got him back,'' the manager said, ''on his terms.''

Newstream managers tend to think that their autonomy is necessary to move with speed; they are equally convinced that the mainstream is too large, cumbersome, and bureaucratic, and that working through mainstream systems would just slow them down. They also believe, like most entrepreneurs, that in a newstream venture one must know one's particular technology or customers to be effective, whereas the mainstream businesses are routinized enough to make it possible for managers to be more interchangeable. One new venture leader expressed concern about what would happen if the newstream business were incorporated into the mainstream organization:

We just got a multimillion-dollar order, and we need to ship a large quantity in a short time. It is not just technical knowledge that accounts for success; we have to have inventory control in place, the proper shipments going out, the right equipment, systems test and systems integration. Our parent has an extremely large organization, and all those parts could be lost in a large organization. When you need to do it in one to two days, it would be impossible. If they move us back [to a mainstream division] they should at least leave us as a separate line of business where we can continue to create the same type of at-mosphere. . . . Yet I would be exposed more and more to the corporate bureaucracy. . . . For instance, for similar product complexities, our parent has two hundred people and we have thirty people. With two hundred people, they are always behind schedule, and they have lots of problems.

The newstream situation thus requires:

- Identifiable, and perhaps separate, physical space for newstream activities, and acceptance of a distinctive newstream culture.
- Design of its own systems and procedures.
- Freedom to use or ignore mainstream services, depending on newstream needs.

But mainstream pressures can reduce newstream autonomy if they include:

- Confusion of newstream and mainstream territories.
- Uniformity requirements—requiring that all activities in the company use the same systems and procedure and be subject to the same controls. Sometimes this is a legal requirement (for example, conformity to equal opportunity rules in hiring), but sometimes it is simply a corporate preference.
- Insistence that newstream projects go through mainstream channels, such as hiring internally or using internal corporate services.

As companies pursue newstreams, then, they face a dangerous balancing act. Newstreams try to slip out from under mainstream discipline, but mainstream requirements can cause newstreams to dry up.

TENSION BETWEEN THE STREAMS

Many examples of well-known corporate venture failures make the mainstream-newstream tension clear. Hollister Sykes, venture manager for now-defunct Exxon Enterprises, performed an autopsy on the effort to move Exxon into high-tech businesses.[11] He attributed most of the problems to mainstream interference. The still-developing ventures were solidified into a corporate division before they were ready and then subjected to standard and highly inappropriate corporate controls. But the business was not well understood by the mainstream strategists, who allocated enormous R&D expenditures to develop projects for an illusory and rapidly changing market. Compensation policies pegged salaries to the size of the activity (small by Exxon standards) and denied equity participation. People were recruited from outside Exxon; no one inside was assumed to have relevant experience because of differences in the businesses, but then these outsiders questioned Exxon's commitment because of the poor pay and corporate controls.

The tensions between the newstream quest for autonomy and the mainstream push for control creates a difference in what makes each powerful. *Power* means different things for mainstream and newstream. Mainstream activities gain power in proportion to their size, the resources dedicated to them, and their strategic significance. The more important they are, the more successful they are likely to be, because of all of the dynamics associated with important activities—attention, visibility, wealth, pressure to succeed. Importance helps maintain mainstream momentum.

But for newstreams, "importance" is likely to reduce rather than increase effectiveness. Among the companies my research group examined in depth there was a considerable range in the dimension of importance: in resource allocation, from a few thousand dollars to develop an idea to several million dollars to develop a stand-alone venture; and in strategic centrality, from peripheral ideas with no consequence if they failed to major quests to find technology or fill market gaps to implement strategic objectives.

The "less important" entrepreneurial vehicles, by and large, performed better than the "more important," in terms of return on investment and fulfilled expectations, if we measure importance in terms of resource allocations and strategic centrality. The success stories in which the returns are greatest proportionally involve modest size and limited power. Kodak's new opportunity process involved less than one percent of total corporate investment, and one of the criteria for business plans that made it to the new venture stage was that the new business not be critical for Kodak's success, or vice versa. Yet at least one venture already looks like a promising new source of revenue for the mainstream business. Teleflex's venture fund was proportionally more important but still modest; resources consumed were just one-half of one percent of sales. Still, CEO Black considers 80 percent of Teleflex's current product line to be a direct result of New Venture Fund investment. One major NVF "win" is a product expected to bring in millions a year in revenue, paying back its development cost out of the first year's profits and providing a toehold in a major new market. By these measures, Raytheon's New Products Center was the least "important" of all: only thirty-five people (in a company of seventy-five thousand), and a yearly budget of less than one two-thousandth of the company's revenues. But this barely discernible drop in the bucket has produced $100 million in incremental sales from a total investment of only $25 million in the NPC.

In contrast, those situations in which the company sank *large* amounts into newstreams because of the strategic significance of the development of new ideas or technology were much less successful. "Barton Machines," a company with about $400 million in sales in 1986, invested $40 million in a portfolio of ventures with a 1987 market value of $29 million, writing off $7 million. Another high-tech company in my study, similarly, identifies strategically significant new ventures and funds them well, while weakly supporting a few smaller, more peripheral ideas. The project most closely tied to the strategic goals of the firm gets the most attention from top management, the most "proven" managers (usually of mainstream businesses), and a continuous infusion of resources. People watching this believe that top management won't let it fail; one critic feels that this safety net means that the project will, in fact, never succeed, because the venture manager lacks the resourcefulness that living on the edge provides, and excessive corporate attention limits experimentation. But the venture that easily turned into a viable business was the "victim" of modest resources and corporate neglect. Recently, that firm's newstream commitment was reviewed and reformulated because of marginal returns compared to expectations.

In case after case, the difference between the typical organizational style required for the creation of new ventures and the more bureaucratic patterns defining established activities leads to predictable tensions—a clash of newstream and mainstream cultures.

"My greatest satisfaction is that we've survived. The new product purveyor works in a hostile world," commented George Freedman, former director of Raytheon's NPC. Newstream creators complain that the rest of the organization doesn't understand them, doesn't cooperate, moves too slowly, stifles their initiative, encumbers them with unnecessary and overly costly procedures, and charges them for services or benefits they would rather not receive. As one new venture general manager put it:

> We get *zero* support from main-line people. Let's take the computer system. I went to their computer people and said that I need XYZ. They wanted to begin a three-month analysis, select a site to test the product, and then evaluate the results. Then and only then would they be ready to select a computer and software. On the other hand, I wanted the computer in the next day. Finally I realized that I had to make the decision myself. Their attitude seemed to be, "Go ahead because we know that you will fail." This was also true in product development and market research.
>
> All the venture people have the same reaction. In fact there is a Venture Management Survival Guide we circulate. Venture people all say: "Stay away from mainstream purchasing and finance." In the corporate purchasing system, one places an order, and nothing happens. We stay away from most of their systems and build our own.

The mainstream managers, in turn, complain that the newstream contingent is given privileges and rewards they don't yet deserve. For example, managers of established activities are locked into corporate compensation policies that compare poorly (in promise, at least) to the opportunity to "get rich" represented by ventures. The head of a major division in a high-tech company pointed out that a counterpart who moved into a new venture within that company is now making close to three times what the division head earns—in a business with much lower revenues.

The venture team's freedom is envied by those managing the routine operations—their freedom from corporate constraints, freedom to spend money as they choose, freedom to create a culture along with a product or business. One established division head was concerned about the morale problem he faced whenever his people visited the new ventures, because of a variety of tangible discrepancies:

> One venture has an inside gym and beer on tap twenty-four hours a day. Another has free meals for the employees and Nautilus equipment; it's a country club. Those guys are funded to the hilt, and no matter how badly they do, they are going to make a lot of money. I send people out there and they come back wondering, "Why am I spending my career here?" Those guys are going to make a lot of money and don't have to deal with a lot of corporate restraints.

A New England Electric mainstream manager spoke about his envy of a newstream executive: "I'm jealous of George Sakellaris because he has a fun company to play with."

Internal entrepreneurs argue, however, that any "privileges" they get are more than paid for by the risks they are taking by leaving the safety of the mainstream, by the dangers they face from living on the edge where there is no job awaiting them if they fail, and by the extraordinary efforts required to nurture new ideas to the point where the product is ready or the business is established or the system is up and running. Although participants in corporate ventures are risking little or none of their own capital (sometimes they "invest" part of their salary), they are potentially jeopardizing their careers. One new venture head wanted to feel that his counterparts in the established businesses could understand this:

> I would say that the overall attitude of my peers is that I'm doing something interesting and exciting; I'm doing something creative. I imagine that they see the pluses and minuses. Certainly the good part is the freedom. On the downside, I expect they think of all the risks; there is no safety net. If the venture fails, we don't have a job to return to. Of course, I believe that there is no security in large corporations anymore. But some people need to think that they have security even if they don't. Even though there is no security in large corporations, people are buffered from the environment. They work toward objectives, meet them, and then go out and party once the goals have been met. The struggle is over. People in the large corporation are so insulated. They have no idea what it is to survive. Within a start-up like ours, the struggle is never over. Every day is a new war. That's the reality.

Newstream participants suspect that the real reason mainstream managers get upset with them is that the newstream people, precisely because they are heading out on their own without a safety net, lack identification with and loyalty to their corporate parent.

The sponsors of newstream programs are often aware of this tension between the streams, and they make sure they link them. Alcan, for example, wants to minimize the differences between mainstream and newstream buinesses. As Chairman David Morton insists, "This is one enterprise, not an enterprise divided into two parts. We are all in the same business, and innovation is everyone's business." Thus, Timothy Tuff, leader of new business development, brings many mainstream managers into the newstream development process. Each new venture is planned by a project team consisting of Tuff and his staff along with mainstream managers who remain in their jobs while contributing to an in-depth study of the venture. One of these managers eventually becomes the venture head. Then, each new business has a small review board consisting of relevant mainstream staff—perhaps legal, financial, and technical. In Tuff's mind, such board members serve not to constrain the venture but to help give it independence:

> We want to have minimum reporting requirements for the new business. The best people suited for that are the gamekeepers turned poachers. The people responsible for protecting the corporate financial integrity are also best at keeping the corporation off the backs of the small business. They can see what's going on and keep the corporation at bay.

The management of the newstream channel, then, needs to be connected to powerful sponsors in the mainstream organization, and it also helps to have mainstream sponsors and supporters for each individual newstream project. Raytheon's New Product Center, for example, established a manager of Product Transfer in direct response to the problems of communication between NPC and the mainstream businesses; his job was to find a mainstream champion for each new product.

Multiple links between newstream and mainstream both enhance the mainstream's perception of benefits and serve as a form of protection for newstreams. Newstreams need this protection because the discrepancies between start-up conditions and management of established activities lead to pulls and tugs on the newstream effort. Managers of the newstream channel, like Tuff at Alcan or Tuite at Kodak, have to mediate and interpret mainstream-to-newstream and newstream-to-mainstream communication. The innovators try to pull their projects farther away from the corporate parents, in systems and procedures if not in physical distance, while the rest of the organization tries to pull them closer by foisting more and more corporate standards and requirements on the venture as it develops. The more strategically important the venture to the parent company, the more it will be visited, scrutinized, and encumbered with help, because the parent cannot afford to let it fail. This help comes with a stiff price tag in requirements for conformity, a price that often is too much for the venture to bear. But still, autonomy must be balanced by accountability. There is a middle ground between the one extreme of so many reporting requirements that, for example, the project group spends more of its time preparing reports than doing the work, and the other extreme of no controls or measures until the end.

If some innovation projects fail because they are *overly constrained* by the need to follow bureaucratic rules and seek constant approvals, others may fail because they are *overfunded and undermanaged* by top leaders, which can remove the incentive to produce results efficiently. Lotte Bailyn learned from her studies of R&D labs that many engineers were subject to overly constraining operational controls while permitted too much "strategic autonomy" to set their own research goals—just the opposite of the combination needed for success.[12]

This can be a particular problem in large new ventures. In one case in a leading corporation, top management generously funded a new venture development effort and then left it alone, assuming that they had done the right thing by providing abundant resources. Because the project was so rich, the team wasted money on dead ends and intriguing but unnecessary flourishes and failed to replan when early results were disappointing. The team did not need to justify their actions to anyone, and the project eventually failed. This is one reason Howard Stevenson and David Gumpert argue that successful entrepreneurship involves *multistage commitments*—smaller amounts of money at more frequent intervals.[13] There is nothing like hunger to motivate the team to clear the next hurdle quickly.

The price paid for project autonomy is to wind up so small or so peripheral that the results are trivial for the company—the benefits are seen as not worth managerial time even if the financial resources consumed are small. If even successful projects are too detached from the mainstream, then the very channel for newstreams is endangered. In the fall of 1988 Colgate-Palmolive closed its Colgate Venture Company, a unit established four years earlier as a conduit for new ideas, despite the profitability of some ventures that had rescued failing products; Gillette, Clorox, and S. C. Johnson (Johnson Wax) also terminated venture subsidiaries. The Colgate unit, on which the company had spent about $10 million and which contributed less than one percent of revenues, was seen as too trivial and too remote from the innovation needs of mainstream businesses for a $5 billion company. Similarly, Kodak's system for growing new small businesses is endangered because it is seen by some managers as no longer necessary once the huge, core film business is turned around.

The key to survival of small newstream units, then, is to demonstrate value to the mainstream. Over time, Raytheon's New Product Center, for example, has strengthened relationships with its mainstream clients; after Bob Bowen took the helm from George Freedman, he increased the interaction between all levels of NPC people and staff in the mainstream businesses, and he instituted a series of visits to facilities all over the country. Comparable reasoning led Teleflex to move leadership of its New Venture Fund from the CEO to the heads of its operating divisions.

Even geography represents a corporate balancing act. If the embryonic venture is situated too close to the parent organization, its distinctive style may arouse those engaged in established activities against it. This political pressure deflects important attention from the creation process itself. But if it is separated by too much distance, the opportunity is lost to develop mutual understanding and eventually join the two streams when the new venture is established.

To ensure a successful newstream effort, top management needs to set the context by defining goals to which potential innovators can aspire, allocating resources for experimentation, and then reintegrating the new venture into the mainstream establishment.[14] Integration and connection are key ingredients for both the first stage and the last stage of newstream development—to stimulate creativity (which benefits from multiple stimuli and cross-area cross-fertilization) and to transfer the results of the development effort into an ongoing business stream. It is only during the development stage itself that the newstream needs to go its own way, separated from mainstream pressures, and allowed to concentrate on learning and without interruption. The managers of the newstream channel, the venture unit, are playing an organizational accordion; they need to open wide to find the many sources of new ideas, close briefly to protect the chosen projects while they take shape, and then open fully again when the start-up takes hold to reconnect the venture to the ongoing businesses.

DIFFERENT STROKES FOR DIFFERENT STREAMS

In the past many large corporations could avoid dealing with these tensions because newstream projects tended to be either unusual efforts undertaken with the special blessing of the top—and therefore granted privileges and immunities—or peripheral activities occurring in hidden corners. But now that entrepreneurship occupies center stage and corporations actively encourage and fund new idea projects, companies must operate in two modes simultaneously—and manage the balancing act caused by the inevitable contrasts and comparisons.

The era in which corporations could operate by the pretense of a single management system for everything is over. Playing in the global Olympics, corporations cannot succeed by valuing uniform treatment over flexibility, adherence to procedures over fast action, and rules over results. Instead, they must recognize that the ability to invest in new opportunities means letting internal enterprises go their own ways. Tailoring the organization style to the business stage will be a necessity for any corporation trying to succeed through post-entrepreneurial strategies.

Changes in the business environment, coupled with the desire of more people for self-expression,[15] mean that, increasingly, companies present people with the opportunity to swim in both newstreams and mainstreams. For example:

- Some people will work simultaneously in both mainstream and newstream projects, holding down a "regular" job while spending some time on a creative task.
- Some people will work sequentially in both streams, moving from established division to start-up and back.
- Managers may coordinate projects in both streams, like the general manager of a television station who juggles the demands and jealousies of the creative program developers and the mainstream administrators.
- Still others may work within the mainstream (which shapes the condition of work) to encourage the beginning of newstreams, like the corporate staff for Kodak's Offices of Innovation or for Barton Machine Enterprises, who act as links between streams.
- And others in the mainstream business will receive the hand-off from entrepreneurs, for example, managing the commercialization of a new product or the integration of a new technology.

In all these cases, effectiveness and success come from understanding the logic of each stream and developing the strokes appropriate for each. The successful post-entrepreneurial manager will be adept at both styles, switching strokes to fit the situation.

TOWARD SWIMMING FREESTYLE

For corporations, the ultimate impact of swimming in both streams comes from teaching more people the freestyle of the entrepreneur. Encouraging newstreams helps companies capture *ideas* but loosens their hold on *people*. Newstreams loosen traditional hierarchial authority, loosen respect for bureaucracy, loosen corporate identification, and loosen career dependence.

First, newstream activity is one more blow to the authority of position and office. Newstream entrepreneurs gain credibility from the power of their ideas, not the power of their offices. Overnight, for example, an obscure middle manager at Ohio Bell can be transformed into a heroic Enter-Prize winner and then a team leader and maybe even a venture president, simply because of an idea. The opportunity for challenge, advancement, and money are not tied to a boss or to a pecking order, but to oneself.

Second, when newstream ideas win freedom from conventional systems and exemption from traditional controls, they raise questions about the logic of requiring these for any activity. If a new corporate venture can do its own purchasing, why should it be required to use the corporate system once it is established? Its success in making this argument paves the way for other established mainstream activities to chart their own course.

Third, newstream projects build commitment and capture extraordinary human energy because of the tasks themselves: highly involving, highly compelling. The lure of the newstream's post-entrepreneurial workplace comes from passion about the idea, the pleasure of creation, and a feeling of personal achievement. But very strong identification with the *project* and close team spirit undermine *corporate* identification. People are not working long hours at an intense pace for Company *X* but for the venture itself. This point is particularly ironic, because the motivation behind some internal venture processes, like that at Tektronix, is to keep good people who would otherwise leave with their ideas. As the experience of several companies illustrates, those same people are now tied to the company only by newstream opportunities and may leave once the venture is established.

Fourth, newstream work weakens people's dependence on mainstream corporate participation in order to have a career. In some cases, compensation for newstream participants is more closely tied to their own and their team's efforts, because of special reward schemes. (Sometimes, newstream participants can be paid well even if the rest of the company does poorly.) Newstream participants see that they are capable of determining their own fates; for some people, this is a change from how they saw themselves while floating along in the mainstream. Their belief in themselves is enhanced, as is their belief in the power of their own ideas. Because of the knowledge that they can create new value, that they can make new things happen, they are more secure in themselves—and more likely to be willing to strike out on their own.

The existence of newstreams creates new distinctions between organizational classes. The "haves" are the people with the freedom to pursue their ideas; the "have-nots" are those people, at "high" as well as "low" levels, stuck with the dictates of established procedures.

It is not clear what mainstream life has to offer the newstream manager, at least in very large corporations that rate managerial status by size criteria (for example, number of staff, revenue base) rather than by the magnitude of accomplishment (for example, creating something from nothing). Most venture managers in the companies I studied would re-enter the mainstream at middle management levels where they would be buried in the middle of a hierarchy after having been at the top of a discernible entity. The ones whose ventures are successful are aware of the status and money they could have gained if they were in a position to take their venture public, instead of having its fate determined by a corporate parent with modest reward to them. One newstream manager mused:

> I am in the middle of my life, and I don't know that the parent corporation offers me that much. I don't think top management is very clear about what they are going to do with me if they reintegrate the venture into the main business. I wouldn't mind making a career here at some corporate level. But is it going to be offered to me? They decided that a venture manager could not go above a certain level in the salary grade. They already put certain restrictions on you so that regardless of how successful I am as a venture manager, I cannot jump ahead of my level, which is unfair and kind of stupid. It precludes your career and your ability to move ahead.

For people whose newstream participation is a welcome and rewarded supplement to their mainstream job, as at Ohio Bell, this is not a problem. For some managers involved more fully in new business start-ups, it creates considerable concern. One company has begun to open a career path for venture managers by moving them from venture to venture; whether this will be sufficient to hold people remains to be proven.

Earlier, I delineated the circumstances under which mainstreams cause newstreams to dry up. But it is clear that newstreams also have an influence on the mainstream business, an influence above and beyond any success in generating new sources of revenue. When newstreams exist beside mainstreams, and when corporate citizens swim in both directions, then the creative boat-rocking spirit of the newstream spills over to infect the mainstream. Unleashing the power of innovation is one more step toward loosening the power of corporate hierarchy and building the post-entrepreneurial corporation.

PART THREE

JOBS, MONEY, PEOPLE:

Consequences of the Post-Entrepreneurial Revolution

CHAPTER 9

From Status to Contribution: The Changing Basis for Pay

*T*he foundations of the traditional corporate hierarchy are rapidly crumbling. Nowhere is this felt more acutely than in the attack on pay.

- In the wake of the turmoil caused by restructuring, middle managers in a company's most profitable division no longer believe that rewards for their contributions will ultimately come with promotions to higher-paid jobs. They want more money now, in the form of bonuses usually given only at higher levels . . . or maybe they should join their bosses in considering a leveraged buy-out.
- As a major company pushes for teamwork and synergy across functions and across product divisions, employees privately wonder why they should bother when all the rewards go to individuals.
- A strategic alliance puts groups of professionals from two partner companies on a high-stakes joint development team. They are doing exactly the same work, using virtually identical skills, but because of differences in partner company size and where their professionals are positioned in the hierarchy, one group's average salary is significantly

lower than the other group's; discovery of this jeopardizes their willingness to contribute fully to the effort.

- In exchange for wage concessions, a manufacturer offers employees an ownership stake. Employee representatives begin to think about total company profitability and start asking why so many staff groups are on the payroll and why they are paid so much.
- To control costs and stimulate improvements, a leading financial services company converts its information systems department into a venture selling to customers both inside and outside the corporation. In its first year, the venture runs at a big profit, and department professionals begin to wonder why they can't get a chunk of the profits they have generated instead of just a fixed salary defined by rank. Or maybe they should leave to start their own firm.

In light of these challenges, old ideas about pay are bankrupt. The post-entrepreneurial agenda—whether synergies or partnerships or newstreams—cannot be accomplished without rethinking matters of money. Innovations in compensation are necessary to succeed at the doing-more-with-less balancing act: simultaneously reducing obligations and stretching capacities, lowering fixed costs and encouraging new ideas. In the post-entrepreneurial corporation, pay must more nearly match contribution.

Status, not contribution, was the traditional basis for the numbers on people's paychecks. The paycheck was a critical element in reinforcing corpocracy. Pay was cemented to hierarchical position, guaranteed regardless of performance. But this system does not square well with the new business realities. It burdens the company with weighty fixed obligations while failing to encourage or reward entrepreneurial behavior.

Who gets the money is one of those controversial questions largely avoided until debates about the competitiveness of American industry brought it out of the closet. The importance of money is not absolute but relative; it often lies not in the amount but in how the amount was arrived at. Money represents both tangible value and a signal of importance.

THE TRADITIONAL SHAPE OF THE PAYCHECK

Every year, several billion paychecks are distributed to Americans in all walks of life, paychecks that ostensibly reflect the "worth" of the work performed by the person named on the check. Ostensibly is the right word. Figuring out how much someone is "worth" has never been a very accurate process.

Traditional corporate pay scales have reflected, largely, such estimated characteristics of jobs as decision-making responsibility, importance to the organization, and number of subordinates. People's pay has been largely a function of the social and organizational positions they occupy. Status was the basis—the standing of a job in the hierarchy of organizational relations. In traditional compensation plans, each job came with an assigned pay level, relatively fixed regardless of how well the job was performed or the real value that performance produced for the organization. If there was a "merit" component, it was usually very small. The surest way—often the only way—to increase the paycheck was to change employers or get promoted. An enormous mountain of systems, traditions, and industrial relations practice was developed to support the fairness of this way of calculating pay.

Traditional pay scales are customarily rationalized by asserting that "the market" ultimately determines pay, just as it supposedly determines the price of everything else that businesses or individual consumers wish to acquire. And many people like, therefore, to deny any fundamental legitimacy to concerns that compensation systems are unfair or inappropriate, that they are capable of "causing" anything, since they are not causes at all, but outcomes. But in fact, precisely because of the fundamental difficulty of directly linking people's compensation to their contribution, all the market really does is reasonably assume that people occupying equal positions tend to be paid equally, and that people with similar experience and education tend to be "worth" the same. And where any given category of job-holder is in shorter (or greater) supply than demand, those prices go up (or down). In the macroeconomic sense, the market "works," but the basis for anchoring pay scales to the actual value of the contributions they reflect is extremely weak. Thus, in the microeconomic sense, the process is circular. We "know" what people are "worth" because in a market that's what they cost; but we also "know" that what people cost in a market is just what they're "worth."

It is therefore not hard to see why achievement-oriented managers looking to competition in the corporate Olympics attack this traditional system as a manifestation of the "paternalistic" benefits offered across the board by Father Corporation. "We've got corporate socialism, not corporate capitalism," charged the head of new ventures for one of the companies I studied. "Everybody gets paid because of rank, despite what they contribute. Is that the American way? We are so focused on consistent treatment internally—no, really, it is homogeneity—that we destroy enterprise in the process."

Traditional pay systems are increasingly less viable or supportable. Economic, social, and organizational changes are bringing the fundamental bases for determining pay under attack. This attack is not theoretical, either. Far from it. Rather, it is literally embodied—thought not always recognized—in the ways post-entrepreneurial companies are already changing their compensation practices.

America is, in fact, already well on its way to transforming the meaning of the paycheck, and some argue that it is none to soon if we are to remain competitive in world markets. Although popular attention has focused on comparable worth—equalizing pay for those doing jobs of comparable value—the most important trend in pay determination has actually been the loosening relationship between job assignment and pay level.

Comparable worth is, however, a highly visible tip of the iceberg in the pay revolution, because it brings to public view a difficult, tension-laden issue: How is pay determined in the first place? The notion of "comparable" worth is obviously dependent on an adequate definition of "worth." And despite the skepticism that greeted the first proponents of comparable worth, major employing organizations are rethinking the meaning of worth itself. And as they are doing so, they are gradually changing the basis for determining pay from *position* to *performance*, from *status* to *contribution*.

This change, which has far-reaching, even revolutionary consequences, is being driven by four separate but closely related do-more-with-less concerns; first, *cost,* the concern that the present system is too expensive for companies that must conserve resources to be competitive; second, *equity,* the concern that the present system is not fair; third, *productivity,* the concern that the present system is insufficient to motivate high performance; and fourth, *entrepreneurial pressure,* the concern that the present system does not adequately reward people for creating new sources of business. In short, pay systems are under attack for neither being cost-effective nor motivating people to do more.

How well do companies now reward contribution? Let's look at merit pay, a conservative and woefully inadequate response to the new demands on the paycheck.

THE MERIT PAY MIASMA

Merit pay is the first logical step in figuring out how to make pay reflect contribution rather than status. It is also the most common "new" pay principle in American organizations, generally the first one adopted when compensation systems are "modernized" to favor the better performers. General Motors made headlines in 1985 when it moved 15,000 employees from twelve divisions to a merit pay system. In 1986 110,000 additional personnel moved to the merit pay plan; at this point GM abandoned the automatic cost-of-living adjustment it had pioneered decades earlier. So did the federal government when it moved the Civil Service to a modest merit system.

The idea is simple. People are paid a base salary defined by the ranking of their job in the overall salary structure—how much the organization feels it must pay to get someone to do that job, with some adjustments for internal equity, to ensure that comparable jobs have similar positions in the structure. Then, increases to base pay—the annual or semiannual "raises"—are determined by judgments about performance and contributions. Increases are calculated as a percentage of base pay.

Merit pay is an essentially conservative approach to the compensation problem. It accepts—indeed, builds on and thus preserves—the status and category distinctions already defined by the organization, the distinctions that determine base pay. In its most common form, it retains—even enhances—the power of superiors over subordinates, as they dole out raises based on their own judgment of contribution. In its individualistic bias, merit pay is also consistent with traditional corporate ideology, which holds the individual alone responsible for his or her fate. It is also one of those apparently good ideas that doesn't really work as intended.

Can anyone be against the idea that people's pay should reflect their performance? Isn't that how the system is supposed to work now? Most Americans share the assumption that pay should reflect worth, and pay increases should be based primarily on performance. Social psychologists have devoted considerable energy to studying the values people hold with respect to the distribution of rewards, and "merit" or performance emerges again and again as number one. The "equity" principle that people should get what they "deserve" based on their contributions wins out over competing principles like "equality"—to each the same. There is a strongly held belief that performance-based reward not only is fairer, but also encourages higher levels of productivity, as people learn that they will get back more if they put more in.[1]

In a typical study, John Fossum of the University of Minnesota involved three groups in making hypothetical decisions about pay increases: college students, line managers, and compensation managers. All three groups agreed that by far the largest consideration should be given to performance—over such other plausible criteria as cost of living, difficulties in replacing someone who leaves, seniority, and organizational budget constraints.[2]

Corporate belief in the importance of individual performance as a determinant of pay increase was documented in a 1981 Conference Board survey of 491 companies. Almost 95 percent of the companies surveyed rated it the most important factor in determining managerial and executive pay increases, and practically 90 percent said it was the most important factor in pay raises for other salaried employees. The next factor, internal equity, was a far-distant second. Moreover, 63 percent of the CEOs surveyed by another research firm said that their pay policies were designed to reinforce highly prized corporate values, especially contribution.[3]

But employees—just as consistently—fail to believe that their pay is indeed based on their performance. In Opinion Research Corporation's longitudinal data bank are the responses of more than 250,000 employees across job categories. From 1970 to 1988, the majority of employees saw little connection between effort and subsequent pay raises.[4] The reasons for this become clear when the *idea* of pay for performance is compared with the reality.

The primary criticisms of merit pay revolve around what are really the only two essential issues in pay: the amount and how it is determined. "Merit pay plans for salaried employees have been facing ongoing challenges during the past four years, which have led many to question their practical value," remarked Bruce Overton, compensation director for R. J. Reynolds. "While conceptually sound, merit pay plans have, in practice, produced little distinction for pay increase amounts based on merit or performance. Moreover, many managers continue to have difficulty making the performance distinctions required in merit pay plans.''

Many merit pay systems involve raises that are simply too small, the complaint goes, to make a difference. In times of high inflation, for example, a 5 percent merit increase can hardly appear meaningful to recipients as an extra reward for their contributions. Estimates of the threshold for a "meaningful" increment range from 10 to 15 percent. One compensation professional, formerly with Pillsbury, pushed strongly for making the entire profit-sharing pool of up to 25 percent of salary performance-based, thereby enlarging the merit increase for the best employees. Pillsbury was "still studying" his proposal two years later.

Some companies engage in a little fine-tuning to try to make small increases appear larger—for example, offering the option of lump sum payments of raises. Aetna, B. F. Goodrich, Timex, and Westinghouse are among them. "They want to make salary increases more flexible and visible," pay expert Edward Lawler commented, "and at the same time, communicate to their employees that they are willing to do innovative things in pay administration."[5] Well, it's a big step.

The determination of merit pay is another sore spot. To make the system fair in the eyes of employees who stand to receive very different treatment, the link between pay and performance has to be clearly established. But for a large number of jobs, this determination is difficult or requires an elaborate and costly process. In a recently implemented Bank of America merit pay system, for example, there are many human and computer monitors of performance. To rate thirty-five hundred employees in the credit card division on twenty specific criteria, the division spends $1 million a year and employs twenty people just to handle the measures. Supervisors listen in on ten randomly chosen calls a week to customer service reps, and outside consultants pose as customers, rating the responses. This might be objective, but to employees it can feel repressive.

Because the price of monitoring and measuring can be so high, many organizations rely instead on the ratings of supervisors in a subjective performance appraisal process with dubious reliability. Far from freeing the energies of employees to seek ways to improve their performance, subjectively based merit pay systems throw them back on the mercy of their bosses. Their earnings depend on the opinions of hierarchical "superiors" about their performance rather than on a more direct assessment of contribution. There is thus, not surprisingly, a fair amount of cynicism about the favoritism and potential for abuse in such a paternalistic practice. For these reasons, several unions are on record in opposition to merit pay, including the one representing employees of Consumers Union, publishers of *Consumer Reports*.

This kind of dependence can make people feel uncomfortable and resentful. Even the most officially powerless among them can retaliate against bosses they resent—by everything from work slowdowns and foot-dragging to outright sabotage—in one case, workers poured motor oil into the lunch pail of a disliked plant supervisor. Bosses soon get the message. Needing everyone's cooperation, they tend to fall back on treating everyone alike in order to avoid the discomfort of defending differential treatment. So it is common in American companies to see supervisors trying to give all their subordinates high ratings so they will "look good" as managers and buy employee cooperation. Companies have had to force "grading on a curve" in order to get any differentiation.

One can easily see how this practice comes full circle. If bosses tend to give everyone average treatment, then the average amount of the merit increase goes down, and the meaning of "merit" is diluted. Criticism two slides right back into criticism one.

Jerold Bratkovich of Hay Associates, a compensation consulting firm, likes the example of the company that tried to get the biggest motivational bang for its limited bucks by offering bosses the option of a meaningful income for just a few—bonuses of up to ten thousand dollars for the best performers. "Not one manager opted to give a bonus," he reported. "They were too afraid of making a judgment and getting the other employees mad at them."

Conflict between supervisor and subordinate—always latent in authority relations—can be matched by the conflict between peers under a pay-for-performance system that forces any degree of differentiation of individuals in the same work unit. This is always a problem, because very few people work alone anymore—even the "traveling salesman." The premise of many merit pay systems is that the individual component of joint output can be singled out. And this can pit group members against one another in competition for scarce rewards.

Here we come upon an interesting organizational Catch-22. There is evidence from stacks of psychological studies that too much difference among group members produces conflict.[6] But, of course, if people do not *know* about the differences, the conflict disappears. So this kind of individual merit pay system may work if the determination of pay is kept secret. But if it is kept secret, the known relationship between pay and performance is weakened. Employees see no evidence to justify the system. Their suspicion increases—of management, if not of one another. And, to take this to its logical outcome, the easiest way to handle such suspicion is to reduce the performance piece of pay still further in order to encourage roughly the same treatment for everyone—which *can* be communicated.

Merit pay plans, then, may end by discouraging high performance in practice. Nor do they offer two desirable attributes for any pay system: looking fair to employees and keeping costs down for the company. These attributes are particularly important for the post-entrepreneurial corporation trying to do more with less.

Every year routine company surveys of employees find greater skepticism about the fairness of traditional pay practices. Every year, the numbers seem to get worse, possibly because traditional practices are skewed toward rewarding the climb to high positions rather then the contribution to organizational success. Top management compensation in particular has been under attack as unjustifiably high, especially when executives get large bonuses just as their company is suffering financial losses, or recovering from them.

While some economists have marshaled data to show that there *is* a positive association between executive compensation and company performance, many professionals still argue that the amounts awarded executives are excessive, reflecting attainment of high status rather than demonstration of high performance. And to employees, the existence of layers upon layers of highly paid managers no longer seems entirely fair; why should they "capture" the return from contributions actually made by those who produce goods and services directly? Employees are beginning to notice. In a well-run leading bank, branch managers get a bonus of up to 30 percent of their pay for excellent branch performance, while the people working in the branch can get only a 6 to 8 percent annual increase. Not only are mangers paid more to begin with, as employees have complained to the personnel department; they are also capturing a greater share of the benefits from *everyone's* effort.

A chorus of voices urges that if executives get bonuses when profits rise, so should the workers who contribute to these profits. There should be an opportunity for all employees—not just management—to share in the gains realized from any enhanced performance to which all presumably contribute.

This line of employee-centered argument (how to encourage people to do more) has been joined with company cost concerns (how to spend less) to produce a solution. Give employees a piece of any increased company profit, but reduce their guaranteed pay in the process. If employees become more like independent entrepreneurs, getting a return from the profit pool, some companies think, they should also take more of the risks, getting smaller guaranteed paychecks. Instead of providing high wages and automatic raises, some companies say, we will give our employees dividends.

THE PROFIT-SHARING SOLUTION: "LET THEM EAT DIVIDENDS"

Facing challenges from foreign and domestic competitors with lower labor costs, companies in every field are seeking ways to reduce the fixed cost of labor. One way to do this is to peg pay to performance— of both the company and the individual. One-time performance awards, spot bonuses, and profit-sharing plans thus begin to seem very attractive as ways to limit guaranteed salaries and wages while holding out the promise of extra earnings for those who truly contribute. The cost reduction potential of this pay scheme can make executives' eyes sparkle with dollar signs.

The fixed part of the paycheck is already beginning to shrink in many American companies, even those that are not in the post-entrepreneurial vanguard. A recent study by the Bureau of National Affairs revealed that one-shot bonus payments, replacing general pay increases, were called for in almost 20 percent of all 1985 union contract settlements outside the construction industry, up from a mere 6 percent in 1984. They were most common in manufacturing, especially in the paper industry, where 52 percent of the contracts included lump sum provisions. Twenty percent of the 564 companies in Hewitt Associates' 1986 compensation survey gave one-time bonuses to white-collar workers, up from 7 percent in 1985. These one-time payments do not raise base pay, nor do they affect overtime calculations. In fact, just the opposite occurs: They reduce the cost of labor. Over two-thirds of the bonus provisions BNA studied were accompanied by a wage freeze or decrease.[7]

Making pay explicitly "float" to reflect company performance is the cornerstone of MIT economist Martin Weitzman's proposal for a "Share Economy." If a significant number of firms can be induced to share profits or revenues with their employees, Weitzman proposed in his 1984 book, the cure for "stagflation" would be at hand. Among other things, firms would have an incentive to create jobs because additional workers are paid only in proportion to what they bring in.[8]

The macroeconomic implications of share ownership are not the issue for companies struggling to compete; they see more immediate benefits from asking workers to take their lumps from business cycles (or, employees would add, poor management decisions) along with the company. Something similar clearly accounts for part of the appeal of employee ownership, especially to companies in industries in which deregulation has created enormous cost competition. At least six major airlines and fifteen trucking firms adopted employee ownership plans in direct response to deregulation, according to Michael Quarrey, Joseph Blasi, and Corey Rosen, authors of *Taking Stock*. More than a dozen pieces of congressional enabling legislation since 1974 also helped by providing a variety of tax incentives and mechanisms. The authors estimate that more than 11 million employees in more than eight thousand firms now own at least 15 percent of the companies employing them.[9]

It is important to note that many firms taking advantage of the new legislation, and the generally favorable climate of opinion surrounding it, did so because of its attractiveness as a financing scheme quite apart from its putative social virtues. Nevertheless, there is little doubt that, properly designed and managed, employee ownership can very positively affect corporate success. Even the New York Stock Exchange came out in favor of it, after commissioning its own study of this capitalistic variant. The Western Airlines case illustrates all these points nicely. After losing $200 million over four years, the airline created the "Western Partnership" for its ten thousand employees, trading a 32.4 percent ownership stake, a meaningful profit-sharing plan, and two seats on the board of directors for wage cuts of 10 to 18 percent. In 1985 Western distributed over $10 million to its ten thousand employees—one hundred dollars each in cash and the rest deposited in employees' accounts. When Western was sold to Delta in 1987, each employee reaped about $8,000 in cash and Delta stock for their average holding of 634 Western shares, shares worth only about $1,650 a year earlier.

Such schemes have obvious advantages over another highly visible alternative for fixed labor cost reduction: two-tier wage systems, which bring in new hires at a lower scale than existing workers. Most of us can see the obvious inequities in pay differences for two groups doing exactly the same job. But pay pegged to actual performance? Earnings tied to company profits? What could be more American in spirit? The clear problem—that lower-paid groups cannot afford swings in income as much as the more highly paid, and that employee efforts are not always directly related to company profitability—do not seem to deter the advocates of profit-sharing. In its many forms, it is seen as one way to move forward what Robert Reich has termed "collective entrepreneurialism."[10]

Profit-sharing is a straightforward arrangement in which a fraction of the net profits from some given period of operation are distributed to employees. The distribution may either be immediate or deferred, and some or all employees may be included. Pacific Telesis included "team awards"—a percent of profits—in its new compensation package, an important aspect of its partnership with the union. Lincoln Electric's plan is particularly generous and well known. The world's largest manufacturer of arc-welding products, Lincoln shares with its two-thousand-plus workers the gains from a level of profitability above the top quartile for Fortune 500 companies. Lincoln has one of the oldest documented gain-sharing plans, touted in a 1951 self-published book, *Incentive Management,* by then-chief executive James Lincoln. The plan is accompanied by an enlightened management system and employee participation in decisions.

Every year Lincoln sets aside 6 percent of profits as a dividend to stockholders—the "wages of capital." Another sum, determined by the board, is set aside as seed money for investment. The balance, paid to all employees, ranges from 20 percent of wages and salary, already competitive with other local companies, to over 120 percent. When added to a wage rate competitive with other companies in the area, this can amount to doubling employees' pay every boom year. The company even remained profitable in the face of sales declines in the 1981–83 recession—to the benefit of employees.

And Lincoln's is by no means the oldest such plan. One of the earliest modern examples of profit-sharing exists at S. C. Johnson and Company, Inc.—more familiarly known as Johnson's Wax—which has included a large fraction of the workforce in its plan since the early 1920s. Indeed, although the company is still owned privately and thus does not publish financial information, it is known that the continuity and amount of profit-sharing at Johnson's Wax is impressive and unusual.

Overall, probably about half a million firms had some form of profit-sharing in 1988, if both deferred and cash payouts are included. By 1983, 13 percent of all production employees, 22 percent of all technical and clerical employees, and 20 percent of all professional and administrative employees in private industry firms other than those categorized as "small business" were already covered by profit-sharing agreements. But these were much more common in manufacturing companies than in services, including insurance and financial services.[11]

The variant known as "gain-sharing" takes profit-sharing one major step further, by attempting, usually with more or less elaborate formulas, to calculate the specific contributions of specific groups of employees (for example, specific production departments or work units), with their contingent pay based on those varying results. Although the basis for calculation varies from one type of gain-sharing to another, they agree on two important principles: First, what is important is that the payout recognize the value of groups rather than individuals (on the theory that teams and collective effort are what count) and second, that the rewards to be shared and the basis for their distribution must be based on definite objective and measurable characteristics (so that everyone can recognize what is owed and when).

For example, General Motors' widely publicized Saturn plant in Spring Hill, Tennessee, will offer gain-sharing, under an agreement with the United Automobile Workers. Workers will get a salary amounting to only about 80 percent of the prevailing UAW standard, but they will be paid productivity bonuses on top of that. GM Chairman Roger Smith has put himself on the public record as squarely in favor of profit-sharing. He said in 1984 that "profit sharing puts entrepreneurship back in the free enterprise system. . . . It offers a tangible and substantial reward for a job well done and an incentive for even close cooperation in the years ahead. . . . Best of all, the record shows that the whole thing works. Employees in profit-sharing businesses do tend to be more productive.'' Such support is particularly striking in light of the attack on this very idea as ''radical'' thirty years ago when the United Auto Workers' leader, Walter Reuther, proposed it.

Scanlon Plans, probably the oldest, best-known, and most elaborate form of gain-sharing, typically distribute 75 percent of gains to employees and 25 percent to the firm. In addition, they are organized around very complex mechanisms and procedures that spell out how employees at various levels will actually participate not only in the control of the gain-sharing process per se, but also in the opportunity to help improve performance continually, and thereby improve their share as well. At Herman Miller, Inc., one of the better-known firms using a Scanlon Plan, it is formally described not simply as a compensation system, but rather as ''a way of life'' for the company. Gain-sharing experts estimate that several thousand companies involving millions of workers have some sort of gain-sharing program. They seem to be growing in popularity, although they still represent the minority of compensation schemes.

Despite this growth in group performance bonuses, top executives are much more likely to capture a portion of the benefits of increased profitability than is the average employee. In a recent Conference Board study of 491 companies, 58 percent had a top executive bonus plan, but only 11 percent had a current profit-sharing plan, 8 percent an all-employee bonus, 3 percent a group productivity incentive, and under 1 percent a group cost control incentive. Performance-related compensation plans generally did not play a significant role in the compensation of employees other than top management and, to a lesser extent, some middle managers. Even in incentive-conscious high-technology firms, gain-sharing is relatively rare. While more than half of the high-tech firms included in a recent Hay Associates compensation survey had cash or stock awards for individuals, only 6 percent had gain-sharing or group profit-sharing programs.[12]

The limited use of gain-sharing can only be attributed to the large number of hierarchy-rattling organization changes it entails. For gain-sharing plans to work, a particular organizational structure and corporate culture are required, including open discussion of the plan to gain employee acceptance, establishment of cross-unit teams or task forces to develop the plan, and adoption of suggestion systems.

Gain-sharing programs also require much more open communication about company goals and company performance. If employees' pay is based in part on company profits, they need to know where the company stands and how their percentage is calculated. Management at Action Instruments, for example, provides their employees with a handbook explaining corporate goals and posts weekly data about orders, shipments, and profits.

Management must thus be ready to accept changes. Steve Bochen, a Canadian Tire executive, warns that gain-sharing's "impact is evolutionary, and it grows in strength like a child. . . . It takes time and hard work to achieve positive results." Is the change worth it? It seems to be, for those who stick with it.

On the employer side, actual monetary benefits vary. The General Accounting Office looked at thirty-six firms with gain-sharing plans; twenty-four provided financial data. Of those twenty-four, the thirteen with annual revenues below $100 million averaged labor savings of 17.3 percent. The other eleven, with greater revenues, calculated savings averaging 16.4 percent.[13] Clearly, these figures cannot be said to be representative in any meaningful sense; nevertheless, a reading of the fairly extensive literature suggests that such figures are not atypical. If anything, they're probably low for established plans. It is even more difficult to pinpoint the bonuses to participants, but it is reasonable to estimate that in good years, people might get as much as 20 percent additional pay.

The majority of firms are positive about their experience with gain-sharing, although it is also possible to find instances in which it simply did not work and had to be abandoned. Experts estimate that about one-third of the programs do not succeed, often because of complexity of administration or poor implementation. The prior state of labor relations and how union involvement is handled also make a difference.

Michael Schuster of Syracuse University studied both successes and failures in depth. The successes generally showed a productivity improvement of 5 to 15 percent in the first year, better work attitudes, product design improvements, and improved product quality. From the workers' point of view, there was more employment stability in difficult and turbulent environments.

The failures have not been insignificant, although, as Schuster notes, "Most managers and companies have been led to believe that there is no down-side risk. This is not the case." The causes for failure are predictable, in light of the two major concerns people have about pay: How much do I get, and how fair is the standard by which I get it? Thus, in Schuster's failures, there were labor problems because of less than expected bonuses, and internal disputes because of inconsistent treatment of different groups. Schuster concludes that success required "assessing the potential for gainsharing in the context of an overall approach to human resource management."[14]

There are some other nagging questions about gain-sharing. What happens when it involves sharing the *loss* as well as the *gain?* The Eastern Airlines case is instructive. Initially enthusiastic when Chairman Frank Borman offered board representation, company stock, and a profit-sharing plan in exchange for wage concessions in December 1983, Eastern employees gradually turned bitter as losses mounted, and management asked for still more concessions. Finally, one of the employee-directors was instrumental in forcing Eastern's sale to Texas International Corporation because of his disaffection with Eastern management.

Gain-sharing can have one further flaw. By treating everybody equally and distributing across-the-board bonuses to rather large work units, the team is strengthened, but the individual pay-and-performance link is weakened. Profit-sharing or share ownership, in which all share equally in total company performance, weakens even further the relationship of the paycheck to the person's own achievements. Is this fair to those who contribute more? Why should the underachievers get the same as the high performers?

So some organizations reason that post-entrepreneurial pay should move in the opposite direction—toward incentives for individual achievements. If we want to encourage employee contributions in particular areas of strategic importance, they argue, why not pay for it? They seek to create a variety of income-earning opportunities for the enterprising by adding special incentives for specific contributions. I dub this aspect of the post-entrepreneurial paycheck "bucks for behavior."

THE PERFORMANCE BONUS SOLUTION: BUCKS FOR BEHAVIOR

Some people associate the idea of pegging pay to the production of specific results with the old-fashioned factory piecework system.

While there are certainly some resemblances, the modern variants are more complex and innovative.

Merrill Lynch's new compensation system for 10,400 brokers, introduced in February 1986, cut commissions for most small trades and discounts, instead rewarding the accumulation of assets under the firm's management, and thereby encouraging brokers to spend more time with larger, more active customers. While total compensation costs may rise, John Steffens, president of the consumer division, also expects earnings to increase as a result of both increase in interest income and savings from processing fewer transactions. The new pay system was developed in direct response to the introduction of new products, such as Merrill Lynch's Cash Management Account. The traditional system, designed for a simpler world, simply did not adequately compensate performance in the new and growing areas.

Commissions and bonuses for sales personnel are standard practice in most industries, of course. What seems to be changing are the amounts people can earn (for example, more than double their salary at General Electric Medical Systems), the greater number of people who can earn them, and the proliferation of ways productivity bonuses can be earned, especially in highly competitive new industries. And spot bonuses or special awards are increasingly used to focus behavior on strategic targets—for example, American Express's One Enterprise awards for projects building synergies across lines of business.

PSICOR's approach was among the more imaginative, and it reflected the kind of constant tinkering that entrepreneurially minded companies are doing. This small Michigan company of 181 employees supplied equipment and professionals (called "perfusionists") for open heart surgery. Perfusionists are in high demand and frequently change employers, so founder Michael Dunaway wanted to find a way to give them immediate rewards, because the standard 10 percent increase at the end of the year seemed too remote.

First he tried random bonuses of one hundred to five hundred dollars for high performance, but tracking them was difficult. Then, in 1982, he hit upon the idea of "continuous raises"—increases in every paycheck, calculated to amount to at least a total of 5 percent a year over base salary, with up to 8 percent added as a lump sum at year's end based on overall performance. Employee response was very positive, but the accounting department was soon drowning in paperwork.

PSICOR's next system involved a combination of quarterly raises, based solely on performance, of up to 5 percent a year, plus a series of bonuses to encourage specific behavior. Regional managers could distribute an average of five hundred to one thousand dollars per employee whenever they saw exceptional work. Perfusionists could earn an additional 10 to 20 percent over base salary in "P-Pay," a bonus based on their actual surgical caseload; out-of-town assignments earn double P-Pay. Other bonuses rewarded operating surgical monitoring devices. Then there was a travel bonus plan, in which points for out-of-town travel can be redeemed for family vacations. Another five hundred dollars could be earned by publishing scientific papers, and one thousand dollars for professional certification. To cap it all, there was a monthly sabbatical every sixth year and use of two resort condominiums.

The employees of PSICOR liked the opportunities for increasing their income. Turnover—understandably—was under 2 percent, and dropped to under 0.5 percent for those employed two years or more. And Dunaway liked the other results for the company. While payroll costs were up, revenue increases more than compensated. Revenues per perfusionist rose from about forty-four thousand dollars in 1982 to well over one hundred thousand dollars (on $17 million in sales) in 1985.

Part of the motivation for performance bonus and incentive pay is to stimulate productivity, particularly targeted to key organizational goals. The other part is retention-oriented—to keep valued employees by giving them ample opportunities to take the initiative to grow their own paychecks.

Florida-based Delta Business Systems, a company that sells, leases, and services office equipment, has taken the proliferation of bonuses almost to its limit. On top of an employee stock ownership plan and managerial salaries geared to objective performance measures (for example, customer satisfaction surveys combined with profitability results for the service managers), DBS offers rewards for meeting certain performance targets.

Praised by the business press for having more than twenty different bonus programs for a mere 315 employees, DBS actually has a changing array of creative options for rather small, personalized incentives, coming and going as they prove to be effective or not. A fifty-dollar monthly "Most Valuable Associate" award used a year ago, for example, was recently dropped in favor of a "Cost Containment Award'' of one hundred dollars to the branch office with the most effective cost-saving ideas; the branch managers decide how to allocate it. When the company was faced with increasing work-related accidents, a bonus program was established to provide a cash award to any branch that completed a six-month period with no workers' compensation claims. There are bonuses for performance within established goals, and bonuses not confined to the job—for new business leads.

While some of DBS's incentives are designed to encourage teamwork (four hundred dollars every two months to the four corporate warehouse workers if they function smoothly as a team), others are purely individualized. For example, one department manager with a base salary of thirty-five thousand dollars a year can earn $750 a quarter more if she runs her department with one person fewer. When this manager lost an employee and submitted a personnel request, management offered her the challenge of running a leaner department while boosting her own pay. Barbara Poole, DBS's director of Human Resources, laughs when she recounts examples like this, saying, "Sometimes I feel we get a little too creative; it makes administering the programs a little crazy." But on the whole, "I'm glad we can get so personalized. I'm certain it's an effective motivational tool."

Not only is this kind of incentive pay complicated to administer, but it often focuses on short-term behavior. So another productivity-oriented pay system has been developed, to concentrate employees' attention on behavior related to longer-term aspects of high performance—pay-for-skill (also known as pay-for-knowledge), in which employee pay is pegged to the number of tasks learned and performed well. This system provides individual incentives for employees to upgrade their performance rapidly—and also creates other productivity benefits to reward the capacity of teams to manage their own work.

A leading consumer goods company has several factories operating successfully under a pay-for-skill system. The basic unit in the factory is the work team, which has responsibility for all aspects of production: operating the machinery, working with suppliers, inspecting the product for conformance to quality standards, and keeping records. With this kind of responsibility, it clearly helps every member of the team to have highly skilled colleagues capable of fully sharing the load.

New employees are hired by the work team after extensive

interviewing, and a training coordinator (also a team member) develops a five-year career plan for how the new employee will progress in skill. This planning is important to the team, because other team members will have to provide coverage for the employee's job while he or she is attending training programs. (In one plant, the work team hired some "temps" because they planned to have two people out for personal computer training.)

Pay grows as the newcomer moves from entry to full team member. There are small pay increments for time served, through the first two years, but the real increases occur as the new team member progresses through as many as several dozen "skill blocks." The skill blocks move from general orientation (learning the plant, operating hand tools, the simplest jobs, and so forth) to on-the-job and classroom training to learn all aspects of one production process. Advanced operating skills involve knowledge of more than one process. The multiskills requirement adds such skills as machine maintenance, quality control, and—one of the payoffs in terms of "self-management"—problem-solving and leadership skills. All of this may occur within five years. By contrast, under the former system in the same plant, it took five years just to move from sweeper to helper to process operator for one process, with no training or responsibility for problem-solving.

To ensure that the increased skill is acutally used on the job, a portion of each team member's pay (25 to 30 percent) is contingent on performance, based on team evaluations. While teams are notoriously unable or unwilling to differentiate among their members when it comes to doling out rewards, this wrinkle does translate informal peer pressure into legitimate opportunities to punish "free riders" who slack off while their teammates toil mightily.

A similar plan is in effect at General Foods' Topeka, Kansas, pet food plant—one of the model "new work systems" often cited by professionals. New employees are paid a starting rate, and then they can advance one pay grade for each job they learn. All jobs earn equal amounts of additional pay, and they can be learned in any sequence. When all the jobs are learned—usually after a minimum of two years—the person earns the top rate, and can gain additional pay only by taking on a skilled trade in addition. Though pay expert Lawler warns of a potential "topping out effect" when many people earn the maximum and have nowhere to go financially, he has not yet seen this occur. Instead, variations have been added, such as giving employees the opportunity to earn more if they learn about the economics of the business.[15]

All in all, pay-for-skills is a clever approach. It stresses individual responsibility but does not have the drawbacks of other pay-for-performance systems that pit team member against team member in contention for the highest ratings. Because there is no limit to the number of people who can reach the highest pay levels, there is little formal inducement to maintain a monopoly of skills or withhold training from newcomers in order to preserve a superior position. It creates a community of nominal peers with a broad range of skills who decide among themselves how best to deploy those skills. Gone are the trappings of hierarchy, from job classifications and grading systems to stacks of supervisors.

A system like this runs counter to the goal many neo-Marxist critics attribute to modern corporations: to ''deskill'' jobs so as to keep more people confined to lower pay levels and to make it easier to accommodate turnover, ensuring that a reasonable proportion of the work force is always new and thus always paid at the lowest rates. The critics think that deskilling keeps the total wage bill low.

So how does an organization ''justify'' in economic terms doing the opposite? The additional costs of higher average wages on the shop floor are paid for out of productivity improvements and savings. Manufacturing executives in the consumer goods company can produce data to show that unit costs of their products are 30 to 50 percent less under such systems than in their more traditional plants. There are also considerable savings in eliminating a large number of supervisory jobs, as the teams take on more and more functions (inspection, purchasing, record keeping) that would otherwise be performed by supervisors and specialized staffs—at higher pay. Then there are the savings from reduced friction in the workplace. Recently a single traditional plant had sixty-six cases under arbitration (actually not a very large number by U.S. industry standards), while the total across over a dozen ''new system'' plants was zero. The productivity gains and cost savings are sufficient, in the company's view, to allow an investment of 10 to 15 percent of total work hours in the additional training and communication required to make the system work. (The comparable figure for their traditional plants is 3 to 4 percent.)

Despite clear advantages, not all distributional problems are solved by a pay-for-skill system. In the beginning, when the system is new and employees are still acquiring skills, the frequent pay increments can be highly motivating. But what happens when people reach the ultimate skill level and the rapid raises disappear? The two traditional responses have been pressures for individual upward mobility, to ensure that the paycheck continues to grow, and collective bargaining, to enhance the whole group's sharing of the economic pie while staying in place. Whether the psychological sense of "ownership" and the actual control over work conditions that the team system creates can offer a third source of satisfaction in the absence of any other monetary reward remains to be seen. Only a few plants under this system have even begun to enter this "mature" phase.

It is an issue that companies now starting to experiment with pay-for-skill decide to duck. Au Bon Pain, a bakery products manufacturer and retailer based in Boston, has just established a pay-for-skill system for the sixty-odd workers in its frozen dough factory. Architect of the system was Au Bon Pain's executive vice-president, Leonard Schlesinger, a former Harvard Business School professor who has written widely on work motivation. In Au Bon Pain's variant, employees enter at $5.75 per hour and can increase their pay to as much as $11 per hour within three and a half years by mastering skill blocks. According to Schlesinger, it will be five years before the company has to face the question of "what next?" By then, he'll be ready for further innovation. Meanwhile, the company will enjoy the productivity gains he envisions.

In general, the tide is moving toward more varied individual compensation based on people's own efforts. Even holdout Digital Equipment moved its sales forces to commissions in the mid-1980s. Post-entrepreneurial principles reach their fullest expression, however, not in the pay-for-performance systems just described, but in the scramble to devise ways that people within organizations can, without actually leaving, act and be rewarded nearly as if they were starting their own business.

THE VENTURE RETURN SOLUTION: OWNING A PIECE OF THE ACTION

The notion of running a piece of a large corporation as though it were an independent business is one of the hottest old-ideas-refurbished in American industry. An emphasis on newstreams alongside main-streams, however, brings problems of pay to center stage. Many companies are not only stimulating a flow of new venture possibilities, but also encouraging potential entrepreneurs to remain within the corporate fold by paying them like "owners" when they develop a new business.

The attempt to simulate the potential-to-make-a-killing incentives that entrepreneurs have when they start their own businesses has led to a very different kind of compensation system operating within traditional corporations. In a style that is pay-for-performance to its fullest extent, venture participants can earn a return, just like founders-owners do, on the marketplace performance of their product or service. Even very traditional organizations without official new-stream programs are looking carefully at the possibility of setting up new ventures with a piece of the action for the entrepreneurs. "If one of our employees came along with a proposition, we'd look at it carefully," a banker executive said. "I'm not sure how anxious we'd be to do it, but ten years ago, we wouldn't have listened at all. We'd have said, 'You've got rocks in your head.' "

The issue of how to pay newstream managers is one of the thorniest ones faced by companies with newstream programs, matching other problems of how to compensate idea developers. A controversy has been brewing in recent years, for example, over how best and most fairly to compensate those from whose efforts new products or technology originate. If an employed scientist creates a patentable invention that is then successfully commercialized, it seems logical that he or she should receive a royalty reflecting the value of that invention to the organization.

But this has not, in fact, been the case in most companies. Traditional practice involved base pay at competitive levels, a small bonus (often $500–$1,000) for patents received, and other, often nonmonetary, incentives to retain the inventor and encourage the next invention. Recognition might range from special awards to promotion to "master" status entailing use of special laboratories, freedom of project choice, sabbaticals, and the like. Cash awards might be involved, but generally were not tied to the returns from the product— for example, IBM's awards for Outstanding Innovation (which could be $10,000 or more) and Invention Achievement (over $2,400). In 1982, IBM distributed $225,000 among the nine inventors of a computer language upon its twenty-fifth anniversary.

These practices have been justified on several grounds. Inventors are on salary, using company resources. The cost of invention is often the smallest piece of investment that needs to be made to successfully commercialize a product. It can be hard to single out individuals as "the" originators when many other people may be contributing ideas and effort. Holding out large monetary rewards can foster competition and secrecy—people "hoarding" their best ideas until developed to the point where rights can be assured. And while some of these concerns could be handled easily by group incentives and team awards, there is still the ultimate fallback argument: If the company doesn't allow others, like marketing or manufacturing staff, to share in the return, inventors shouldn't share in it either.

Besides, the argument runs, creative people may be motivated more by ego than by money anyway. George Freedman of Raytheon's New Products Center agrees with this. As the contributor of more than twenty patentable inventions himself, most achieving considerable marketplace success, his biggest financial rewards were five hundred dollars a patent and occasional larger-than-average salary increases. But he and his staff kept churning out inventions "for the ego trip," he says. "When we see ads for our products, we know that we were the ones to do it. That's the thrill that makes it all worthwhile."

There is some evidence to support the "ego trip" argument for technical professionals. A group of ten technically oriented companies collaborated on a survey of nine hundred of their engineers and scientists. The high-priority sources of motivation for these employees included such ego-oriented opportunities as having support and recognition for doing innovative work and having budgets to carry on special projects—both highly important to more than 85 percent of the sample. But cash bonuses based on individual contribution were also highly valued by professionals in their thirties and forties.

Opportunity and challenge count, but so does money. Leaders of one newstream venture I studied wondered how long they can keep people if they cannot depart from the parent corporation's pay system and instead provide rewards based on the venture's performance. For the first few years, this venture was able to entice people because of the entrepreneurial setting, but there were already signs that this would not be enough. Fancy titles—higher-sounding than one could achieve in the parent at that pay grade—were one motivator, but with such a small group, career paths would be flat and titles static. The venture head said:

When I hire people, what I use to entice them is "This is the place where you can really do something." This is particularly important to engineers. They can pick what they do. I'll let the engineer make decisions. They have the chance to identify things to do, to use their capabilities and to go ahead and do it.

But another manager made it clear that the absence of entrepreneurial rewards would soon hurt:

The motivation *now* is having a small, new, different place [to work], making it work, and learning. But eventually, the reputation for poor pay will hurt retention. Tentative plans for extending the performance-based compensation plan further down the organization are being discussed.

Clearly the joy-in-work hypothesis goes only so far. Among the strong arguments on the other side is one that strikes a national nerve: In 1959 Japan worked on a law tying employed inventors' compensation to the market value of their inventions. Although I cannot find evidence that it was enacted, in 1967 Japan passed the United States in per capita patent applications.[16] This record was disturbing enough for Congress to consider several bills covering patent rights for inventors.

The situation is beginning to change. In recent lawsuits, inventors have won large awards from employers for inventions that proved profitable. Robert Beasley, a former Lockheed engineer, complained publicly that his twenty-thousand-dollar award for inventing high-temperature-resistant tiles for the space shuttle was inadequate in light of the $50 million in contracts Lockheed received on the basis of it. Hearing about Beasley, two other Lockheed inventors eventually sued the company after receiving $1,250 apiece for an invention they estimated had a value of $330 million to the company; a trial court awarded them $2.6 million, which Lockheed quickly appealed. The lower court judgment was subsequently overturned, and the inventors got nothing. In fact, Lockheed's inventor awards program is a good one by industry standards—"one of the most generous patent programs in the world," a company spokesman said. There's a bonus of $500 when a patent application is filed, $1,000 when the patent is issued, and royalties of 20 percent on the first $100,000 in returns, 10 percent on the next $400,000, and 5 percent thereafter. But even under a "generous" program, the money question is clearly troublesome.

Some companies, particularly entrepreneurial start-ups, do not have to be forced to pay inventors differently. One of these is Wilson Laboratories, a growing computer test equipment manufacturer in California in the $5 million range that wants entrepreneurial incentives for its engineers. Founder and CEO Randall Wilson reasons that "ordinary income is not enough for an employee who wants to feel that he's at least partially in business for himself." Indeed, engineering vice-president Jim Dietz felt that the employees themselves would not stand for a system in which they turned over an idea that made big bucks for the company and received nothing more than their salary.[17]

When a product development project is initiated, Wilson and key aides determine a royalty amount based on the product's perceived market potential and longevity. Royalties may go as high as twenty-five thousand dollars, although as the opportunity has gradually been extended to smaller projects that won't contribute as much to the company, the average amount has gone down to about 20 to 50 percent over base salary. At first, only the senior engineers were eligible but now, Deitz says, "It's open to pretty much anyone involved in a large project."

Royalties are tied to schedule and performance—in part as a necessity for opening the opportunity to a wider group. "The first people involved were more than willing to put in the extra hours and the hard work," Dietz reports, "but now that the base has spread, we're running into people who aren't quite as gung-ho. The penalties for being late give them the incentive they need."

Engineers today, tomorrow the rest of the workforce? Dietz recognizes that Wilson Laboratories may need incentive plans for all employees soon, because there is already some jealousy on the part of other professionals in the organization.

High-technology firms like Wilson Labs are particularly dependent on the contributions of individual innovators, especially when it is easy for them to leave to start their own firms. So entrepreneurial incentives are more frequent, and perhaps even a necessity in these organizations. For example, a 1983 random sample of the 105 Boston-area firms employing scientists and engineers compared with the high-tech ones dependent on R&D for new product development with their more traditional, established counterparts. The high-tech firms tended, on average, to pay a lower base salary but offer more financial incentives of other kinds, such as cash bonuses, stock options, and profit-sharing plans.[18]

Furthermore, across high-tech competitors, special incentives and other entrepreneurial forms of compensation tend to be more widely used by the most financially successful firms. One study of sixty-six companies compared the twenty-four "best" companies in terms of financial results with the other forty-two (a five-year average increase in net profit of 9.4 percent for the "best," compared with an average loss of 5.9 percent for the others). The better companies were much more likely to tie rewards to frequently communicated priorities. One common financial award program involved pools of money provided to senior managers to recognize employees for significant contributions to the organization, with substantial publicity. (Interestingly, the "best" were also more likely to use team or group incentives along with individuals ones, acknowledging joint contributions to outcomes.)[19]

Similarly, for another group of sixty-four high-tech companies ranging in size from $20 million to over a billion dollars in sales, more than half provided financial returns to key contributors in some form. Spot awards involving a lump sum cash payment were by far the most common, used by 80 percent of the companies with a special incentive program. These cash awards could add up to one hundred thousand dollars to the paycheck, although the usual amount was around five thousand dollars. Stock options or stock grants were also used by 50 percent of them.[20]

Wherever it is thought that employees can perform as well—or better—for the company if they are also in business for themselves, the entrepreneurial component of the paycheck is on the rise. And this means not only in high-tech, but in no-tech companies as well. Au Bon Pain, with $30 million in revenue from forty stores nationwide, launched a partnership program that will turn over a big piece of the action to store managers. Revenues over $170,000 per year per store will be shared fifty-fifty with the "partners." In 1987 two store managers with salary levels of $25,000 under the old system earned well over $100,000 each under the new.

Providing direct payoff for new revenues generated is an integral part of many newstream programs, such as Ohio Bell's Enter-Prize program. Ohio Bell leaders are reluctant to discuss the reward system for Enter-Prize winners. One manager, "concerned about publicizing the amount of the reward," grimaces when he speaks of going from fifty-dollar checks for suggestion winners to fifty-thousand dollar checks for an Enter-Prize winner. This award—the largest so far—went to a team of software developers.

Enter-Prize bonuses represent perhaps 5 to 10 percent of the money saved or profit made from projects. At the display booths at Ohio Bell's Innovation Fair, a poster above each project gave an estimate of the money saved or new revenues accrued—clearly Ohio Bell is keeping track of the financial impact of the Enter-Prize program. An executive in charge reported that the aspect of the program he worried about most at the start was evaluating the projects and assigning a value to their impact on the bottom line and then translating that figure into a cash award for the innovator. The precedent of the graded percentage of savings was taken from the previous Suggestion Plan. To ensure the integrity of the awards—and reduce the potential for bitterness among employees—the Enter-Prize program's champion convinced both the budgetary people from the engineering departments and the corporate-level revenue management group to be involved in measuring the bottom-line impact of each project. He especially saw the need to have verification of the value of the projects from the corporate financial staff—a group that reported to the president.

Furthermore, to encourage department support, the boss of an Enter-Prize winner receives a "drawing account" that boosts the superior's budget. The amount in the account is about 1 percent of the savings realized from an innovation. The money is given to encourage other people to innovate and to recognize managers who are supporting innovation. The money can be used as the manager wishes, from sending people to seminars to buying equipment.

Although the monetary award had significant meaning for some employees, other Enter-Prize winners also enjoyed the recognition they received. Substantive attention, rather than monetary reward, was in some cases more highly prized. For example, Al Wallenhorst, who designed an elegant system for the rehabilitation of cross connect boxes, claimed he was not at all concerned with a potential cash prize. Instead, he was glad that his design is saving money for Ohio Bell—a company for which he has worked for forty years.

As idea development gets more complex, and newstream activities are separated from the mainstream more sharply than in the Ohio Bell case, entrepreneurial incentives increase. Companies with new ventures resembling start-up businesses have elaborate systems for giving participants a piece of the action. Most such schemes pay the venture participants a base salary, generally equivalent to their former job level, and ask them to put part of their compensation "at risk"; their percentage of "ownership" is determined by the part they put at risk. This then substitutes for any other bonuses, perks, profit-sharing, or special incentives they might have been able to earn in their standard job. Sometimes the return is based solely on a percentage of the profit from their venture; sometimes it comes in the form of internal "phantom stock" pegged to the mother company's public stock price. Payout may occur at several intervals in the development of the venture, rather than forcing the corporate entrepreneurs to wait the seven to twelve years it can take to earn a profit in a new venture. So "milestone bonuses" for meeting established targets may be used, with further incentives for timeliness added—if you're late, the payoff goes down.

Clearly, potential corporate entrepreneurs cannot get as rich under this system as they could if they were full owners of an independent business, sharing ownership with their provider of venture capital, but they are also taking much less risk. The parent corporation offers them more services than just that of a banker or a board of directors. Some companies factor in the resource access they are providing the venture participants (for example, a market research department, a corporate name, technology expertise, and other benefits from their tie to an established company) by putting a cap on the dollar amount venture managers or their teams can earn from the venture.

AT&T began its venture development process—still labeled only an experiment—just before divestiture. By 1986, seven venture units were in operation, one started in 1983, three in 1984, and three more in 1985. The intent was to design a compensation plan outside their pay system that would increase the amount of risk people were willing and likely to take, and to seed new businesses, a few of which might eventually grow into large ones. Each venture is sponsored by one of the existing AT&T lines of business.

William Stritzler, the AT&T executive responsible for overseeing this process, offers venture participants three compensation alternatives. These correspond to three levels of risk—to find what Stritzler calls a "rational midpoint" halfway between the risk/return opportunity offered by venture capital financing on an independent basis and the normal development of a new business by salaried employees within a corporation. All participants in the venture—manager and team members alike—must be on the same plan. (The largest venture is currently up to ninety employees.)

Pay option one allows venture participants to stick with the standard corporate compensation, keeping the salary level associated with their previous position. In short, they get a paycheck based on job grade, augmented by any team bonuses or individual merit increments other employees might get, just as if they were holding a regular job rather than growing a new business. Not surprisingly, none of the seven venture units has chosen this option.

Pay option two takes both the risk and the return up a notch. People agree to freeze their salaries at the level of their last job until the venture begins to generate a positive cash flow, and the AT&T investment is paid back (or, with the concurrence of the venture board, when certain important milestones are met). At that point, venture participants can get a one-time bonus, up to 150 percent of their salary. That's it, except for any salary adjustments to reflect increased levels of responsibility and performance. Five of the seven venture teams have selected this.

The third option, chosen by two self-confident bands of risk-takers, comes closest to simulating the independent entrepreneur's situation. Venture participants can contribute from 10 to 15 percent of their salary to the capitalization of the venture, which is taken out of each paycheck for that period until the venture begins to make money and generate a positive cash flow. The only limit is that they cannot reduce their salary below the minimum wage—to avoid legal problems and prevent people from putting their own personal funds into the venture. The payoff is up to eight times their investment from the cash coming into the venture, once certain criteria have been met.

These last venture participants have invested about 12 to 25 percent of their salaries. One of the two ventures has had some distributions already. The project began in October 1984, and employees elected to invest from 8 to 25 percent of their thirty- to eighty-thousand-dollar salaries for three years. Benefits (typically 25 to 30 percent of salaries) were invested at the same rate. By 1987 the company had paid several bonuses, just below the maximum payout rate of eight times the salary invested. And a computer graphics board venture housed outside Indianapolis could return $890,000 to its eleven employee-investors in the near future.

As a sign of just how attractive this program is to AT&T employees, ideas for new ventures started coming to Stritzler and his staff even before the program was formally announced. In the first year, three hundred potential entrepreneurs brought ideas to Stritzler based on what they had heard through the grapevine. Perhaps two thousand ideas have been offered since, netting a venture formation rate of about one out of ever 250 ideas. People have been funded at every level, from first-line supervisor to the fifth level, which in AT&T parlance is roughly equivalent to a department head just below the officer ranks. In principle, AT&T is willing to offer this option to nonmanagers, too.

Entrepreneurial pay is spreading. It is in the air and on the lips of leaders. One executive justifies his company's entrepreneurial incentives by citing a story he had heard about Ross Perot, founder of Electronic Data Systems, the company Perot later sold to General Motors. "This may be folklore," he said, "but when Ross Perot was a salesman for IBM, there was a cap on commissions. Perot had filled his quota by April or May one year, so he went to the boss to point this out and to seek additional commission. The boss turned him down. So Perot spent the rest of the year at IBM's expense, designing EDS. Now plainly," he concluded, "we don't want that to happen here. We don't want to turn people off, and we want to make sure that people can be as productive as possible. If compensation has to change in order to allow that to happen, we have to develop the appropriate system."

THE CHALLENGE TO HIERARCHY: TENSIONS AND DILEMMAS

As the paycheck continues to move in a post-entrepreneurial direction, toward contribution as the basis for earnings, it unleashes a set of forces with far-reaching potential to transform work relationships as we know them now. The transformation will probably begin in benign ways, as organizations take modest steps to make "bureaucratic" pay more "entrepreneurial."

Take the case of a large bank moving into new financial service areas. Upon buying a brokerage firm, the bank found that it had also acquired a very different compensation system. A generous commission arrangement makes it fairly common for employees to earn regularly twice their salary in bonuses, and once in a while five times. In 1985, at least three and perhaps as many as six people made as much in salary and commissions as the chairman did in his base salary—that is, roughly five hundred thousand dollars. Those people all made much more than their managers and their managers' managers and virtually everyone in the corporation except the top three or four officers, a situation that would have been completely impossible a few years ago. "Traditionally," one of the bank's executives said, "there's no way that people would have been able to earn more than their boss, and absolutely no way that people would have been able to earn money approaching the compensation of the chief executives. That simply would have been prevented no matter what the rationale for it."

Now it cannot be prevented, and the executive admits—although his attempt to do so is why I am not naming the bank—it is also hard to keep it quiet. "People in the trade know perfectly well because they know the formula, they see the proxy statements, and they are busy checking out the systems by which we and everybody else are compensating these people."

But in anything but the shortest run, the idea of earning more than the boss seems insupportable in traditional organizations, and to some people, troublesome. It is "embarrassing," in the words of a senior bank officer, when people can readily earn more than their boss. It is equally tense in the other direction, when lower-level employees get a 6 to 8 percent increase while their manager gets a 30 percent bonus for results that they know perfectly well they helped create. People are getting angry and are beginning to push hard for a more equitable arrangement. "We agree," a bank officer confesses. "We just don't know what to do about it."

An attempt to spread the profits further comes up against a classic problem in compensation. Dividing the manager's bonus among his or her subordinates would so dilute it that it could become meaningless. If a few people can gain the benefit of even a modest increase, then it may be worth doing. If the increase is shared more broadly, it may become so small as to lose value. (Remember the common assumption that a payment needs to reach 15 percent of base pay in order to represent a meaningful difference.)

There are some organizational precedents for situations in which people in "lower-ranked" jobs are paid more than those above, but it is not a very happy or comfortable situation for most traditional corporations. Field sales personnel paid on commission can earn more than their managers under some compensation schemes. Star scientists in R&D laboratories may earn more than the administrators nominally "over" them. Hourly workers can make more than their supervisors with the addition of overtime pay or because of union-negotiated wage settlements. But these have generally been clear exceptions, and disturbing ones to boot.

To get a feeling for just what kinds of difficulties nonhierarchical pay causes for traditional status relations, let's look at a less extreme situation, in which the gap between adjacent hierarchical levels is reduced, even if the hierarchical sequence of more for each higher level is retained. This is called "pay compression," and it is a source of concern to traditional corporations who believe in maintenance of the value of the hierarchy.

On an American Management Association survey of 613 organizations, of which 134 were corporations with over one billion dollars in sales, 67 percent reported that they were experiencing compression problems. What is most striking about the expressed concern is that the gap between adjacent levels is still great, and only a few percentage points divide those organizations identifying a problem from those that do not. For example, the average earnings differences between first-line production supervisors and the highest-paid production workers was 15.5 percent for organizations reporting compression problems, but not much higher than that, at 20 percent, for organizations with no self-reported problems. In the maintenance area, the difference was even less: 15.1 percent average earnings difference for those who said they had a problem and 18.2 percent for those who said they did not.[21]

It is hard to avoid drawing the conclusion that the organizations concerned about compression are not responding to any actual problem. Instead, they appear to be driven by a perceived threat that the hierarchy will crumble because of new pay practices. This becomes even clearer when we look at what those organizations reported they would *not* do to solve compression problems. While 67.4 percent of those concerned about compression agreed than an instant bonus program would help, 70.1 percent said their companies would never do it. While 47.9 percent said that profit-sharing for all salaried supervisors would help, 64.7 percent felt that their companies would never do it. In fact, the least-likely-to-be-accepted solutions were all the ones that could change the nature of hierarchy: reducing the number of job classifications, establishing fewer wage levels, and granting overtime compensation for supervisors (in effect equalizing their status with that of hourly workers). On the other hand, the most-favored solutions involved aids to upward mobility (more training, more rapid advancement) *within* the existing promotion structure, maintaining the structure of hierarchy intact.

The structure of hierarchy is indeed challenged by post-entrepreneurial pay systems, whatever form they may take. Social psychologists have shown that the maintenance of an authority relationship depends on a degree of inequality. If the distance between boss and subordinate—social, economic, or otherwise—declines, so does automatic deference and respect. The key word here is "automatic." Bosses can still gain respect by their competence, their treatment of subordinates, or their help. But power in the relationship has shifted. The situations are more equalized.

Equalization is further aided by the existence of objective measures of contribution. Once high performance is established, once the standards are clear and clearly achieved, the subordinate no longer needs the good will of his or her boss quite so much. One more source of dependency is reduced, and power again becomes more equalized. Proven achievement in higher earnings than the boss's produces security. Security produces risk-taking. Risk-taking produces speaking up and pushing back.

The relationship between a "star" editor in a publishing house and various people "above" who have tried to "manage" him comes to mind. Well-paid—extremely well-paid—because of his obvious best-seller track record, he simply stands outside the hierarchy rather than within it. Coddled and wheedled rather than ordered about, he maintains entrepreneurial independence within a corporate bureaucracy, because this company is willing to breach the official pecking order to pay for performance wherever it is found.

The boss is thus forced to move from a relationship of authority to one that is more collegial. But there are positive implications for the boss as well. If the subordinate can earn more than the boss while staying in place, one of the incentives to compete with the boss for his or her job is removed. Gone is the tension that can be created when an ambitious subordinate covets the boss's job and will go to extremes to discredit or displace him or her.

In short, if some of the *authority* of hierarchy is eliminated, so is some of the *hostility* of hierarchy. But if tensions upward are sometimes reduced, tensions among peers can be exacerbated.

The jealousy potential inherent in some forms of post-entrepreneurial pay is an explicit problem, especially when only part of the organization has this option. In two different companies with new venture units that offer equity participation, the units are being attacked as unfair and poorly conceived because participants can earn so much money for what the attackers see as only modest or trivial contributions to the overall corporation, while those who keep the mainstream businesses going—the businesses responsible for the big revenues and big profits—face salary ceilings and insignificant bonuses.

The conflict between two different systems is self-inflicted in companies that establish new enterprise units. But sometimes the conflict comes as an unwelcome by-product of a company's attempt to expand into new businesses via acquisition. In the case of the bank that acquired a brokerage operation, the contrast in earning opportunities—high in brokerage, lower in the bank—became a source of considerable tension. To avoid the employment equivalent of a "run on the bank"—everyone from managers to secretaries trying to transfer to the brokerage operation—the corporation was forced to establish performance bonuses for branch managers and even some piece-rate kinds of systems for clerical workers, though these are not nearly as generous as the managers' extra earning opportunities.

This system, though it solves some problems, creates others. The bank's human resources executive recognizes that although these income-earning opportunities are pegged to individual performance, individuals do not work in isolation. Branch managers' results are really dependent on how well their employees perform, and so are the results of nearly everyone except those in direct sales—and even there, a team effort can make a difference. Yet, instead of teamwork, the bank's practices may encourage dysfunctional competition—hoarding good leads or withholding good ideas until one person can claim the credit. "We talk about teamwork at training sessions," one executive said, "and then we destroy it in the compensation system."

Team-based pay raises its own questions and generates its own problems. There is the "free rider" problem, in which a few nonperforming members of the group benefit from the actions of productive members. There are problems caused by resentment of dependency, especially if people of very different traditional statuses are involved—for example, nominally "higher-level" people who resent having their rewards pegged to the performance of a group including those "lower" than themselves.

There are also pressure problems. Gain-sharing plans, in particular, can create very high peer pressure to do well, since the pay of all depends on everyone's efforts. Theodore Cohn, a compensation consultant, likes to tell about the Dutch company, N. V. Philips, in which twice-yearly bonuses are up to a significant 40 percent of base pay. "Managers say that a paper clip never hits the floor—a hand would be there to catch it," Cohn recounted. "If a husband died, the wake was at night so that no one would miss work. If someone went on vacation, somebody else was shown how to do the job. There was practically no turnover." At Lincoln Electric, where the performance bonus results in pay that is twice the average factory wage, Cohn has claimed that peer pressure can be so high that the first two years of employment are called "purgatory."

BALANCING THE PAYCHECK

The post-entrepreneurial organization seeks to balance two ends of an apparent contradiction: reduce fixed asset costs while investing in the active pursuit of new value. Contribution-based pay is a consequence of this pursuit.

Contribution-based pay has several virtues. It increases perceived system fairness when it gives employees a share of increased company performance. It helps companies keep fixed costs relatively low. It can raise productivity by steering behavior toward strategic goals. And it allows those who create new value for the company to earn a return on it.

But contribution-based pay also opens a Pandora's box of choices and dilemmas. The three principal post-entrepreneurial pay systems—profit sharing, performance bonuses, and venture returns—themselves encompass a multiplicity of possibilities. Thus, managing post-entrepreneurial pay is one of the ultimate corporate balancing acts. There are five key trade-offs:

- Rewarding individual or group contributions.
- Rewarding whole company or unit performance.

- Distribution controlled by management (and therefore discretionary or subjective or both) or automatic upon hitting established targets.
- Amounts relative to base pay or determined by value of contributions to the company.
- A single system for the whole company or multiple systems.

Because assessing contribution is a complex matter, the paycheck of the future will also be more complex. If it is impossible to disaggregate the individual contribution in team performance or decide whether to reward divisions for their own performance regardless of the whole company's fate, then the solution lies in making pay reflect an element of each. While merit pay and executive bonuses tend to reward individual performance, gain-sharing and team profit-sharing tend to reward group performance—so organizations may need to do some of both. As companies struggle for balance, the paychecks they distribute will be based on a dramatically more complex set of calculations. As many as five variables will determine the final numbers: for example, a guaranteed small base amount based on organizational level and position plus an individual merit component plus a group or division gain-sharing component plus an overall company profit-sharing component—and these four amounts supplemented from time to time by one-shot, short-term bonuses and recognition awards for exemplary individual and team contributions. Sophisticated information systems will help manage this complexity.

If pay systems reflect authority systems, then the weakening of traditional control systems based on a hierarchy of statuses plus the rise of commitment-based systems that stress employee responsibility and initiative make performance-based pay inevitable. The traditional system worked only as long as it was viewed as legitimate by those subject to it. The changing business environment and new demands on employees and leaders to solve problems, improve performance, and open new opportunities undermine the legitimacy of the traditional status-based system. Economic imperatives that could be avoided by traditional oligopolistic bureaucracies in a more stable world must be confronted head-on by organizations faced with global competition and a turbulent environment. Thus, there is a movement afoot in many companies to both control costs and motivate performance targeted to strategic objectives by changing the pay system to one with lower fixed wages and salaries but higher variable earnings opportunities.

Ultimately, those pay systems that work will not be ones that encourage the competition-focused corporate cowboys to rise again, getting what they can for themselves without taking the broader goals of the company into account. Instead, the successful systems will be those that balance the drives for individual achievement with the cooperative effort of the whole corporate team.

CHAPTER 10

The New Workforce Meets the Changing Workplace: Opportunity and Overload

*W*ill "busier-than-thou" replace "holier-than-thou" as the way Americans show off their importance to one another?

The post-entrepreneurial revolution in American business has broken down taboos and opened up endless possibilities. It has multiplied the pressures people feel to prove they are contributing—to prove that their job "adds value" in case the company plays musical chairs with the structure, or to make sure they earn their performance-based pay. Sometimes there seem to be no limits. Companies scan their ranks for new ideas and encourage collaboration between departments, partnerships outside start to take the place of command-and-control systems inside, and new pay systems encourage people to do more to get more.

The excitement comes with a price tag. In a world in which anything is possible, but nothing is guaranteed, and the failure to pursue opportunity may be a worse sin than making a mistake, how much work, how much activity, how much effort is enough? In a post-entrepreneurial workplace, "enough" is defined not by some pre-existing standard like the length of the workday but by the limits of human endurance. And this standard, in turn, changes the shape of professional and personal life.

Post-entrepreneurial organizations engender some underlying tensions—the soft underbelly of aggressive, creative, lean organizations. The celebrated new breed of corporate entrepreneurs—in hot pursuit of new opportunities, dynamic, fast-moving, and constantly innovating—lead exciting but overloaded lives. Post-entrepreneurial organizations vastly increase the complexities people must deal with and multiply the responsibilities they bear. The lure of the post-entrepreneurial workplace makes some people *want* to do more, at the same time that it thrusts more upon them, willing or not.

And as work demands threaten to get out of control, life itself threatens to get out of balance.

Some Americans are working harder (or at least *longer*) than ever—the ones in the "better" jobs. Among the groups with the longest hours of work in a recent Harris poll are those in what are considered the most "desirable" occupations: entrepreneurs in smaller businesses, especially retailing, at 57.3 hours per week; professionals at 52.2 hours per week; and those with incomes over fifty thousand dollars at 52.4 hours per week. A *Wall Street Journal* survey of top executives found that 88 percent of them worked ten or more hours a day, 18 percent worked twelve or more; 94 percent worked at least an hour every weekend, 33 percent worked six or more; 56 percent had seven or more days of business travel per month; and 80 percent spent some of their leisure time with work colleagues. The evidence suggests that executive time is expanding. A Korn-Ferry survey of 1,362 senior executives from Fortune 500 and Service 500 companies in 1985 showed that the modal respondent worked 56 hours a week, three more than in 1979. Vacation days were down by two (from sixteen to fourteen). Sixty percent of the CEOs surveyed by another research firm in 1984 spent over sixty hours a week working, as against 44 percent in 1980.[1]

For those engaged in new ventures, work hours can be even longer. A New England group reported having under five hours of leisure time a week. For participants in corporate newstream activities, a six-day and sixty-hour workweek seemed normal. At Millitech, a young high-tech firm in western Massachusetts, the parking lot was typically still one-third full at 6:00 P.M.

The long hours can make certain high-paying occupations look less good on a per-hour basis. The Harvard Business School student newspaper ran an April Fool's Day parody recruitment ad for an outfit called "MBA temps." The ad touted the financial virtues of working as a typist at $15 an hour compared with the $10-an-hour starting salaries for novice investment bankers ($1,000 a week divided by 100 hours worked). In another spoof, a Michigan law firm offered regular starting pay of $43,000 for 1,700 billable hours per year, or a "New York Associate" track: $70,000 for 3,000 hours. It was a joke, but still, the work style for many lawyers in New York has been characterized as a "grim ritual of all-nighters, tepid take-out dinners, bleary-eyed vigils at printing houses, Dial-a-Cabs, atrophied social lives, and neglected marriages."[2]

WORKAHOLICS, WORKFORCE EXPLOITATION, OR WORKPLACE CHANGES: WHY ARE WORK HOURS RISING?

There are three common explanations for why some people work long hours. The first view is psychological, finding hard work a kind of addiction and labeling the practitioners "workaholics." Workaholics are driven to do more than they need to and are unable to let go of work, unable to rest or vacation. The drive to work all the time is tied not to a particular ends or particular situations but to inner compulsions beyond the person's control.

A second perspective, associated with radical sociologists, views the modern corporation as an example of a "greedy organization," as Lewis Coser puts it,[3] ever-eager to consume more and more of the person, obliterating other choices, subordinating the rest of life to the demands of the company. By making the worker dependent on the rewards it holds out, the company can exact as much work as the person can bear, especially when the rewards include corporate status and power. An executive recruiter's comments in a national magazine lend unwitting support to this sociological critique:

> The 80-hour man [sic] has far more sizzle. Nine out of ten companies will take the guy who's always there, whose example is one of brute force of effort. His example filters down to those beneath him.[4]

Generally, it is the highly paid occupations in which hours worked are highest, but the link between money and time is not direct. In those cases in which professionals bill their time at high hourly rates, earnings clearly go up as hours increase (corporate law and management consulting are two examples), but in many firms, the income from extra hours does not always accrue to the individual—reinforcing Coser's greedy organization hypothesis. Furthermore, there is no such direct relationship between hours and income for most corporate citizens; managers and professionals in the category called "exempt" are not subject to wage-and-hour laws requiring overtime pay. In some of the corporate newstream ventures I studied, participants were acutely aware that their especially long hours were not tied to any additional compensation, except modest proportions of the venture's returns. "When you are in an internal venture," one newstream manager reported, "you do not work just nine to five like other people, yet you may not have generous stock options or ownership share as do outside ventures." But despite this sore point, those interviewed admitted that they would still put in every extra hour they had to make the venture succeed.

Both the "workaholic" and "workforce exploitation" theories view people who work long hours as victims out of control, although they differ on the origins of the victimization, internal or external. The psychological theories can thus more easily explain long hours of voluntary work, while the sociological theories direct us to see the pressures companies impose on people. Yet both make "excessive" work, beyond the forty-hour norm, seem distasteful and pathological.

A third perspective is more cynical, questioning whether the long hours are entirely what they seem. The late sociologist Erving Goffman coined the term "facework" to describe a person's manipulation of images to control others' impressions. "Face time" has become a popular expression for creating the appearance of spending long hours in order to make a good impression. The time used may be nonproductive or even non-work-related, but the impression is there. For example, one ambitious manager used to leave handwritten notes on executives' desks: "7:30 A.M., stopped by to see you, sorry to miss you." Those skilled at "face time" might not even be at work at all—for example, leaving the impression that they are elsewhere in the building while going shopping.

None of these theories, however, accounts for the pattern of who works longest, or for the fact that hours worked are increasing. They also have difficulty explaining the positive relationship between hours worked and job satisfaction. Jobs rated as more desirable also tend to take the most time, and recent studies show that job satisfaction is highest where people are working the longest hours.[5]

Overload does not necessarily result from driven individuals neurotically compelled to work until exhaustion, nor from a soulless economic system conniving to grind people up in the relentless pursuit of profit. To understand fully this work style, we must turn to the nature of the workplace itself, and how it is changing as post-entrepreneurial strategies take hold. At the simplest level, of course, reduced employment security from corporate restructuring can produce career anxiety, which leads to hard work to demonstrate irreplaceability. As one person put it, "When you see people being laid off all around you, you'd have to be irrational not to put your nose to the grindstone." And the loss of organizational slack as companies get leaner can leave more work for a small number of people; tasks often do not disappear even when staffs are cut. But post-entrepreneurial strategies not only increase productivity pressures, they also fundamentally alter the nature of the work itself.

Post-entrepreneurial workplaces increase the lure of work. The chances to earn performance bonuses, or share in productivity gains, or get funding for newstream ventures, or work more closely with PALs outside the company—all of these increase, rather than decrease, time demands. When there is greater opportunity, there is also greater overload. People want both to do more and have more heaped on them. This is not a matter of individual preferences; it comes from working in more complex, more emotionally involving, more time-consuming situations. And it is not merely a workload that the corporation imposes on employees; employees invest themselves in more challenging and interesting work or opportunities to participate in organizational problem-solving.

When work is more exciting, people want to do it longer. In fact, sometimes, the *organization* tries to place limits on work hours in order to avoid "burnout"; otherwise employees might keep right on going. A Chicago insurance company locks doors at seven o'clock weekdays, and all but four hours over weekends, to make sure employees don't overwork.[6] Sequent, a Tektronix venture, tells people to take time off, has a mandatory three-week vacation, and locks the doors of the building on holidays.

But when work is more interesting, people will just take it home. In one company, secretaries on a task force found themseives carrying piles of paper home for the first time in their careers. The task force was important, its mission was interesting, and suddenly they had a project with goals that required reflection beyond the time permitted in the office. It is common to see lower-echelon employees who are members of problem-solving groups or who are being coached to propose newstream ideas using their lunch hour to hold meetings, reporting on ideas they had at home, because they are committed to the goals of the group.

At Ohio Bell, for example, one newstream innovator cared enough about his project *and* his "normal" job to do both, taking the project work home. He reported;

> The only company time I spent on my project was making phone calls or traveling. I developed procedures and everything else at home. It was a major mistake not asking to be taken off the job. I didn't ask to be taken off the job because I was the only person in the company able to do it. It would have taken two months to train somebody else and I didn't want to take that time. I didn't predict the problems and setbacks that would come. When I faced them I needed time and energy to resolve them—time and energy that I didn't have because I was still working my regular job. . . . The biggest obstacle I faced was my workload. I wanted flexibility and I didn't have that.

A Tektronix venture manager agreed that the work went home with his people, mentally if not actually:

> We were "always thinking about the business." Even if someone were at home, he could wake up at two A.M. and suddenly remember something that needed to be done in the office. Or he could stay at the office until two A.M. and then leave a note on someone else's desk, suggesting that X needed to get done.

Similarly, the leader of a new venture team at Eastman Kodak reported that the effort

> required that we work sixty-hour weeks in the beginning. Saturdays were a normal day of business. [Interviewer: What drove you?] We had a

tremendous sense of accomplishment. We could see the business grow in the course of just a couple of months. That was a unique feeling.

Another Kodak newstream manager said that this was the requirement for success:

> Once you get rolling down this track, there is probably nothing that can stop you. In fact if there is something that can stop you, you are probably not the person who should be doing the venture. You just have to become so wrapped up and believe in it so much. . . . It was seven days a week and all night.

Even the normal overload can be increased by a crisis. At Sequent, a crisis required everyone to pull together to meet a market deadline. People who had been working twelve-hour days and Saturday started to come in on Sunday, and instead of leaving at midnight, they would stay a few more hours. Some did not go home at all, and others had to look at their watches to remember what day it was.

The opportunity-overload mix is not just a managerial or white-collar phenomenon. Blue-collar workers in so-called "high commitment" workplaces face similar overload problems because of doing-more-with-less strategies. And while overload dilemmas find their fullest expression in fast-paced high-tech businesses, in start-ups, among top executives, and in deal-making professions, they also extend well down the ranks to workers in traditional industries, as a consequence of "work reform" efforts designed to offer more power and opportunity, more responsibility and more chance to contribute ideas. In the 1970s and 1980s, productivity improvement efforts in the United States increasingly have taken the form of empowering workers through opportunities for greater control over their work, often through the formation of teams and the elimination of layers of management, like other restructuring efforts to build synergies. One review of more than eight hundred studies of several thousand workplaces with productivity improvement projects found that the most common workplace changes were toward flat, lean structures, multiskilled employees, and team configurations.[7] Couple these features with the extra meetings required by partnerships, the attraction of new idea programs and contribution-based pay, and "average" workers too experience the conditions for higher work absorption and overload.

One of the best and most widely acclaimed examples of the new blue-collar workplace is NUMMI (New United Motors Manufacturing, Inc.), a joint venture of Toyota and General Motors in California, with the active cooperation of the United Auto Workers union. NUMMI represents the convergence of all three major post-entrepreneurial strategies: partnerships, restructuring to get leaner, and actively tapping employee ideas. Assembly work at NUMMI is done in teams, job classifications have been reduced to a bare minimum, and compensation is fairly uniform with minimal distinctions of "level," reflecting a lack of emphasis on hierarchy. Many NUMMI management concepts derive from the Japanese partner, although the American partner appears to dominate daily operations, and Japanese management is not particularly visible to observers.

In the early days of NUMMI, there was excitement, enthusiasm, and a high level of after-hours voluntary participation, just as in many post-entrepreneurial workplaces. People would arrive early at the plant to maintain their equipment or do calisthenics, and teams would hold problem-solving meetings or design projects on their own time. Team members would not let their peers slack off or duck involvement. Longer hours spent at work or thinking about work were an inevitable consequence. If blue-collar workers are treated like entrepreneurs, managing their own part of the business, aspects of their work style will come to resemble that of entrepreneurs.

Later, another source of overload was imposed at NUMMI as a result of doing-more-with-less imperatives. Assembly line pressures intensified because of sales problems, creating a push for higher volume. It was difficult to argue about the new pace, however, because it was no different from the speed of work in Japan. But as NUMMI commentators pointed out, the American workers were on the average ten years older than their Japanese counterparts (forty versus thirty), and the American workers lacked the career mobility opportunities to move away from physical work and into design or sales offered to Japanese workers. Only part of a Japanese system was being adopted, but for a very different American workforce and without compensating career incentives. As a result of productivity pressures, in the shadow of partnership misunderstandings, fatigue was common, weekends were often spent recovering from work, and levels of voluntary after-hours participation declined.[8]

How Post-Entrepreneurial Workplaces Produce Overload

The post-entrepreneurial organization operating under do-more-with-less imperatives tries to stretch its reach while reducing its staff. While there may be fewer duplications, redundancies, procedural hoops, managerial checkpoints, and gatekeepers preventing access, there is also much less slack. Each person carries more of the responsibility.

But it is not simply a matter of fewer people doing the *same* work. The *nature* of the entrepreneurial workplace also creates *more* work. Four characteristics contribute.

The communication imperative. More challenging, more innovative, more partnership-oriented positions carry with them the requirement for more communication and interaction. One needs more time for meetings in a post-entrepreneurial workplace, where divisions interact in the search for synergies, job territories overlap, people might report to more than one manager, and projects require the coordination of a number of people, each with specialized responsibility. But groups often taken longer to do certain kinds of work than do individuals, even if the quality of the solution is higher. Furthermore, management tasks are different under a post-entrepreneurial system in which responsibility is delegated downward to reduce management layers, or managers work with outside partners rather than inside employees. In these more participative circumstances, people need to spend more time selling ideas rather than commanding. They need to spend more time explaining goals, keeping staff or allies up to date with timely information, and making sure they understand where their responsibilities fit into the whole task.

Evidence suggests that the greatest proportion of an executive's time is spent communicating, often in short fragments on a large variety of topics.[9] Thomas Bolger, CEO of Bell Atlantic, a company now actively engaged in developing new ventures in the United States and overseas, repeatedly calls subordinates at home as early as 7:00 A.M. "People who work for me should have phones in their bathrooms," he says. Even his vacation house has seven phones, including ones in the garage and the sauna.[10] Now the communication imperative extends down the ranks.

In the post-entrepreneurial corporation, communication demands, and therefore time demands, are up. Digital Equipment, a company thriving on innovation and thus with a need for communication across diverse entities, established its own in-house helicopter service to link a score of New England facilities. Concerned about travel time and costs, the company then established an elaborate teleconferencing system to allow people to communicate without traveling. But instead of reducing travel costs, the teleconferencing capacity actually *increased* them, because more people, who could communicate more easily, found even more reasons to get together.

Post-entrepreneurial organizations vastly increase the complexities that managers and professionals deal with and multiply the responsibilities that they bear. After all, they are no longer simply following established procedures or working solely within their own circumscribed area; they are also developing joint projects with other units in pursuit of synergies, and they are coordinating closely with customers, suppliers, and other external partners. The more integrated and synergistic the organization, the more time is spent in communication. In one successful transnational corporation, Philips, Christopher Bartlett and Sumantra Ghoshal found that over two thousand managerial hours a year were spent just on global communications.[11]

Two ingredients combine to put most post-entrepreneurial players in a state of permanent overload. The first is an oversupply of tasks, and the second is an assumption that all of those tasks must be done no matter how many there are. For a variety of reasons, it is not easy to redistribute the tasks or establish priorities that reduce the workload to more manageable proportions; indeed, efforts to solve the problem often themselves add another set of temporary tasks.

It seems to go with the post-entrepreneurial territory. At one particularly fast-moving company, there was a well-understood norm that people come early and stay late. Thus, a wave of cynicism greeted the recent circulation of a Corporate Values Statement that called for a balance among work, family, and community life. Indeed, the manager who drafted it typically arrived at his office at 7:30 A.M., with the parking lot already half full. By 6:00 P.M., he often faced two more hours at his desk preparing for a dinner meeting that would take him to midnight.

It is not the number of *people* reporting to a manager that creates the problem, but the number of *projects*. Professionals with no supervisory responsibilities face exactly the same situation. As a consequence, much of their time is spent in meetings. At one major manufacturing company, this was a matter for company jokes. Even at lower white-collar levels, it was reported that 40 to 70 percent of office time was spent at meetings, and a key technical manager estimated that the figure for him was over 95 percent. He had little time, while in the office or anywhere near it, to be by himself. On weekends, he spent at least six hours going through the mail and memos he couldn't get to otherwise. On his office desk was a pile of paperwork almost four inches high, which he chipped away at between meetings, but it was replenished every day to the same level.

The post-entrepreneurial workplace generates an embarrassment of information riches. High-activity organizations that value open communication not only produce information at a rapid rate, they also like to circulate it. While open communication means that everyone can easily find out what is going on, it also means that important signals for a particular person or group may be lost in all the other information noise. The task of weighing the significance of information is added to all of the other tasks. And because, indeed, the latest unfiltered information package may include something of importance, it cannot be neglected either.

The expandable activity slate. Overload is also associated with change, whether from restructuring or from the encouragement of newstreams. In companies geared to innovation, there is always some new task coming up. And the people already in place have to do it. Even if there were not a bias toward staying lean and keeping headcount low, there would still be many reasons why new tasks are assigned to old people—to have high-risk items handled by known quantities, for example, or to get the task done now without taking the time to educate an outsider.

There is also no standard for how much is "enough." This is always a difficulty, of course, in high-discretion jobs with broad goals and the mandate to seize new opportunities—exactly what characterizes more and more of the jobs in post-entrepreneurial firms. In circumstances in which it is felt that any letting down allows a competitor to steal a march, or in which failure to do everything possible may mean missing something, "enough" seems to be defined only by the limits of human endurance. When one is oriented to opportunity, there is always something more than can be done.

Indeed, in some post-entrepreneurial organizations, anyone who appears to get through all of his or her work is automatically suspect. One CEO was particularly distressed that a key manager rarely arrived before 9:00 A.M. and was always out of the office by 5:30. "He must not be working hard enough," the boss said to me. The manager had a different view: "I'm just a good delegator, and besides, I don't think everything always has to be done instantly," he claimed in his own defense. But exactly that attitude worried the CEO, a dynamic perfectionist who used every spare moment to think of still more opportunities for the company to pursue. He fired the manager.

A dramatic increase in the number of people who can initiate. This is a fringe benefit of a more synergistic, integrative organization, one that encourages cooperation among the various areas of its business. It also comes with empowering more people, at ever-lower levels, both inside (employees) and outside (suppliers or customers), to take initiative to propose new ideas. And it is a by-product of piling special projects on top of basic responsibilities. As a senior Digital executive, Win Hindle, observed, "Our company is more frenetic than others." Projects started at first-rung levels can overlap and bump into one another. Employees work for two or more bosses. "That's great for creative exchange," Hindle says, "but it's trying when an employee can't be in two places at once."[12]

The initiation of tasks does not even have to be direct—one person making a demand on another. The hidden output of one group's innovative effort is often to create more work for another group. It is typical in consumer products companies, for example, for the marketing department for one set of brands to devise an exciting new promotion without being fully aware of what other brand teams are doing. Each separately could be handled by manufacturing and sales; together they would be a disaster in the making. Communication overload is one of the reasons why marketing teams fail to see the problem.

The experience of Donna Dubinsky at Apple Computer—a tale immortalized by Todd Jick in a Harvard Business School teaching case[13]—illustrates the ways in which widespread empowerment in a post-entrepreneurial workplace makes overload spread geometrically. I first met Dubinsky at one of Apple's leadership workshops at Pajaro Dunes, the beach resort, in the spring of 1985. One of the striking things about that so-called retreat was that no one had really left the job behind. The forty or so upper-middle managers all seemed preoccupied by back-home events. The issue preoccupying Dubinsky was a proposal by a manufacturing manager to make radical changes that would impinge on her area, distribution. Without involving Dubinsky, the manager had developed a plan and taken it to the executive committee. Suddenly Dubinsky found her work multiplying. In the midst of the Christmas season, a busy time for distribution anyway, she had to prepare a response to the manufacturing manager's proposal, then serve on a task force reviewing distribution that met weekly for four months. Besides the formal meetings, there were counter meetings and lobbying efforts and phone calls at home. In the end, her views prevailed, but not until a thorough rethinking of the distribution function had been undertaken, involving still more people on her staff in studies and analyses. In short, the initiative taken by a leader in another area triggered a series of events that amounted to still more work for Donna Dubinsky.[14]

The exhilaration of living on the edge. In the organizations I observed, from Apple and Digital to Kodak and Pacific Telesis, there was remarkably little complaint about this obvious—and sometimes dysfunctional—overload. Instead, the situation was presented with a kind of pride: It must take very special people to live in this environment, and we really have to be awfully good to do all of this and more. These difficult circumstances let us demonstrate our extraordinary abilities. And what we're doing must be very important.

The implicit argument that underlies such pride goes something like this: *If we were in an organization that had a modest number of tasks, and we had adequate time to do them all, probably anybody could do them. Moreover, that probably means that there is some fat in the system or some extra cost that should be taken out. Therefore, we are among the very few people who can cope effectively under these circumstances.*

A multitude of projects, combined with the need to respond to unforeseen events, means that even top people do not control their own time. The demands of some tasks that suddenly increase in value interfere with the completion of other tasks, thus adding unintentionally to the workload of someone else, someone who was dependent on the initial tasks' getting done. For example, in a successful corporate giant very effectively reshaping itself for the global Olympics through a rapidly changing product portfolio, one division is particularly plagued by overload. Because it is central to the constant changes, its people are highly vulnerable to expanded activities. It is typical for people to be called out of a meeting by their pink-slip-bearing secretaries and told to report to somewhere else or to tackle some other job. They simply excuse themselves and disappear. The meetings might go on, but they clearly are not the same, and important decisions are delayed—thus requiring still another meeting to be scheduled.

Geography is no barrier to this kind of overload. The general manager of a business unit in that company flew to Europe on the Concorde one afternoon, checked into his hotel and went immediately to the hotel's restaurant for dinner. He was just taking his first bite when he was summoned to the telephone. It was his boss, telling him about an impending competitive crisis. His response—the right one for his company—was to pick up his bag, go to the airport, and fly home to make sure that other people were responding to the situation. In fact, he did not work on the problem himself; he simply talked with others to make sure it was handled. But rather than frustrating him, the whole episode made him feel even more important.

Thus, in the post-entrepreneurial workplace, predictable hours and predetermined responsibilities would seem to be things of the past.

FROM INTELLECTUAL ABSORPTION TO EMOTIONAL ABSORPTION: PERSONAL RELATIONSHIPS IN THE POST-ENTREPRENEURIAL WORKPLACE

When work is absorbing, the workplace becomes the site for absorbing relationships. When the workplace consumes not only people's time but also their intellectual energy by giving them challenging problems to ponder, it is only one more step to become the center of emotional life as well.

In the traditional bureaucratic corporation, roles were so circumscribed that most relationships tended to be rather formal and impersonal. Narrowly defined jobs constricted by rules and procedures also tended to stifle initiative and creativity, and the atmosphere was emotionally repressive. The post-entrepreneurial corporation, in contrast, with its stress on teamwork and cooperation, with its encouragement of imagination and commitment to the process of building the new, brings people closer together, making the personal dimension of relationships more important.

This is illustrated by looking at one increasingly common form of personal relationship at work, attractions between men and women.

If life in the post-entrepreneurial workplace has a frantic quality, it can also have a romantic quality. The romance associated with post-entrepreneurial work is occasionally literal as well as figurative. The presence of large numbers of women working alongside men as peers combines with the special circumstances of post-entrepreneurial work to make personal attachments more common. After all, when people are working long hours, the workplace is more likely to be the setting for fulfilling personal needs. The sheer number of hours and the absorption in the tasks at hand make it less likely that they have the time or energy to look outside. In fact, the "couple" is now a more acceptable presence in many corporations. Because of the increasing frequency with which couples were forming in the post-entrepreneurial workplace, in the mid-1980s many companies started relaxing policies that had required one member of a couple to leave. Almost 60 percent of 547 responding companies on an American Society for Personnel Administration survey cited such relaxed policies.[15] Martin-Marietta even has an affirmative hire-a-couple policy; it adds about a hundred couples a year to its workforce, with the proviso that one member of a couple cannot supervise the other.

One of the new personal challenges arising in the wake of the shift toward post-entrepreneurial management, then, involves a new temptation: close emotional attachments between men and women. When men and women work in close proximity in post-entrepreneurial situations, such attachments are both more likely and more troublesome. It is not merely the presence of women in the upper reaches of the workforce in greater numbers that breeds this temptation, but the nature of the contact made possible by empowering assignments and activities, and by the new requirements of rapidly changing organizations.

Men and women have always been attracted to one another, but the workplace was generally not the vehicle through which this attraction developed, for several reasons. First, men and women were generally separated by status barriers that either minimized contact (for example, the all-male executive ranks) or defined contact in terms of domination and subordination (which, in some cases, led to sexual harassment rather than to emotional attachments). Second, the tasks both men and women performed were more likely to be routinized and formalized by bureaucratic norms that depersonalized interactions. Even if men and women were in contact, much of their work together was simply too boring and mundane to produce emotional intensity. And the rare attachments that were produced were generally not linked to task performance, so their organizational implications were minimal.

The advent of post-entrepreneurial management has changed all that. It has increased the number of situations that stimulate emotional attachments. Although only a small proportion of those exposed succumb, there are enough examples to make such attachments a new corporate dilemma. In the instances I have observed, three circumstances contributed in the development of a couple relationship. Note that these circumstances are necessary but not sufficient; the parties themselves must be susceptible. And note also that mere exposure to these circumstances does not automatically create attachments; they are still rare, and certainly do not encompass all working relationships between men and women.

Open-ended and informal contact across levels and functions. Such contacts between men and women are both the most obvious and the least deterministic condition for the formation of emotional attachments. People need to meet each other first, and the more meetings there are, the greater the odds of emotional attraction. High-innovation organizations are defined more by networks than by hierarchies. People are constantly coming into informal contact—through task forces, interdisciplinary projects, conferences, training programs, and even social events, like the Friday afternoon pizza party with rock bands and dancing that I attended in Lotus Development Corporations's parking lot one warm spring day. Indeed, status differences are played down in favor of first names, creative (but nonhierarchical) titles, and emphasizing the importance of everyone's contribution. Under these circumstances, personalities emerge out of faceless roles. The interest men and women share in working for the same exciting project may evolve into an interest in each other.

Innovation assignments: to change something, fix something, invent something, create something. As innovation assignments increase, and when they involve a small number of people, the groundwork for intimacy is laid. Newstream work is inherently absorbing and empowering. People are encouraged to break constraints, to go beyond convention, and to ignore the usual rules governing their organizations and the relationships within it. The risk is exhilarating; the responsibility feeds a sense of individual potency as well as dependency on partners. It is common for the people paired in innovations to feel that they are alone against the world—and together they will conquer it.

A man and a woman in this already emotionally charged atmosphere may occasionally find that their intense love affair with their work translates into a love affair with each other. Some emotionally involved managers remind me of Bonnie and Clyde, adventurers whose romance made them so high on their own power that they developed illusions of omnipotence. But without going to that extreme, work situations that involve scaling new heights or performing the impossible can create a special bond with the work partner.

In most of the corporate couples I encountered, exactly this kind of situation encouraged their attachment. Typically, the man was slightly senior to the woman, and they were jointly responsible for making a major change or developing a new approach. She reported directly to him in some cases; in others they were linked because of a common professional field and a special assignment. Whether the setting was a bank, a computer company, an industrial products manufacturer, or a consumer marketing firm, the partners felt that they were, together, the lone force for the new ways allied against all the voices of tradition in the company.

Fantasy settings. Also contributing to the temptation of attachments are the romance-breeding settings in which those working on high-priority projects find themselves. Overnight travel or late-night meals put men and women together at a time of day most dreamlike, most conducive to fantasy, and often in fantasy settings like dimly lit restaurants that surround people with "servants," luxuries, and a flow of alcohol. When a male and a female banker exploring acquisitions flew in for business meetings the night before and met for dinner, the setting was exactly as if they were "dating," and conversation easily led them toward intimacy. Romantic attraction is not difficult in worlds designed for romantic illusion.

What happens when the workplace is the site for social life? From the corporation's perspective, there seem to be few problems when work life intrudes on personal life, taking time as well as physical and emotional energy—time and energy that could otherwise be spent with families and nonwork friends. Some fast-growing high-tech companies and professional firms make a point of organizing social life for their overloaded professionals and managers. A large consulting firm characterized by long hours and constant travel sponsors enticing parties and excursions to resorts on weekends. It thereby captures whatever free time people have left under the guise of giving them great benefits; it thereby also ensures that all of their social contacts are with other firm members. Indeed, one goal of team-building sessions at off-site retreats, like the ones Apple held at Pajaro Dunes, complete with "outdoor exercises" and meditative beach walks in small groups, is to create strong emotional bonds that will persist when people return to work. But if friendships and romances come from among work peers, then people are in effect never off the job.

Problems with personal relationships come, from a business standpoint, when emotional attachments are not kept within bounds, when personal life intrudes on work life. Special friendships, "old boy" loyalties, and corporate romances are potentially threatening because they can too easily fall into a danger zone where members begin to show favoritism instead of objectivity and close off access of other people to them. Part of the bond in close relationships is the ability to exclude others, to be "special" to one another, to have experiences and knowledge not shared by anyone else. But this runs counter to what a post-entrepreneurial organization needs: people willing to work together across widespread areas to pursue synergies, the flexibility to redeploy people to new tasks. The same newstream ventures that generate work intensity also require trust that the best decisions will be made in the light of high uncertainty, a trust jeopardized by wondering whether friendship or emotional attraction are clouding judgement.

Family-based businesses run into these problems, even when they have reached the size and status of large corporations. In one family-held service conglomerate with revenues approaching a billion dollars a year, family members had the inside track on all top management positions; inexperienced young relatives were often assigned to experienced nonfamily professionals to learn the ropes before leapfrogging over them. Furthermore, family members shared strategic information only among themselves; senior staff officers often could not get the data that affected their planning. The result: a dampening of enthusiasm and a reduction of initiative on the part of nonfamily managers. Personal bonds were seen as taking precedence over the needs and goals of the company. Not surprisingly, much of the business was stagnating.

It is in the post-entrepreneurial corporation's interest for its members to have a generalized team feeling and emotional absorption in the work itself, but not to center feelings on particular people. Any strong attachment to something or someone other than the task at hand is likely to pose a threat to the openness, inclusion, collaboration, and trust essential to post-entrepreneurial organizations.[16] It limits the flexibility to redeploy people. It is distracting to both those participating in it and those observing.

Post-entrepreneurial organizations, in short, want people to form close relationships—but not too close.

The workplace as a center for social life and the workmate as a candidate for marriage mate is, on one level, a convenience for overloaded people who have absorbing work that leaves little time to pursue a personal life outside. It is also an inevitable consequence of the new workforce demographics. But on another level, the idea is profoundly disturbing. What about the large number of people whose personal lives are not contained within the corridors of the corporation? What about the people with family commitments outside the workplace? The same overload and intensity that draw people together in the workplace also spill over to affect the nature of family life.

CONSEQUENCES OF OVERLOAD: EXACERBATING HISTORICAL WORK-FAMILY TENSIONS

The overload induced by the post-entrepreneurial workplace has important human consequences. The spillover into personal life threatens relationships that are not easily accommodated to the demands of the workplace. For example, when I asked successful corporate innovators what their accomplishments *cost,* their answers were revealing: gaining weight, getting a divorce, getting in trouble with the family.

The trouble may be only temporary, during periods of peak overload, but it is clearly there. At one corporate venture, the first two years were so overloading that, a participant recalled, "No one took a vacation. Our spouses did not agree to this." But after start-up, venture group members used their bonuses to finance "many expanded vacations to Florida, California, and Mexico. Now we can afford the time and have the money." When the intense effort of post-entrepreneurial activity has a clear goal and a financial payoff, family harmony is more clearly maintained. Entrepreneurs in stand-alone start-ups report having less than five hours of leisure time a week, and 50 percent of a group surveyed by New Enterprises Associates called loss of family time the biggest cost of starting a business. But that did not necessarily result in divorce or discord because families shared the entrepreneur's dreams.[17]

Traditional corporate work, however, did not necessarily have the four characteristics that make entrepreneurial work hours tolerated by families—control, clear project goals, defined milestones permitting temporary relaxation, and large potential payoffs. Furthermore, families of traditional corporate workers were generally not allowed to be their partners.

Ambivalence about family responsibilities has a long history in the American corporate world.[18]

If any one statement can be said to define what is still the most prevalent corporate position on work and family, it is the "myth" of separate worlds. The myth goes like this: In a modern industrial society, work life and family life constitute two separate and nonoverlapping worlds, with their own functions, territories, and behavioral rules. Each operates by its own laws and ought to be kept separate. "A myth," Sebastian de Grazia has reminded us, "is not a lie. It is something almost everyone wants to believe. In believing it, he sometimes embraces a cold [idea] too warmly."[19] The myth of separate worlds, however, is a relatively recent historical development. Let's take a brief excursion into corporate history to see how this came about.

Historically and cross-culturally, organizations of all kinds, especially those making a radical break with the past, have attempted to exclude or neutralize particular ties that might compete with the loyalty and the commitment the organization demands from its members. The family is an especially insidious source of competing loyalties. For one thing, it combines both emotion and authority. Emotion—especially sexuality—was for a long time considered the enemy of work discipline, and its expression was excluded from the workplace. But the authority represented by the traditional institution of family is equally threatening to organizations for which its own authority is the sine qua non of its existence. The authority of parents over children, husbands (in the traditional model) over wives, and (in even more traditional systems) elder kin over younger ones—all might compete with the authority of the organization. That family members choose one another (in the case of marriage) or find themselves together (in the case of birth) for reasons totally unconnected with the organization's purposes further threatens to undercut its authority.

The dilemma for a loyalty-demanding organization, then, is this: whether to try to incorporate and thus co-opt the family into serving the organization's ends, or to try to exclude it by either replacing its functions or planning them clearly outside the boundaries of the workplace.

Recent histories of the family's relation to the evolving capitalist-industrial system indicate that the family was first incorporated into organizational life and then pushed outside. In the early years of the Industrial Revolution, the authority of the organization was absolute, and families were often uprooted and fragmented by the demands of their labor. But at the same time, in the first few decades of the nineteenth century, the family became an important work unit in city factories in England, as it was somewhat later in New England. Spinners in textile mills chose their wives, children, and near relatives as assistants, generally paying them from their own wages. Children entering the factory at eight or nine worked for their fathers, perpetuating the old system of authority and the traditional values of parents training children for occupations. In the 1820s and 1830s this system began to decline in England, partly to undermine the traditional economic authority of spinners.[20] But familial influences and ties in early industrial organizations were maintained much longer in the United States—for example, in the Amoskeag Corporation of Manchester, New Hampshire. Before the evolution of modern management systems, which were developed largely between 1890 and World War I, the family often functioned as a labor recruiter, a housing agent, an influence on the job placement of its members, and even a unit that could affect daily job control. Before personnel and recruitment systems were devised, organizations often relied on workers to bring in members of their families, and this was a large source of new women employees in factories during World War I. (A few prominent privately held companies like Steelcase in Michigan still rely heavily on family-based recruitment.) But the degree to which the family could exercise some control over and within the workplace was very much a function of ethnic group and industry; it was not true, for example, in steel mills.

Eventually, action against nepotism was taken in order to extend the control of managers over formerly more independent workers. In factories, at least, the unformed (children) or the unattached (young married women) were often the preferred workers, because of the assumption of their greater malleability. The textile mills of Connecticut, Rhode Island, and southern Massachusetts replaced the "family system," in which whole families were employed and wages and tasks assigned by age and sex, with a "boarding house system" devised by Boston financiers that employed young unmarried women from rural areas as temporary workers and housed them in company facilities.

Such systems were eventually ended by labor laws protecting children and women from exploitation. But by then, factory owners had managed to train a generation in appropriate work habits and thus to create its own labor force. Organizations at this time, primarily the proprietors, found it to be in their interest to break the family's control over work and workers, and this was an important consequence of the movement toward "systematic" or "scientific" management in America.

Other attempts to cope with the family problem in early industrialization involved swallowing the family and taking over its functions. One move was to make workplaces into "total institutions" in the form of company towns and company lodging. Some independence was lost to the family in such settings, and the organization had access to the private or nonworking aspects of workers' lives. Corporate "welfare" programs at the turn of the century, such as those of the H. J. Heinz Company of Pittsburgh in the 1880s and 1890s or the kindergartens run by National Cash Register in Dayton, often employed the imagery of the company as a "family," and in some cases there were intrusions into workers' homes—inspections to see if they were living respectable lives. This solution was never widely accepted, although there are still textile mills in the South where the integration of the family into the workplace extends organizational control over workers.

With the growth of cities, schools, and an organization-habituated labor force, antinepotism rules prohibiting the employment of close family members (usually husbands and wives) began to define the corporation's policy toward families. In the factory, the family no longer entered the system of production. New ideologies assumed that work was a central life interest and that people at work had no other responsibilities.

For the white-collar classes, the growth patterns of cities helped separate the family from the organization. Because industrialization was not a pleasant process, the ideology of home and hearth as the preserve of tradition and humanity grew through the nineteenth century. Those who could afford to remove their residences to "pastoral" surroundings, far from places of employment, often did so, also removing, in the process, points of contact between the rest of the family and the organization. It was the well-paid people—the least replaceable, with the most control over organizations' resources— whose loyalty, and hence freedom from particular ties, organizations needed most. And it was these same workers who perhaps tended to have the strongest degree of work-family territorial separation.

Territorial separation between residential and commercial/industrial districts, reinforced in the twentieth century by the advent of zoning and by striking architectural differences (until office buildings and high-rise apartments became indistinguishable), confirmed the tendency to see work and family as entirely separate. It is the middle-class family, after all, upon which many social images of America are based, and suburbia has in many ways become the American version of "traditional society." It is hardly surprising to note that, until the 1970s when women's labor force participation shot up, for much of the time large stretches of suburban residential areas were populated only by women and children, the people who were assumed to transform an individual male worker into a "family" with a "family life." (For years researchers studied the activities and attitudes only of women when they looked at "family life," thus reinforcing the myth of separate worlds.) The man was plugged in when he appeared, but he was *not* seen as carrying with him family membership when he went off to work. Employed women, however, were presumed to have, or want to have, a family.

Separation of the occupational and family sectors of society came to be considered by intellectuals essential to the smooth functioning of each and thus to the integration of society as a whole. This view rested, first, on a definition of the norms of each sector as "incompatible." Occupational life, in this perspective, is seen as organized around impersonal and objective standards of competence linked to the technical content of a function. These norms are directly opposed, a prominent sociologist of the 1950s argued, to those of the family, which instead rest on custom and particular and emotional standards and define roles by age and sex rather than "objective" performance criteria.[21] This same reasoning, of course, helps account for the tensions surrounding attachments at work.

But the sociologist took his argument a step further by concluding that a strong separation of the two sectors enabled each to function with a minimum of interference from the conflicting standards of the other. The work world's interests were served, in this theory, by making sure that only *one* member of a nuclear family played a "fully competitive" role in the work world, and that workplaces were clearly distinct from residences. The family's interests were also served by this separation (and the exclusion, then, of married women from paid careers), for intimacy and solidarity required, according to this theory, that husband, wife, and children not engage in direct competition for prestige or rate performance by impersonal standards.

If this argument now sounds like an apologia for the 1950s, it is because it was. The popularization of such theories coincided with the recognition of the "organization man"—and the first rumblings of discontent that would later disprove them. The traditional corporation reached its zenith in the 1950s and is only now being fully transformed. It pushed the family aside and excluded it from "business," while favoring managers with a private support system that would handle nonwork responsibilities without letting them interfere with work. The corporation's edict to its members could be phrased as: "While you are here, you will *act as though* you have no other responsibilities, no other life."

Thus, historically, *married* men and *single* women were the most likely to succeed in the most powerful and best-paid corporate positions. Married men not only were considered more stable, they also brought with them an unpaid support system that managed their home lives so that there were no conflicting demands, and sometimes assisted with business-related activities. All that, of course, is in the process of change with the virtual disappearance of the classic "corporate wife" and the advent of two-career couples in the workplace. Yet the conflict between the family and the organization is still unresolved and is reflected in subtle hiring preferences. Data from the *Wall Street Journal* poll of executives in 1987 make clear that divorce stigmatizes top executives and is still relatively rare due, analysts speculate, to pressure to keep the marriage together (and no time for divorce proceedings anyway). But executive recruiters are also beginning to note a change, ranging from acceptance of divorce to an active preference for single or divorced men—because, it is said, they can focus their energies on the job and save the costs of family relocation or spouse job searches.[22] Indeed, one of the corporate entrepreneurs attracted by new venture opportunities at Tektronix reported that his motivation for involvement was to have a project to throw himself into after a divorce, to absorb him so much he could forget about his personal problems. He was the only person who confided this motive, yet the sprouting of a connection between singlehood and the ability to participate in the post-entrepreneurial workplace cannot be ignored.

OLD ASSUMPTIONS, NEW REALITIES

The old assumptions, the "act-as-though" principles of the traditional corporation, were based on the premise that any strong personal attachment outside of work would be a distraction, a pull on the attention or energy of the employee. It was not even so much the time that family responsibilities took that was the issue; it was the competition for the employee's emotions. When United Airlines flight attendant Mary Sprogis was fired upon marrying a pilot in 1966, United claimed that unattached women were a "business necessity"; married ones would be worrying about their children instead of the passengers.[23] (She sued United for sex discrimination and won.)

Today married women join married men in the new workforce, and *both* worry about their children. In a 1986 *Fortune* survey of four hundred men and women with children under twelve, fathers were almost as likely as mothers to say that the job interferes with family life and somewhat more likely to claim they would sacrifice career opportunities that would cost them time away from their family (although less than a third of either group felt this way). Furthermore, there is evidence that responsibilities to children can take a toll on productivity for both men and women. AT&T sociologist John Fernandez's surveys show that 41 percent of working parents lost one day in a three-month period; 77 percent of the women and 73 percent of the men took time away from work attending to children, from phone calls to long lunches to more significant blocks of time.[24]

But if child care is increasingly an issue shared by men and women, other family responsibilities are not. Women still do the bulk of household work. In a nationwide survey analyzed by sociologist Catherine Ross, 76 percent of the women employed full-time still do the majority of the housework. In a Media General–AP poll of 1,473 adults nationwide in the spring of 1986, 93 percent of the respondents said spouses *should* share household cleaning equally when both work full-time outside the home, but women actually *do* more in 57 percent of the homes where there are two workers. In a survey of seventeen hundred women in nontraditional roles with children under two, seven out of ten of their husbands were said to offer significant "help," but mostly with car, maintenance and repair of equipment, and baby-sitting. The rest of the work was the woman's responsibility. Overall, women had 25 percent less leisure time than men in a 1987 survey of six hundred people with incomes over twenty-five thousand dollars a year.[25]

Is the changing workplace creating a major problem for a large proportion of the workforce? The new workforce contains an ever higher proportion of women with even greater education and even greater aspirations, along with a higher proportion of men married to such women. But the very people who are pressing for higher-level positions may also carry with them heavier outside-of-work demands, particularly centering on family responsibilities. In recognition of these demographic shifts, the number of companies offering subsidized daycare centers jumped almost 50 percent from 1984 to 1987, to about three thousand.[26] But still, relatively few new workplace systems involve flexibility, time off, or support for family responsibilities. U.S. Labor Department data in 1988 showed that only 11 percent of American companies offer child-care benefits to their workers. And while more than 20 percent of American workers have now alternative work schedules such as flextime, compressed work weeks, or regular part-time job sharing, according to a Work in American Institute study, there is little evidence that use of such alternatives extends to people in leadership positions or those involved in entrepreneurial assignments.[27]

Despite the rising career consciousness of newer cohorts of employed women, there still exists a conflict between the demands of work and the needs of family. There is scant evidence that women in their thirties begin to lose their career ambitions when they express a desire for children. The careers they have been educated to want, however, do not accommodate less than fully committed—and even overburdened—people. Thus, the opportunity-overload connection of the post-entrepreneurial workplace presents a danger of excluding half the workforce—women—from the better jobs. While equal employment opportunity policies open up hopes of higher positions for women, new work systems (designed with many of the same liberal goals in mind) may increase the barriers to getting them.

In the beginning of the equal opportunity push, it looked as if organizations characterized by high-participation, high-involvement work systems would also create more opportunities for women. It was thought it would happen because these organizations favored diversity and flexibility, in contrast to bureaucratic structures that kept women who were concentrated in "stuck" (low-mobility) positions from ever getting access to opportunity. But recent data from Silicon Valley show the paucity of women in significant positions in some of the most entrepreneurial companies in the country.[28] Many of the most compelling examples of effective innovation in highly entrepreneurial organizations show that sixty-plus-hour workweeks full of occasional all-nighters and midnighters and midnight trips to act on an inspiration are confined almost entirely to young men without families.[29] When married women with children engage in such activities, they are often working side-by-side with their husbands, as in the case of Elena Prokupets at Kodak's Edicon venture. Thus, it becomes clear that women do not automatically do better in innovative corporate environments unless there is also significant support for personal life and family responsibilities.

Outside-of-work responsibilities have not declined as work hours go up. The amount of leisure time is dropping *faster* than the increase in hours worked. A 1985 Harris survey identified a steady and inexorable decline in leisure time. Since 1973, the median number of hours worked by Americans (in paid work) increased by 20 percent while the amount of leisure time available to the average person dropped by 32 percent.[30] Market researchers call the dinner party a casualty of long work hours.[31]

There is a clear strain in the system here. As organizations loosen up and begin to operate on less hierarchical premises, giving more people an opportunity to participate in decisions, tackle challenging projects, and take on exciting tasks, they also become more absorbing of people's time, energy, and emotions. If they are allowed to absorb more of the person without providing support for other responsibilities, they will either become even more antagonistic to the family than they have been in the past or eliminate the prospect of ever reaching equal opportunity goals in the more challenging, higher-level, and better-paying positions.

Bumping up against old assumptions are new realities. Post-entrepreneurial organizations cannot afford rules and practices that exclude part of the workforce. Furthermore, work that is absorbing and overloading is reaching further down into the ranks, as organizations shift to post-entrepreneurial principles governing more and more jobs. For employees simply to put in their time is not good enough; they must put in their thoughts, their energy, and their commitment as well. In any case, the sheer amount of daily time it takes to succeed in post-entrepreneurial settings is greater than in the traditional workplace. But it can no longer be assumed, as in the traditional workplace, that responsibilities and commitment to personal and family life can be ignored.

MANAGING THE PERSONAL BALANCING ACT

Post-entrepreneurial management is essential to restoring the competitiveness of American companies, and it is appropriate for this work style to keep spreading. But the success of these leaner, more cooperative, more innovation-seeking companies cannot rest solely on the backs of overloaded employees.

Two ingredients combine to put most key personnel in a state of permanent overload. The first is an oversupply of tasks, and the second is a standard that requires that all tasks be done, no matter how many there are. When it is not easy to redistribute the tasks or establish priorities that reduce the load to more manageable proportions, people are stuck in a permanent state of overload. But even in post-entrepreneurial settings, workloads are less burdensome under three conditions.

1. When authority is delegated along with responsibility. This old lesson has some new implications. Consultants William Oncken and Donald Wass have distinguished four kinds of demands on management time: boss-imposed, system- or peer-imposed, subordinate-imposed, and self-imposed (discretionary)[32] Of the four, subordinate-imposed demands are the most controllable, because many of them involve a failure on the part of managers to delegate responsibility.

Instead, subordinates initiate (by presenting problems or ideas), but the manager still executes. Managers can reduce overload by increasing subordinates' ability to follow through without involving them, a principle that is even more important under the new post-entrepreneurial strategies than in traditional companies.

2. *When the number of simultaneous changes are minimized.* Another prime source of overload is the creation of new initiatives. Managers usually try to start and continue everything at once, and because of the constant motion surrounding important projects, employees find it difficult to focus and follow through on them. I have sat through many executive retreats that generate long lists of "action items," each one with an immediate deadline. This kind of overload can be controlled by declaring a moratorium on smaller projects or less significant initiatives, which allows the larger and more significant tasks to be accomplished.

The old lesson—setting clear priorities—has new, more urgent implications in the post-entrepreneurial workplace. Change requires a measure of stability. If everything is in flux, nothing can be counted on or accomplished.

3. *When simplicity is emphasized over complexity.* Robert Hayes and Kim Clark have observed that one productivity depressor in American factories is the sheer number of different items and options that must be handled.[33] There is a managerial and professional equivalent in too many choices and unique situations in the post-entrepreneurial workplace. Unnecessary complexity also results from the tendency in many organizations for activities and regulations, once institutionalized, to continue forever. But workloads can be made more manageable by invoking the organizational equivalent of sunset laws for roles, tasks, procedures, and programs that have outlived their usefulness. A large division of Exxon U.S.A. conducted a "hog law" review (the label is Texan) to see what old requirements still being adhered to could be pruned or eliminated.

Overload problems are exacerbated, then, by poor management. Still, in a post-entrepreneurial world, there is no guarantee that reducing bureaucratically induced overload would do much to reduce entrepreneurially driven overload—the desire to accomplish something of value however long it may take. When people choose to work hard, because of their involvement in their projects, how can they manage the rest of life?

The usual "solutions" can be arrayed along a continuum—from

individual "quasicelibacy" at one end to full-fledged corporate welfare systems at the other. At one extreme, some people clearly opt for a minimal personal life outside of work, remaining single (as the old-fashioned "career woman" used to do) or ignoring family bonds and abdicating any family responsibilities (as some high-level executives still do). But the celibate option neither appeals to the growing share of the population in entrepreneurial workplaces nor makes sense for the needs of society as a whole. So at the other extreme, the corporation could become the locus for emotional as well as professional life, as it does for "singles" who have no chance to meet "dates" except at work. The company could provide for all of the outside-of-work responsibilities of its employees—from child care to housing to grocery purchases to housecleaning services—as indeed many did in the past in the old company towns, and some do in more moderate forms today.

Neither extreme is particularly attractive. Almost by definition, personal life is something we all want to remain personal. But where should the balance be struck?

A first step is simply the official corporate acknowledgment of the nonwork responsibilities people bear, making it legitimate for both men and women to participate actively in family life and adding to their fringe benefits the resources to do this effectively.

Time, however, is the scarcest of resources. As long as post-entrepreneurial situations entice (or force) people to work to their fullest, time for personal life outside of work will be limited. Yet this does not necessarily mean that balance is impossible. Elizabeth Cook McCabe, Director of the Boston Advertising Club, coined the slogan, "You can have it all—but not all at once." Perhaps the solution to the post-entrepreneurial workplace dilemma lies in just that concept of long-term rather than short-term balance. Just as high-intensity new-stream projects involve a different work rhythm, with periods of extraordinary involvement ending as projects are completed and periods of rest following them, so too might we measure balance not in days or weeks but in months or years.

A second step, then, is acknowledgment of this long-cycle rhythm, a rhythm that already characterizes many entrepreneurial lives— periods of immersion in work and others that are more relaxed. This could mean organizing work around projects, and careers around cycles of involvement and relaxation. A point of payoff, when the project has achieved a major goal and rewards for contribution can be garnered, could be the signal for a period of rest or rededication to family. Apple Computer is moving toward this concept by offering sabbaticals after five years of employment.

The ultimate personal balancing act in this post-entrepreneurial era involves not just time but emotions. Highly absorbing work makes it harder to be emotionally available for personal relationships that are not tied to work. Post-entrepreneurial situations make it more likely that work responsibilities will intrude on attention as well as availability to family members. At the same time, the post-entrepreneurial workplace also makes it more likely that strong emotional attachments will arise in the midst of work.

Traditional assumptions about the separation of work life and personal life are no longer viable, but we have not yet created a coherent set of new values and beliefs to take their place. The "organization man," after all, is rapidly becoming obsolete, and the "cowboy" is not what American business needs either. Men and women alike hold leadership roles in a world requiring creativity and cooperation. The post-entrepreneurial contributor, to stay in shape for the competition, must lead a balanced life.

Thus, the post-entrepreneurial age is engendering a variety of balancing acts centering on personal responsibilities and relationships. Help in achieving balance can come from better personal time management, better organizational systems, and better institutional supports. But tensions and conflict between work life and personal life will never be fully resolved; they are almost inevitable by-products of post-entrepreneurial aspirations. Instead of trying to wish away the dilemma, we must give people the support they need to pursue business opportunities fully without shortchanging the human relationships that are of equal importance.

CHAPTER 11

From Climbing to Hopping: The Contingent Job and the Post-Entrepreneurial Career

*T*he traditional corporate career may soon share the fate of the dad-at-work-mom-at-home-two-kids nuclear family: an oft-invoked ideal that applies to fewer and fewer people.

Ask "Arnie" how different his career is today from what he expected five years ago, when he was happily ensconced in a strategic planning managers' job at an industrial products company, one more step in a certain pathway to a presidency. Now, with twenty-five years before retirement, he is scrounging for consulting jobs and thinking about buying a franchise because a change of focus wiped out his job, and he didn't want to take a downgrade.

Or ask "Estelle" how she "plans" her career after leaving an upper-level bank job for an insurance company offer—losing her place in line for the top officers' jobs and a number of profit-sharing and pension

298

benefits tied to longevity—only to find that the insurance company disappeared in a merger. So she looked a little longer and landed another good job, but that one too dissolved before she even got there because the company was taken over. To say that Estelle is aggravated doesn't do justice to her feelings. Now she has plunged into an entrepreneurial venture (a piece of which she might sell back to her old bank) with some partners who need her industry expertise, and she hopes to make an immediate killing big enough to compensate her for the loss of those profit-sharing benefits and the shot at the high-paying executive suite she gave up when she moved off the bank's career ladder.

Or ask "Paul" if he would ever go back to middle management now that he is an internal "venture capitalist" for his mid-sized company, having the fun of nurturing start-ups and getting paid in part by how well they do. Or look at the hope of growing numbers of Harvard MBAs: to be in business for themselves after five to ten years, to run their own smaller companies rather than slowly making their way to the top of larger companies. In short, they know they'd better count on themselves rather than on the traditional corporation.

The post-entrepreneurial revolution is reshaping the relationship between employers and employees; it is shifting the nature of work careers. As corporate jobs change in number, in mix, in substance, and in the characteristics of their incumbents, people have to rethink their careers. Bureaucratic-corpocratic assumptions about a steady, long-term rise up a hierarchy of ever-more-lucrative jobs give way to new realities and new expectations: long-term uncertainty, the need for portable skills, the likelihood of a stab at being in business for oneself. Climbing the career ladder is being replaced by hopping from job to job. Reliance on organizations to give shape to a career is being replaced by reliance on self. These circumstances generate personal dilemmas, dilemmas concerning loyalty and commitment. And while they touch a growing number of corporate employees at all levels, nowhere are they more clearly reflected than in the dramatic changes affecting the upper ranks.

TOWARD NEW CAREER PREMISES: FORCES ALTERING BUSINESS CAREERS

The three major post-entrepreneurial management strategies—restructuring in search of synergies; increasing reliance on external alliances, with suppliers of labor substituting for permanent internal employees; and the encouragement of innovation and entrepreneurship—are dramatically altering the nature of the corporate career.

Restructuring

The increasing uncertainty and instability of corporate careers is a direct result of restructuring. People at all levels, of course, are affected by the massive dislocations that accompany restructuring, and the costs are often much higher for those in lower-income and lower-skill categories. But the changes in the nature of managerial careers are most dramatic for what they presage about the declining ability of large organizations to provide the long-term security of traditional careers.

Between 1981 and 1986 nearly 11 million people were classified by the Bureau of Labor Statistics as "displaced workers," almost 10 percent of the civilian labor force. Almost half of these were experienced workers on the job for three or more years. The bureau further stated that more of this displacement was due to permanent separation, not temporary layoffs as in previous recessions. While 56 percent of the displacement occurred in factory-related positions, almost 40 percent took place among white-collar groups most likely to have had safe corporate careers in the past; 15 percent of the displacement was from the managerial and professional ranks; 22 percent from technical, sales, and administrative support.[1]

Between 1983 and 1987, according to another estimate, nearly ten thousand companies changed hands, and well over 2 million people saw their jobs disappear or deteriorate. The *Wall Street Journal* estimated that in the year 1985 alone, six hundred thousand middle managers were squeezed out in corporate belt-tightening, mergers, and takeovers. Indeed, one executive search firm found that 52 percent of the top management group leave a company within three years after a takeover.[2] In a 1985 Korn-Ferry survey of 1,362 senior executives about the biggest threats to an executive career, "mergers and reorganizations" stood out as the number one threat, cited twice as often as the factor next in line, "being in a slow-growth industry."

Large firm managers and professional staff are disappearing, and with them go a set of career expectations. In the 1980s, total employment in companies with one thousand or more workers fell by 1.2 million. By 1986, only 11.88 percent of the American labor force was employed by the Fortune 500 companies, down from 15.4 percent in 1977. Numerous examples make clear why bureaucratic career ladders are crumbling even in the absence of mergers and acquisitions. After reducing total employment at Xerox by about 20 percent, CEO David Kearns still felt about another third of the jobs in management and administration could come out. At Exxon the corporate headquarters staff went from 2,300 people in 1975 to 325 in 1987. More than three hundred major companies cut back their workforces between January 1985 and June 1986, including Apple, which lost 1,200 employees (20 percent of the previous total); and Eastman Kodak, which lost 13,700 by the end of 1985 (10 percent).[3]

Career expectations are changing in response to organizational restructuring. A 1986 Harris–*Business Week* poll of managers at the one thousand largest companies found that nearly 50 percent expected the company to reduce its salaried workforce in the next few years. They saw there was no connection between how well they did their job and how secure it was. On a Heidrick & Struggles survey of 545 top executives, 73 percent agreed that upper-level managers were beginning an exodus from Fortune 500 firms. Only 37 percent had confidence in the future of big companies. Fewer than half were willing to relocate for their company. Only one-third believed loyalty meant "support and commitment to corporate goals and strategies." And on a Hay survey of middle managers at sixteen hundred companies from 1975 to 1985, the percentage with a favorable view of their opportunity for advancement showed a precipitous drop from ten years earlier. In 1975 over 75 percent had a favorable view; by 1985 just under 40 percent did.[4]

Many middle managers in traditional large companies have always felt powerless anyway, squeezed between the demands of implementing strategies they don't influence and the ambitions of increasingly independent-minded employees. But at least they were well paid, had job security, and could expect a steady if slow rise. Now their privileges are eroding rapidly. They must cope with the classic difficulties of their positions while explaining why their positions exist at all. As Paul Hirsch put it: "Wall Street's advice to managers searching for excellence . . . has been to tell them to become excellent at searching for new jobs."[5] And managers, reading the handwriting on the corporate wall, are increasingly accepting incentives to retire early or simply departing before their numbers are called. Loss of faith in the corporation to provide a long-term career has been matched by the recognition that there may be better earning opportunities in other situations. It is not just loss of faith in individual employers that is involved but a more fundamental loss of faith in the very notion of the orderly, single-company career path.

Contracting Out

The second force influencing careers is the growth of what has been termed a "just-in-time workforce," or the "externalization of employment"—in other words, hiring temporary help or replacing internal departments with external suppliers of services.

There is ample evidence of the contracting out of jobs formerly done by full-time employees and the growth of "contingent" rather than "permanent" employment. Between 1963 and 1977 the number of temporary help service firms increased by 240 percent, payrolls by 468 percent, receipts by 469 percent in constant dollars, and employment by 450 percent. Between 1977 and 1981, there were increases of another 137 percent in payroll and 450 percent in employment. By 1986, 735,000 workers were employed by temporary help agencies, and the industry had almost doubled in size since 1982, growing 21 percent faster than the electronic computing equipment industry from 1979 to 1984.[6] For the United States as a whole, the number of people employed by temporary agencies rose from 400,000 to 804,000 between 1982 and 1986. In Massachusetts alone the rise was from about 25,000 to 37,000 in the same years. At a time of dramatic declines in unemployment in general, temps were one of the fastest-growing segments of the state's labor force.[7] And according to the Bureau of Labor Statistics data, the number of American workers whose primary income was earned in temporary jobs rose from 471,800 to 835,000 from 1983 to 1986.

More than half the new jobs created since 1980 have gone to contingent workers. The number of part-time workers in 1986 was 34.3 million, up from 28.5 million in 1980, and it is estimated that they will become 30 to 33 percent of the U.S. workforce by 1990, according to a Conference Board economist, who argued that perhaps half of these are involuntary part-timers.[8] Eighty-five to 95 percent of American corporations currently use temporary workers. By the year 2000, the Bureau of Labor Statistics indicates, about 80 percent of jobs will be in the service sector that uses 75 percent of temporary employees.[9]

Furthermore, there has been a shift in the nature of temps from those doing routine work to those with professional skills for special projects. The temporary business is booming for legal and medical professionals, for example. The computer makes it easier for some kinds of professionals to offer services without attachment to a firm. Cambridge Contract Engineering, to take one case, for ten years virtually owned the market of supplying professionals for high-tech firms; now there is an upsurge in competing firms. Typical CCE work orders are for chemical engineers at thirty-five dollars an hour; technical editors, twenty-one dollars an hour; or software engineers, forty dollars an hour. Professional temps report liking the freedom to move around, the high pay, and the absence of office pressures and politics. Charles Church, a thirty-nine-year-old software engineer, commented: "You come in specifically to get a job done, and that's what you concentrate on. I don't worry about office politics, and I don't get headaches from wearing neckties."[10]

Temporary agencies have themselves become big corporations. Norrell Corporation, number four in the industry in revenues, provides a variety of office and security services; it staffs mail rooms, file rooms, cash receipts areas, and data processing departments, among others. Norrell has grown from 49 offices with $22.5 million in sales in 1978 to 310 offices with $308.5 million in sales in 1987—and 130,000 "employees." By 1984, recognizing that more and more large corporations were using temps not only to gain flexibility in handling business fluctuations but also to replace whole categories of employment for routinely used functions, Norrell began touting its "permanent temporary services." Interestingly enough, Norrell itself is a post-entrepreneurial hybrid: part corporation, where managers (many of whom are recruited from among the temporary professionals) can climb a traditional career ladder; and part network of venture partners, including the eighty-five franchise owners who helped Norrell expand quickly.

As contracting out continues, and companies substitute supplier alliances for permanent employment, more people can expect to find their career in "producer service" industries—such as advertising, computer and data processing, personnel supply, management and business consulting, protective and detective services, building maintenance, legal services, accounting and auditing, and engineering and architecture—the fast-growing employment areas. But this sector also offers, on average, more uncertainty and less security than the traditional corporate career. In 1986, 15 percent of the self-employed were found in producer services, and one of the most rapidly growing segments of the industry was "personnel supply," a fact accounted for by the dramatic expansion of temporary help agencies placing contingent workers.[11]

Corporations are increasingly handling the demand for professional knowledge and services by contracting out rather than by adding permanent employees, and they are transferring whole departments to specialist companies like Norrell.

Opportunities for Creative Contribution

The third force altering the nature of careers is more positive. While traditional, perhaps more bureaucratic, managerial jobs are being eliminated at a record rate, and managers face growing career uncertainty, changes in the content of jobs provide new kinds of opportunities. As corporations try to develop newstream business, they are establishing venture units or venture funds that allow managers to run their own businesses or get support for special projects—and earn a direct return. Furthermore, the general move toward contribution-based pay begins to eliminate the need for promotion up a career ladder in order to increase earnings.

In the workplace that is emerging as companies gear up for the global corporate Olympics, opportunity goes to those who can *create* the job, not those who inherit a pre-determined set of tasks defining a hierarchical position. One example of how far this emphasis on inventing one's job extends is the comment made to me by an Apple manager after my first visit that I should "grow my own job"—and I was only a consultant. One Silicon Valley manager described it this way:

> In my position, the nature of the duties can change a lot depending on the expertise and interest of the individual. For example, if I were really anxious to travel and instruct, I could look around for some topics that aren't well documented and make myself an expert on those topics, and tell management that someone needed to go out and teach a course in that. In general, there's more work to do than people to do it, so you look at your position and you say, there are lots of things that would be appropriate for me to do. If I have a conscience I'll do what needs to be done. If I'm selfish, I'll do what I want to do. So there's a lot of flexibility.[12]

While full of opportunity, this workplace style is also full of uncertainty. The very chance to invent, shape, or grow a job puts career responsibility squarely in the hands of the individual. If jobs are fluid and created by their incumbents, how can organizations define orderly career paths? Making it possible for people to swim in newstreams, developing innovation projects, only underlines the idiosyncratic nature of the careers that evolve from individually determined jobs. Those working in corporate newstreams are not "contingent" employees in the same way that "temps" are; yet they still may not be able to envision a future with the corporation beyond the current project.

Post-entrepreneurial business strategies thus alter the context in which careers take shape, especially for the "white-collar elite" of professionals and managers who once felt their careers were secured and assured. To understand the impact of this shift, it is important first to consider how the traditional career paths are changing. I distinguish three principal "pure" career types—what social scientists call "ideal types"—into which most people's careers once fell: "corpocratic" (or bureaucratic-in-business) careers; professional careers; and entrepreneurial careers. Post-entrepreneurial management is rapidly making the bureaucratic type obsolete.

THE DEMISE OF "CORPOCRATIC" CAREERS

For much of the recent past, the idea of a career in the business world meant to most people a series of almost-automatic promotions to bigger and better jobs inside a company—a career pattern like the civil service of the government bureaucracy. Such a bureaucratic career is defined by the logic of *advancement*. The bureaucratic career pattern involves a sequence of positions in a defined hierarchy of positions. "Growth" is equated with promotion to a position of higher rank that brings with it greater benefits; "progress" means advancement within the hierarchy. Thus, a "career" consists of formal movement from job to job—changing title, tasks, and often work groups in the process. Indeed, these very characteristics were at the heart of social theorist Max Weber's original definition of bureaucracy in government.[13] These elements also describe the career systems of traditional, large companies, systems that can be called "corpocratic."

In the typical corpocratic career, all of the elements of career opportunity—responsibilities, challenges, influence, formal training and development, compensation—are closely tied to rank in an organization. Indeed, this—of the three major types—is the quintessential *organizational* career, for which employment by an organization is a necessity for the managerial job ladder to have any meaning at all. There could be no corporate career "ladder" without a structure of ranks and grades, defining by level who can do what and who can get what. For example, eligibility for membership on key policy committees may be tied to level, with an untested assumption that those who have attained higher levels have the "best" qualifications simply by virtue of attaining that level. Or pay may be tied to rank through the job grading system, common in American corporations; because there is a ceiling on how high salaries can go within ranks—regardless of performance—the person must be promoted, must advance to a "higher" position, in order to make more money.

The structuring of career incentives in the corpocratic pattern serves to induce those eligible for higher ranks to seek them. It thus encourages a proliferation of ranks and grades—sufficient distinctions so that there is apparent "progress" at sufficient intervals of time. It also encourages *weak* attachments to task or work group, since movement is the name of the game, but *strong* attachments to organizations, since ultimate rewards (financial and political) will come only with sticking it out with one employer long enough to get to the highest positions on the ladder. The manager in a corpocracy thus accumulates "organizational capital"—knowledge of a particular company, its traditions, its politics—as a chief career asset.

The bureaucratic business career had its moments of historical dominance in the United States with the rise of the large twentieth-century industrial corporation based on mass-production mechanical technologies favoring routinized jobs, and American economic hegemony, which allowed companies to get "fat." But as other nations come to the fore, as the global marketplace and international competition expand, as technology becomes more complex and more rapidly changing, as women and minorities seek access to the better jobs, and as growth slows (or reverses) in traditional industries, it is harder to sustain the assumptions on which the corpocratic pattern was based. Among those bureaucracy-inducing assumptions:

- A limited pool of competitors for higher positions, with the "losers" accepting their place, thus permitting a pyramidal distribution of people and maintenance of the legitimacy of hierarchy.
- Continuing organizational growth, so that opportunity could be offered through expanding the width of the pyramid.
- Long-term employment, so that eventually, over the career, rewards forgone now would be received later, at higher ranks.

The traditional corpocratic career, with its slow climb up the corporate ladder, was already on the decline even before the advent of today's restructuring pressures. Innovative organizational structures in newer industries provide many variations in managerial career paths. Highly decentralized organizations with matrix structures or project assignments tend to provide general management responsibilities for many more people, much earlier in their careers, thus giving them a taste of the entrepreneur's profit-and-loss orientation. For example, a product manager may feel like an "owner" of his or her line of business, negotiating with functional managers for the right team to design, manufacture, and sell the product.[14] At the same time, a consequence of flattening the hierarchy is that other managers will remain "professionals" for much longer in their careers. In neither case is promotion up a long ladder of jobs the most important factor any longer in determining "rewards." Entrepreneurial opportunities for some coupled with longer professional service for others means that the bureaucratic career pattern applies to fewer and fewer people.

Of course, the bureaucratic career logic never applied to all corporate jobs; the career logic associated with jobs varies even within the same corporation.[15] Companies provide career ladders for some jobs, but not for others; the length of ladders and the salary "height" they reach can vary greatly. For example, product managers with MBAs may have a long progression of promotions ahead of them in some companies, but internal human resource consultants in those same firms may find that their entry and terminal positions are roughly the same, meaning few if any promotions. One of the major thrusts of equal employment opportunity programs for women and minorities is to eliminate this difference in bureaucratic opportunity—to generate career ladders for people at lower levels who were denied access to promotions because their jobs were not viewed as leading to other, "higher" jobs. In large corporations as well as in the federal bureaucracy, upward mobility programs begun in the 1960s have indeed opened entry-level administrative positions to people.[16] But there is an irony here. The proportion of lower-level managerial jobs filled internally began to increase at just the same time that many companies, like Kodak, started looking outside for top talent previously found only from within. Thus, there are more competitors for middle management jobs while the jobs themselves are scarcer and less likely to automatically lead to top management.

At the same time that traditional career ladders are being built at the bottom, the higher rungs are being lopped off. More people at lower levels have *theoretical* access to promotion while the *actual* number of slots ''above'' is declining. If a company restructures to find synergies and combines operations with an acquired company or downsizes and reduces management layers, there are fewer ''high-level'' jobs. If a company handles expansion by using temporary workers and contracting out to suppliers, there are fewer chances for promotion, since promotion depends in part on expansion.[17] And promotion chances decline precipitously if the company deliberately cuts back at higher levels. One management consultant, who praises the virtues of downsizing, advised companies to remain lean in management and in employment in general:

> Make it hard to get hired. Develop detailed selection criteria. . . . Deliberately understaff. Use contractors and part-time employees as buffers to even the swings of cyclical business. Continually look for ways, short of hiring people, to get low value-added work done.[18]

The survivors of restructuring efforts are thus well aware that while they may still have a *job,* they may no longer have a *career*—at least in the traditional ladder sense. A manager in a corporation that restructured to gain focus by selling off a major chunk of the business found herself facing this dilemma. She said:

> I have mixed feelings about the divestiture. Because they cut so many people above me and collapsed the corporate and divisional departments into one, I have a much bigger job. Much bigger. More responsibility and excitement than anyone my age in other places. But that also puts me as high as I can go. There's no place to move into here. This is *it*. If I want to move up, I have to leave. Or try something else. Promotions seem like a thing of the past.

The corporate ladder is collapsing because it can no longer carry the weight. As post-entrepreneurial strategies take hold, they put more burdens on the traditional corpocratic career ladder than that career system can possibly handle. People's expectations for growth can no longer be fully accommodated by a corpocratic career pattern, because long sequences of jobs "above" no longer exist in many companies. People's hopes for achieving security by accumulating "organizational capital"—favors owed by peers, the good will of "superiors," knowledge of company routines and traditions—are diminished as restructuring continues to create new organizational combinations, and as external alliances become more important centers of strategic action.

Expectations of automatic earnings increases tied to attainment of "higher" positions are dashed by a shift toward contribution-based pay, making pay contingent on performance rather than on position. Even America's "corporate welfare system"—pensions and benefits offered to permanent employees of particular companies by those companies—is rendered obsolete by the shift to post-entrepreneurial principles. Most of those corporate entitlements are based on an assumption of longevity—that one person sticks with one company (itself an entity that is assumed to be unchanging).

Clearly, the bureaucratic pattern has to go. But what do we replace it with? And what about the security it brought to people, a security many still crave? However, before indulging in nostalgia for the traditional ladder career, we should also recall the rigidities associated with the corpocratic form of organization. Among other things, seniority is a poor guide to assignments and rewards in the performance-conscious corporate Olympics. Instead, professional and entrepreneurial career forms are better suited to innovative organizations operating in an uncertain and turbulent environment with high demands for change; and it is out of those roots that the new post-entrepreneurial career takes shape, with new forms of security beginning to blossom.

THE SPREAD OF PROFESSIONAL CAREERS

The professional career structure is defined by craft or skill, with the possession of valued knowledge the key determinant of occupational status, and reputation the key resource for the individual. Career "growth" for professionals does not necessarily consist of moving from job to job, as it does for corpocrats, and "advancement" does not have the same meaning. Instead, those on professional career tracks may keep the same title and the same nominal job over a long period. Opportunity in the professional form, then, involves the chance to take on ever-more-demanding or challenging or important or rewarding assignments that require greater exercise of the skills that are the professional's stock in trade. "Upward mobility" in the professional career rests on the reputation for greater skill.

Professional careers do not necessarily unfold within a single organization—as an employee of Company X. Professionals may be highly organizationally embedded (for example, engineers and teachers) or weakly organizationally embedded (for example, physicians in private practice affiliated with hospitals but not "employed" by them). In fact, the professional "community" or industry may be a more important organizing factor in the professional career model than an employing organization that writes the paycheck. For example, consider the Hollywood film industry, characterized by a system of recurrent ties among major participants working under short-term contracts for single films. Those with records of success are in a better bargaining position for the next round of contracting.[19] Indeed, journalist Bruce Nussbaum observed that Hollywood could soon be the model for work in big companies; film producers move from one studio to another, loyal only to themselves and their profession, and television producers jump from one station to another.[20] Similar examples include professionals and entrepreneurs coming together for high-technology development projects, financial deals between bankers and international clients, and real estate development.[21] One job-hopping manager commented that in biotechnology "We are all gypsies. You work for an industry, not a company." His own career, for example, took him from a Ph.D. in chemistry to Polaroid to a medical diagnostics start-up.[22]

In such cases, careers are produced by *projects* rather than by the hierarchy of jobs in a single organization. And the key variable in success is *reputation*. Reputation counts for both those people pulling projects together, so they can attract the best talent, and those professionals who want to find the best projects. Each project, in turn, adds to the value of a reputation as it is successfully completed. So people make their commitments to projects rather than to employers.

Professionals thus exhibit weak loyalty to particular employing organizations. As an observer of computer professionals at Apple and other Silicon Valley companies put it, the "right place to work" is a matter of the appeal of particular projects:

> There is no single or permanent right place, of course. It varies depending on the current desires and skills of the individual, and how these match up with the currently available array of work options. Since both change, negotiating a career in Silicon Valley is best viewed as an intricate free form dance between employees and employers that rewards continuous monitoring but cannot be fully choreographed.[23]

As occupations "professionalize," then, their members not only command greater remuneration for services because of their enhanced collective reputation and the skills monopoly they can enforce through associations that provide "credentials," but they also exhibit a weaker attachment to employers, except perhaps for firms of fellow professionals. Indeed, firms of professionals, such as law firms, management consulting firms, or firms of architects and designers, can flourish precisely because of portable skills that can be exercised on behalf of many different organizations rather than dedicated to one. Because of the portability of reputation—and the relationships with clients or project formers that flow from it—talent raids of professionals are common in some industries. Between December 1987 and January 1988, Dean Witter hired away eighty-two stockbrokers from E. F. Hutton, including three whose gross production was over $1 million a year and one whose gross production was almost $4 million. But when Dean Witter itself was acquired by Sears in 1981, other firms lured its talent. This practice is especially prevalent in stock brokerage because of the bond between broker and client. At Shearson, according to outsiders' estimates, about one-quarter of its experienced brokers leave each year. The only way to get loyalty seems to be by buying it—deferring compensation or offering products that tie a broker's customers to the firm.[24]

The professionalizing of managerial work—the growth of specialized skills in such areas as financial analysis, strategic planning, compensation, and marketing—means that even a manager's fate is no longer tied to a single corporation; most managers acquire a knowledge base and a set of skills that are transferable to other organizations. What economists call "firm-specific knowledge" derived from long experience with a single company is also declining in value relative to more generalizable expertise because of a rapidly changing business environment. When change and innovation are the issue, the skills to be flexible and learn are more important as a way to build the future than long-term company experience that helps to preserve traditions and routines.

The professionals' reliance on reputation stands in great contrast to the anonymity of the bureaucrat. Professionals have to "make a name for themselves"; for corpocrats, the "name" that confers status is the company name. And the determination of career fate by fellow professionals through peer review also stands in great contrast to the determination of a corpocrat's fate by hierarchical "superiors"—a ridiculous label anyway, since it refers to decision-making rights and may have nothing at all to do with whether bosses are indeed "superior" in skill. The mobility of the professional career depends upon establishing a value in the external marketplace that is reputation-based. This reputation is conferred by others—by peers (as in reviewers for professional journals or Pulitzer Prize boards or Cannes Film Festival voters or Deming Quality Award selectors in Japan), or sometimes by "fans" or "constituents" whose "votes" select the "best."

The creation of star quality is a hallmark of the dynamics of a professional career. It serves, certainly, to increase opportunity dramatically for those so recognized, but it also serves to confer professional status on the entire profession, by indicating that there are high objective standards attained by the best practitioners—standards that exist independently of what specific organizations may seek to attain. Thus Deming Awards for manufacturing quality in Japan help professionalize blue-collar industrial work by setting and rewarding universal quality standards.

Some of the changes in the organization of work occurring in the United States and Canada, sometimes derived from models used in Japan, West Germany, and Scandinavia, thus involve attempts to substitute professional career structures for corpocratic ones—increasing professional opportunities for growth. One good example is the pay-for-knowledge system, which provides individual incentives for employees to upgrade their skills rapidly. Such trends as these pose yet another alternative to climbing the corporate ladder.

In an increasing number of circumstances, then, the corpocratic career model has been replaced by more professional career structures. Why should teachers have to become administrators in order to earn more or have their greater mastery of their field acknowledged? Why should skilled craftworkers in factories face a salary ceiling if there are still more ways they could contribute within their current job title? Why is a proliferation of hierarchical "levels" reflected in changing job titles necessary to motivate performance in the United States if Japanese organizations are more productive with far fewer levels and classifications?

One of the attractions of offering professional opportunity is that it is inherently less limited than corpocratic opportunity, in that "growth" is not dependent on either widening the pyramid or heightening the hierarchy—or on someone else moving out of a position. Hence its advantage in times of slower economic growth or awareness of the costs of excessive hierarchy. Furthermore, professional opportunity involves setting high performance standards and incentives to master them—another benefit in competitive economies.

THE BURGEONING OF ENTREPRENEURIAL CAREERS

The third major career pattern is the classic entrepreneurial one. The term "entrepreneur" has come to be associated with the formation of an independent business venture or with ownership of a small business, but these meanings are too restrictive. Instead, an entrepreneurial career is one in which growth occurs through the creation of new value or new organizational capacity. If the key resource in a bureaucratic career is hierarchical position, and the key resources in a professional career are knowledge and reputation, then the key resource in an entrepreneurial career is the ability to create a product or service of value.

Thus, for Kenneth Olsen, founder and chairman of Digital Equipment Corporation in 1957, career "growth" has involved no changes of title or job or position; yet, he has greatly increased his power, remuneration, and responsibilities by leading the growth of the organization around him to much larger size—and reaping a direct return from the economic value he has created. This entrepreneurial career pattern is not restricted to the single founder. It occurs for everyone in the same organization who "stays in place" but leads the growth of the territory for which he or she is responsible. Recently formed and rapidly growing businesses often offer entrepreneurial careers in many areas, to many people. In a small financial firm, the director of auto industry projects began with three people, and then, as the business grew, she found herself managing several levels of staff across several cities, with a bonus tied to the profits of her area.

Instead of *moving up,* those in entrepreneurial careers see progress when *the territory grows below* them—and when they "own" a share of the returns from that growth.

The risk of entrepreneurial careers is certainly greater than that of corpocratic careers or even of professional careers. The essence of corpocratic careers is certainty and security, in return for which people will sometimes take a lower wage than they might receive if they were in business for themselves. Professionals have taken on the mantle of skill or knowledge, which commands a price in the marketplace. Independent entrepreneurs have only what they grow. But then, they can also capture a much higher proportion of the returns if they succeed.

Freedom, independence, and control not only over one's tasks (as the professional supposedly has) but also over one's organizational surroundings are associated with the classic entrepreneurial career. But so is greater uncertainty about the future, about how the career will unfold. The freedom to fail is an integral part of this career pattern, especially in entrepreneurial pockets like Boston's Route 128 or California's Silicon Valley. But some venture capitalists argue that an entrepreneur who has gone bankrupt with one idea can come back and get the capital to start another idea.[25]

There are ways to limit risks as an independent entrepreneur, of course, with franchising preeminent among them. The number of franchise-format businesses in the United States, over 2,000 in 1986, is more than double what it was ten years earlier, according to Commerce Department data. These companies operated over 300,000 units in 1986, compared to 220,000 in 1976. In 1986 sales were about $576 billion, up from $365 billion in 1981, a 58 percent jump. There are more than 2,200 franchisers in more than 60 industries. Many are services like home remodeling, carpet cleaning, painting, dry cleaning, oil changes, tune-ups, temporary employment, and even franchised business consulting. Notable among them, if only for their ingenuity, are Duds 'n Suds, a combination laundry and singles bar;

Hemorrhoid Clinics of America; and Molly Maid, a service providing cleaning women in frilly English maid uniforms. There were 1,942 *varieties* of franchising businesses in 1984. The total number of units in the United States as of 1986 was 328,812, up over 26 percent compared to the 260,555 units in 1981.[26]

Risks are minimized for franchisee-entrepreneurs. A 5 percent discontinuance rate in the first year compares with a 30 to 50 percent rate of small business failures in the first year, according to Small Business Administration statistics. Commerce Department figures indicate a discontinuance rate in 1984 of 3.2 percent (not including franchises that are sold back to the parent, often at distress prices).

Franchising has gotten a boost from corporate restructuring; laid-off middle managers sometimes use their severance pay to start businesses. Industry insiders observe:

- I am seeing a lot of former middle managers in their 40s and 50s who are realizing that they won't have enough from a corporate pension for a comfortable retirement. (Terry Fairbanks, whose company, Copy Mat, has sold 75 copy center franchises since 1984)
- The best market for potential franchisees is coming out of the middle management ranks. (Carol Green, Chairperson of Denver's Franchising Network)
- . . . A corporate team player may be better suited to franchising than an entrepreneurial maverick, who may chafe at the rules and procedures any franchiser will impose on him. (John James, director of entrepreneurial services at Arthur Young in Houston)[27]

Consider the examples of Charlie and Linda, now married and in business together as store owners. Charlie, an engineer, had been laid off and had to stand in unemployment lines. A suggestion at a party sent him to look at property for a sandwich store, a "Subway," in Fort Lauderdale. He started his franchise with six thousand dollars in the bank and a ten-speed bike, which he used to make bank deposits, riding through the summer rains. Meanwhile, Linda left her job as an executive trainee at Macy's in San Francisco to tend bar "until I could have my own business." A casual visit to a Subway in her parents' home town of Eugene, Oregon, got her thinking about a Subway franchise. She opened one in Los Angeles and ran it until she and Charlie married. They met in a franchise advisory committee meeting.[28]

Whether forced out or opting out, big company managers and professionals are going into business for themselves in record numbers. Added to the restructuring victims, who have no choice because their jobs have disappeared, are two other groups: corporate escapees who see no chance for progress because entrenched managers are blocking their way up the ladder and self-confident risk-takers who want more autonomy and the chance to capture the returns from their labors more directly.

A spate of new service businesses in Boston, for example, have been formed by "stuck" middle managers who see fewer slots above them, and those higher positions that do exist unlikely to be vacated soon. Going into business for themselves is thus a way to break loose. This version of the entrepreneurial dream revolves around autonomy rather than wealth, around "being my own boss" rather than building an empire. It is a response to the strains of subordinacy. One outplacement counselor, for example, claimed that 90 percent of her clientele of dismissed executives think of starting their own company, to avoid being in a position where they could be powerless and get fired again. Only 30 percent actually do start a business.

At a time of shrinking big-company payrolls, a desire to convert the fixed costs of employment into the variable costs of subcontracting, and closer alliances across companies that promise a continuing flow of business, independent entrepreneurship has to represent a desirable alternative to corporate employment. From the point of view of the individual, there are more opportunities for small firms and independent contractors to pick up the tasks of disappearing departments—and be treated as a valued ally in the process. From the point of view of the large corporation, helping former employees start businesses may be easier than helping them find another job—and may allow the corporation to keep the services the employees provide.

Thus, it is now a routine part of outplacement counseling to test entrepreneurial skills and desires. The idea is growing in other realms, too. The State of Washington is experimenting with a plan to encourage laid-off workers to start their own businesses by giving them lump sum payments of up to six thousand dollars from a Labor Department grant. There are some legal and political hurdles, but support is growing, including support in Congress. Franchising is increasingly seen as a middle ground for displaced managers who want to start businesses but also want the security of attachment to a business already established in the marketplace and providing detailed operating procedures to follow.

Take the case of Alan Shaver, age forty-nine, out of a job after twelve years as General Foods' corporate secretary because of the company's acquisition by Philip Morris. He chose to resign after feeling that his assignments were now only make-work. Ironically, Shaver himself had been responsible for shrinking his department by 50 percent to cut administrative costs to help "save" General Foods. Getting onto another corpocratic ladder had to look like a dubious proposition to him. Of four serious job interviews in his first months of looking, one company was then taken over and two were identified as takeover targets. Shaver has increasingly focused on buying a small business or a franchise.[29]

Add reluctant entrepreneurs like Shaver to the self-employed and sole proprietors, and the growth of the new career logic becomes clear. Between 1974 and 1984, self-employment in the United States tripled, with women accounting for most of that growth. In 1987 self-employment accounted for almost 10 percent of the nonagricultural workforce over twenty-four years old—nine million people.[30]

In general, the entrepreneurial career pattern offers many of the elements often found to be associated with motivation for high productivity: control over one's own work, ability to set one's own pace, the joy of seeing something emerge out of nothing, monetary rewards tied directly to what one has accomplished. From a company's standpoint, offering jobs that resemble entrepreneurial situations can have the additional virtue of reducing fixed labor costs—because pay varies with how much people actually bring in. Hence, salespeople paid on commission often have "entrepreneurial" careers. Even though "employed" by large organizations and subject to the direction of managers, they develop their own territory and reap the rewards thereof—a condition both highly motivating in a potentially frustrating occupation like selling, and risk-reducing for the employer who does not have to pay unless there are results. In fact, it is often hard to get top salespeople to leave the entrepreneurial track; the bureaucratic pace of a managerial career seems unappealing.

Corporate trends further add to the number of people who taste some form of entrepreneurship sometime in their work life. Some American corporations are trying to establish entrepreneurial options as an alternative both for individual careers and for business growth.

Newstream ventures within otherwise traditional corporations can offer venture participants the chance to earn a return, just as founder-owners do, on the marketplace performance of their product or service. While this alternative was relatively rare five years ago (as of 1984 only 6.9 percent of 1,618 AMA member organizations in a 1984 American Management Association survey had special venture funds or entrepreneurial opportunities),[31] interest in newstream vehicles is growing among leading companies. Changes in pay also open entrepreneurial career options to workers otherwise stuck in corpocratic systems; for example, employee stock ownership or gain-sharing. These plans offer opportunities to increase earnings and sometimes even influence and control without having to wait for a promotion. The revolution in pay practices allows growing numbers of people to begin to see themselves as resembling entrepreneurs in business for themselves, even if nominally an employee of a larger corporation.

If corpocratic opportunity is inherently limited (because it is tied to "openings" in higher-level positions), entrepreneurial opportunity is expandable. And the entrepreneurial career path is also more directly attuned to creating new value rather than simply preserving old ways.

THE POST-ENTREPRENEURIAL BLEND

Careers shaped by professional and entrepreneurial principles better fit the needs of businesses struggling to compete effectively in the corporate Olympics. The skill of the professional and the innovation of the entrepreneur are important assets for the economy as a whole. Like it or not, more and more people will find their careers shaped by how they develop and market their skills and their ideas—and not by the sequence of jobs provided by one corporation. More people will be in and out of business for themselves at more points in their careers, as they enter and leave corporations, as they start and grow businesses, as they combine with peers to offer professional services for still other businesses and corporations. Some post-entrepreneurial careers will still unfold within the embrace of a large corporation, but they will be marked less by promotions to greater administrative responsibility and more by project opportunities blending professional skills and innovative ideas.

Overall, the power of the position is giving way to the power of the person. A formal title and its placement on an organization chart have less to do with career prospects and career success in a post-entrepreneurial world than the skills and ideas a person brings to that work. This model can produce world-class athletes in Olympic contests for corporations that know how to develop and tap skills, wherever they are found. This model can open vast opportunities for people as well, if the training, coaching, and financial backing is available to help them move with their skills and their ideas. But this model is also fraught with risks and uncertainties. The changing shape of careers produces its own set of corporate balancing acts.

CHAPTER 12

The Pursuit of Skill and Reputation: Security and Loyalty in a Post-Entrepreneurial World

To the Chinese, opportunity and danger are conveyed by the same symbol. To post-entrepreneurial corporations and their people, opportunity and danger are also found together in the new career patterns.

The opportunities are clear: an adaptive workforce for which getting ahead means getting better—growing in skills, growing ideas, or finding ever more challenging arenas in which to apply skills and ideas. Companies that know how to learn because their people know how to learn.

The dangers are equally clear: cutting people loose from corporate security without offering anything else to make them focus on building for tomorrow, not just complying with today's demands. If people are encouraged to rely on themselves, then how can the corporation rely on them? A response is urgently required. The "contract" between corporations and their people must be rewritten to provide new forms of security that, in turn, engender a new, more powerful kind of loyalty.

THE NEW SECURITY: "EMPLOYABILITY"

The overall impact of post-entrepreneurial strategies is to weaken the power of hierarchy and loosen the employment bond between corporation and person. The impact of changes in the content and context for managerial jobs, for example—corporate venture opportunities, rewards for contribution, and the professionalizing of managerial work—is to reduce the necessity for long-term employment with a single organization in a sequence of ever-higher jobs as the only way to earn increasing career rewards. At the same time, long-term employment is rapidly disappearing, leaving those who counted on it adrift in a sea of insecurity. Even for those who remain with one employer, the logic of their careers is less likely to resemble the bureaucratic pattern of an orderly progression of ever-higher-level and more remunerative jobs. Instead, they are more likely to move from project to project, rewarded for each accomplishment, like professionals; or to create their own opportunity by developing newstream ideas and getting a piece of the action, like entrepreneurs.

The post-entrepreneurial career, then, is a blend of professional and entrepreneurial principles, premised on more "contingent" jobs. Although some jobs are "contingent" in the fullest sense—temporary, a matter of subcontracting with few benefits or promises—all jobs today have a greater contingency factor. One's pay, one's future, is ever more contingent on individual performance, on the company's ability to remain in business or continue as an identifiable entity, on strategic decisions about which services to supply inside and which to buy on the market.

If security no longer comes from being *employed*, then, it must come from being *employable*.

In a post-entrepreneurial era in which corporations need the flexibility to change and restructuring is a fact of life, the promise of very long-term employment security would be the wrong one to expect employers to make. But *employability security*—the knowledge that today's work will enhance the person's value in terms of future opportunities—that is a promise that can be made and kept. Employability security comes from the chance to accumulate human capital—skills and reputation—that can be invested in new opportunities as they arise. No matter what changes take place, persons whose pool of intellectual capital or expertise is high will be likely to find gainful employment—with the current company or with another company or on their own. Timothy Tuff, President of Alcan Aluminum U.S.A., offers no guarantees of continued employment to the people he entices out of the mainstream to head Alcan's newstream businesses, but he does tell them, "If they give the new business a whirl, they will be a better and more saleable person for it."

In many high-tech firms, where people understand the uncertainties of the environment, there is already a realization that employability security is the appropriate career foundation. There, employment is seen as dependent on continuing hard work and growth in skills, and security on the ability to generate income regardless of the fate or good will of any particular employer. But what makes a company attractive, in turn, is its ability to provide learning opportunities—chances to grow in skills, to prove and improve one's capability—that enhance the person's ability to keep employable. Training and retraining or challenging jobs on significant projects are more important, in this calculus, than benefits programs like pensions contingent on long service. Apple Computer, for example, had a billion dollars in revenue and thousands of employees before it had a pension plan.

Even in cases in which employment security is promised, the *employment* guarantee is only possible because of programs aimed at ensuring *employability*. The new forms of employment security rest on a base of employability security. In the Pacific Bell–Communications Workers of America business partnership, the company offered employment security in exchange for greater flexibility in deploying people, and an Agreement on Employment Security was the first step in forming the alliance. But what the company was in fact offering was human capital investments to secure people's future, not a guarantee that they would always remain in their jobs. The company was offering to invest in retraining and career counseling that would continually upgrade people's skills so that they would always be employ-*able*, though their jobs might disappear and they might have to prove their abilities to contribute to the company over and over again throughout their careers.

Some prominent companies have always been able to attract top talent even when they had stringent up-or-out systems for younger managers, with no security at all, because they were seen as a training ground, a good place to learn and a good place to list on one's résumé. One of those was General Electric, traditionally tough on new hires but still getting the best because of its learning opportunities—and then full of long-term security for those who made the cut. But GE is now even more geared toward promising only employability security, and no other guarantees. After eliminating a whopping one-fourth of General Electric's workforce, CEO Jack Welch understood that the company's ability to attract and motivate people would not come from the promise of job security but from the attractiveness of opportunities for achievement: "The job of the enterprise is to provide an exciting atmosphere that's open and fair, where people have the resources to go out and win. The job of the people is to take advantage of this playing field and put out 110 percent."[1]

The new, post-entrepreneurial GE system would be fine for the Silicon Valley computer professionals Kathleen Gregory studied, who take exciting opportunities as they arise, without planning formal careers. Said one of the managers in her study:

> The word "career" is an interesting one that I think is almost inappropriate to this industry and this Valley, because "career" to me implies some sort of planning. I think of people who graduated with an MBA and go to work for a large company and they have their career path laid out in front of them. That's something I don't see happening here at all. People are attracted for a variety of different motivations. They come, they do their thing, and they may evolve into other jobs or they leave the company and go somewhere else. At least if you ask most people, "What do you think you'll be doing in ten years from now?" they'd be hard pressed to give you an answer. But, there is a great deal of confidence that when they're ready to move on, something for them to move on to will be there.[2]

Even where companies *want* to keep the same employees long term and promise them a job for life, they can only afford this is they keep people growing and learning through elaborate retraining, as IBM did to avoid layoffs in 1985—in short, keeping them *employable* within the same corporation. Continuing upgrading of skills and pursuit of new opportunities is a lifelong proposition even inside a single corporation. Of course, it is essential in the wake of restructuring.

For people who think about their careers, the pursuit of learning opportunities and reputation may be overtaking the pursuit of promotion, as post-entrepreneurial strategies take hold. In many corporations, managers now work with one eye on their résumé. Assignments that used to be seen in terms of their political value in the promotion game are now assessed for their résumé value, viewed in terms of how they will position the person in the external labor market or how they provide learning that will help the person with the business he or she hopes to start someday.

In short, what people are increasingly working to acquire is the capital of their own individual reputation instead of the organizational capital that comes from learning one system well and meeting its idiosyncratic requirements. For many managers, it might be more important, for example, to acquire or demonstrate a talent that a future employer or financial investor might value than to get to know the right people several layers above in the corporation where they currently work.

This shift to investment in reputation can produce more skillful and self-directed business contributors. It can also produce cynics who distrust any attachment to the corporation. Chuck loyalty, the cynics say—it's a burden, not a virtue—and invest in self. *Fortune* magazine columnist Walter Kiechel advises managers to jump at jobs at other companies when they can, because when they are forced out of their present companies those jobs may not be there. Kiechel's version of the "New Employment Contract" holds that:

> Hereinafter, the employee will assume full responsibility for his own career—for keeping his qualifications up to date, for getting himself moved to the next position at the right time, for salting away funds for retirement, and, most daunting of all, for achieving job satisfaction. The company, while making no promises, will endeavor to provide a conducive environment, economic exigencies permitting.[3]

Similarly, Paul Hirsch, who calls career planning "a random crapshoot," offers this advice in a career handbook for the new management era: Remain emotionally separate, resist the temptation to get drawn into a corporate surrogate family, maintain visibility, marketability, generality, credibility, and mobility. Do this by cultivating networks, returning recruiters' calls, avoiding overspecialization, and avoiding long-term and group assignments. Overall, Hirsch cynically advises career management geared to the résumé. He says that managers should ask themselves about every assignment: Will having this experience on my résumé make me more attractive to future employers?[4]

This cynical career strategy is confirmed by a shift in assignment preferences uncovered in an informal survey of major banks and *Fortune* 500 companies. Jobs once considered plum assignments and prerequisites for top executive posts are now judged dead-end spots to be avoided because they do not translate to jobs in other companies or keep people in the mainstream of the job finding networks.[5] The standard for the résumé game players, then, is no longer whether the job is important to the current employer, but whether it has "résumé value."

But concerns about employability do not have to result in this kind of game playing, which puts personal welfare above company welfare. There are many people who know that the substance behind the items on the résumé matters even more in a post-entrepreneurial world, and thus they seek a track record of accomplishments by taking on change projects that can provide clear benefits to the company. If anything, their own fate and the fate of their projects are more closely intertwined in post-entrepreneurial companies; unless there are company payoffs, these people may be cast adrift without additional reputational capital.

It was more typical than not, in the companies I worked with, to find that the uncertain and contingent quality of post-entrepreneurial careers compelled people to look for ways to demonstrate their value to the company—if there were opportunities for leadership of significant projects and no abrupt transitions in the wind that would make it hard to complete them.

In one case, a ten-person project team was designing a new cost-saving system for a major unit of a large company; every person on the team had a different career stake in the project. The project manager knew it was a chance to demonstrate his capacity to run the entire department once the system was installed; another manager used it to gain new skills so she could move into a different kind of work, maybe for the current company, maybe not; a third professional who had been ready to quit to go into consulting on his own found the project an exciting challenge that kept him at the company; a fourth manager was explicitly interested in having experience with that kind of system to add to her résumé. Despite the differences in career hopes and expectations—differences that themselves reflected post-entrepreneurial variety—each team member shared a concern for producing a high-quality product that would quickly demonstrate its value to the company. In fact, the knowledge of these career stakes in a world without guaranteed employment motivated the team to work especially hard to make the project valuable for not just their own department but for every other business unit in the company.

If post-entrepreneurial career prospects sometimes create cynics unconcerned with corporate performance, then they can also create professionals passionately concerned about making strategic contributions to the company's success. The difference lies in whether the company shows its own concern for its people by treating them fairly at times of transition, giving them ample notice of changes so they adjust gradually, investing in their learning and growth, giving them opportunities for innovative contributions, and rewarding their performance directly.

It is hard to tease out all of the consequences of the post-entrepreneurial career logic, however, by looking inside the corporation, because the changes in commitments and behavior are subtle and not always observable. So I looked for cases that would put the changes under a magnifying glass to make them easier to see. The impact of the career revolution is seen most dramatically in cases in which people move from being employed managers to being outside contractors for their former employers. In these instances, similar tasks are performed by the same people for the same organizations. But the people are no longer employees occupying positions in a hierarchy with promotion expectations; instead, they are suppliers in business for themselves. These examples help us see the financial consequences for the individual-turned-supplier, the productivity consequences for the employer-turned-customer, and the relationship consequences for everyone.

Take the case of Stanley Collins. Collins made the transition from manager to entrepreneur after thirty-four years on the career ladder of a big company.[6] In 1986, Collins lost his job as director of corporate relations, with twenty-one direct reports, when Owens-Corning Fiberglas restructured to fight a hostile takeover bid and eliminated all but two people from the thirty-one-person public affairs department. A reluctant entrepreneur ("I never had any burning desire to do it"), Collins quickly joined forces with the manager of Owens-Corning's video-communications operation, also let go, to buy the video labs and set up shop as SK Associates, producers of corporate communication tools.

A number of things stayed exactly the same. Collins worked in the same building, renting space Owens-Corning had available because of the downsizing; for the first few months, Collins and his partner even kept their old offices. He worked with many of the same people, because Owens-Corning was the business's first customer. Contacts still inside the company provided advance intelligence about departments with public relations needs.

But these superficial signs of continuity masked more dramatic signs of change. The basis for Collins's earnings was different. While Collins could do very well financially if the business expanded, for the first year he was making less than half of the eighty thousand dollars plus he had earned as an employee and had no corporate benefits. First-year partnership income was better than initial projections, offering Collins and his partner the prospect of substantial returns in the future. But the risks were equally real. The business was started with loans secured by mortgages on the partners' homes.

Collins's use of time was also different. The partners were eager to reduce dependency on Owens-Corning, so selling became a much bigger part of Collins's workday. Adjusting to the lack of support services, the entrepreneurs were required to put in their own time on everything from insurance to the purchasing of equipment. As Collins said:

> You don't realize when you're in the corporate womb how protected you are. Before, when I needed a copy machine, I said, "Get me a copy machine." This time, I went to the stores and looked at forty-eight models.[7]

Relationships were different, too. It was sometimes awkward to serve as a contractor to former subordinates, making the transition from treating them as employees to be *handed* tasks to treating them as customers who *provided* tasks. One can also wonder how long the new business could continue to get "insider" market intelligence on Owens-Corning.

Overall, then, post-entrepreneurial careers presage a number of important changes.

Changes in Economic Well-Being: Fluctuating Income

One of the integral pieces of the corpocratic career logic was the expectation of linear progress: Tomorrow will be better than today. But moving off a corporate ladder can mean severe income fluctuations or a reversal of fortunes. Professional and entrepreneurial careers are not linear in the same sense as bureaucratic careers. Post-entrepreneurial careers can provide much greater economic opportunity for some, and the chance to expand earnings well beyond the limits of a corporate paycheck, but this chance comes with more risk and less security.

Take the case of displaced managers. To find out what happens to them, *Fortune* magazine surveyed 250 laid-off managers who sent résumés to a search firm in the first half of 1986. Over half (56 percent) found new jobs, but for 79 percent of the 141 who found jobs, the search took a minimum of four months. For 45 percent of the job-finders, the pay was higher in the new job, for 20 percent it was the same as their previous job (now many months behind them), and for 35 percent the pay was lower. The companies tended to be smaller (in 60 percent of the cases), and well over half the job-finders had fewer people reporting to them.[8]

Fortune saw this as evidence for optimism. But it makes a better case for a temporary downward economic slide for perhaps 75 percent of the original group—those who still haven't found jobs plus those who took lower pay plus those who went back to their old pay after time out of work (assuming severance pay did not cover the entire search period). If smaller companies and fewer direct reports also indicate less expansive future prospects, in terms of progression "up" a pay scale, the *Fortune* survey provides evidence of diminished economic well-being for those displaced from corpocratic career ladders.

Similarly, Columbia professor Katherine Newman watched over a period of eighteen months as eighty-five members of Forty Plus, a club in New York for job-seeking executives, found jobs. Her results were more discouraging than *Fortune*'s: one-quarter were making more than they had, one-quarter earned the same as they had in the job they had held one to two years earlier, and one-half earned less than they had. Overall, Newman estimated that six million Americans experienced downward mobility between 1981 and 1986. She arrived at her figure by adding four groups: those who took salary cuts, the unemployed, those who moved from full-time to part-time work, and those who left the labor force altogether.[9]

I present these data not to elicit sympathy for the reduced fortunes of highly paid managers but to consider the meaning of the shift away from secure corporate careers. One inevitable result is greater fluctuations in earnings. A freelance software engineer, for example, could earn over sixty-five thousand dollars in a good year, concentrating on his profession instead of organizational politics. But in a bad year he was unemployed almost five months, living on cash advances from credit cards. Or consider the case of "R.P. of Arlington," who commented on this new career pattern in Juliet Brudney's advice column in the *Boston Globe:*

> Yuppies become fallen stars overnight, not only the middle-aged professionals described in your column. When I was 31 and on a rise a few years ago, the company was sold. The buyer fired me and others. I expected a flood of offers. None. I looked hard. Nothing. I finally found a job in another field at a dip in salary. I'm on my way up, but also moonlighting to develop a new service so I have something to fall back on if I'm hit again.[10]

Will fluctuating incomes drive Americans deeper in debt, or will this be the impetus to increase the national savings rate? It depends on whether we accept the shift in career patterns and plan for fluctuation, not automatic progress.

Changes in Productivity: Discretionary Time and Energy

In some industries, such as broadcasting and film, the lack of corporate loyalty has not prevented the growth of enormously successful companies and might even have helped.[11] But critics argue that nonpermanent jobs harm productivity because people who do not anticipate a future in a company have none of the loyalty to the company that can motivate extra effort and no stake in assuring that their work is well done. "I don't think part-time people do shoddy work," commented the personnel director for a machinery manufacturer that used temporary services extensively, "but there's a tacit understanding that we won't ask them to go the extra mile and that they won't have to."[12] Others argue just the opposite: that temporary workers are likely to do work that regular employees won't, constituting a "reserve army of temporary labor power" working harder than permanent employees and thereby increasing the performance pressure on those employees by reminding them that they could become contingent, too.[13]

It is clearly not the case that productivity decreases when the same task is done by a supplier under contract rather than by an employee under a job assignment. When employees become entrepreneurs, they may have a greater incentive for good performance, because under entrepreneurial logic they capture returns directly from it, and under professional logic they need the boost to reputation that builds future work. So those in post-entrepreneurial careers have a *higher* stake than bureaucrats in productivity. Furthermore, many of the things done for employees to get them up to speed—from training to coaching and supervision—can be done just as well by suppliers; even "firm-specific knowledge" can be passed on to newcomers by contract professionals who are old hands with a particular company client. Indeed, suppliers of specialized services may set higher performance standards than a company could manage with its own employees. A case in point is Servicemaster, which provides cleaning staffs for schools and hospitals and has impressively high financial returns. Its success secret is elaborate training to infuse janitorial work with dignity and professional values.

Work may or may not be done better under the new career logic, but it is undeniably done differently. The difference in the basis for future progress—counting on oneself instead of counting on the company—affects the allocation of discretionary time and energy. For example, for those working with corporations as contractors or on a project basis as well as those employees whose careers consist of movement among projects instead of promotions "upward":

• Networking and selling occupy a great deal of time. The necessity of selling the next job can undercut attention to the present job. In consulting, for example, it is quite common for a sense of accomplishment to come from selling the work even more than from carrying it out successfully. Successful completion may mean the *termination* of a job.

• The benefits of new ideas are often retained by the person. Innovation potential can be withdrawn from the corporation. "Free time" for learning, creating, or inventing is channeled toward ends that enhance the person. It is uncertain whether any of this is channeled back to the organization.

Kate McDonough's switch from vice-president of customer affairs at Citibank to a position in a professional firm illustrates the shift in time use. At Citibank, she reported, she worked from nine to five-thirty, spending half her time supervising five people and none of it contributing to revenues by bringing in customers. At the public relations firm, she works twelve-hour days and many weekends, devoting about 10 percent of her time to finding new clients, 60 percent to serving them, and 30 percent to managing nine people.[14]

Overall, people in post-entrepreneurial careers face much more significant consequences of whether they produce results for an ultimate customer or user of their work than do people buried in bureaucracies who carry out one piece of a project but are shielded from direct accountability for the results of the whole. In post-entrepreneurial careers, access to the *next* job is much more directly tied to excellence in the last one. I believe that productivity can be higher under these circumstances, but so is anxiety.

Changes in Relationships: Status, Stature, and Belonging
The shift from hierarchical to post-entrepreneurial careers affects more than just task relationships. In the last few decades in America, many symbols of status have come in the form of corporate perquisites: private jets, club memberships, and golf outings. Such status symbols are declining both for those still employed in corporations, because many companies feel expensive perks can't always be justified, and for independent entrepreneurs, because they are spending their own money. Visible signs of status thus disappear except for the flashiest of wealthy entrepreneurs—fewer fancy offices, company cars, or private executive-only dining rooms.

What also disappears is the stature that comes from occupying the "office," with all the implied power of the big firm behind it. The "office" and the "company name" lent stature to people regardless of the magnitude of their talents and often out of proportion to them. Ordinary people were elevated to larger-than-life status because they could commit large amounts of company money or because they had company resources and influence behind them. But when they leave the company, their ascribed status is reduced. Now only their own achievements, their own personal name, counts. For those corporate careerists who had no opportunity or inclination to "make a name for themselves" before moving off the corporate ladder, the shift in status is a shock.

I watched many managers leave companies assuming they would have an easy time establishing themselves as consultants because of all the contacts they had in other companies, all the invitations to speak at conferences—only to find that there was no interest in their services. People they thought respected them for their individual talents turned out to have been interested in them only because of their corporate positions. Without impressive institutional affiliations and the trappings of office, they are "nothing." Their personal stature has diminished with the shift of career logic. On the other hand, people who had made their own name count, who had relied less on corporate stature, had a much easier time adjusting to post-entrepreneurial careers.

A number of identity anchors and social anchors also disappear when the corporate ladder collapses. Large corporations provided many minor symbols of belonging, from company T-shirts and souvenirs of corporate conferences to awards earned in recognition programs. And as people climbed the corporate ladder they acquired social affiliation, membership in a club of permanent members of the corporate family. Many aspects of personal and social life—as well as access to prestigious community opportunities—were defined by this membership.

Under the new career logics, people are more literally "on their own." People have to feel good about what they produce, not about external trappings designed to make them feel important. They must rely on the power of their ideas, not the power of their position. Their chief asset is their own name, not the company's name.

SHIFTING LOYALTIES

These changes in the nature of careers in turn change the meaning and locus of loyalty in the workplace. Professional performance standards and a new basis for ethics have to emerge.

Trust and Mistrust

Those managers and professionals who once made up the committed core of the traditional corporation's white-collar ranks have had their faith and trust stretched to the breaking point. While belief in the American economic system remains strong, belief in the large corporation and the safety of a corporate career are rapidly disappearing. Resentment toward employers influences not only the attitudes of those who have been displaced, but also the attitudes of those still laboring inside the corporation. Adjustment to the new career logic thus involves loyalty not to company but to self, commitment not to organization but to task.

The positive side of this phenomenon, of course, is the triumph of the entrepreneurial values of self-reliance and enterprise over "organization man" politicking and conformity. The negatives are equally clear. Among them is the mistrust accompanying the transition, which is most visible for the reluctant entrepreneurs forced out of corporate careers.

One indicator of the residue left by involuntary displacement is the upsurge in lawsuits. The American Arbitration Association reported that the number of employment cases filed for breach of contract in nonunion situations rose from 231 in 1985 to 330 in 1987, and the value of claims from about $25 million to $40 million.[15] Since other evidence shows that older displaced managers may have a more difficult time finding jobs, employers worry about age discrimination suits.

But even when the transition out of a corpocratic career to a post-entrepreneurial one seems benign, hostility and resentment are just below the surface. One corporation converted a large segment of its human resources department to "entrepreneurial" (independent contractor) status, offering free rent and a guarantee of the first year's worth of consulting contracts to any of the professionals who wanted to start their own businesses. The company saw this as a winning proposition all around—reducing the corporate's payroll while helping employees to become entrepreneurs, selling their services at fees that could go much higher than their salaries with the prospect of building a profitable business to boot. Four staffers, excited about the idea of an entrepreneurial venture, formed a consulting company working closely with their former employer. But an undercurrent of anger and hostility grew stronger as the months went by. The insecurity of their position became clear when they had a hard time selling their service to other businesses. The guaranteed work from the former employer made them feel dependent, which, in turn, increased their resentment. After all, if there was enough work to keep them busy for a year, why were they taken off the payroll and forced to lose their benefits? Soon their anger was a recurrent theme in all their conversations, and relationships with still-employed colleagues soured. They put in as little time as possible on the contract work and took all they could, from supplies to support staff assistance. What began as an attempt to handle a restructuring creatively became, instead, an occasion for anger and sabotage.

The shock of a sudden shift in career prospects undercuts other attempts to build trust and commitment in the workplace. For example, labor expert Charles Heckscher reports on the emotional distance maintained from employer's attempts to create commitment via participation at a manufacturing company with the "best" kinds of practices:

Teamwork was stressed everywhere; everyone was very aware of guiding principles and referred to them often (sometimes by initials!); status distinctions were minimized. Yet interviews with workers revealed very high levels of resentment. They did not subscribe to the hyped-up language of the plan, in which workers were, for instance, referred to as "associates." They felt the company was prying into their personal lives by encouraging them to participate in "wellness" programs. Most of all, they felt the rhetoric of participation was not carried out in reality. When a large number of "associates" were abruptly and unilaterally laid off, it only confirmed their cynicism.[16]

Bitterness is not the only response, however. Reactions depend on how much *employability* help is provided. Professionals and managers whose companies gave them opportunities to build their stock of "human capital" through education or résumé-enhancing assignments show much more positive attitudes, even after displacement. For example, one Polaroid engineer who had earned his MBA in a company-sponsored program felt "indebted" to the company despite the fact that Polaroid's downsizing led his career astray.[17] Thus, offering employability security can help mitigate the resentment caused by a loss of employment security.

It is the people *without* reputational capital, those whose careers had been only bureaucratically based, who suffer the most. Katherine Newman summarized her findings about the feelings of people who move from secure and well-paid jobs to more marginal positions:

> Feelings of anger or dismay, a sense of injustice—these are the responses to downward mobility shared by most of its victims. They worked hard for what they had, deferred gratification when necessary, and sacrificed when called upon by their country or their families. But the experience of downward mobility makes it abundantly clear that this is not enough. Attaining a responsible white-collar job, a skilled blue-collar job, or a stable marriage is no key to a lifetime of security. One can play by the rules, pay one's dues, and still be evicted from the American dream. There is simply no guarantee that one's best efforts will be rewarded in the end. Few people come to this pessimistic conclusion until after calamity strikes. And it is the violations of their older, more optimistic expectations, the uncovering of the naked truth about how precarious comfort is, that makes downward mobility so difficult for them to bear.[18]

But the individualistic career emphasis of managers leads them to question themselves, not meritocracy, Newman argues, when they slide. Even when a company pushes hundreds of managers out, the collective character of their displacement fades from view. Consider her interview with a former manager, out of work for over a year after his entire division was eliminated:

> A policy is a policy and a procedure is a procedure. That's the way you operate. If you're part of the corporate world you understand. It doesn't make you feel better; it doesn't smooth anything, but that's the way you do it. You accept it . . . otherwise you can't work in that environment. . . . If I got back into the game, I'd play it the same way. And I would expect the same things to happen to me again.[19]

Other observers also point to a continuing belief in the corporation among the displaced managers:

> Most [of a group of job-seeking managers] retain a zest for business and a belief that all the upheaval—and the sweeping away of whole management layers, including their own—is for the country's good.[20]

But the corporate believers also face the strain of reconciling their faith in the system with the realities of their situation:

Studies show, ironically, that the managers who are hurt worst in any firing are those who believe most strongly in the work ethic so prized by employers. Managers who personally identify most closely with their jobs and companies also suffer the worst stresses when their positions are eliminated.[21]

Survey data confirm these impressions. A national *Business Week–Harris* poll of six hundred middle managers found that 56 percent had assumed on beginning work that if they did a good job they could work for their current employer as long as they liked, but now 56 percent were no longer sure this was the case, because 55 percent of the employers had cut back the salaried workforce within the last five years. Only 37 percent thought they would get a better job if they were laid off. Yet, despite this violation of *individual* assumptions, 75 percent did *not* see laying off or buying out managers as a "betrayal of trust," and 72 percent felt that people who lost jobs in companies that had reduced salaried employment over the past few years had been treated fairly by their employers, despite the fact that 79 percent of this middle management group indicated that top management gets the best treatment in reductions. Eighty-one percent agreed that cutbacks were usually necessary for the long-term well-being of the corporation, but 65 percent felt that salaried employees were less loyal to their companies than ten years ago. Fifty-four percent of a sample of Americans, compared to 32 percent of a sample of Japanese on another Harris poll, felt that employees should work primarily for their *own* satisfaction and success rather than that of the organization they work for.[22]

In short, belief in the *system overall* remains strong, while faith in *particular employers* is eroding. If a person cannot trust the employer, the only locus for trust is in oneself, in one's own skills and goals.

The decline of the corpocratic career and the vast displacement accompanying it touches not just those who are forced out or opt out. It also affects the loyalties and commitments of those who witness the changes as survivors of layoffs and cutbacks. Psychologist Joel Brockner examined the attitudes and behavior of "survivors" both in controlled laboratory experiments and in restructuring corporations. He concluded that survivors' commitment to the *organization* would be more strongly affected than would their commitment to their work. Survivors often *work harder* after a layoff, but they also often feel much more negatively about both the organization and their cowork-ers, toward whom competitive feelings are aroused.[23]

Loyalty in a Post-Entrepreneurial Corporation

The growth of a contingent managerial and professional workforce is a significant factor affecting loyalty and commitment. But this gloomy picture is only one side of the equation; the other side is far sunnier. Equally significant is the growth of the post-entrepreneurial career logic inside corporations.

For one thing, for the people left after cutbacks, for the managers and other employees remaining in the "permanent" core of the company, there is often new opportunity to tackle challenges, take on bigger jobs, and operate more entrepreneurially without levels of stifling bureaucracy above. One staff professional whose job had been humdrum, for example, became a department head after her company restructured and led the development of new advertising campaigns, new compensation plans, and joint ventures with marketing partners— activities and a level of responsibility possible only because of the company's shift to post-entrepreneurial strategies. Still, by the old standards, she was less "loyal" despite the improvement in her job. She chose tasks with a glance at the marketplace for her skills, and there were some "necessary" meetings she politely refused to attend.

What *is* corporate loyalty in a post-entrepreneurial organization? Does loyalty mean adopting the company line and accepting the constraints or requirements of people higher in the chain of command? Or does it mean challenging tradition and questioning explicit orders in pursuit of new value for the company? Is loyalty equivalent to mindless conformity to present demands, or is it exhibited in doing what one thinks is best for the organization in the long run? While corporate citizens have always confronted these questions, post-entrepreneurial organizations heighten the tensions surrounding them.

In the traditional corporation, loyalty had a clear object; one was loyal to the next person in the hierarchy, who represented the chain of command. Just as in the military, obedience to commands counted for more than results; superior performance that involved breaking a rule was punished. For example, a regional manager in an insurance company led his region to dramatic increases in productivity and profits, but he used some unconventional rewards after being warned against using them; his official performance appraisal was lower than the financial results warranted because of his violation of company norms.

Post-entrepreneurial organizations, on the other hand, offer the prospect for a different definition of loyalty, for five reasons.

First, there is often no such thing as a "chain" of command, and people may work under different leadership for different purposes. Multiple reporting relationships and fluid groupings are considered assets, giving the organization both needed flexibility and helpful cross-fertilization across areas. I was asked by a reporter recently whether "insubordination" was on the rise in American corporations; my answer was that "subordination" was on the decline. Under post-entrepreneurial management there is less dependence on one boss and fewer limits to creativity and dissent.

Second, there is explicit encouragement for people to test limits, challenge traditions, chart their own courses, and move in new directions. Even when leaders say this without really meaning it, still the idea has been planted in people's minds that innovation of any kind is a good thing.

Third, decentralization of decision-making responsibility puts more power in the hands of more people at lower levels to exercise their own judgment about the best course of action.

Fourth, the increasing professionalism of many key jobs that changes career commitments also provides standards for conduct and performance that transcend the particular requirements of particular bosses or particular corporations. Human resource or finance or marketing professionals know what excellence is, even if the boss views it differently.

Finally, post-entrepreneurial organizations produce so much change that they cannot offer the same incentive for unquestioning obedience that traditional corporations could: promotion into ever-more-rewarding positions. To do something organizationally questionable is better, in the opinion of many of the post-entrepreneurial managers I interviewed, than to do something professionally questionable, since their future depends more on their own abilities and reputation than on the fate of the particular organization for which they happen to be working at the moment.

The new loyalty issues that are most difficult for today's corporate citizens are not the ones that arise at ethical extremes, such as clear cases of rule violation or moral trespass. While important (and growing in importance in the wake of numerous corporate and Wall Street scandals), these are also more easily understood. What plagues thoughtful people instead are loyalty questions of a more subtle professional kind, when there are conflicts that come down to matters of judgment and taste.

A striking proportion of the complaints managers have expressed to me in recent years concern just such matters. Here's how it typically goes: "They've put me in this job to improve our performance; then they won't let me do it. And they let me know that I am being disloyal by being unhappy with the situation." Or: "I know the right thing to do, but I can't get anyone to listen. They just want a robot who follows orders." Or: "I was asked to find out what was wrong with our process. I discovered some things that no one higher up wants to hear. If they didn't want the information, why did they ask me to get it?" In each of these instances, the person was highly devoted to the company and fervently wanted it to succeed. And in each instance, he or she was torn between competing definitions of corporate loyalty— loyalty to bosses versus loyalty to standards of excellence.

A major industrial products company lost a talented senior executive over just these issues. He had risen through the manufacturing ranks to the senior position, with the mandate to build a world-class manufacturing capacity. He took this mandate seriously, developing long-range strategies to innovate in both technology and human systems, revitalizing existing facilities as well as building new ones on new models. Partway through the execution of his strategy, he was asked by top management to move to another technical position at the same level with higher pay, as part of the normal managerial rotation, freeing his slot for another executive being developed who was not nearly as innovative, nor likely to continue the manufacturing revitalization effort. The senior manager argued vociferously for the desirability of continuity in the manufacturing slot, but the decision was firm. Loyalty to the company, in the leadership's view, meant accepting any assignment and going where needed—a "good soldier" ethos. But loyalty to the company, in the manager's view, meant executing strategies that would improve long-range performance. He quit over the difference—to the considerable surprise of the top executives, who couldn't understand why anyone would leave a good company over a small matter like which function he led.

Sometimes conflicts of loyalty reflect judgments different from those of the current leaders about the right way to bring about change. A major communications company embarked on an ambitious program of "cultural change" to build a new spirit for operating in a more competitive marketplace. So zealous was a powerful executive in support of this program that he made it clear to all managers that "if you want to keep on working for this company, you'll use this program—and nothing else." This push put some key professionals in a bind. Their own judgment and experience told them that the solid positive benefits of the program were accompanied by some serious hidden costs. What were they to do? Where did their loyalty lie? Quitting in protest seemed a ridiculous extreme, but so did wholeheartedly endorsing something that had such significant flaws. It was a balancing act of major proportions. Ultimately, they saluted the program in public but found every opportunity to offer compatible alternatives to their own people without overtly criticizing the program. That way, they were covered. They could present themselves as supporters who were enthusiastic enough to want to build on and augment the official program.

When companies encourage their managers to become more professional and more entrepreneurial, they are also encouraging them to develop their own judgment about what the company needs. It should not be a shock that managers take this directive seriously. Yet it often is. The CEO of an innovative service company was surprised that the manager he put in charge of "building the culture to accelerate our growth" came back to tell him that his behavior was one of the major roadblocks to realizing that culture. The CEO considered that a major act of disloyalty and insubordination. The manager called him on that, citing the enormous loyalty he had exhibited to the company through the years, always putting organizational welfare over personal gain. (Although cynics may wonder, my own observations confirmed this.) It was only after a difficult and lengthy confrontation that the CEO calmed down enough to accept the manager's interpretation and stop trying to find excuses to fire him.

The economist Albert Hirschman once posted the choices of organizational members with a difference of opinion as "exit," "voice," or "loyalty."[24] Either they can leave, as my first example did; speak up, as my second and third examples did, however subtly; or keep quiet and accept the rightness of the organization's way— Hirschman's "loyalty" alternative. But I am arguing that as organizations adopt post-entrepreneurial modes, loyalty is no longer a simple or straightforward matter. Exit and voice may also be forms of loyalty. It is a new corporate balancing act.

CAREERS AND COMMITMENTS IN PERSPECTIVE

As post-entrepreneurial principles take root, people potentially gain something—the freedom to innovate, the excitement of creation, the chance for direct rewards from their own contributions—but they also just as certainly lose something. If fewer and fewer careers consist of a steady climb up a corporate ladder, people gain a measure of independence. But that independence is purchased at the price of old-fashioned security.

The new career patterns are one more blow to the dominance of hierarchy. Even inside large corporations, the nature of the managerial task changes when contingent career conditions prevail. Managing temporary employees, consultants, and suppliers requires an emphasis on skills different from those used to manage subordinates—skills such as negotiating terms and rates, coordinating across the boundaries of many organizations. Once more, influence and persuasion must replace command and coercion. Furthermore, under traditional conditions, the pay and prestige of managers derives in part from the size of their staffs. Now, with a value placed on shrinking internal staffs, the traditional indicators of importance decline. But skillful brokering among consulting firms and independent contractors clearly cannot produce the same career benefit as controlling a large staff; instead, managers must demonstrate the value of their own expert contributions or risk being eliminated as just "middlemen" themselves. The meaning of a corporate career thus changes in substance as well as in promotion opportunities.

Furthermore, there are a number of losses of traditional values—of long-term employment security, of the loyalty of employer to employee and employee to employer. Some wonder how we can sustain productivity, quality, and innovation under these circumstances; don't these stem from the mutual commitment of employer and employee? Others wonder about the human consequences of the inevitable displacement, the transition costs that must be borne.

These would be problems indeed if nothing replaced the traditional values. But rigid forms of employment security can be replaced by the more flexible employability security. This suggests, for one thing, an extension of social safety nets to help people cover the costs of transition. A society that encourages investment in human capital via continuing education, training, and support for venture creation can help people feel secure even when they move across companies or invent their own jobs. And corporate loyalty—surely a mixed virtue in the past in any case—can be replaced by a needed emphasis on professional standards and personal ethics.

Conclusion

Beyond the Cowboy and the Corpocrat: A Call to Action

Slowly but surely, America is waking up to the emerging economic realities. Across the business landscape, companies in many different industries, of many different ages and sizes, are reshaping themselves into contenders in the global corporate Olympics. The motivation for adopting the new forms is mixed. Companies are as much pushed by their need to reduce costs and manage constrained resources as they are pulled by the lure of entrepreneurial opportunities as barriers to worldwide business activity fall away. The changes are implemented poorly in some cases and well in others. For people, the new business forms are accompanied by insecurity and overload at the same time that they generate more exciting and involving workplaces and give more people more chances to operate like entrepreneurs, even from within the corporate fold.

But despite the unsolved problems, slowly but surely, America is learning how to compete in the corporate Olympics.

Rapid change in the business environment makes the Olympic contest sometimes resemble the croquet game in *Alice in Wonderland,* as I pointed out in Chapter 1. In that kind of game, every element is in motion—technology, suppliers, customers, employees, corporate structure, industry structure, government regulation—and none can be counted on to remain stable for very long. It is impossible to win a game like that by using the old corporate forms: elaborate hierarchies and slow decision-making processes; in-house rivalries and adversarial relationships with stakeholders; risk-averse systems that crush new ideas not directly related to the mainstream business; and rewards geared to climbing the ladder from position to position rather than to accomplishment or contribution.

But even though that game is fraught with uncertainty and lack of control, there is a way to win it. A contest that puts a premium on responsiveness and teamwork can be won by employing four *F*'s: being Focused, Fast, Friendly, and Flexible.

For corporations to get in shape for Olympic competition, then, they must evolve flatter, more focused organizations stressing synergies; entrepreneurial enclaves pushing newstream businesses for the future; and strategic alliances or stakeholder partnerships stretching capacity by combining the strength of several organizations. Together, these strategies constitute the strategic, business action agenda.

SYNERGIES

The first major component of post-entrepreneurial strategy is to seek that combination of businesses, array of internal services, and structure for organizing them that promotes synergies—a whole that multiplies the value of the parts. Olympic contenders need leaner, more cooperative, more integrated organizations. Compared to the traditional corporation, post-entrepreneurial companies have fewer layers of management and smaller corporate staffs; they minimize the interveners that delay action. A key concept guiding the post-entrepreneurial corporation is focus: ensuring that people at all levels are able to concentrate on contributing what they do best, in a company itself fully focused on maximizing its core business competence.

Driven by an imperative to make sure that all activities "add value," post-entrepreneurial companies decentralize some functions, putting them close to the business unit those functions support; they contract out for some services, turning to suppliers that are specialists in that area and reducing the need for the company to manage activities largely unrelated to their core business competence; and they convert some service departments into ''businesses'' that compete with external suppliers to sell their wares both inside and outside the company. Such organizational changes allow post-entrepreneurial companies to do more with less, because their staffs are smaller, their fixed costs are lower, resources are available closer to the site of the business action, and all departments are more clearly focused on their contributions to the business.

To move from simply adding value to multiplying it, the post-entrepreneurial company also builds the connections between its various products or businesses, encouraging such cooperative efforts as cross-selling, product links in the marketplace, exchange of technological or market information, resource sharing to apply one unit's competence to another's problem, or letting each division serve as the ''lead'' for particular innovations. This means that the typical post-entrepreneurial company is less diversified than the traditional corporation, tending to add only those businesses that build on existing competence or can extend it.

But the search for synergies is sometimes forgotten in a corporation's rush to restructure. Many cut costs without considering the consequences. They work on the ''use less'' side of the equation but not the ''achieve more'' side. Or they acquire new businesses because theoretically there is a ''fit,'' but then foster rivalries that interfere with getting benefits from that strategic fit. Reshaping an organization to create more value runs the risk of subtracting value rather than adding it. The issue is how to restructure thoughtfully instead of downsizing mindlessly. There are two principal problems: poor management of the transition itself and setting up contests that produce ''winners'' and ''losers.''

First, top management typically overestimates the degree of cooperation it will get and underestimates the transition costs. Among the by-products of significant restructuring are discontinuity, disorder, and distraction—all of which tend to reduce productivity. People can lose energy, projects can lose key resources, and initiative can grind to a halt. Faith in leaders can be diminished, and power differences are made uncomfortably visible, showing many people that they lack control over their own fates. But even if some of these transition problems are temporary, a more permanent residue can be left: an undermining of commitment to the future. ''Shall I write the list of our locations in pencil?'' one manager asked.

The second danger is inducing the ''mean'' along with the ''lean''—a cowboy style of management that encourages groups to shoot it out with one another in internal competitions. Such in-house rivalries can stem from any situation that promotes battles over scarce resources among groups with a reason to be antagonistic to one another—for example, the conquerors and the vanquished after an acquisition, parallel start-ups with the goal of only one survivor, or creeping market boundaries that cause divisions of the same company to seek one another's customers. But in-house competition undermines goal achievement, leading groups to emphasize defeating their rivals instead of strong task performance. It can drive out innovation and lower standards.

The management challenge is to retain value and increase it by handling transitions so that they reinforce commitment and build the cooperation that brings synergies. This means, first of all, managing with an eye on the past and the future as well as the present: in any major change, minimizing the losses people have to face while allowing grieving about the past; providing positive visions of the future; and reducing the uncertainty of the present by active communication. After a transition, it means actively organizing to motivate the search for synergies: championing the cause from the top, providing forums to help managers identify opportunities outside their own areas, offering incentives and rewards for teamwork, making resources available for joint projects, and promoting relationships and communication to help people know one another and share information across diverse areas—to perceive that their fate is shared and they can help one another.

The post-entrepreneurial emphasis on synergies decreases the ''vertical'' dimension of organization, reducing elaborate corporate hierarchies and large central staffs, and increases the ''horizontal'' dimension—the direct cooperation between peers across divisions and departments.

ALLIANCES

The second major component of post-entrepreneurial strategy involves developing close working relationships with other organizations, extending the company's reach without increasing its size. Strategic alliances and partnerships are a potent way to do more with less. They permit the company to remain lean, controlling costs, while gaining access to more capacity than what is owned or employed directly. The traditional corporation was stuck with the limitations of do-it-oneself-or-don't-do-it-at-all mentalities. Partnerships are a flexible alternative to acquisition, with a more modest investment and the ability to remain independent. The leaner organization that contracts out for services depends on the suppliers of those services and therefore benefits from close cooperation with them. Furthermore, in a rapidly changing business environment, alliances with other organizations on whom one company depends are a powerful way to ensure that all change in the same direction, thereby reducing uncertainty. The traditional corporation's mistrust of outsiders and desire for control made it impossible to plan jointly with customers or suppliers.

Post-entrepreneurial companies find a number of benefits in coalitions with other companies: information access, windows on technology, speed of action, and mutual accommodation to innovation that creates faster payback.

Post-entrepreneurial companies pool resources or link their systems to create even greater joint capacity in a variety of ways. There are groups of companies contributing to consortia that provide a special service for all of them, joint ventures to pursue particular business opportunities, and partnerships between a company and its suppliers, customers, or even unions.

Strategic alliances and partnerships blur the boundaries between organizations, permitting them to take advantage of one another's capacities and to coordinate their activities for mutual benefit. This coordination requires degrees of information-sharing unprecedented in the traditional corporation. And it is not only the external ally who gets more information; it is also the managers inside who have to know more in order to be intelligent representatives to the partnership. In general, effective alliances create multiple links between the allies: joint planning at the strategic level, technical data exchange at the professional level, and direct data links at the production level. The connections multiply. One partner company may make investments in the other that resemble the investments a corporation might make in one of its divisions: management conferences to review business plans, staff training programs, performance appraisal programs, and recognition events. The relationships may get even more intertwined when companies are both suppliers and customers to one another.

Becoming "PALs" with other organizations makes the post-entrepreneurial corporation different from the traditional corpocracy in a number of ways; it changes what and how managers manage. Alliances can rapidly move a company to a participative standard; instead of commanding subordinates in a hierarchy, alliance managers engage in discussions with partners of similar standing over whom they have no formal authority and whose careers they do not control. Thus the skills they must exercise are different. They must understand how to balance the interests of multiple constituencies (for example, their company's desires and those of the partner), how to establish egalitarian relationships, how to identify shared goals and search for consensus, how to earn respect when it is not automatically coupled to rank, and how to be sensitive to symbols and signals that affect the level of trust in the relationship.

Alliances and partnerships are thus vulnerable to a number of management failures. Sometimes they fall apart because of shifts in the strategy or circumstances of one of the partners, which means that the alliance is no longer valuable or desirable. But more often they suffer because the companies entering into them simply do not do what it takes to achieve the benefits of alliance. Successful partnerships imply a degree of equality to which some companies and some managers are unwilling to move; they would rather try to duplicate traditional command conditions by manifesting less commitment than the partner, maintaining an imbalance of resources or information or starving the partnership by not supplying enough of these, and monopolizing the benefits. The partner, in turn, may have prematurely placed trust in the relationship, arousing so much resentment when the trust is violated that cooperation ceases. Or the domain for the alliance may be so circumscribed that effective action to derive benefits for all parties is impossible; the organizations fail to link their systems or plan together or find a framework for resolving differences, and meanwhile, each has other loyalties that conflict with the partnership, including the pull of internal corporate politics.

Clearly, partnerships are not a casual matter, and they should not be entered into casually, or they will absorb time and energy without bringing benefits and raise expectations only to frustrate them, which is more disappointing than never to have been promised anything. For all the fanfare surrounding industry research consortia like Bellcore for the regional telephone operating companies or the Microelectronics and Computer Corporation, experience suggests that the companies entering into such alliances are only weakly committed, and, in turn, the consortia produce little that they define as benefits—reinforcing their lack of commitment in a vicious circle. Being only casually a partner is like being only somewhat pregnant.

The management challenge, then, is to select only those relationships that are sufficiently important that they will be entered into with full commitment and with a willingness to invest the resources and make the internal changes that successful external partnerships entail—the sharing of information, the linking of systems, and the establishment of agreements for governing the partnership. The "six *I*'s" of successful alliances—Importance, Investment, Interdependence, Integration, Information, Institutionalization—make it possible for the post-entrepreneurial corporation to use partnerships to do more with less. But they also require major shifts away from bureaucracy and hierarchy.

NEWSTREAMS

The third major post-entrepreneurial strategy is to actively promote newstreams—a flow of new business possibilities within the firm. To do more with less in the demanding context of the global Olympics means being able to capture and develop opportunities as they arise, to ensure that good ideas don't slip away and that new ventures are ready to join the mainstream business or lead the company in new directions. Thus, post-entrepreneurial companies extend the domain for invention well beyond the R&D department, and the domain for new venture formation well beyond the acquisition department. They are unlike traditional corporations in giving more people, at more levels, the chance to develop and lead newstream projects.

While post-entrepreneurial companies want a climate for innovation in which every employee feels that innovation is part of his or her job, they do not just depend on the lucky break of an innovation's spontaneously arising in some corner of the company and making its way to a leader's attention. Instead, they create official channels to speed the flow of new ideas: for example, special funds to support new ideas without eating into mainstream business budgets; centers for creativity to speed the application of new ideas; incentives to find and nurture employee-led projects; incubators to grow new ventures; or investments in new technology ventures outside that can be linked to established businesses inside. The managers who preside over newstream channels may simply act as scouts to find ideas already under development, or they may more actively coach potential project developers and inspire them to come forward.

But simply establishing newstream channels does not automatically assure that newstream projects will be successful. Just as with the other two post-entrepreneurial strategies, success depends on the effectiveness and appropriateness with which the strategy is implemented; it requires a management sensibility not part of the traditional repertoire. The very existence of newstreams generates tensions and dilemmas because the requirements for nurturing a new venture conflict with management systems geared for running mainstream businesses—or at least better tolerated by the mainstream.

For one thing, "planning" for a newstream means placing bets rather than being able to predict a relatively assured set of results from a known line of business. Newstreams are not yet routinized; they are characterized instead by unexpected events, which makes scheduling difficult. Newstreams are uncertain in a number of respects; their course is bumpy, and they rock boats because they are controversial. Newstream projects are intense; they absorb more mental and emotional energy than established activities, generate new knowledge at a rapid rate, require excellent communication among those with fragments of knowledge, and are thus more dependent on teamwork and more vulnerable to turnover. Finally, newstreams benefit from autonomy—perhaps places of their own for the projects, removed from the mainstream and allowing experimentation, but certainly newstreams need a separation of style and procedures so that development projects can move quickly without the constraints deemed necessary to control the established mainstream business.

When newstreams dry up without producing benefits for the company, it is often because of a failure to understand the requirements for newstreams. Sometimes companies expect quicker and greater financial returns than the newstream can support; sometimes they choose newstreams only for their financial promise and not for the ways they might be useful to the mainstream business; sometimes they place a few big bets rather than nurturing a flow of many more modest newstream ideas. When a company counts on newstreams for more than they can handle, it often kills them with management attention, imposing mainstream systems that hinder rather than help.

There is also a tension between the streams that makes traditional mainstream managers uneasy; the newstream quest for autonomy conflicts with the mainstream push for control. Mainstream people may resent the "privileges" newstream people have in being freed from traditional constraints; newstream people may argue, in turn, that they are more vulnerable, taking greater career risks. In many ways, the existence of newstreams flowing alongside the mainstream business loosens traditional hierarchical authority, undermines respect for bureaucracy, weakens corporate identification in favor of project identification, and teaches people they can rely on themselves, thereby reducing their dependency on the corporation to give them a career. The corporate "haves" become the people with the freedom to pursue their ideas; the "have-nots" are those still encumbered with the shackles of bureaucracy.

THE COMING DEMISE OF BUREAUCRACY AND HIERARCHY

The three post-entrepreneurial strategies can change sluggish organizations into agile, athletic champions in the global corporate Olympics. They can show bloated, overweight corpocracies how to dance. But they are not quick fixes; they are fundamentally different ways of organizing to get the work done, with revolutionary consequences for management. They simply do not work when companies try to employ them mindlessly or casually: for example, using a slash-and-burn approach to restructuring, cutting staff to the bone without rethinking how the work gets done; spending large sums to acquire promising businesses without dedicating resources to integrating them well; heralding "alliances" without making the underlying commitment to behave more cooperatively; or throwing money into new ventures without giving them the ability to produce results. Instead of being able to do more with less, companies that do not move in more people-sensitive and less bureaucratic directions, more cooperative and less hierarchical directions, will find themselves doing less with more.

The corporation itself is being turned inside-out, like a reversible garment worn out on one side. Some executives I know are beginning to draw their organization charts upside-down, with managers at the bottom supporting the line employees at the top. But inside-out is an even more accurate image for the new organization. There is more "detachment" of what was once "inside" the corporation's protective shell (for example, employees being replaced by contingent workers and staff departments being spun off as independent contractors) and more "attachment" to what was once "outside" (for example, closer, more committed relationships with suppliers, customers, and even competitors). We are watching a simultaneous loosening of formerly strong relationships and strengthening of formerly loose relationships. Those groups brought closer clearly benefit, but those cast out are often cast adrift.

The new corporate ideal involves a smaller fixed core, but a larger set of partnerlike ties. There is less "inside" that is sacred—permanent, untouchable, unchangeable people, departments, business units, or practices—but more "outside" that is respected, representing opportunities for deal-making or leverage via alliances. This ideal represents a reversal of the old corporate imperative to get as big as possible, in order to have power and control over the business environment. In an environment of turbulence and high uncertainty, vast size can instead produce rigidity and sluggishness—like the overage, overweight former athletes many large American corporations have become. Increasingly today the corporate ideal lies in how *small* an organization can be and still get the job done.

Other analysts have noted this reversal in a number of different ways. TRW economist Pat Choate has heralded the coming of a "high flex society," pointing to the new social policies required to increase business flexibility by helping individuals be more flexible in their job choices over their lifetimes. Michael Piore and Charles Sabel, writing on *The New Industrial Divide,* point to the competitive virtues of the small, focused company involved in a network of other companies providing complementary skills—a virtue they label "flexible specialization." Raymond Miles has argued that the new corporation will resemble a "switchboard"—a small communications center managing a network of relationships.[1]

This post-entrepreneurial style of management is not simply another fad, another one-shot program to be added to all the other things corporations are attempting to do. It represents a fundamentally different set of organizing principles from bureaucracy, a different way of conducting corporate life. These values and practices are often present as a matter of course in new ventures, but now they are increasingly finding their place in established corporations as well. Whereas bureaucratic management is inherently preservation-seeking, entrepreneurial management is inherently opportunity-seeking. The major concern of bureaucracy is to administer a known routine uniformly, guided by past experiences, whereas the major concern of an entrepreneurial organization is to exploit opportunity wherever it occurs and however it can be done, regardless of what the organization has done in the past. The post-entrepreneurial organization brings entrepreneurial principles to the established corporation.

All of these developments represent a dramatic new corporate ideal, one very different from the old-style corpocracy:

• Bureaucracy tends to be position-centered, in that authority derives from position, and status or rank is critical. Post-entrepreneurial organizations tend to be more person-centered, with authority deriving from expertise or from relationships.
• Bureaucratic management is repetition-oriented, seeking efficiency through doing the same thing over and over again. Post-entrepreneurial management is creation-oriented, seeking innovation as well as efficiency.
• Bureaucratic management is rules-oriented, defining procedures and rewarding adherence to them. Post-entrepreneurial management is results-oriented, rewarding outcomes.
• Bureaucracies tend to pay for status, in the sense that pay is position-based, positions are arrayed in a hierarchy, and greater rewards come from attaining higher positions. Post-entrepreneurial organizations tend to pay for contribution, for the value the person or team has added, regardless of formal position.
• Bureaucracies operate through formal structures designed to channel and restrict the flow of information. Post-entrepreneurial organizations find opportunities through the expansion of information, through the ability to maximize all possible communication link—with coalition partners inside and outside the organization.
• Bureaucracies assign specific mandates and territories, to circum-scribe the action arena. In post-entrepreneurial organizations, charters and home territories are only the starting point for the creation of new

modes of action; furthermore, opportunities come from the ability to make relationships across territories.
• Bureaucracies seek ownership and control. Post-entrepreneurial organizations seek leverage and experimentation.

Thus, to use an overworked expression, the dominant business paradigm is changing.

Three principles emerge from observing the new organizational strategies in practice, intertwined post-entrepreneurial principles that create the flexibility required to meet the strategic challenge of doing more with less:

• Minimize obligations and maximize options. Keep fixed costs low and as often as possible use "variable" or "contingent" means to achieve corporate goals.
• Find leverage through influence and combination. Derive power from access and involvement, rather than from full control or total ownership.
• Encourage "churn." Keep things moving. Encourage continuous regrouping of people and functions and products to produce unexpected, creative new combinations. Redefine turnover as positive (a source of renewal) rather than negative.

In this context, each of the popular management buzzwords and fads of the last decade seems a way station on the road to a more comprehensive rethinking of corporate strategy and organizational form. For example, participative management and employee involvement, "intrapreneurship" and "quality circles" have each found their niche and reached their logical limits in many companies. Advocates have rightly praised these corporate innovations for their benefits— usually local increases in productivity, quality, or innovation. Skeptics have rightly condemned them for being faddish, superficial, quick fixes with fragmented implementation. Still, in retrospect, each has been important in moving corporations toward challenging the old managerial assumptions, loosening their structures, and experimenting with new practices. One offshoot of many of these programs is the weakening of hierarchy and the reduction of levels of organizations as employees are given more opportunities to influence decisions and exercise control.

Alongside the *propeople* corporate policies popular in the last decade, however, are a number of other business maneuvers often characterized as *antipeople:* financial manipulation and a takeover binge leading to involuntary restructuring and job displacement. Ironically, these manipulations also tend to create leaner, less hierarchical organizations, as acquirers seek to reduce costs by eliminating corporate staffs and unnecessary layers of management or divesting business units that can function alone, thereby, giving them entrepreneurial independence. But when done for financial speculation rather than to enhance long-term capacity, this strategy can subtract value rather than add it.[2]

The post-entrepreneurial principles I have identified clearly have both an upside and a downside. At their best, they increase opportunity, giving people the chance to develop their ideas, pursue exciting projects, and be compensated directly for their contributions. At their best, they encourage collaboration across functions, across business units, and even across corporations. The business benefits from the use of these principles are lower fixed costs and increased entrepreneurial reach.

But at their worst, the same strategies can lead to displacement instead of empowerment, rivalries instead of teamwork, and short-term asset-shuffling and one-night stands with the latest attractive deal instead of long-term commitments to build capacity. The same strategies executed unwisely and without concern for the organizational and human consequences will not produce continuing business benefits—especially if people withhold effort and commitment for fear of being displaced or to hedge their own bets against change.

It is not the strategies themselves but their execution that make the difference in whether the consequences for people are expanded entrepreneurial opportunity or anxiety, insecurity, and loss of motivation to produce.

LIFE IN A POST-ENTREPRENEURIAL WORLD: THE HUMAN CONSEQUENCES

We are witnessing a crumbling of hierarchy, a gradual replacement of the bureaucratic emphasis on order, uniformity, and repetition with an entrepreneurial emphasis on creativity and deal-making. But at the same time, we are also watching new societal dilemmas arise in the wake of this change.

The post-entrepreneurial revolution changes not only the organization and management of the corporation, but also the lives people lead in the business world. There are more contingencies, more uncertainties. The very rigidity of the traditional corporate bureaucracy also provided a measure of security; if people had to "know their place," at least that place was relatively stable and unchanging from day to day and year to year. But today, companies must either move away from bureaucratic guarantees to post-entrepreneurial flexibility or they stagnate—thereby canceling by default any commitments they have made.

Post-entrepreneurial strategies hold out the promise of more satisfaction and rewards for people, but more of those benefits are contingent on what the individual—and the team—does and not on what the corporation automatically provides. The three forms of contribution-based pay—profit-sharing and gain-sharing, performance bonuses, and a share of venture returns—give people the power to grow their own earnings and distribute the corporation's rewards more fairly to those who deserve them, and they do not force people to wait in line for promotions as the only way to make progress. The excitement of projects in which people are empowered to act on their own ideas make work more satisfying and more absorbing, increasing the sense of accomplishment. The opportunity to be essentially in business for oneself, inside or outside the large corporation, puts more control in the hands of smaller groups. And because these consequences of the shift to post-entrepreneurial strategies are more motivating for people, the corporation should reap benefits, too, in increased productivity.

The post-entrepreneurial revolution has a dramatic impact on people's careers—the sequence of jobs that constitute their life's work—and this illustrates both the potential and the problems that ensue. The three major strategies that give flexibility to the corporation (corporate restructuring, which eliminates some jobs altogether or shuffles employers; greater comfort with alliances, which increases reliance on suppliers outside the firm rather than on employees inside; and the encouragement of newstream ventures) also shift the center of career action from promotion up a ladder to ad hoc projects. The bureaucratic career is disappearing; the corporate ladder is losing rungs and stability. The traditional corporation is in such turmoil that it can no longer carry the weight of people's hopes and dreams, or society's expectation of permanence, to which a variety of welfare benefits and pension funds are tied.

Success in a post-entrepreneurial career combines the knowledge base and search for reputation of the professional with the entrepreneur's ability to move from project to project creating new value. People's careers are more dependent on their own resources and less dependent on the fate of a particular company. This means that some people who know only bureaucratic ropes are cut adrift. It means that incomes are likely to fluctuate rather than increase in an orderly fashion every year. It means more risk and uncertainty. It does not necessarily mean lower productivity, for professional standards and concern for reputation may be sufficient incentives and also the best guarantee of continuity of employment even with the same corporation. No longer counting on the corporation to provide security and stature requires people to build those resources in themselves, which ultimately could result in more resourceful people.

But these benefits do not accrue as yet to everyone, because not all companies have as yet moved fast enough or far enough to the post-entrepreneurial style. Some companies try to go halfway and flub it, and others have not changed at all. Furthermore, because most American social policy is still geared to the assumption that the traditional corporation is alive and well, there are problems emerging in the wake of the post-entrepreneurial revolution that are not yet well understood or well handled. Some people joyously leap off the corporate ladder into post-entrepreneurial careers, but others are shoved off callously, without a safety net or help in getting back on their feet. Some people are absorbed in more exciting work, but others are working harder just to pick up the slack when companies cut staff and get wage concessions yet still expect the same amount of work to be done.

The first major problem that must be addressed in the post-entrepreneurial world is the tension between corporate flexibility and individual security. Businesses want and need the flexibility to restructure, to change shape, and to pursue newstreams, while employees want the security of knowing there is a place for them. Yet even that is too simple. Fewer and fewer people are really counting on a permanent career in one company anymore; but still, they want to have a measure of control over their careers, instead of being cast adrift without the resources to begin again, and they want to feel that they are making progress with each career step. Income security has not been a cornerstone of recent American social and business policy; but employment security has been central—for example, a key element for unions that know that wage rates cannot continue to rise without limit, and therefore shift to job security as a bargaining principle. Job security has also been an implicit part of the employment contract for managers and professionals in large corporations. It was this security that apparently produced commitment and loyalty, the ability to plan for the long term, and the desire of both employer and employee to invest in each other's success. The post-entrepreneurial strategies make that guarantee of long-term employment more difficult to sustain—even if it were still desired.

In the post-entrepreneurial world, the best source of security for people is a guarantee not of a specific job or a specific employer, but of their *employability*. Employability security means offering people the chance to grow in skills and accomplishments so that their value to *any* employer is enhanced—the present one or a future one or themselves as independent entrepreneurs. In the future companies will invest in people not because they are stuck with them for life but because employability security produces better performance from more highly skilled people.

Workplace overload is a second significant problem, one that spills over into personal and family life. People are working long hours because leaner organizations put pressure on the remaining staff to do more work, because there are more exciting opportunities to pursue projects that bring great rewards, and because post-entrepreneurial strategies increase complexity and the need for communication. The absorption with work goes up when people can earn performance bonuses, share in productivity gains, get funding for newstream ventures, develop joint ventures with other divisions, or work more closely with partners outside the company. Flexible organizations that innovate, that seek synergies, have more changes to keep up with, and they are more complex. As more people are empowered, more people can initiate activities that create work for still others; the slate of activities is continually expanding. It becomes difficult to set limits, difficult to determine how much work is "enough."

It is not hard work or long hours per se that pose the problem; after all, if companies are going to win in the corporate Olympics they need this kind of Olympic effort. But not all the overload is necessary; some reflects frenzy and chaos rather than crisp focus. More significantly, this work style tends to turn the workplace into the prime site for absorbing relationships, a center of emotional life for single people (and sometimes for married ones as well). It eats into personal life and exaggerates the conflict between work and family.

In some cases, workplace overload could be reduced through better management: by delegating authority along with responsibility, minimizing the number of simultaneous changes, and emphasizing simplicity over complexity. That helps some. But businesses must also make space for personal life. It is a matter not simply of making arrangements to make sure that children are cared for (although I consider it a given that more child care must be made available), but also of providing time for families to be together, uninterrupted by work. Nor is it realistic, in the post-entrepreneurial era, to expect many people or companies to tolerate reduced hours every day or every week. Instead, time-out should be organized around the longer cycles of post-entrepreneurial work rhythms, the rhythms of projects. Periods of intense work should be matched by periods of relaxation and renewal. Rewards should come at the ends of projects, not on a calendar that is the same for everybody regardless of the work they do; and these moments of reward should mark a clear ending of one intense effort and a pause for personal life before beginning the next.

IN SEARCH OF THE POST-ENTREPRENEURIAL HERO: INDIVIDUAL SKILLS FOR SUCCESS

If the post-entrepreneurial corporation requires a different kind of work system and career system, it also requires a very different set of individual skills. We need a new image of the hero in business—the kind of leader who can manage the balancing act and guide us to victory in the corporate Olympics.

Our archetypal images of business leadership have themselves derived from the two poles that define today's corporate balancing act. We could choose between the conservative resource preserver (what Howard Stevenson and David Gumpert called the "trustee") and the insurgent entrepreneur (Stevenson and Gumpert's "promoter").[3] In popular lore, the former was reflected in images of the "organization man" or "corpocrat," while the latter was described as a "maverick" or "cowboy," each character occupying one end of the conserve-or-build spectrum.

The corpocrat has long been the target of well-deserved criticism, and the corpocratic style is gradually disappearing from progressive businesses. But despite glorification of the maverick in the 1980s entrepreneurial revival, the cowboy is also too extreme to be entirely satisfactory as a leadership image—just as John Sculley found at Apple Computer. It is easy to see the weakness in both styles when cowboys and corpocrats clash. From Steve Jobs's problems at Apple to Ross Perot's clash with General Motors after GM purchased his company, EDS, these are the typical sources of tension:

• The cowboy lives in a world of immediate action; the corporation manager wants review and deliberation. What the cowboy views as time-wasting, rear-covering conservatism the corporation manager may see as the consensus-building necessary to implement decisions that many people control.
• The cowboy wants to seize every opportunity, betting big—but if he loses he's wiped out. The corporation manager makes complex resource-allocation decisions balancing the protection of past investments with the pursuit of new opportunities; after all, the corporation is the trustee of other people's assets.
• The cowboy strains limits, but the corporation manager has to establish limits to guide the actions of multitudes of people efficiently. The cowboy breaks rules and gets away with it, but the corporation manager thrives on controls and the uniform application of rules. There are few worse morale-plungers in a corporation than the realization that some are more equal than others.
• The cowboy motivates by personal loyalty, surrounded as he is by just a few trusted cronies who love the work the way he does. The cowboy's direct control means that he can manage through impulse and whim, ''shooting from the hip.'' But the corporation manager has to make complex and longer-term agreements that make whim out of place, and he or she seeks an impersonal commitment to the philosophy of go-anywhere-do-anything regardless of personal ties or feelings about the job.
• The cowboy rejects fancy ''citified'' trappings, living simply at work—just one of the folks, regardless of wealth. But the corporation displays symbols of affluence to make people believe in its importance; it establishes gradations of privilege and perquisites to motivate people to seek the highest ranks.

The large corporate manager's suspicion of the cowboy, then, is not necessarily a politically motivated bias against mavericks who fight oppressive authority or speak unpleasant truths. It comes from a recognition that the cowboy personifies a challenge to the very premises on which a large corporation operates. Allow too many cowboys, and the foundations of hierarchy begin to crumble—but so does the basis for cooperation and discipline.

Without the bold impulses of take-action entrepreneurs and their constant questioning of the rules, we would miss one of the most potent sources of business revitalization and development. But without the discipline and coordination of conventional management, we could find waste instead of growth, unnecessary risk instead of revitalization. Just as Kodak and Pacific Telesis needed more cowboys, Apple and Digital needed more corporate discipline and cooperation.

Today's corporate balancing act requires a different style from either extreme, a post-entrepreneurial style better suited to playing in the corporate Olympics. Our new heroic model should be the athlete who can manage the amazing feat of doing more with less, who can juggle the need to both conserve resources and pursue growth opportunities. This new kind of business hero avoids the excesses of both the corpocrat and the cowboy. Where the former rigidly conserves and protects, the latter relentlessly speculates and promotes. But the business athlete has the strength to balance somewhere in the middle, taking the best of the corpocrat's discipline and the cowboy's entrepreneurial zeal. Again the four *F*'s come to mind: Focused, Fast, Friendly, and Flexible. Business athletes need to be intense, lean and limber, able to stretch, good at teamwork, and in shape all the time.

There are seven skills and sensibilities that must be cultivated if managers and professionals are to become true business athletes.

First, they must *learn to operate without the might of the hierarchy behind them.* The crutch of authority must be thrown away and replaced by their own personal ability to make relationships, use influence, and work with others to achieve results. Business athletes stand—and run—on their own two feet, rather than being propelled automatically by the power of their position, just as a member of any athletic team is revered not for wearing the uniform but for his or her own performance. The traditional corporate hierarchy is rapidly crumbling, and title or formal position count for less anyway, in a world of negotiations involving internal collaborations or strategic alliances or the formation of new ventures. In strategic partnerships, for example, there is no room for faceless bureaucrats sending impersonal memos. Partners become more exposed and available to one another as people, as the Grotech joint venture participants and the Pacific Bell managers began to realize. Or in newstream ventures, the manager has little more to offer to potential members of the venture team than the excitement of trying because of the power of his or her vision. In many ways, business athletes have to count on their use of self, not their use of organizational status, to achieve results.

Second, business athletes must *know how to "compete" in a way that enhances rather than undercuts cooperation.* They must be oriented to achieving the highest standard of excellence rather than to wiping out the competition. In the new game, today's competitors may find themselves on the same team tomorrow, and competitors in one sphere may also be collaborators in another. Even America's trade adversaries are potential partners, and it would be a mistake for the conduct of temporary competition to undermine the ability to cooperate later. Thus, business athletes must be skillful collaborators. Whether companies are seeking synergies through internal collaboration across business units or seeking leverage through strategic alliances and partnerships, the lesson is clear. Successful managers in the corporate Olympics must not only be good negotiators, seeking the best deal for "their" unit, but also understand when and how to share resources, to combine forces, to do things that benefit another group—in the interests of superior overall performance. This relationship orientation means knowing how to assess and value what is good for all parties in the long run, not simply analyzing the "fairness" of a single transaction.[4]

Third, and related, business athletes must *operate with the highest ethical standards.* While business ethics have always been important from a social and moral point of view, they also become a pragmatic requirement in the corporate Olympics. The doing-more-with-less strategies place an even greater premium on trust than did the adversarial-protective business practices of the traditional corporation. Business collaborations, joint ventures, labor-management partnerships, and other stakeholder alliances all involve the element of trust—a commitment of strategic information or key resources to the partners. But the partners have to rely on one another not to violate or misuse their trust. Even newstream ventures involve a high degree of trust, in the willingness to commit corporate resources to untried and uncertain activities with a minimum of monitoring. The trust required for all of these new business strategies is built and reinforced by a mutual understanding that each party to the relationship will behave ethically, taking the needs, interests, and concerns of all others into account.

A fourth asset for business athletes is to *have a dose of humility* sprinkled on their basic self-confidence, a humility that says that there are always new things to learn. Just as other kinds of athletes must be willing to learn, willing to accept the guidance of coaches, constantly in training, and always alert to the possibility of an improvement in their techniques, so must business athletes be willing to learn. A learning attitude is a clear necessity for swimming in newstreams, for exploring uncharted waters, but it is also a necessity for seeking synergies and for discovering the benefits of strategic alliances, many of which form so that partners can learn from one another.

I have seen this attitude emerge in companies and people that used to be closed in every sense. At Apple Computer in 1985, for example, I was often told that "we have nothing to learn from anyone else"; but by 1988, Apple was actively creating strategic alliances for learning, and a major effort to reshape the finance function began with visits to other companies. Of course, to learn from others, people must— literally—learn to speak their language, whether Japanese, Spanish, or computer-ese.

Fifth, business athletes must *develop a process focus*—a respect for the process of implementation as well as the substance of what is implemented. They need to be aware that *how* things are done is every bit as important as *what* is done. My case studies and comparative data make it clear that execution may matter more than strategy. Whether restructuring builds synergies or leaves dead bodies in its path, whether alliances and partnerships indeed stretch capacity or simply stretch relationships to the breaking point, whether newstream investments lead to effective projects that produce results or to nothing—all this relies not only on the quality of the big strategic idea behind it but also on the concern for excellence of implementation.

Both Eastern Airlines and Western Airlines, for example, faced the same do-more-with-less pressures in the early 1980s, both made the bold strategic move of seeking wage concessions from employees in exchange for an announced "business partnership," and both were later acquired by other airlines. Yet the contrast in how each implemented its strategy could not be more striking. Eastern botched it by showing poor faith and not quite taking the steps that would make the employee partnership work, and since a hostile acquisition by Texas Air (resisted by management and sought by demoralized employee leaders), Eastern has been hurt financially by public displays of employee discontent, including claims of safety problems. Western, in contrast, as I showed earlier, managed the same strategic move by a careful attention to process and netted a more valuable company that merged smoothly with Delta to the benefit of employees, shareholders, and customers.

Sixth, business athletes must *be multifaceted and ambidextrous,* able to work across functions and business units to find synergies that multiply value, able to form alliances when opportune but to cut ties when necessary, able to swim equally effectively in the mainstream and in newstreams. There is no room for narrow or rigid people in the new business environment. Each component of the new business strategies that I have described relies heavily on the ability to form teams, to make connections, and to integrate functions. Business athletes must bring their own professional or functional skill to the team, but also must know how to connect it to the skills brought by others.

Seventh, business athletes must *gain satisfaction from results* and be willing to stake their own rewards on them. The accomplishment itself is really the only standard for the business athlete. With post-entrepreneurial pay-for-performance a growing reality, and with the middle management hierarchy dismantled, the measure of success must, in any case, shift from status to contribution, from attainment of a position to attainment of results. Promotion cannot be a reward at a time when there are fewer layers of management and employment security is being undermined or redefined. At the same time, the shift toward doing-more-with-less strategies opens up new kinds of opportunities for achievement and rewards—whether via participation on the frontiers of partnerships, where more power and responsibility fall upon partner representatives, or via involvement in newstream ventures that turn ordinary employees into entrepreneurs.

These seven managerial skills also point toward the individual skills required to manage a career at a time when climbing the corporate ladder has been replaced by hopping from opportunity to opportunity:

- A belief in self rather than in the power of a position alone.
- The ability to collaborate and become connected with new teams in various ways.

- Commitment to the intrinsic excitement of achievement in a particular project that can show results.
- The willingness to keep learning.

All of these attributes constitute an investment in one's own human capital rather than a reliance on accumulating organizational capital. Ultimately, this new loyalty to project rather than to employer can be better for the company, too, because it produces results-oriented, entrepreneurially inclined employees who are dedicated to their activities instead of being dedicated to corporate politics and position enhancement. And certainly it is better attuned to the workplace realities of the emerging business strategies.

FROM CORPORATE POLICY TO NATIONAL POLICY: THE POST-ENTREPRENEURIAL CHALLENGE

Of the many challenges we will face in the next decade, the transition to a positive post-entrepreneurial style, in both our business and our personal lives, will be among the toughest.

America has a set of policies and programs, expectations and aspirations, which are tied to a traditional system that is rapidly disappearing. If we continue to presuppose the corporation of the past, with its apparent stability and longevity, we will make very bad social policy. Some things will be tense and produce seemingly irresolvable conflict. For example, there could be pressure on corporations to guarantee employment levels, even when that restriction on flexibility reduces the competitiveness of the firms—unless we develop policies and programs that acknowledge that continuing change is now a fact of life. In short, we must gear national policy to the business forms of the future.

Education and training, continuing education and retraining, have to be at the top of the agenda. If an educated workforce has been America's number-one asset in the past, it is even more critical in the rapidly changing world of the global corporate Olympics, in which innovation renders old skills obsolete and requires new ones, including the professional knowledge to produce those innovations. Training needs must be addressed both inside and outside of industry.

Certainly corporations can be encouraged to invest in constant upgrading of the skills of their workforce, to improve performance ''in place" and tie rewards to those performance improvements; to redeploy people into new jobs in new areas as a means for avoiding layoffs in the face of acquisitions or shifts in technology or markets; and to attract the best people by providing the kind of education that increases their desirability on the job market when internal promotions and a permanent career can no longer be assured. Corporate education programs should be a matter of national interest, for they are an important extension of secondary and higher education. Not only do they help companies improve their competitiveness—a matter of public concern—but they also ensure that the labor force remains employable regardless of the fates of particular units of particular companies. A human resource tax credit for training investments, particularly in technological areas, would encourage the spread and deepening of this public service. Ironically, America has had tax credits for research-and-development investments, but not for development of the human skills that R&D requires. It is time to give the same priority to education and training.

However, only larger corporations tend to be wealthy enough to carry their own educational staffs and mount their own educational programs. And as corporations get leaner by turning to consultants and contractors for internal services, and as restructuring makes the population of "employees" an unstable one, it is clear that we cannot expect to rely on individual corporations to meet the retraining needs of the nation. Just as alliances between companies in the form of research consortia with government assistance are springing up to pool resources for R&D that would be too costly if done individually, so can industry-level training partnerships produce a skilled workforce for many companies—and a vehicle for retraining when a company restructures or an individual wants to seek opportunity elsewhere.

There are models for these partnerships at the state level; for example, the Machine Action Project in Massachusetts, which is helping smaller machine tool companies reposition themselves in the global economy by retraining the workforce.[5] Such training partnerships could be designed and governed by a coalition of leaders from business, labor, government, and education—from public universities to private training contractors. They would be a flexible resource, yet one that is stable and institutionalized—a continuing capacity for the industry or the region.

In addition to job-specific training, educational policy should ensure that schools across the nation better prepare all their students in two critical skills for competing in the global corporate Olympics: technological literacy and facility in other languages, including Asian languages. Because of the cross-functional emphasis of post-entrepreneurial corporations, because of the number of boundary-spanning partnerships involving transfer of technological knowledge, more people at more levels of business organizations will need to feel comfortable with learning about technology, with assessing it, with incorporating the benefits of new technologies into their repertoires. One kind of technology in particular, information technology, will be a primary tool in communication, permitting the interactions that build synergies across units with wide geographic dispersion, permitting partners to share data and link their planning systems. But technological literacy alone will not permit Americans to gain the benefits of global operations or cross-national partnerships unless we also have language skills. The partner that must work through translators loses time, opportunity, and information.

At the state level, again, there are excellent efforts underway to build these competences. New York State, for example, has a major program to teach about technologies of all kinds in high schools across the state. I can only wonder what the infusion of federal dollars and federal leadership would mean—and how quickly we could see results. What if every high school in America were to teach Japanese? What if colleges continued this education? In a half-dozen years would we see an improvement in the ability of American companies to compete in and with Japan? Of course, teaching subjects like these requires teachers able to do so. We must reach out to nontraditional sources for teachers competent in these nontraditional subjects—not just those with formal "teaching credentials": for example, retired executives, engineers with release time from their company, or foreign residents in the U.S. It should be a national priority to tap this kind of talent and link it to school systems everywhere.

Also on the public policy agenda should be a new role for unions as partners in planning for workplace changes. The "business partnership" between Pacific Bell and the Communications Workers of America enhances both the competitiveness of the company, giving it the ability to get workforce cooperation in moving quickly to employ new technology and restructure jobs, and the security of the people— as union leaders collaborate with company managers to design new career paths and train for new skills. Yet the current labor law framework still tends to assume an adversarial relationship between labor and management, not a relationship that involves joint planning for the workplace of the future.[6] Furthermore, when employees get more involved in partnership activities, they run the risk of crossing a line into "making managerial decisions," which makes them ineligible for union membership. It is time to rethink labor law to make it better fit the emerging collaborative, partnership-oriented framework American business so desperately needs.

Pay for contribution rather than for position is another idea whose time has come. It helps businesses be more competitive by motivating performance, increasing the variable component of pay and reducing the fixed costs, making the system fairer in the eyes of employees, and reducing the emphasis on promotion as the only way to earn more, thus helping limit excessive layers of hierarchy. Pay-for-performance systems also help people gain more control over what they earn. There should be incentives to encourage more companies to establish profit-sharing and gain-sharing programs, and there should be favorable tax treatment of performance bonuses and gains from internal venture returns—treating them more like long-term capital gains than like ordinary income (assuming the distinction returns to the tax code). At the same time, large executive bonuses or stock options should not be allowed at all unless comparable bonus systems exist for employees in general.

Sharing the profits with those who help produce them is one way to put reality behind the oft-stated corporate slogan that "people are our most valued assets." While we want people to share in the benefits of good times, we must also put some social safety nets under them to cushion their fall during bad times. Setting minimum standards for severance benefits (including for continuation of health insurance), especially after a change in ownership, would help; while many companies would surely exceed the minimum, the policy would move more firms into the "good employer" category (and spread the costs more evenly). I support the proposal that employers pay into a worker retraining account as a hedge against the time when corporate change sends those workers out on their own. A modest "contribution" of this sort would help companies keep their freedom to make changes.

The corporation is an artificial construct; nothing about its definition says that it must endure or that it must be the central instrument for ensuring social welfare. But the corporation is also much more than a bundle of transactions; it is infused with meaning and value by all those who devote their life to it and who, therefore, find that it is indeed the primary determinant of their families' welfare. We have counted on corporations to take care of people, and to take care of them for the long term. Today, however, even those corporations with strong values and concern for their people must make more gut-wrenching changes more rapidly. Nostalgia for a world with corporate stability and longevity should not blind us to the need to provide social safety nets outside of the corporation, via government—the way nostalgia for the traditional nuclear family with stay-at-home wives meant waiting decades for the needs of working parents to receive attention in Washington.

Next, then, we should move forward quickly on meeting the needs of working parents for high-quality, affordable child care (this means *facilities,* not just tax credits) and for time to be with their families. In addition to parenting leave at birth or adoption and flexible work hours on a daily or weekly basis, there should be a newer idea: the flexible year. A "flex-year" would involve long periods of time off or time on less intense activities between high-intensity, time-demanding projects. We should develop work rhythms that alternate between times of high work involvement and times of rest and renewal—making legitimate a break of a month or two as projects end before plunging people into a new one. These minisabbaticals can be devoted to family or to education or simply to personal revitalization.

It is also time to acknowledge that changes in career patterns require flexibility in the administration of unemployment and severance benefits. An increasing number of people go into business for themselves rather than looking for another employer. Thus, the idea of unemployment insurance as a bridge for the time between employers is less relevant to them; what they need is capital to establish their business. Lump sums could be provided to invest in start-ups upon presentation of a business plan, as in the State of Washington experiment. Such lump sum payments, if used to create a business, could receive a tax treatment different from that used as bridge income between employers. Not only would this kind of system better meet the needs of individuals in post-entrepreneurial careers, but it also would help rev up the entrepreneurial engine that is responsible for so many of America's new jobs.

Finally, we must replace the assumption of longevity—that one or a few employers will provide for the individual's lifetime needs—with the assumption of mobility. Pensions need to be made portable, tied to the individual rather than to the employer and administered by third-party partners. One model is the Teachers Insurance and Annuity Association–College Retirement Equities Fund (TIAA-CREF) for college, university, and secondary school personnel. While organizations pay into it as part of their benefits programs, the accounts move with the individuals.

These ten recommendations for national policy—a human resource development tax credit; industry-level training partnerships; accelerated technology and language education; union-management partnerships to plan workplace changes; incentives for profit-sharing and performance bonuses; stronger safety nets for displaced employees; day care; flex-year opportunities; flexible use of severance and unemployment benefits; and portable pensions—would make it possible to support flexibility for corporations while still providing security for people.

We must encourage corporations to do their part, but we must also establish the means outside individual corporations, at the industry level or community level or in partnership with government. There is a need for new kinds of consortia to fill the gaps in a world that is less stable—interstitial or bridging mechanisms that will facilitate alliances between organizations or handle issues such as training or day care for a variety of organizations.

TOWARD VICTORY IN THE CORPORATE OLYMPICS

Baseball great Yogi Berra put it best. "The future," he once said, "ain't what it used to be." Corporations, individuals, and America as a nation have to face up to and manage a very different economic environment, a competitive global Olympics that requires post-entrepreneurial strategies and business athletes for success.

How do we get people to welcome change, particularly changes of the magnitude of those I have described? There are many ways that resistance to change can be overcome. Uncertainty and anxiety can be handled by ample information and communication, by role models, by training in the new skills, by transition periods in which the old way and the new way coexist.[7]

But the most powerful way to encourage people to embrace change is to develop a shared vision of an even more positive future, a vision created jointly by all of a corporation's stakeholders—its customers, suppliers, employees—and its potential industry and government partners.

While "vision" is sometimes thought to be the task of leaders,[8] people at all organizational levels have a role to play in bringing the post-entrepreneurial corporation to life. Indeed, it is heartening to know that leadership to move companies in more cooperative, innovative directions can come from many places, not just from the chief executive's office. Certainly the goals set by John Sculley at Apple, Jim Robinson at American Express, Gerry Grinstein at Western Airlines, or Colby Chandler, Kay Whitmore, and Philip Samper at Kodak were critical ingredients in moving those companies toward post-entrepreneurial strategies; but so were the new models designed and championed by numerous division general managers, staff executives, and imaginative professionals. Ed Voboril launched the search for global synergies as a PPG group executive, Ron Payne envisioned supplier partnerships from his post as Digital's corporate purchasing officer, Ben Dial and Lee Cox pushed the union partnership as respective heads of human resources and the operations department at Pacific Telesis, and Raytheon's George Freedman, like Bob Tuite and Bob Rosenfeld at Kodak, invented a newstream channel from technical staff positions, often swimming against the current to prove its usefulness and win top management support; and all had allies among their peers. The new modes of action they created, whether cross-area synergy projects or strategic alliances or innovation programs, stimulated still other people—the organization's "employees" or its "partners"—to cooperate in finding new opportunities, as Elena Prokupets did for Kodak, or in dramatically improving the performance of existing businesses, as Carol Twigger did for Ohio Bell.

In short, the post-entrepreneurial organization is created by a three-part mix: by the context set at the top, the values and goals emanating from top management; by the channels, forums, programs, and relationships designed in the middle to support those values and goals; and by the project ideas bubbling up from below—ideas for new ventures or technological innovations or better ways to serve customers. Leaders have a role to play in each element. They explore and communicate values and strategies; they authorize the structures, mechanisms, and programs to enable others to contribute; and they select from among the promising ideas presented to them those that get resources and rewards, those that should be spread elsewhere, or those that will be moved into the company's mainstream.

Leadership of all the kinds I have described is essential to move American companies toward higher performance. That bright future is clearly possible for American business, if we can let go of the assumptions of the past, unlock the shackles of bureaucracy, and marry the entrepreneurial spirit with corporate discipline in the post-entrepreneurial corporation. After all, even while other nations field Olympic-class business teams, America has incredible strengths to draw on: some of the best universities and research centers in the world, still the sites for technological leaps forward; large domestic markets where we should have the home-team and home-field advantage in selling our wares; abundant natural resources; an entrepreneurial tradition that causes mavericks with new ideas to rise and strike out on their own; a diverse society with ties to many parts of the world; and a democratic distaste for closed status systems that suppress talent.

The task ahead is to design corporations and careers that can capitalize on these strengths rather than waste them, that can tackle wide opportunities while living within resource constraints. Meeting the challenge of doing more with less is the ultimate balancing act. We must combine the power of corporate teamwork and cooperation with the creativity and agility of the entrepreneur, without slipping into the excesses of either corpocrat or cowboy. To succeed in the global business climate we face, we must deepen our skills at both cooperating and creating, and we must spread them—person by person, team by team, project by project.

Each successful project, each short-term victory, and each move away from bureaucracy and toward synergy, partnership, and innovation, will bring us closer and closer to the ultimate long-term achievement—a sustainable competitive economy. Then, the American way of management can once again be a point of pride for its practitioners, a source of well-being for the public, and an admired model for the world.

Notes

Chapter 1

1. Joseph Bower, *When Markets Quake: The Management Challenge of Restructuring Industry* (Boston: HBS Press, 1986).
2. To his credit, Tom Peters, coauthor of *In Search of Excellence*, the book that started the excellence boom, is not pushing capital-E Excellence anymore either. Compare Thomas J. Peters and Robert Waterman, *In Search of Excellence* (New York: Harper and Row, 1982), with Tom Peters, *Thriving on Chaos: Handbook for a Management Revolution* (New York: Alfred A. Knopf, 1987).
3. Peter G. Peterson, "The Morning After," *The Atlantic*, vol. 26, no. 4 (October 1987) pp. 43–69. See also Cuomo Commission on Trade and Competitiveness, *The Cuomo Commission Report* (New York: Simon and Schuster, 1988).
4. U.S. Bureau of the Census, *Statistical Abstract of the United States: 1988*, 108th ed. (Washington, DC: U.S. Government Printing Office, 1987).
5. U.S. Department of Commerce data, cited in Claudia Deutsch, "U.S. Industry's Unfinished Struggle," *New York Times*, February 21, 1988, sec. 3, p. 7.
6. U.S. Bureau of the Census, op. cit.
7. Ibid.
8. Ibid.
9. Ibid.
10. Ibid.
11. Daniel Burstein, *Yen! Japan's New Financial Empire and Its Threat to America* (New York: Simon and Schuster, 1988).

12. U.S. Bureau of the Census, op. cit.
13. *Common Sense on Competitiveness* (Atlanta: Carter Center Conference Report Series), vol. 1, no. 1; U.S. Department of Commerce, Survey of Current Business, various issues. See also Council of Economic Advisers, *Economic Report of the President* (Washington, DC: U.S. Government Printing Office, 1987).
14. Peterson, op. cit., p. 48.
15. Rudiger Dornbush, James Poterba, and Lawrence Summers, *The Case for American Manufacturing in America's Future* (Rochester, NY: Eastman Kodak, 1988).
16. Burstein, op. cit.
17. M. R. Kleinfield, "Hanging on in the Mini Market," *New York Times*, November 29, 1987, sec. 3, p. 1. "Japanese Banks in California," *Western Banker*, April 1987, p. 13.
18. Burstein, op. cit.
19. Benjamin Friedman, "Sorting Out the Debt," *New Perspective Quarterly*, Fall 1987, p. 23.
20. Burstein, op. cit.
21. Katherine L. Bradbury, "The Shrinking Middle Class," *New England Economic Review*, September–October 1986, pp. 41–55.
22. Congress of the United States, Joint Economic Committee, *Working Mothers Are Preserving Family Living Standards*, May 9, 1986.
23. Data come from the Council on Competitiveness, the private group formed out of the Reagan Presidential Commission on U.S. Competitiveness.
24. U.S. Department of Labor, Bureau of Labor Statistics, "Usual Weekly Earnings of Wage and Salary Workers, 4th Quarter, 1987," February 1, 1988.
25. Paul Hirsch, *Pack Your Own Parachute: How to Survive Mergers, Takeovers, and Other Corporate Disasters* (Reading, MA: Addison-Wesley, 1987).
26. David Sanger, "U.S. Chip Makers Recovering," *New York Times*, May 26, 1987, p. 1.
27. Cuomo Commission, op. cit., p. 4.
28. David M. Gordon, "Private Debt Dwarfs Uncle Sam's," *Los Angeles Times*, January 20, 1987, p. 3.

Chapter 2

1. "Has the World Passed Kodak By?" *Forbes*, November 5, 1984, p. 188.
2. Thomas Moore, "Old-Line Industry Shapes Up," *Fortune*, April 27, 1987, p. 26.
3. John Sculley with John Byrne, *Odyssey: Pepsi to Apple . . . A Journey of Adventures, Ideas, and the Future* (New York: Harper and Row, 1987), p. 134.
4. Ibid., p. 238.
5. Ibid., p. 379.
6. "Apple Launches Mac Attack," *Time*, January 30, 1984.
7. Sculley, op. cit., p. 273.

8. Ibid., p. 241.
9. Ibid., p. 394.
10. Ibid., p. 321.

Chapter 3

1. Michael Porter, "From Competitive Advantage to Corporate Strategy," *Harvard Business Review*, vol. 65, no. 3 (May–June 1987), pp. 45–59. H. Donald Hopkins and Robert A. Pitts, "Acquisitions and Performance: Why Don't Acquisitions Help?" unpublished paper, Temple University, 1987.
2. Ibid.
3. Robert H. Tomasko, *Downsizing: Reshaping the Corporation for the Future* (New York: AMACOM, 1987).
4. Paul Hirsch, *Pack Your Own Parachute* (Reading, MA: Addison-Wesley, 1987).
5. Myron Magnet, "Help! My Company Has Just Been Taken Over," *Fortune*, July 8, 1984, p. 44.
6. David B. Jemison and Sim B. Sitkin, "Corporate Acquisitions: A Process Perspective," *Academy of Management Journal*, 11 (1986), pp. 145–163.
7. Richard Behar, "We'll Get Back to You on That," *Forbes*, April 6, 1987, pp. 42–43.
8. Hirsch, op. cit., p. 55.
9. Aimee L. Stern, "General Foods Tries the Old Restructure Ploy," *Business Month*, November 1987, pp. 37–39.
10. Allan J. Hamilton, "Why Trammell Crow's Star Salesman Is Persona Non Grata," *New York Times*, March 22, 1987.
11. Alfie Kohn, *No Contest: The Case Against Competition* (Boston: Houghton Mifflin, 1986).
12. Ibid., p. 53. See also Peter Blau, *Exchange and Power in Social Life* (New York: Wiley, 1964).
13. David W. Johnson, Geoffrey Maruyama, Roger Johnson, Deborah Nelson, and Linda Skon, "Effects of Cooperative, Competitive, and Individualistic Goal Structures on Achievement: A Meta-Analysis," *Psychological Bulletin*, vol. 89, no. 1 (1981). pp. 47–62.
14. Jonathan Kwitny, "Science Follies: At CDC's AIDS Lab Egos, Power, Politics and Lost Experiments," *Wall Street Journal*, December 12, 1986, p. 1.
15. Allan Cohen and David Bradford, *Managing for Excellence* (New York: Wiley, 1985).
16. Theresa Amabile, *The Social Psychology of Creativity* (New York: Springer-Verlag, 1983).
17. Kohn, op. cit., p. 63.
18. In situations in which many parties compete, weaker players can sometimes band together to provide a convincing alternative, gaining strength in union—for example, trade associations of very small companies, such as the Independent Grocers Association, which can provide some of the same clout big companies

have. But this is unlikely in internal corporate competitions of the sort described here.

19. Judith A. Howard, Philip Blumstein, and Pepper Schwartz, "Sex, Power, and Influence Tactics in Intimate Relationships," *Journal of Personality and Social Psychology*, 51 (1986), pp. 102–109.

20. "Inside MCorp's Corporate Banking Merger," *ABA Banking Journal*, October 1986, pp. 135–36.

21. See also Cynthia Ingols and Paul Myers, "The Human Side of Mergers: The Western/Delta Story," in R. M. Kanter, B. A. Stein, and T. F. Jick (eds.), *The Challenge of Change* (New York: Free Press, forthcoming).

Chapter 4

1. D. Quinn Mills, *The IBM Lesson* (New York: Times Books, 1988).

2. James L. Heskett and Sergio Signorelli, "Benetton," Harvard Business School case study, 1984.

3. For more extended discussion of this concept, see Raymond E. Miles and Charles C. Snow, "Fit, Failure, and the Hall of Fame," *California Management Review*, vol. 26, no. 3 (Spring 1984), pp. 10–28; and "Organizations: A New Concept for New Forms," *California Management Review*, vol. 28, no. 3 (Spring 1986), pp. 62–73. Miles has used the switchboard metaphor only in working papers, but the press picked up on it, most notably in a 1985 *Business Week* cover story on the "hollow corporation." So the image is now established. Tom Peters is pushing a similar concept; see Tom Peters, *Thriving on Chaos: Handbook for a Management Revolution* (New York: Knopf, 1987).

4. Aimee L. Stern, "General Foods Tries the Old Restructure Ploy," *Business Month*, November 1987, pp. 37–39.

5. Oliver E. Williamson, *Markets and Hierarchies: Analysis and Antitrust Implications: A Study in the Economics of Internal Organization* (New York: Free Press, 1975).

6. Richard G. Hamermesh and Nasswan Dossabhoy, "Cleveland Twist Drill," Harvard Business School case study, 1984.

7. Michael Porter, "From Competitive Advantage to Corporate Strategy," *Harvard Business Review*, vol. 65, no. 3 (May–June 1987), pp. 43–59.

8. Christopher Bartlett and Sumantra Ghoshal, *Managing Across Borders: The Transnational Solution* (Boston: Harvard Business School Press, 1989).

9. Steve Swartz and Steve Weiner, "Stalled Synergy: Many Firms Back Off from Offering Arrays of Financial Services," *Wall Street Journal*, November 12, 1986.

10. Stern, op. cit.

11. John J. Sherwood, "Creating Work Cultures with Competitive Advantage," *Organizational Dynamics*, 16 (Winter 1988), pp. 5–27.

12. Julie Solomon and Carol Hymovitz, "Team Strategy: P&G Makes Changes in the Way It Develops and Sells Its Products," *Wall Street Journal*, August 11, 1987.

13. Monci Jo Williams, "Synergy Works at American Express," *Fortune*, February 16, 1987, pp. 79–80.
14. Swartz and Weiner, op. cit.
15. Dwight B. Crane and Robert G. Eccles, "Commercial Banks: Taking Shape for Turbulent Times," *Harvard Business Review*, vol. 65, no. 6 (November–December 1987), pp. 94–100. See also Robert Eccles and Dwight Crane, *Doing Deals* (Boston: Harvard Business School Press, 1988).
16. Alfie Kohn, *No Contest* (Boston: Houghton Mifflin, 1986), p. 69.
17. Swartz and Weiner, op. cit.
18. Robert Axelrod, *The Evolution of Cooperation* (New York: Basic Books, 1984).
19. Peter F. Drucker, "The Coming of the New Organization," *Harvard Business Review,* vol. 66 no. 1 (January–February 1988), pp. 45–53.

Chapter 5

1. Roy D. Shapiro, "Toward Effective Supplier Management: International Comparisons," Harvard Business School working paper (9-785-062), 1986.
2. D. Burt, *Proactive Purchasing* (Englewood Cliffs, NJ: Prentice-Hall, 1984), cited in R. Shapiro, op. cit., p. 107.
3. R. Shapiro, op. cit.
4. Michael Porter and Mark Fuller note that "while coalitions are not new in international competition, their character seems to be shifting. Coalitions are becoming more strategic, through linking major competitors together to compete worldwide. More traditional coalitions were often tactical." Porter and Fuller, "Coalitions in Global Strategy," in M. E. Porter (ed.), *Competition in Global Industries* (Boston: Harvard Business School Press, 1986), pp. 315–43; the quote is from p. 315. The evidence on usage of international coalitions comes from Pankaj Ghemawat, Michael E. Porter, and Richard A. Rawlinson, "Patterns of International Coalition Activity," in the same book, pp. 345–65.
5. Kathryn R. Harrigan, *Strategic Flexibility: A Management Guide for Changing Times* (Lexington, MA: Lexington Books, 1985).
6. Joseph Badaracco, *Citadels Under Siege: How Knowledge Is Transforming the Boundaries of the Firm* (tentative title), forthcoming.
7. The two studies are cited in "Corporate Odd Couples," *Business Week*, July 21, 1986, pp. 100–105. For data and arguments supporting the view that joint ventures may be undertaken for temporary advantage and therefore with a "self-liquidating strategy," so that dissolution or eventual merger can be a sign of success, not failure, see Benjamin Gomes-Casseres, "Joint Venture Instability: Is It a Problem?" *Columbia Journal of World Business*, vol. 22 no. 2 (Summer 1987), pp. 97–102.
8. Susan R. Helper, "Supplier Relations and Innovation: Theory and Application to the U.S. Auto Industry," unpublished doctoral dissertation, Harvard University, September 1987. See also Michael E. Porter, *Cases in Competitive Strategy* (New York: Free Press, 1982).
9. This is the conclusion I draw from studies such as P. Mariti and R. H. Smiley,

"Cooperative Agreements and the Organization of Industry," *The Journal of Industrial Economics*, vol. 31 (1983), pp. 437–51. In seventy cooperative agreements identified from announcements in the European business press (in each case managers were interviewed), technology and marketing goals dominated; economies of scale and risk-sharing were less common goals. But auto industry firms were more likely to be looking for cost reduction through scale economies; computer industry firms were concerned about the speed and diffusion of technological innovation. Note that this study predated a major set of changes in the auto industry, putting pressure on firms for faster absorption of technological innovations in electronics and materials—which should cause this industry, too, to move away from scale economies toward innovation as a goal for partnerships.

10. Ralph Biggadike, *Corporate Diversification: Entry, Strategy, and Performance* (Boston: Harvard Business School, Division of Research, 1976).

11. With respect to the AT&T–Philips joint venture (APT), my Harvard Business School colleague George Lodge reminded me that neither were very clear as to what they expected from each other. AT&T thought it was getting access to European telecommunications markets. But Philips had no reputation in high-tech telecommunications. In 1986, the French government gave its digital switch business to Ericsson of Sweden instead of to APT, partly because the French perceived Philips as the maker of light bulbs on the Eiffel tower, not digital switches.

12. Robert J. Eccles, "The Quasi-Firm in the Construction Industry," *Journal of Economic Behavior and Organization*, vol. 2 (December 1981), pp. 335–57.

13. American Electronics Association, 1988 Productivity Survey, conducted by Pittiglio Rabin Todd and McGrath and KPMG Peat Marwick (Santa Clara, CA: AEA, 1988).

14. George Lodge and Richard Walton, "The American Corporation and Its New Relationships," *California Management Review*, forthcoming.

15. Eric von Hippel, *The Sources of Innovation* (New York: Oxford University Press, 1988).

16. Benson Shapiro, "Close Encounters of the Fourth Kind," Harvard Business School working paper, 1987.

17. William J. Hampton, "How IBM Wooed Ford into a More Meaningful Relationship," *Business Week*, March 30, 1987, p. 87.

18. Thomas Kochan et al., *The Transformation of American Labor Relations* (New York: Basic Books, 1986).

Chapter 6

1. Roy D. Shapiro, "Toward Effective Supplier Management: International Comparisons," Harvard Business School working paper (9-785-062), 1986.

2. Chester I. Barnard, "Organizations as Systems of Cooperation," reprinted in Amitai Etzioni and Edward W. Lahman, A *Sociological Reader on Complex Organizations*, 3rd ed. (New York: Holt, Rinehart, and Winston, 1980), pp. 11–14.

3. "Corporate Odd Couples," *Business Week*, July 21, 1986, pp. 100–105.

4. Andrew Pollack, "Uniting to Create Products," *New York Times*, January 14, 1986, sec. D, p.1.

5. Newspaper articles have provided the data base for several important studies of coalition activity, thereby tending to overcount those kinds likely to be announced with fanfare to the financial community (e.g., joint ventures or licensing agreements opening up totally new product-market possibilities) and undercounting those that have less intrinsic "glamour" (e.g., a closer relationship between existing suppliers and customers that improves existing products, speeds line extensions, lowers costs, brings faster innovation, etc.). For example, one major study using announcements in *The Wall Street Journal* found more examples of what the researchers called "Y" type coalitions (which involved shared performance of an activity by the partners, as in a joint venture) than "X" type coalitions (which involved a division of labor, as in supplier-customer relationships); the researchers also expected the "Y" type to be longer-lasting. See Pankaj Ghemawat, Michael E. Porter, and Richard A. Rawlinson, "Patterns of International Coalition Activity," in M. E. Porter (ed.), *Competition in Global Industries* (Boston: Harvard Business School Press, 1986), pp. 345–365. But I think these findings seriously understate the growing importance and longer-term viability of stakeholder partnerships. Because these are more difficult to identify from public sources, researchers must go directly to companies for information—a more time-consuming process, but ultimately more valid.

6. Norm Alster, "Dealbusters: Why Partnerships Fail," *Electronic Business*, April 1, 1986, pp. 70–75.

7. "Corporate Odd Couples," op. cit.

8. William Davidson at the University of Southern California is the source for the item about U.S.–Japan joint ventures with no U.S. managers. See also Steven Prokesch, "Stopping the High-Tech Giveaway," *New York Times*, March 22, 1987, sec. 3, p. 1. Thomas McCraw of the Harvard Business School has pointed out that for every American studying in Japan, there are fifteen Japanese—from a much smaller population pool—studying in the U.S. "They simply know us better," he commented in an interview in the Harvard Business School *Bulletin*, "and have consequently outclassed us in all kinds of negotiations."

9. Prokesch, op. cit.

10. Jeffrey A. Trachtenberg, "Why Things Go Better with Coke," *Forbes,* November 18, 1985, p. 41.

11. Prokesch, op. cit.

12. "Corporate Odd Couples," op. cit.; Alster, op. cit.

13. Alster, op. cit.

14. "Corporate Odd Couples," op. cit.

15. Alster, op. cit.

16. Jane Mayer, "CBS, Fox Film Drop Cable TV Operation from Joint Venture," *Wall Street Journal*, June 8, 1982, p. 16.

17. William J. Hampton, "How IBM Wooed Ford into a More Meaningful Relationship," *Business Week,* March 30, 1987, p. 87.

18. Benson Shapiro, "Close Encounters of the Fourth Kind," Harvard Business School working paper, 1986.
19. "Corporate Odd Couples," op. cit.
20. David Card, "Metheus–CV: The Synergy Unravels," *Electronic Business*, April 1, 1986, p. 74.
21. Among Michael Porter and Mark Fuller's most important criteria for selecting a long-term coalition partner are that the partner possesses the desired source of competitive advantage that would create a disadvantage if a rival had it, and that the partner is unlikely to become a competitor. See Porter and Fuller, "Coalitions and Global Strategies," in Porter (ed.), *Competition in Global Industries*, op. cit., p. 341; and John Stopford and Louis T. Wells, Jr., *Managing the Multinational Enterprise* (New York: Basic Books, 1972).

Chapter 7

1. There is suggestive evidence of an association between an interest in new markets and lines of business and both internal venture activity and external acquisition-seeking. In one study, firms with the largest number of successful new ventures tended also to spend more on marketing-related activities and seek more acquisitions, but to spend less on "classic" (stand-alone) R&D. In short, the emphasis was on the potential to exploit new ideas to open new markets, rather than on research for its own sake or to contribute to existing lines of business. See Richard Klavans, Mark Shanley, and William M. Evan, "The Management of Internal Corporate Ventures: Entrepreneurship and Innovation," *Columbia Journal of World Business*, vol. 20 (Summer 1985), pp. 21–27.
2. George Freedman, *The Pursuit of Innovation: Managing the People and Processes That Turn New Ideas into Profits* (New York: AMACOM, 1988), p. 206.
3. Norman D. Fast, "The Future of Industrial New Venture Departments," *Industrial Marketing Management*, vol. 8 (November 1979), pp. 264–73.
4. Zenas Block and P. N. Subbanarasimha, "Corporate Venturing: Practices and Performance in Japan and the United States," unpublished manuscript, New York University, forthcoming; Zenas Block, "Can Corporate Venturing Succeed?" *The Journal of Business Strategy*, vol. 3 (Fall 1982), pp. 21–33; Zenas Block, "Some Major Issues in Internal Corporate Venturing," in J. A. Hornaday, J. A. Timmons, and K. H. Vesper (eds.), *Frontiers of Entrepreneurship Research* (Wellesley, MA: Babson College, 1983).
5. The very factors that create success for a venture capital operation can compromise its ability to serve the parent company's diversification objectives, as there can be a conflict between, for example, the organizational independence required to make good investments and the limitations on the kinds of companies invested in presented by the parent company's business strategy (i.e., a desire to find synergies with existing businesses). See G. Felda Hardymon, Mark J. DeNino, and Malcolm S. Salter, "When Corporate Venture Capital Doesn't Work," *Harvard Business Review*, vol. 61 (May–June 1983), pp. 114–20.

6. For an extended discussion of the phases of innovation (from idea generation to full-fledged use), and the conditions associated with higher levels of creativity and support for new ideas, see Rosabeth Moss Kanter, "When a Thousand Flowers Bloom: Structural, Social, and Collective Conditions for Innovation in Organizations," *Research in Organizational Behavior*, vol. 10 (Greenwich, CT: JAI Press, 1988).

Chapter 8

1. Edwin Mansfield, John Rapoport, Jerome Schnee, Samual Wagner, and Michael Hamburger, "Research and Innovation in the Modern Corporation," in Robert R. Rothberg (ed.), *Corporation Strategy and Product Innovation* (New York: Free Press, 1981), pp. 416–27.
2. Jim Powell, "Bootstrap Entrepreneurs at GTE TeleMessenger," *GTE Together*, Winter 1985.
3. Ralph Biggadike, "The Risky Business of Diversification," *Harvard Business Review*, v. 57 (May–June 1979), pp. 103–111.
4. Rosabeth Moss Kanter, *The Change Masters: Innovation and Entrepreneurship in the American Corporation* (New York: Simon and Schuster, 1983).
5. James Brian Quinn, "Managing Innovation: Controlled Chaos," *Harvard Business Review*, vol. 63 (May–June 1985), pp. 73–84. My Harvard Business School colleague Robert Hayes pushed me to wonder why internal venturers are so unhappy about corporate controls in their desire for total autonomy when independent ventures tend to be under strict surveillance by venture capitalists and banks. I conclude that it is a different kind of control. Pure investors and lenders may watch expenditures, but they are not as likely as a corporate parent to insist on the use of particular systems, procedures, and services—useful to the venture or not.
6. Quinn, op. cit.
7. Ralph Katz, "Project Communication and Performance: An Investigation Into the Effects of Group Longevity," *Administrative Science Quarterly*, vol. 27 (1982), pp. 81–104.
8. Thomas Peters and Robert Waterman, *In Search of Excellence* (New York: Harper and Row, 1982).
9. Jay Galbraith, "Designing the Innovating Organization," *Organizational Dynamics*, vol. 10 (Summer 1982), pp. 5–25. See also Rosabeth Moss Kanter, "When a Thousand Flowers Bloom: Structural, Social, and Collective Conditions for Innovation in Organizations," *Research in Organizational Behavior*, vol. 10 (Greenwich, CT: JAI Press, 1988).
10. Quinn, op.cit.
11. Hollister B. Sykes, "Lessons From a New Ventures Program," *Harvard Business Review*, vol. 64, no. 3 (May–June 1986), pp. 69–74.
12. Lotte Bailyn, "Autonomy in the Industrial R & D Lab," *Human Resource Management*, vol. 24 (1985), pp. 129–146.
13. Howard Stevenson and David Gumpert, "The Heart of Entrepreneurship," *Harvard Business Review*, vol. 64 (March–April 1985), pp. 84–94.

14. Joseph Bower developed the seminal framework for understanding resource allocation decisions as an interplay between the context set by the top of the organization and the proposals brought by the middle; see Bower, *Managing the Resource Allocation Process* (Boston: Harvard Business School Division of Research, 1970). His perspective informs many other attempts to define where new ventures should fit into corporate strategy and what the role of top leadership should be. See Robert A. Burgelman, "Corporate Entrepreneurship and Strategic Management: Insights from a Process Study," *Management Science*, vol. 29, no. 12 (December 1983), pp. 1349–64; Phyllis Mason, *Managing Internal Corporate Ventures: A Process Approach*, unpublished doctoral dissertation, Columbia University, 1986. A comprehensive examination of one company's mainstream/ newstream linkages is found in Robert A. Burgelman and Leonard R. Sayles, *Inside Corporate Innovation* (New York: Free Press, 1986).
15. Michael Maccoby, *Why Work?* (New York: Simon and Schuster, 1988).

Chapter 9

1. Gerald S. Leventhal, "The Distribution of Rewards and Resources in Groups and Organizations," in *Advances in Experimental Social Psychology*, vol. 9 (1976), pp. 91–131. For examples of empirical evidence, see Wayne M. Alves and Peter H. Rossi, "Who Should Get What? Fairness Judgments of the Distribution of Earnings," *American Journal of Sociology*, vol. 84, no. 3 (November 1978), pp. 541–64.
2. John A. Fossum and Mary K. Fitch, "The Effects of Individual and Contextual Attributes on the Sizes of Recommended Salary Increases," *Personnel Psychology*, vol. 38 (Autumn 1985), pp. 587–602.
3. Charles Peck, "Compensating Salaried Employees During Inflation: General vs. Merit Increases," Conference Board study, no. 796 (New York: Conference Board, 1981).
4. Opinion Research Corporation, *Managing Human Resources in 1983 and Beyond* (Princeton, NJ: Opinion Research Corporation, 1983). See also Opinion Research Corporation, "Statistics on Employees' Perceptions of Pay and Performance," unpublished data, 1988. These data show that in 1986–1987 only 42 percent of managers, 30 percent of exempt employees, and 21 percent of nonexempt employees saw a correlation of pay and performance.
5. Edward E. Lawler III, *Pay and Organization Development* (Reading, MA: Addison-Wesley, 1981). See also Lawler, "Reward Systems," in J. R. Hackman and J. L. Suttle (eds.), *Improving Life at Work* (Santa Monica, CA: Goodyear, 1977).
6. Levanthal, op. cit. See also Steven E. Markham, "Pay-for-Performance Dilemma Revisited," *Journal of Applied Psychology*, vol. 73, no. 2 (1988), pp. 172–80.
7. *Facts for Bargaining: What's New in Collective Bargaining Negotiations and Contracts*, Part 2, Bureau of National Affairs, no. 1117, March 24, 1988. See also "1986–1987 Salary Increase Survey" (Chicago: Hewitt Associates).

8. Martin L. Weitzman, *The Share Economy: Conquering Stagflation* (Cambridge, MA: Harvard University Press, 1984).

9. Michael Quarrey, Joseph Blasi, and Corey Rosen, *Taking Stock: Employee Ownership at Work* (Cambridge, MA: Ballinger, 1986).

10. Robert Reich, *Tales of a New America* (New York: Times Books, 1987).

11. U.S. Bureau of Labor Statistics, *Employee Benefits in Medium and Large Firms, 1982*, no. 2176 (Washington, DC: U.S. Government Printing Office, 1983), p. 48; Hewitt Associeates and Profit Sharing Council of America, *1988 Profit Sharing Survey* (Chicago: Hewitt Associates, 1988).

12. Peck, op. cit. See also Michael F. Spratt and Bernadette Steel, "Rewarding Key Contributors," *Compensation and Benefits Review*, vol. 17 (July–August 1985), pp. 24–37.

13. General Accounting Office, "Productivity Sharing Programs: Can They Contribute to Productivity Improvement?" AFMD-81-22, March 31, 1981.

14. Michael Schuster, "The Scanlon Plan: A Longitudinal Analysis," *Journal of Applied Behavioral Science*, vol. 1 (1984), pp. 23–28.

15. Lawler, op. cit.

16. David Stipp, "Lab Legacy: Inventors Are Seeking Bigger Shares of Gains from Their Successes," *Wall Street Journal*, September 4, 1982.

17. Ellen Wojahn, "In Search of the Retentive Incentive," *INC*, May 1984, pp. 211–16.

18. Jay R. Schuster, *Management Compensation in High Technology Companies* (Lexington, MA: Lexington Books, 1984).

19. Jay R. Schuster, "Compensation Plan Design: The Power Behind the Best High-Tech Companies," *Management Review*, vol. 74 (May 1985), pp. 21–25.

20. Spratt and Steel, op. cit.

21. James W. Steele, *Paying for Performance and Position: Dilemmas in Salary Compression and Merit Pay* (New York: AMA Membership Publication Division, 1982). Data in the following paragraph are from the same study.

Chapter 10

1. Amanda Bennett. "Early to Bed . . . A Look at the CEO Workweek," *Wall Street Journal Executive Style*, March 20, 1987. See also Ford S. Worthy, "You're Probably Working Too Hard," *Fortune*, April 27, 1987

2. David Margolick, "On Taking Pity on the Downtrodden Associate," At the Bar column, *New York Times*, January 8, 1988.

3. Lewis Coser, *Greedy Organizations: Patterns of Undivided Commitment* (New York: Free Press, 1974).

4. Worthy, op. cit.

5. Christopher Jencks, Lauri Perman, and Lee Rainwater, "What Is a Good Job? A New Measure of Labor Market Success," *American Journal of Sociology*, vol. 93, no. 6 (May 1988), pp. 1322–57.

6. Worthy, op. cit.

7. Barry A. Macy, "An Assessment of U.S. Work Improvement and Productivity

Efforts, 1970–1985,'' Annual Meeting of the National Academy of Management, August 1986.

8. Daniel Forbes, "The Lessons of NUMMI," *Business Month,* June 1987, pp. 50–52.

9. Henry Mintzberg, *The Nature of Managerial Work* (New York: Harper and Row, 1973).

10. Daniel P. Wiener, "Astride the Bounciest Baby Bell: Thomas Bolger," in "The Year's 50 Most Fascinating Business People," *Fortune,* January 5, 1987, p. 87.

11. Christopher Bartlett and Sumantra Ghoshal, *Managing Across Borders: The Transnational Solution* (Boston: Harvard Business School Press, 1989).

12. Dyan Machan, "DEC's Democracy," *Forbes,* March 23, 1987.

13. Todd D. Jick and Mary Gentile, "Donna Dubinsky and Apple Computer, Inc." Harvard Business School case study, 1986.

14. Ibid.

15. Susan Jacoby, "Business Affairs," *New York Times Magazine,* November 29, 1987.

16. Research I did years ago on people's attachment to strong communities led me to propose that any attempt to build a strong team or community is associated with frowning on exclusive couple relationships; see Rosabeth Moss Kanter, *Commitment and Community* (Cambridge, MA: Harvard University Press, 1972).

17. "Families Bear the Brunt of the Entrepreneurial Dream," *Wall Street Journal,* September 11, 1986.

18. The discussion that follows draws heavily on my more extended writing on historical work-family tensions; original references to sources are to be found there. See Rosabeth Moss Kanter, *Work and Family in the United States* (New York: Russell Sage Foundation, 1977).

19. Sebastian de Grazia, *Of Time, Work and Leisure* (New York: Twentieth Century Fund, 1962).

20. Neil J. Smelser, *Social Change in the Industrial Revolution: An Application of Theory to the British Cotton Industry* (Chicago: Universuity of Chicago Press, 1959).

21. Talcott Parsons, "The Social Structure of the Family," in R. N. Anshen (ed.), *The Family: Its Function and Destiny* (New York: Harper & Bros., 1949).

22. Cynthia Crossen, "A Lingering Stigma," *Wall Street Journal Executive Style,* March 20, 1987.

23. Martha Brannigan, "The Pioneers: Women Who Fought Sex Bias on Job Prove to Be a Varied Group," *Wall Street Journal,* June 8, 1987, p. 1.

24. Fern Schumer Chapman, "Executive Guilt: Who's Taking Care of the Children?" *Fortune,* February 16, 1987.

25. Catherine E. Ross, "The Division of Labor at Home," *Social Forces,* vol. 65 (March 1987), pp. 816–33. See also Associated Press, "Are Women Getting Their Fair Shake?" *Boston Globe,* June 17, 1986. See also Trish Hall, "Why All Those People Feel They Never Have Enough Time," *New York Times,* January 2, 1988.

26. Stephen J. Simurda, "Child Care," *Boston Globe,* February 26, 1988.

27. "New Work Schedules for a Changing Society," Work in America Institute study, 1981.
28. Everett M. Rogers and Judith K. Larsen, *Silicon Valley Fever: Growth of High-Technology Culture* (New York: Basic Books, 1984). Myra K. Strober and Carolyn L. Arnold, "Integrated Circuits-Segregated Labor: Women in Computer-Related Occupations and High-Tech Industries," in H. Hartmann (ed.), *Computer Chips and Paper Clips* (Washington, DC: National Academy Press, 1987).
29. Tracy Kidder, *The Soul of a New Machine* (Boston: Little, Brown, 1981).
30. Louis Harris. *Inside America* (New York: Vintage Books, 1987).
31. Trish Hall, "The Dinner Party Quietly Bows to More Casual Alternatives," *New York Times,* February 24, 1988.
32. William Oncken, *Managing Management Time: Who's Got the Monkey* (Englewood Cliffs, NJ: Prentice-Hall, 1984).
33. See Jeffrey G. Miller and Thomas E. Vollmann, "The Hidden Factory," *Harvard Business Review,* vol. 85, no. 5 (September–October 1985) pp. 142–51. See also H. Thomas Johnson and Robert Kaplan, "The Importance of Long-Term Product Costs," *McKinsey Quarterly,* Autumn 1987, pp. 36–48; and Alan Kantrow (ed.), *McKinsey Quarterly,* Spring 1988, entire edition.

Chapter 11

1. U.S. Bureau of Labor Statistics data, compiled and integrated in Katherine S. Newman, *Falling From Grace: The Experience of Downward Mobility in the American Middle Class* (New York: Free Press, 1988).
2. Paul Hirsch, *Pack Your Own Parachute* (Reading, MA: Addison-Wesley, 1987), pp. 30, 52.
3. Bruce Nussbaum, "The End of Corporate Loyalty," *Business Week,* August 4, 1986, pp. 42–49.
4. Hirsch, op. cit., p. 102.
5. Ibid., p. 30.
6. Jeffrey Pfeffer and James N. Baron, "Taking the Workers Back Out: Recent Trends in the Structuring of Employment," in B. Staw and L. Cummings (eds.), *Research in Organizational Behavior,* vol. 10 (Greenwich, CT: JAI Press, 1988). Also based on D. Mayall and K. Nelson, *The Temporary Help Supply Service and the Temporary Labor Market,* final report submitted to Office of Research and Development, Employment and Training Administration, U.S. Department of Labor, 1982. See also Max L. Carey and K. L. Hazelbaker, "Employment Growth in the Temporary Help Industry," *Monthly Labor Review,* April 1986, pp. 37–44.
7. Bruce D. Butterfield, "Being a 'Temp' Takes on New Meaning," *Boston Globe,* November 3, 1987.
8. Daniel Forbes, "Part-Time Work Force," *Business Month,* October 1987, pp. 45–47.
9. Philip H. Wiggins, "Temporary Help in Great Demand," *New York Times,* March 4, 1988.

10. Butterfield, op. cit.

11. John Tschetter, "Producer Service Industries: Why Are They Growing So Rapidly?" *Monthly Labor Review*, December 1987, pp. 31–40. Producer service industries have been growing much more rapidly than other areas of nonagricultural employment. While the industry grew at an average rate of 6.2 percent from 1959 to 1982 (about double the rate of services in general and by 1972 triple that of industry as a whole), between 1982 and 1986 it expanded by 8.5 percent (compared to 2.7 percent for nonagricultural employment growth overall). Most of the expansion through 1986 seemed to be accounted for by increased contracting out for services by manufacturing companies, rather than by "unbundling"—the transfer of whole departments to specialist companies. There does, however, seem to be displacement of clerical and building services from corporate payrolls to firms specializing in supplying these services to many companies. But, as Tschetter pointed out, his data cannot address the question of whether unbundling is occurring for individual companies, as more anecdotal evidence about the dismantling of corporate staffs in the largest corporations suggests. His study also did not examine whether nonmanufacturing corporations are unbundling staff services and transferring them to specialist firms.

12. Kathleen L. Gregory, *Signing Up: The Culture and Careers of Silicon Valley Computer People* (Ann Arbor, MI: University Microfilms [doctoral dissertations], 1984), p. 207.

13. Max Weber, edited by Talcott Parsons, *The Theory of Social and Economic Organization* (New York: Free Press, 1947).

14. Rosabeth Moss Kanter, "Variations in Managerial Career Structures in High Technology Firms," in Paul Osterman (ed.), *Internal Labor Markets* (Cambridge, MA: MIT Press, 1984).

15. Statistical support for this notion comes from a study of jobs in one hundred organizations. There was only weak support for hypotheses linking job ladders to organizational or sectoral imperatives, but more support for links to firm-specific skills, organizational structure, technology, occupational differentiation, and custom. See James N. Baron, Alison Davis-Blake, and William T. Bielby, "The Structure of Opportunity: New Promotion Ladders Vary Within and Among Organizations," *Administrative Science Quarterly*, 31 (1986), pp. 248–73. In my own study of the company I called "Industrial Supply Corporation," I found striking difference in the length of career ladders in various sectors of the company, creating differences in opportunity. See Rosabeth Moss Kanter, *Men and Women of the Corporation* (New York: Basic Books, 1977).

16. Thomas A. DiPrete, "The Professionalization of Administration and Equal Employment Opportunity in the U.S. Federal Government," *American Journal of Sociology*, 92 (January 1987), pp. 879–909.

17. Jeffrey Pfeffer and James Baron made a similar point when they observed that "recent trends imply an increasing interorganizational division of labor, as work formerly conducted within the boundaries and under the administrative countrol of a single enterprise is parcelled out to more specialized organizational entities. . . . It may reduce the ease with which workers can build careers by

moving upward within single organizations.'' Pfeffer and Baron, op. cit., p. 269.

18. Robert Tomasko, ''Running Lean, Staying Lean,'' *Management Review*, November 1987, p. 36.

19. Robert R. Faulkner and Andrew B. Anderson, ''Short-Term Projects and Emergent Careers: Evidence from Hollywood,'' *American Journal of Sociology*, 92 (January 1987), pp. 879–909

20. Nussbaum, op. cit.

21. Robert J. Eccles, ''The Quasi-Firm in the Construction Industry,'' *Journal of Economic Behavior and Organization*, 2 (December 1981), pp. 335–57.

22. Nussbaum, op. cit.

23. Gregory, op. cit.

24. Alison Leigh Cowan, ''Hutton Buyer Assails Talent Raids,'' *New York Times*, January 27, 1988.

25. Cheryll Aimee Barron, ''Silicon Valley Phoenixes,'' *Fortune*, November 23, 1987, pp. 127–34.

26. Matthew Heller, ''The Perils of Franchising,'' *Forbes*, August 25, 1986, pp. 66–69. See also Ellen Paris, ''Franchising—Hope or Hype?'' *Forbes*, December 15, 1986, pp. 42–43.

27. Ibid.

28. Ripley Hotch, ''Franchising,'' *Nations Business*, June 1986, pp. 51–54.

29. Dyan Machan, ''Life in the Outside Lane,'' *Forbes*, October 5, 1987, pp. 220–22.

30. W. J. Howe, ''The Business Service Industry Sets Pace in Employment Growth,'' *Monthly Labor Review*, April 1986, p. 34; see also U.S. Department of Labor, Bureau of Labor Statistics, *Employment and Earnings*, January 1988, p. 186.

31. Goodmeasure, Inc, ''The Changing American Workplace: Work Alternatives in the 80s,'' AMA survey report (New York: American Management Association, 1985).

Chapter 12

1. Robert Tomasko, ''Running Lean, Staying Lean,'' Management Review, November 1987, p. 37.

2. Kathleen L. Gregory, *Signing Up: The Culture and Careers of Silicon Valley Computer People* (Ann Arbor, MI: University Microfilms [doctoral dissertations], 1984).

3. Walter Kiechel III, ''Your New Employment Contract,'' *Fortune*, July 6, 1987, pp. 109–10.

4. Paul Hirsch, *Pack Your Own Parachute* (Reading, MA: Addison-Wesley, 1987), p. 127.

5. Carol Hymovitz, ''More Executives Finding Changes in Traditional Corporate Ladder,'' *Wall Street Journal*, November 14, 1986.

6. Amanda Bennett, ''Growing Small: As Big Firms Continue to Trim Their Staffs,

2-Tier Setup Emerges," *Wall Street Journal,* May 4, 1987. The Stanley Collins case Bennett describes is similar enough to examples I found in my own field research that I have chosen to use it as an illustration here because it has already been reported in the public press. Many of the former managers whose career shifts I observed expressly requested that I either not use their experiences in ways that might identify them, or report only in generalities. Thus, it is convenient to use a "public" case to illustrate more general themes I uncovered in extensive field research.

7. Ibid.

8. Peter Nulty, "Pushed Out at 45—Now What?" *Fortune,* March 2, 1987. pp. 26–30.

9. Katherine S. Newman, *Falling from Grace* (New York: Free Press, 1988).

10. See Hilda Scott and Juliet Brudney, *Forced Out* (New York: Simon and Schuster, 1987).

11. Bruce Nussbaum, "The End of Corporate Loyalty," *Business Week,* August 4, 1986, pp. 42–49.

12. Daniel Forbes, "Part-Time Work Force," *Business Month,* October 1987, pp. 45–47.

13. Jeffrey Pfeffer and James Baron, "Taking the Workers Back Out," in B. Staw and L. Cummings (eds.), *Research in Organizational Behavior*, vol. 10 (Greenwich, CT: JAI Press, 1988).

14. Nulty, op. cit. Again, I chose to use a "public" case so I could identify a person and company by name. My field research cases are very similar.

15. Claudia H. Deutsch, "Why Being Fired Is Losing Its Taint," *New York Times,* Jaunary 24, 1988.

16. Charles Heckscher, *The New Unionism: Employee Involvement in the Changing Corporation* (New York: Basic Books, 1988), p. 101.

17. Alex Beam, "When the Grass Isn't Greener," *Business Week,* August 4, 1986, p. 44.

18. Newman, op. cit., p. 229

19. Ibid., p. 77.

20. Nulty, op. cit.

21. Hirsch, op. cit., p. 79.

22. *Business Week*–Harris Poll, "No Job Is Forever," *Business Week,* August 4, 1986.

23. Joel Brockner, "The Effects of Work Layoff on Survivors," in B. Staw and L. Cummings (eds.), *Research in Organizational Behavior*, vol. 10 (Greenwich, CT: JAI Press, 1988).

24. Albert Hirschman, *Exit, Voice, and Loyalty: Responses to Decline in Firms, Organizations, and States* (Cambridge, MA: Harvard University Press, 1970).

Conclusion

1. Pat Choate and J. K. Linger, *The High-Flex Society: Shaping America's Economic Future* (New York: Knopf, 1987); Michael J. Piore and Charles F.

Sabel, *The Second Industrial Divide: Possibilities for Prosperity* (New York: Basic Books, 1984), Raymond E. Miles and Charles C. Snow, "Organizations: A New Concept for New Forms," *California Management Review*, vol. 28, no. 3 (Spring 1986), pp. 62–73.

2. Corporate raiders looking for quick financial gains represent one abuse that U.S. policy may already be moving to prevent—by disallowing tax deductions associated with hostile takeover costs, by placing limits on deductions for debt service when takeovers are involved, by barring "greenmail" payments designed to make a raider go away, or by protecting employee pension funds against their use to finance a takeover bid. But even if hostile takeovers are reduced in number or frequency, the buying and selling of corporate assets by corporations is likely to continue. Ensuring that these have positive rather than negative consequences for the companies involved, the shareholders, employees, and the American economy is a harder task, because managerial skill is involved. Allied Corporation embarked on a major restructuring in the early 1980s (changing its name in the process), buying many companies for financial reasons; though "synergy" was often invoked as an ideal, it was hard to find in practice. Over time, Allied sold many of the assets it had acquired. A few years ago the company spun off a group of losing companies as the Henley Group, under the leadership of an executive whose goals were involved *long-term investment and revitalization*. The "losers" are now outperforming the parent company.

3. Howard Stevenson and David Gumpert, "The Heart of Entrepreneurship," *Harvard Business Review*, vol. 64 (March–April 1985), pp. 84–94.

4. This attitude is related to the new feminist view of morality as encompassing not just analytic "justice" or "rightness" in the abstract but also maintenance of relationships.

5. Michael S. Dukakis and Rosabeth Moss Kanter, *Creating the Future* (New York: Summit Books, 1988).

6. Charles Heckscher, *The New Unionism: Employee Involvement in the Changing Corporation* (New York: Basic Books, 1988). Thomas Kochan et al., *The Transformation of American Labor Relations* (New York: Basic Books, 1986).

7. See Rosabeth Moss Kanter, "Managing the Human Side of Change," *Management Review*, March 1985; also on videotape as *Managing Change: The Human Dimension* (Cambridge, MA: Goodmeasure, Inc., 1984).

8. For an eloquent statement about the ways leaders learn to develop visions, see Warren Bennis, *Becoming a Leader* (Reading, MA: Addison-Wesley, 1989).

Acknowledgments

A few years ago I wrote a short magazine column on recognition, listing forty-five ways to say "thank you" to employees. I worried that it was really too basic, since many of the steps outlined were matters of simple human courtesy, albeit with a creative flair. To my surprise, it became one of the magazine's most widely requested pieces. Is singling people out for recognition still so rare that American managers need checklists on how to do it? Is saying "thank you" something we need to be reminded to do? I hope not. But that is why I think the acknowledgments in a book are so important. It is one way to make clear that even the lonely, solitary act of writing—just me facing the moment of truth in front of a yellow pad or word processor—is the product of much collaboration, much teamwork and support. It is one way to say "thank you" publicly. I hope to find other ways to recognize and applaud my colleagues as well, but this is a start.

Through my years of investigation, I had many excellent partners who helped with everything from library research to field interviews to telephone fact checking to tackling tough consulting projects on which we were inventing new solutions to new business problems. Often, we worked as a team of three to six people. Because there were so many separate projects and there was overlapping team membership, I will thank people here in alphabetical order: Ann Bernstein, Wendy Brown, Wendy D'Ambrose, William Fonvielle, Janet Frohnmayer, Cynthia Ingols, Robin Johnson, Paul Loranger, Erika Morgan, Paul Myers, Jeffrey North, Janice Nyquist, James Phills, Elisabeth (Lisa) Richardson, Tobias Seggerman, Barry Stein, David Summers, Ruth Wagerman, Alistair Williamson, Luke Yang, and Joseph Zolner. In addition, I shared a research/consulting project with Harvard Business School colleague Janice McCormick. Kathy Chaudhry cheerfully typed drafts, and Mignon Chan and Willa Reiser helped with the final stages.

Before I came to the Harvard Business School, research funding was provided by Goodmeasure, Inc. From 1986 on, when I joined the Harvard faculty with the Class of 1960 professorship, generous research support was provided by the Harvard Business School Division of Research. I especially want to thank Senior Associate Dean Jay Lorsch for his important backing of the research as well as his tough-mindedness. The wise and supportive hand of Dean John McArthur was also felt at important times. And the stimulating intellectual atmosphere at the Harvard Business School, grounded in the real world but always pushing the frontiers of knowledge, taught me a great deal as I participated in numerous faculty seminars.

Exceedingly intelligent comments on pieces of the manuscript as they evolved were provided by Professors Chris Argyris, Warren Bennis, Joseph Bower, Amitai Etzioni, Richard Hackman, Robert Hayes, Paul Lawrence, Dorothy Leonard-Barton, George Lodge, William Sahlman, Malcolm Salter, Benson Shapiro, Jeffrey Sonnenfeld, Howard Stevenson, Richard Walton, and Eleanor Westney. I hope I benefited from the judgment of these excellent colleagues, as well as from comments by the staffs of many of the corporations mentioned in the book, but of course I alone bear responsibility for what is said here. The ideas were also "field-tested" in numerous presentations to numerous executives—too many, in fact, to mention, but people like Gene Bell, Joan Bok, Sidney Boren, Debi Coleman, Roxanne Decyk, Ben Dial, Charles Eberle, Don Gevirtz, Carol Goldberg, Gerald Grinstein, Doris Holzheimer, John Lillie, Ron Payne, Philip Samper, John Sculley, John Sims, Deborah Smith, and Mike Szymancyk deserve special thanks for pivotal events along the way. So do Tom Peters, Sue Cook, and Allan Cohen.

As research findings were generated and my thinking evolved, I published some specialized articles from which I have drawn for this book, benefiting in the process from editors' and readers' comments. These included: "The New Alliances: How Strategic Partnerships Are Reshaping American Business," in *Business in the Contemporary World,* edited by Herbert Sawyer, University Press of America, 1988; "Managing Change, in Innovative Organizations," in *Productivity and Quality through Science and Technology,* edited by Y. K. Shetty and Vernon Buehler, Quorum Books, 1988; "When a Thousand Flowers Bloom: Social, Structural and Collective Conditions for Innovation in Organizations," in *Research in Organizational Behavior,* edited by Larry Cummings and Barry Staw, JAI Press, 1988; "Encouraging Innovation and Entrepreneurs in Bureaucratic Companies," in *Handbook for Creative and Innovative Managers,* edited by Robert L. Kuhn, McGraw-Hill, 1988; "The Attack on Pay," *Harvard Business Review,* March–April 1987; "From Status to Contribution: Organizational Implications of the Changing Basis for Pay," *Personnel,* January 1987; "The New Workforce Meets the Changing Workplace," *Human Resource Management,* Winter 1986; "Stimulating and Managing Corporate Entrepreneurship: The Auto Industry Connection," in *Entrepreneurship in a Mature Industry,* edited by John C. Campbell, University of Michigan Center for Japanese Studies Papers in Japanese Studies, no. 14, 1986; and "Supporting Innovation and Venture Development in Established Companies," *Journal of Business Venturing,* Winter 1985.

I also "leaked" the concepts I was developing—and learned from the responses I got—in twenty-four monthly columns I wrote for *Management Review* magazine from 1985 to 1987. Some of these were coauthored with Cynthia Ingols, Paul Myers, Barry Stein, Joe Zolner, Erika Morgan, Toby Seggerman, Bill Fonvielle, and Bob Gandossy. Erika Morgan also coauthored with me a report on the Pacific Bell–Communications Workers of America partnership, which appeared as a Harvard Business School Working Paper. During this period, I drew on my research on managing teams, conducted while working with the Goodmeasure staff, to compile guidelines for quality improvement programs. These guidelines were published in *Solving Quality and Productivity Problems: Goodmeasure's Guide to Corrective Action,* American Society for Quality Control Press (310 West Wisconsin Avenue, Milwaukee, Wisconsin).

Special gratitude is owed to my most recent full-time Harvard

Business School research assistants, Lisa Richardson and Jeffrey North, for they very competently bore the brunt of the final push to fill in all the gaps that would link separate studies and put American business and American society in context. Lisa, whom I first knew when she was a Yale undergraduate, shows enormous potential to be a "star" in the business firmament someday. I look forward to watching her post-entrepreneurial career evolve.

My editor, Frederic Hills, and his colleague, Burton Beals, understood right away what I was trying to do in this book, even when I didn't. They believed me when I said I typically wrote four drafts before I was satisfied, and they patiently provided very insightful comments that moved the process forward. Since Fred also wears an executive hat at Simon and Schuster, I enjoyed his intelligent appreciation for all the corporate balancing acts I was documenting. Of course, the knowledge that my friend Richard Snyder, an executive admired for the high standards he sets, was at the helm of Simon & Schuster Inc. provided additional incentive to do the best job I could. Dick paid me the ultimate compliment of using me as a consultant— showing that publishers can read and believe in their own books. Martin Davis, respected CEO of parent company Gulf + Western, also played an important role in motivating me by his own personal backing for my previous Simon and Schuster book, *The Change Masters*.

Finally, there is family. My family is enormously important to me. The losses of my mother, Helen Moss, and my father, Nelson Moss, a few years ago were blows to all of us who loved them so much, but especially to myself and my sister, Myra Moss-Horvath. Their memories join that of Stuart Kanter, who died prematurely in 1969; by a twist of fate, I am carrying on his work. But I am so lucky in the closeness of my husband, Barry Stein, and son, Matthew Moss Kanter Stein—a competent nine-year-old as I write this—that I have always been able to embrace the future with energy and joy. If only more corporations could see that family can be not a drain on productivity but an enhancer of it!

Barry takes pride in being my "secret weapon"—a brilliant colleague with accomplishments of his own who not only collaborates with me in everything from consulting to cooking but also cares deeply about improving organizational effectiveness. His new company, Goodmeasure Software, makes many of the ideas we developed jointly available to managers in software packages, a creative and useful innovation. Matthew, for his part, takes pride in his frequent-flyer miles, earned from circling the globe with us on business trips on which he has learned to be fluent in room service in several languages. More importantly, Matthew's curiosity, interest, willingness to help (thinking up titles or screening phone calls while Mom is writing), and sheer zest for life are invaluable to Barry and me.

All parents want their children to have a bright future. Matthew, if this book can contribute to the success of the American economy, then it is a way of saying "thank you" by brightening your future and that of your whole generation.

Boston, Massachusetts, October 28, 1988

Index

About the Author

Rosabeth Moss Kanter holds an endowed chair as Professor of Business Administration at the Harvard Business School, and is the author of *Men and Women of the Corporation* and *The Change Masters*. An adviser to many Fortune 500 corporations, she was a founder of the Boston consulting firm Goodmeasure, Inc. One of the most sought-after business speakers in the world, she was named by a leading national magazine as one of the 100 most important women in America and cited as the "guru of the corporation." The author lives in Cambridge, Massachusetts, with her husband, Barry Stein, and her son, Matthew.